International Perspectives on the Management of Sport

International Perspectives on the Management of Sport

Editors

Milena M. Parent
Trevor Slack

AMSTERDAM • BOSTON • HEIDELBERG • LONDON
NEW YORK • OXFORD • PARIS • SAN DIEGO
SAN FRANCISCO • SINGAPORE • SYDNEY • TOKYO

Butterworth-Heinemann is an imprint of Elsevier

Elsevier Academic Press
30 Corporate Drive, Suite 400, Burlington, MA 01803, USA
525 B Street, Suite 1900, San Diego, California 92101-4495, USA
84 Theobald's Road, London WC1X 8RR, UK

This book is printed on acid-free paper.

Library of Congress Cataloging-in-Publication Data
International perspectives on the management of sport / editors Milena M. Parent, Trevor Slack.
    p. cm.
    Includes bibliographical references and index.
    ISBN-13: 978-0-7506-8237-4 (alk. paper)
    ISBN-10: 0-7506-8237-X (alk. paper)
    1. Sports administration–Cross-cultural studies.   I. Parent, Milena M.   II. Slack, Trevor, 1948–
III. Title.
GV713.I58 2007
796.06′9–dc22

2007004179

British Library Cataloguing-in-Publication Data
A catalogue record for this book is available from the British Library

ISBN 13: 978-0-7506-8237-4
ISBN 10: 0-7506-8237-X

For all information on all Elsevier Academic Press publications
visit our Web site at www.books.elsevier.com

Printed in the United States of America
07 08 09 10 11 12 10   9 8 7 6 5 4 3 2 1

To Trevor and to all my graduate students

MMP

To Jim Biddle,

a good teacher and a good friend

TS

Contents

Foreword xiii
Preface xvii
Acknowledgments xix
Contributors xxi

1 Introduction (Parent, Gerrard, and Slack) **1**
   Organization Theory 2
   Economics/Finance 5
   Future Research 9
   References 11

I   Institutions and Environments   **15**

2 Athletic Fundraising and Institutional Development:
   Friend or Foe? (Stinson and Howard) **17**
   Research Stream Overview 19
   Central Findings/Themes 20
   Conclusions/Implications 32
   References 35

3 Understanding Sport Participation—A Cross Level
   Analysis from the Perspectives of Neo-Institutionalism
   and Bourdieu (Skille and Skirstad) **37**
   Norwegian Sport 38
   The Sports City Program (SCP) 39
   Theories of Field: Neo-Institutionalism and Bourdieu 43

Explaining Sport Participation: Different Levels of Analysis . . .   48
Concluding Remarks   55
References   56

4 **Network Perspectives on Organizations**
(Quatman and Chelladurai) **61**
What Are Networks?   63
What Is the Network Perspective?   64
The Network Perspective and Organizations   76
Practical Applications of a Network Perspective   77
Summary and Conclusions   79
References   79

5 **The Political Economy of Managing Outdoor
Sport Environments** (Trendafilova and Chalip) **81**
The Tragedy of the Commons   84
The Coase Theorem   85
Collective Action   87
Public Policies and Regulations   88
Voluntary Cooperation   90
Subcultures and Sport   91
Implications   93
References   94

6 **The Institutional Dimension of the Sports Economy
in Transition Countries** (Poupaux and Andreff) **99**
The Collapse of the Soviet-Style Sports Economy   100
Institution Building and Economic Transformation in
    Transition Economies   102
Assessing Institutional Change in Transitional
    Sports Economies   110
Concordance between Sports and Economic Institutions in
    Transition Countries   116
Conclusion   122
References   123

II Professional Leagues   **125**

7 **National Dominance in European Football Leagues**
(Goossens and Kesenne) **127**
Theoretical Model   129
Benchmark: No Broadcasting/Sponsorship, Closed Labor
    and Product Market   130

Introduction of Live Broadcasting and Shirt-Sponsorship. 136
Introduction of the Champions League with
    an Open Labor Market and Large Increase in
    Broadcast Rights. 137
A First Empirical Verification 140
Conclusions 142
References 144
Appendix 7.1 145
Appendix 7.2 146
Appendix 7.3 146
Appendix 7.4 146
Appendix 7.5 147
Appendix 7.6 147
Appendix 7.7 148

8 **Beyond Competitive Balance**
    (Kringstad and Gerrard). **149**
    Uncertainty of Outcome, Competitive Balance and the
        Theory of Professional Sports Leagues 151
    Competitive Balance in the Simple League Context 155
    Competitive Balance in More Complex
        League Structures 161
    Measuring Competitive Balance in the North American
        Major Leagues and European Club Football 165
    Some Concluding Thoughts. 169
    References 171

9 **Transactions Cost Variation and Vertical Integration:**
    Major League Baseball's Minor League Affiliates
    (Winfree, McCluskey, and Fort). **173**
    Vertical Integration in MLB 174
    Transaction Costs and Demand Variation: Specification 176
    "The Seven Hypotheses": Results and Further Evaluation. 182
    Ownership Structure and Vertical Integration. 186
    Conclusions 187
    References 188

10 **Organization Specific Training and Player Salaries:**
    Evidence from the National Basketball Association
    (Darling and Maxcy) **191**
    Data and Models 193
    Discussion of Results. 198
    Conclusions and Suggestions for Future Research 201
    References 202

III Event and Voluntary Organizations   205

**11 The Governance of the International Olympic
Committee** (Kübler and Chappelet) **207**
The IOC's Management 208
Managing the IOC's Management 212
The IOC's Regulatory Mechanisms 216
Harmonizing the Regulatory Mechanisms 219
The Metagovernance of the IOC 222
Conclusions 224
References 226

**12 Structural Factors Influencing the Volunteer-
Professional Staff Relationship in Large-Scale
Sporting Events** (Parent and Slack) **229**
Methodology 230
Results and Discussion 232
Conclusions 241
References 242

13 A Typology of Sponsorship Activity
(Thompson and Speed) **247**
Taxonomy and Typologies 249
Conceptual Framework 253
The Dimensions of Classification: Targets and Objectives 254
Sponsorship Typology 257
Empirical Use of the Typology 264
Theoretical Use of the Typology 264
References 266

**14 Understanding Control in Voluntary Sport
Organizations** (Byers, Henry, and Slack) **269**
Past Research 270
Underpinnings of a New Conception of Control 273
Methods 275
Results and Discussion 276
Conclusions 281
References 283

15 Sports Clubs—Computer Usage—Emotions
(Friederici and Heinemann) **287**
Thematic Elements 289
Computer Technology in Sports Clubs 298

Emotions in Computer Usage 299
Concluding Remarks................................ 311
References 312

Index... **315**

Foreword

In 2002, the *Economist* devoted one of its special reports to world football, in particular the effects of globalizing markets on the organization of football. Among other trends, the authors noted that Europe's three top leagues were siphoning the world's best young players from their homelands, which was hurting those local teams and leagues. There were other effects. Jorge Valdano, who played for Argentina's 1986 World Cup champions and later served as sporting director of Real Madrid, put it this way: "Twenty years ago it was easy to say that Latin American football was about technique and talent, and European football was about organization, speed, and fighting spirit. But with television and player transfers, all these trends are coming together."[1]

Sociologists have cautioned against glib conclusions about such trends. As Grant Jarvie has argued, global or international visions/versions of sport may coexist with local visions/versions. Just because everyone wears Nike products does not mean that everyone plays Nike's game.[2] Moreover,

---

[1] Jorge Valdano, "Passion, pride, and profit: A survey of football," *Economist* 6, 9 (June 1, 2002) 12.

[2] Grant Jarvie, "Internationalism and sport in the making of nations," *Identities: Global Studies in Culture and Power*, 10 (2003), 537–551. For other balanced views of global sport see the special issue of the *Sociology of Sport Journal*, 11, 4 (December 1994); Alan Bairner, *Sport, Nationalism, and Globalization* (Albany: SUNY Press, 2001); Toby Miller, Goeffrey Lawrence, Jim McKay, and David Rowe, *Globalization and Sport* (London: Sage, 2001).

the last century and a half witnessed alternating currents of convergence-divergence-convergence in the modes and manners of sports around the world. The period between 1870 and 1914 (which contained the "golden age" of global capitalism) saw a certain sporting convergence as athletes and promoters on widespread continents embraced particular forms of sport from England (association football), America (baseball and basketball), and Canada (hockey). From 1914 to the 1970s, however, the currents diverged as nations dealt with hot wars, depressions, and cold wars. It was this period that spawned "Brazilian" football or "Russian" hockey. The last four decades have seen another shift in the tides, back toward the convergence that Valdano described.[3]

What have been the effects on the management of sport organizations? Does the notion of "Brazilian" football or "Russian" hockey extend beyond playing techniques and coaching tactics, to organizational dynamics and management theory? These are big questions for academics and practitioners alike. There is much to sort out. Milena Parent and Trevor Slack have assembled an international team of outstanding scholars to help us begin this inquiry.

Scholars, topics, and theoretical and methodological approaches in vibrant fields—these three are always in flux, growing in scope and strength by accretion and deletion, just the way sports grow and change. Old hands in sport management will see some well-known and some new names among the authors. Some of the topics are of long standing but still contentious inquiry—e.g., the impact of athletic success on institutional fund-raising, factors related to competitive balance, the effects of vertical industry integration, the role of governing bodies, sponsorship, and control. But readers will take away something new on each of these topics. The book includes some less-studied topics that reflect a changing world in the last three decades as global capital has reasserted itself and sports models begin to converge: transition economies, sports clubs and voluntary organizations, and the impact of new technologies. Finally, there are some fresh theoretical and methodological perspectives such as Skille's and Skirstad's use of Bourdieu, Trendafivola, and Chalip's use of the "Coase Theorem"; Quatman and Chelladurai's use of network analysis; and Friederici and Heinemann's very interesting emotionology.

Parent and Slack offer a compelling introduction that places the chapters into a coherent framework of past, present, and future developments in scholarship. That alone is worth the price of admission. The editors have chosen almost all North American and European scholars and topics.

---

[3]For an extended discussion of these phases, see Stephen Hardy and Andrew Holman, "Periodizing Hockey History: One Approach," Annual General Meeting of the Society for International Hockey Research, Moncton, New Brunswick, May 2006. We will use this framework in our forthcoming book on hockey history.

Will this help us understand what is happening in South African soccer or Dominican baseball or Saudi hockey? Time will tell. The world of sport management is changing quickly in a global age. *International Perspectives on the Management of Sport* will reward any reader seeking to understand the how and the why of this process.

Stephen Hardy
University of New Hampshire

Preface

This is an exciting time for sport around the world. Not only is sport a multibillion dollar industry (many times over and still growing), but research that examines the management of sport in its various forms is expanding. This book offers the cutting edge research in sport management being done in various countries around the world.

The people who have written for this book are among the best in the world; they are all-stars, if you pardon our pun. We have primarily divided them up into two groups, the sport economists and, for want of a better term, the organizational theorists. This is not to say that good, theoretically-informed work does not occur in other areas, such as sport and the law or marketing and sponsorship. Rather, we have chosen not to focus on these issues in the present book.

These all-star sport management researchers are each paired with a current or recent doctoral student with a promising career. Our goal was to present leading sport management research from around the world while providing promising graduate students an opportunity to publish, with the assistance of their (current or former) supervisor. That is why each chapter's first author is the student.

The chapters in this book range from those that deal with small voluntary sport organizations to those that deal with the International Olympic Committee. Issues that confront the three major spectator sports [football (soccer to North Americans), basketball, and baseball] are also examined, as are some of the issues that face multisport events and those that confront single sports. The theoretical frameworks used vary, and it is the problem that confronts the particular organization that determines the theoretical approach taken. The authors of Chapters 2–15 come from nine different countries, thus demonstrating that issues related to sport are global problems and not restricted to one particular geographic area.

Thus, this book offers (as its title states) an international perspective on various aspects of sport management by current and future leaders in the sport management field. This book is meant for anyone interested in knowing the latest research related to sport: students (undergraduate and graduate), researchers, sport managers, and sport volunteers.

Acknowledgments

This book would not have been possible without the enthusiastic support of all contributors and of Elsevier for recognizing the excellence of the authors and the emergence of an important area of research, sport management. We would also like to thank our respective families for their support, as they know the time and effort it takes to produce quality research.

We would both like to thank the authors who have contributed to this book. They come from nine different countries. They are current and former editors of the *Journal of Sport Management*, the *European Sport Management Quarterly* (formerly the *European Journal of Sport Management*), the *International Journal of Sport Finance*, and the *International Review for the Sociology of Sport*. Their articles and books form the backbone of current work on the management of sport.

We would like to thank Steve Hardy for writing the Foreword to this book and Bill Gerrard for his help with the introduction, particularly the section on economics. We would also like to thank Dennis McGonagle and Elsevier for agreeing to publish this book.

Milena would like to thank her parents, Marc and Ingrid Parent, for their support during her studies and now as a new professor. Milena would also like to thank Trevor for being a true mentor.

Trevor would like to thank Milena Parent for being a good coauthor and supporting him through a difficult time. Trevor would also like to thank Susan Davis for her help with typing the manuscript. Last but not least, Trevor would like to thank his wife, Janet. Janet has always loved him and supported his many projects, both prior to and during his illness. To her he owes the greatest debt.

Dr. Milena M. Parent, Ph.D. and Prof. Trevor Slack, Ph.D.

Contributors

Andreff, Wladimir
Wladimir is a full Professor of Economics at the University Paris 1 Panthéon Sorbonne. He holds a Ph.D. in Economics from the University Paris 9 Dauphine. He previously was a full professor in Economics at the Limoges University and a full professor in Economics at the University of Social Sciences of Grenoble 2. He has published 10 books and more than 300 articles relating to economics. His work has been translated into a number of different languages, and he is a consultant on economics to a number of organizations and governments. His research interests are in the economics of sports and the economics of postcommunist countries.

Byers, Terri
Terri Byers is a Principal Lecturer at Coventry University in the Faculty of Strategy and Applied Management. Her main research interests are in organization control and change, particularly in the voluntary sector, although she has also published work related to commercial organizations in the areas of strategy in small firms and managing quality and performance in sport organizations. Having served several years on the board of *European Sport Management Quarterly*, Terri is now on the editorial board for the *International Journal of Sport Management and Marketing* and is currently working on a special issue for this journal. She has commissioned a book by Sage (coauthored by Milena Parent and Trevor Slack) on *Key Concepts in Sport Management*.

Chalip, Laurence

Laurence is a Professor in the Department of Kinesiology and Health Education at the University of Texas at Austin, where he also serves as coordinator of the graduate and undergraduate sport management programs. He earned his Ph.D. in policy analysis at the University of Chicago. His research focuses on issues of sport marketing and policy. He has published three books, three research monographs, and more than 70 articles and book chapters. His research has been funded by grants from the Gerald R. Ford Foundation, Hankook Ilbo, the Australian Research Council, the Social Sciences and Humanities Research Council, the Sustainable Tourism Cooperative Research Centre, and the Texas Department of State Health Services. He is a Research Fellow of the North American Society for Sport Management, which conferred the Earl F. Zeigler Award upon him in 2005. He has been given two service awards from the Sport Management Association of Australia and New Zealand, and in 2000 was named to the International Chair of Olympism by the International Olympic Committee and the Centre for Olympic Studies. He was the founding editor of *Sport Management Review*, and is past editor of the *Journal of Sport Management*. In addition, he serves on the editorial board of five other journals.

Chappelet, Jean-Loup

Since 1993, Jean-Loup has been a Professor of public management at IDHEAP, the Swiss Graduate School of Public Administration associated with the University of Lausanne, Switzerland. He has also been the IDHEAP Director since 2003. Born in Morocco in 1953, he obtained a Ph.D. from the University of Montpellier, France, and a M.Sc. from Cornell University, New York, where he held teaching and research positions. In the 1980s, he worked for five years as head of the IT department within the International Olympic Committee (IOC) administration. Jean-Loup specializes in sport management, sport policy, and sport politics, with a particular emphasis on the IOC and the organization of Olympic Games and other sport events as regional and national public policies.

Chelladurai, Packianathan

Packianathan ("Chella") secured his Ph.D. in Management Science from the University of Waterloo in Canada. He is a tenured full Professor of Sport Management in the College of Education and Human Ecology at The Ohio State University specializing in organizational theory and organizational behavior in sport. He has published articles in leading journals, such as the *Journal of Sport Management, Journal of Sport and Exercise Psychology, International Review of Sport Sociology, Research Quarterly for Exercise and Sport*, and *Quest*. He has authored more than 20 chapters in books, two monographs, and four books. He was the editor of the

Journal of Sport Management and continues to serve on its editorial board and that of the *European Sport Management Quarterly*.

Darling, Joshua J.

Joshua ("Josh") received his M.S. degree in sport management from Ithaca College in 2006. Josh is from the greater Albany, New York area and is a lifelong sports fan. He earned his B.S. degree from the Park School of Communication at Ithaca College in 2001. He is currently pursuing opportunities in sport communications and sport management in both professional and college sports.

Fort, Rodney

Rodney is Professor of Economics in the School of Economic Sciences at Washington State University. He received his Ph.D. from the California Institute of Technology in 1985. He serves on the editorial boards of the *Journal of Sports Economics*, the *International Journal of Sport Finance*, and the *Eastern Economic Journal*, and as a vice-president for the International Association of Sports Economists. His publications are too numerous and diverse to list and have appeared in the *American Economic Review, Journal of Political Economy, Journal of Economic Literature, Economic Inquiry, Scottish Journal of Political Economy*, and the *Journal of Sports Economics*. His books with James Quirk (*Pay Dirt* and *Hardball*, Princeton University Press) are obligatory references and he is author of the best-selling textbook *Sports Economics* (2nd edition, Prentice Hall). Professor Fort has been a panelist on sports economics issues at many universities around the world (United States, Switzerland, Cologne, Rio de Janeiro, and Gijon). He has also testified before the U.S. Senate Subcommittee on Antitrust concerning competitive balance issues in baseball and before the New Zealand Commerce Commission on the establishment of a Premier Division in New Zealand Rugby Union. He frequently renders expert opinion in legal cases concerning sports, has appeared on the CBC's Hockey Night in Canada, and is frequently interviewed on National Public Radio.

Friederici, Markus

Markus is an Assistant Professor in Sociology. His research interests include organizations, theory of emotions, and cultural studies. He obtained a diploma in sociology, psychology, and political sciences. He obtained a Ph.D. in sociology (magna cum laude). He was a visiting professor at the University of Pernambuco (Recife, Brazil). He has published about emotions in organization, social implications of technologies, and cultural differentiation in sports organizations. He worked as the editor of the *Hamburg Review of Social Sciences* (www.hamburg-review.com) and as a consultant.

Gerrard, Bill

Bill is a Professor of Sport Management and Finance at Leeds University Business School. He is also visiting professor at Trondheim Business School in Norway. Bill is a graduate of the University of Aberdeen (M.A., 1982), Trinity College, Cambridge (M.Phil., 1983), and the University of York (D.Phil., 1995). He is a past editor of the *European Sport Management Quarterly*, associate editor of the *International Journal of Sport Finance*, and a member of the editorial boards of the *Journal of Sport Management* and *Journal of Sports Economics*. He was awarded the European Association for Sport Management Scientific Excellence Award in 2004. Bill has published extensively on the economics and finance of professional team sports. His main areas of focus are performance analysis and asset valuation. He has acted as an expert witness in a number of sports legal cases and worked as a consultant for a number of professional sports teams particularly in UK soccer. Bill regularly comments in the national and international media on sport business. His sporting allegiances in soccer are Celtic, Leeds United, and Scotland.

Goossens, Kelly

Kelly is currently a Ph.D. student in applied economics at the University of Antwerp. She is also a research and teaching assistant in the Economics Department at that same institution. Her research interests are in sports economics, particularly competitive balance. She has published in *Rivista di Diritto ed Economia dello Sport* [*Journal of Law and Economics of Sport*].

Heinemann, Klaus

Klaus was a full Professor of sociology at the University of Hamburg (Germany). He received a Ph.D. and habilitation in sociology at the Technische University Karlsruhe. He was previously a full professor of sociology at the University of Trier. He is currently an Emeritus Professor in sociology at the University of Hamburg. His research emphasis is on the sociology of organizations and economy, sociology and economy of sport, and methods of empirical research. He has published 30 books and more than 180 articles on these subjects. He was chair of the Scientific Advisory Board of the German Sport Federation from 1978 to 1990, a member of the board of the Federal Institute for Sport Sciences and editor-in-chief of the *International Review for the Sociology of Sport* from 1988 to 1996.

Henry, Ian

Ian is a Professor of Leisure Policy and Management at Loughborough University. He is currently the Director of the Centre for Olympic Studies and Research, which is a joint research center of the British Olympic

Foundation and Loughborough University. He is an author, coauthor, and editor of a number of research texts in this field, including *Sport in the City* (Routledge, 2001) edited with Chris Gratton, *The Politics of Leisure Policy* (2nd edition, Palgrave 2001), and *Transnational and Compara- tive Research in Sport: Globalization, Governance and Sport Policy* (Routledge, August 2007).

Howard, Dennis

Dennis is the head of the Marketing Department and Philip H. Knight Professor of Business in the University of Oregon's Lundquist College of Business, where he teaches sports business courses at the Warsaw Sports Marketing Center. Dennis formerly served as the Director of the Graduate Program in Sport Management at The Ohio State University. Dennis has authored or coauthored three books and close to 100 articles on sport and leisure industry topics. His book with John Crompton, *Financing Sport*, is the first comprehensive textbook on the many traditional and innovative revenue acquisition methods available to sports organizations. In 1998, Dennis received the Earle Zeigler Award from the North American Society for Sport Management in recognition of his outstanding research contribu- tions to the field of sport management. Currently, Dennis serves as the Editor of the *International Journal of Sport Finance* and on the editorial board of the *Journal of Sport Management*. Since joining the University of Oregon business faculty in 1997, Dennis has received the Undergradu- ate Teaching Award and the Harry R. Jacobs Distinguished Teaching Award.

Kesenne, Stefan

Stefan is a Professor of economics at the University of Antwerp and part- time at Leuven. He holds a Ph.D. in economics from the Catholic University of Leuven. He teaches classes in sports economics, labor eco- nomics, and applied econometrics. His major field of research is sports economics. He is vice-president of the International Association of Sports Economists (IASE) and a member of the Scientific Committee of the International Center for Sport Studies (CIES) at the University of Neuchâtel, Switzerland. He is a member of the editorial board of the *Journal of Sports Economics* (JSE) and the *European Sport Management Quarterly* (ESMQ).

Kringstad, Morten

Morten is an Associate Professor at Trondheim Business School in Norway and a Ph.D. student at Leeds University Business School in the United Kingdom. He has a graduate qualification in economics and business administration from the Norwegian School of Economics and Business Administration. His principal research area is the business and economic aspects of professional team sports. He has presented at several NASSM, EASM, and IASE conferences.

Kübler, Brenda

Brenda is a part time research associate at the Swiss Graduate School of Public Administration (IDHEAP) in Lausanne. She holds a Bachelor of Arts from the University of Nottingham, England and a postgraduate technical languages diploma. She worked in the International Olympic Committee Administration and in other international organizations. She is also a freelance translator and editor.

Maxcy, Joel G.

Joel joined the University of Georgia, Department of Kinesiology as Associate Professor and coordinator of the sport management program in 2006. He was previously an Associate Professor and coordinator of the Sport Management graduate program at Ithaca College and has been on faculty at the State University of New York—Cortland and Eastern Oregon University. Joel earned an M.A. degree from the University of Maine and received his Ph.D. in economics from Washington State University. He teaches courses in sports finance and economics. His research interests include economic and legal applications to amateur and professional sports.

McCluskey, Jill

Jill is Associate Professor in the School of Economic Sciences at Washington State University (WSU). Her research focuses on theoretical and empirical issues related to quality and consumer perceptions. She has published 42 peer-reviewed journal articles, in such journals as the *Review of Economics and Statistics, Journal of Applied Econometrics, Journal of Environmental Economics and Management, American Journal of Agricultural Economics,* and *Land Economics.* She received her Ph.D. in 1998 from the University of California, Berkeley with specializations in economic theory, industrial organization, and environmental and resource economics.

Parent, Milena M.

Milena is Assistant Professor in the School of Human Kinetics at the University of Ottawa. She is also the Interim Director of the Research Centre for Sport in Canadian Society. Her areas of expertise are organization theory and strategic management. Her research focuses on organizing committees and stakeholders of large-scale sporting events, such as the Pan American Games, the *Jeux de la Francophonie,* and the Olympic Games. She is also interested in community, sport-based partnership management, as well as characterizing youth engagement in sport. She has published in the *Journal of Sport Management, European Sport Management Quarterly*, and the *International Journal of Sport Finance*. She is also the coauthor of the 2nd edition of *Understanding Sport Organizations: The Application of Organization Theory* with Trevor Slack. Her research has been featured at various conferences including the North American Society for Sport Management conference, the Administrative Sciences Association of Canada conference, and the Academy of Management conference.

Poupaux, Sandrine

Sandrine was a Ph.D. student at University Paris 1 Sorbonne. Her research interests include sports economics and institutional changes in postcommunist economies. She has published in *Revue Juridique et Economique du Sport* and *The Handbook on the Economics of Sport* (S. Szymanski, ed.).

Quatman, Catherine

Catherine graduated in 2006 with a Ph.D. in sport management from The Ohio State University. Her doctoral dissertation was titled "The Social Construction of Knowledge in the Field of Sport Management: A Social Network Perspective." She has published on leadership and motivation in sports in the *Olympic Coach,* and has presented four papers in scholarly forums. Catherine is currently serving as an Assistant Professor of Sport Management at Texas A & M University.

Skille, Eivind

Eivind received his Ph.D. from the Norwegian School of Sport Sciences in 2005. He is currently an Associate Professor of Sport Sociology at Hedmark University College.

Skirstad, Berit

Berit is currently academic head of the Department of Culture and Social Studies at the Norwegian School of Sport Sciences. She is also an Associate Professor at that same institution responsible for sport management. She is President of EASM and a leader of the scientific committee for the European Sport Management Conferences. She has edited two books in English and two in Norwegian and published numerous chapters. She has also participated in sport conferences and presented papers over the last 35 years. She has been a board member of the Norwegian University for Sport and Physical Education for several years and a member of several committees and an executive board member of several sport organizations both nationally and internationally. She holds executive board positions in skiing, orienteering, Sport for All and European Women, and sport at an international level.

Slack, Trevor
Trevor is a Professor at the University of Alberta. In 2002, he suffered a stroke and this book is the second he has published since that time. He has published in such sports and leisure journals as *Journal of Sport Management*; *International Journal of Sports Marketing & Sponsorship*; *Sport Management Review*; *European Sport Management Quarterly*; *International Review for the Sociology of Sport*; *Journal of Leisure Research*; *Leisure Studies*; *Culture, Sport Society*; and *International Journal of Sport Finance*. He has also published in *Organization Studies, Journal of Management Studies, Human Relations, European Journal of Marketing, Journal of Applied Behavioral Science*, and the *Academy of Management Journal*. He has also published a number of books and chapters on the management of sport.

Speed, Richard
Richard is Associate Dean for Faculty Resources & ANZ Professor of Marketing Strategy at the Melbourne Business School, University of Melbourne. Richard and Peter Thompson published a paper on consumer response to sponsorship in the *Journal of the Academy of Marketing Science*.

Stinson, Jeff
Jeffrey is an Assistant Professor of Marketing at North Dakota State University. He earned his Ph.D. in Marketing from the University of Oregon in 2005. His research interests center on the influence of intercollegiate athletics on the behavior of private donors to colleges and universities.

Thompson, Peter
Peter has an MBA from the Melbourne Business School. He is a lecturer in marketing at Monash University and is currently a doctoral student at the Melbourne Business School. Peter and Richard Speed published a paper on consumer response to sponsorship in the *Journal of the Academy of Marketing Science*.

Trendafilova, Sylvia
Sylvia is completing her doctoral studies in sport management at the University of Texas at Austin, where she also teaches in the Department of Kinesiology and Health Education. In addition, she serves as a mentor for student athletes through the Department of Athletics. In 2004 and 2006, she won the Alderson Teaching Excellence Award. She earned two Masters degrees at Baylor University, one in environmental science and one in sport management. She is a certified official for U.S.A. Track and Field. Her work on environmental management in sport has been presented at three conferences of the North American Society for Sport Management.

Winfree, Jason

Jason has a Ph.D. in Economics and is an Assistant Professor of Sport Management at the University of Michigan. His primary research focuses on professional and collegiate athletics. This research encompasses fields of applied microeconomics and econometrics such as Industrial Organization, Labor Economics, and Public Economics. He studies the factors that affect attendance, ownership, and pay in Major League Baseball. He has published in these areas in such journals as *Journal of Sports Economics*, *European Sport Management Quarterly*, and *Applied Economics*.

1

Introduction

Milena M. Parent, Bill Gerrard, and Trevor Slack

Sport management research includes many areas: organizational theory, organizational behavior, strategy, finance/economics, marketing and sponsorship, law, ethics, policy, leadership, and education, just to name a few. The North American Society for Sport Management (NASSM) was created in 1985 to bring together researchers interested in sport management. Since then, the field has grown in size and quality of research.

This book presents the cutting edge research of two key areas of sport management, organization theory and finance/economics. Organization theory has evolved over the years from examining the role of organizations in society and who controls the organizations, to understanding organizational structures, processes, and activities in order to make the organization more efficient and effective (Clegg, Hardy, and Nord, 1996). Pugh and Hickson (1997) separate organization theory research into six main areas: the structure of organizations, organizations and their environments, management, decision making, people in organizations, and organizational change and learning. In turn, sport finance and economics cover a wide range of topics over and beyond how to do budgets. Examples of areas of interest include: team/club/league objectives, demand versus pricing, player labor markets, stadium funding and naming rights, economic impact analyses of events, economic impacts of such issues as television broadcasting and discrimination, economics of various amateur versus professional leagues, fundraising and sponsorship, and public versus private funding (Howard and Crompton, 2004; Sandy, Sloane, and Rosentraub, 2004).

This introductory chapter is structured as follows. First, we provide an overview of organization theory in the sport management literature and discuss what this book's chapters add to this field. We do the same for finance/economics. Finally, we provide avenues for future research.

Organization Theory

Organization theory is an important aspect of research in sport management, as we all have to deal with various types of organizations in our lives. If we understand them, we can make them better and, in turn, make our lives easier. As mentioned earlier, organization theory deals with all that relates to organizations. As such, organization theory provides us with a macro view of organizations, as opposed to organization behavior's more micro view. There are many perspectives and theories that fit within organization theory, such as network theory, institutional theory, population ecology, structuration theory, contingency theory, and critical perspectives. While organization theory research within the broader management literature has an extensive base—having concepts dating back to Adam Smith's *Wealth of Nation*, first published in 1776—that is not the case within sport management, due in part to the relative newness of the sport management field (NASSM was only created in 1985 to help define and develop the field). The following provides an overview of our knowledge in sport management organization theory research, as well as what the chapters in this book contribute to that knowledge.

Organization Theory in Sport Management

Organization theory-related research in sport management started with the work of one of the coeditors of this book, Trevor Slack, and his colleagues (notably Bob Hinings, Lisa Kikulis, and Lucie Thibault). Slack began by focusing on a sport organization's structural and design aspects. Kikulis, Slack, Hinnings, and Zimmermann (1989) and Kikulis, Slack, and Hinings (1992) offered a structural taxonomy of, and archetypes for, national sport organizations. Thibault, Slack, and Hinings (1991, 1993, 1994) examined more specifically the impact on the structure and operations of national sport organizations when increasing the number of professionals in the organization, as well as the types of strategies a national sport organization may choose. Slack and Hinings (1992, 1994) also began exploring change in national sport organizations, whereas Amis and Slack (1996) further explored the size-structure relationship in sport organizations. Amis, Slack, and Berrett (1995) took an organizational theory perspective to examining conflict in organizations, as did Kikulis, Slack, and Hinings (1995) in their study on decision making.

Other areas of organization theory have also been studied using sport organizations. Notably, Chelladurai and his colleagues examined goals and effectiveness of sport organizations. For example, Trail and Chelladurai (2002) focused on intercollegiate athletics goals, whereas Chelladurai, Szyszlo, and Haggerty (1987) offered a national sport organization effectiveness psychometric scale. Finally, Chelladurai and Haggerty (1991) focused on process effectiveness perception differences between volunteers and professionals.

As well, power and politics have been examined in sport organizations using an organization theory perspective. For example, Sugden and Tomlinson (1998) studied power in relation to the governance of football. Palmer (2000) explored the researching of elites in sport, whereas Hoye and Cuskelly (2003) examined board power and performance.

More recently, institutional theory, strategic alliances/partnerships, and critical perspectives have been areas of interest for sport management organization theorists (Parent, 2006). For example, O'Brien and Slack (1999, 2003, 2004) used institutional theory to examine deinstitutionalization processes, roles and strategic behaviors of organizational actors, and organizational change in the English Rugby Union. Institutional theory was also used by Silk, Slack, and Amis (2000) to examine organizational processes in the 1995 Canada Cup of Soccer. However, much remains to be done in relation to sport management and institutional theory, such as establishing institutionalization patterns within sport systems, examining (institutional) pressures from the environments and whether (and how) resistance to these pressures is possible, and examining institutional change within national and international, amateur and professional sports.

Another area of interest has been strategic alliances, partnerships, and networks. While these terms are often used interchangeably, they are distinct: a partnership is a formal or informal association of two or more actors (individuals, groups, organizations) formed for various reasons (outputs, learning, assistance, and so on), a strategic alliance is a formally negotiated partnership between two or more actors based on organizational learning, whereas a network is a skill-based partnership formed between more than two partners (cf. Child and Faulkner, 1998). Partnerships, strategic alliances, and networks have begun to be examined, especially structurally, within the sport management literature: Cousens and Slack (1996) examined antecedents of partnership formation; Glover (1999) provided partner selection guidelines; and Chadwick (2000) highlighted the importance of an actor's position within a network. Nevertheless, basic concepts such as which form (partnership, strategic alliance, or network) is best for sport organizations have yet to be determined, as these are issues of the management and sustainability of such organizational relationships.

A third recent area of interest for sport management organization theorists is the use of a critical perspective. Critical perspectives are based on different combinations of one or more of the following developments in Western thought: 1) the complexity of the human project (e.g., Freud); 2) the issue of power/knowledge (e.g., Foucault, Nietzche); 3) socially constructed accounts of language and experience (e.g., discourse analysis); and 4) an historically-based social conflict theory (e.g., Marx and his critical theory). Critical theory is increasingly used by sport management researchers to examine social and economic trends in sport (e.g., Harvey and Saint-Germain, 2001) and to examine the quality of sport management research (e.g., Chalip, 1996). It is also used as a framework for examining different actor perspectives (e.g., King, 1997). Unlike many management researchers who stop at critiquing what is wrong in the world (using critical theory for example), sport management researchers are also using this perspective to improve the plight of various groups through action-research. For example, Frisby, Crawford, and Dorer (1997) used action-research to assist women in accessing local physical activity services, while Burden (2000) used action-research for examining community building and volunteering. While this is a good start, a wider variety of organizations and cultures should be studied as, by virtue of its nature, we cannot generalize findings from a critical theory-based study.

Contributions from this Book

When examining the organizational theorists' contributions to this book, it is clear that they are making significant advances to the field. First, Skille and Skirstad (in Chapter 3) combine a current issue in sport, sport participation, with two increasingly popular theoretical perspectives, institutional theory and Bourdieu's sociocultural theory of practice. This chapter exemplifies the theoretical advantages to using two perspectives, as well as providing practical reflections on supply and demand for sport participation. Second, Quatman and Chelladurai (in Chapter 4) argue for the examination of sport organizations from a network perspective. The authors explain how using such a perspective is not only useful for organizational theorists but also for practitioners. Third, Trendafilova and Chalip (in Chapter 5) address sport-related prevention and redress of environmental degradation using the "tragedy of the commons" and the Coase Theorem. The authors make the case for interventions to be targeted to sport subcultures in order to foster change in environmental values and norms. While this may be a slow process, the authors suggest regulations for more immediate impact.

Fourth, Kübler and Chappelet (in Chapter 11) examine the International Olympic Committee's (IOC) governance in depth at five different levels and provide informed comments as to the IOC's progress and potential. Fifth, unlike most research in sport management, which examines the individuals in the volunteer-professional (paid) staff relationship, Parent and Slack (in Chapter 12) take an organizational theory perspective and propose structural factors that can impact the relationship. Sixth, Thompson and Speed (in Chapter 13) distill the sponsorship literature in order to provide a typology of sponsorship activity, thereby allowing different sponsorship opportunities to be compared appropriately. The authors also provide both empirical and theoretical uses for the typology. Seventh, Byers, Henry, and Slack (in Chapter 14) examine conflict in a holistic manner in a type of organization poorly studied in this topic, voluntary organizations. They highlight the fact that while administrative, social, and self-control mechanisms may operate simultaneously, it is social and self-control mechanisms that had a more significant impact on the organizations' members. Finally, in answering the dearth of technology-related research in organization theory, Friederici and Heinemann (in Chapter 15) explore the impact of the introduction and use of computers on sport club managers' emotions. They link computer usage and emotions with organizational theory concepts such as structure, stability/change, authority, division of labor, formalization, and control.

Economics/Finance

Economics and finance provide a highly formalized approach to understanding the behavior of individuals and organizations. Economic and financial behavior is conceptualized as allocative choices in which individuals and organizations must resolve the fundamental dilemma of scarcity. In almost all real-world situations, the possibilities of alternative courses of action far exceed the available resources. So choices must be made. For example, professional sports teams have limited salary budgets to spend on players determined by their revenue streams. Teams must make hard choices on which current players to retain and which to cut, which rookies to draft and which free agents to recruit. The economic perspective is one of individuals and organizations continuously making decisions over how to allocate scarce resources between alternative possibilities.

Economics and finance adopt an instrumentalist notion of rationality in which the allocation of resources is the means (i.e., inputs) by which individuals and organizations seek to attain the end of maximizing their economic well-being (i.e., outputs). This conceptualization of individual and organizational behavior allows choice to be modeled mathematically as constrained optimization using the tools of differential calculus. This yields the general optimal condition that individuals and organizations should allocate resources to any particular use only up to the point at which the marginal benefit of allocating another (infinitesimally small) increment of resource equals the marginal cost of so doing. Ultimately, the application of economic and financial analysis involves defining appropriately and valuing the benefits and costs of alternative choices. In the case of goods and services that are traded on a market, valuations are directly observable in the form of market prices. When it comes to the costs and benefits associated with items that are not traded on a market, valuations can only be obtained indirectly as implicit prices inferred from observed choices.

The study of markets and the determination of observed market prices is a key aspect of economic and financial analysis. The basic theory of price determination is demand-and-supply theory that proposes that the market price of any traded commodity tends toward the market-clearing equilibrium level at which the total quantity required by buyers (i.e., demand) equals the total quantity offered for sale (i.e., supply). The market price shifts if either the demand conditions and/or the supply conditions change. Hence, it is crucial to understand the various factors that influence the demand for a commodity and the supply of commodity. It is also crucial to investigate the structure of the market. The demand-and-supply theory of price only holds provided there are many buyers and sellers in the market with no individual or group of buyers or suppliers having sufficient market power to set the market price. If the supply side of the market is dominated by one seller (or a group of sellers acting together), then it can be profitable for the sellers to restrict the quantity traded in order to charge a higher price. This situation is known as monopoly power. Similarly, if the market is dominated by one buyer (or a group of buyers acting together), then the market price can be set below the market-clearing level to the advantage of the buyers. This is known as monopsony power. Typically, the regulatory authorities try to limit the extent of monopoly or monopsony power to prevent one side of a market from being exploited by the other side.

Economics/Finance in Sport Management

The application of economic and financial analysis in the management of sport has been a real growth area in recent years, particularly in the study of professional team sports. This is not surprising since the sub-discipline of sports economics has been an established area of research for many years. However, there is an important distinction between sports economics *per se* and the economics and finance of the management of sport. The distinction is one of motivation and emphasis. Economists have long been attracted to professional team sports as an empirical context to test economic theory. Apart from the intrinsic interest in sport and its high profile, it is an industry that is highly competitive, data-rich and very transparent to the outside observer. What other industry offers a mountain of statistics on the current performance and career histories of employees (i.e. players) and managers (i.e. coaches) as well as regular observations on the production process (i.e. games) and its outputs (i.e. wins and losses)? In addition there is detailed information on the number of consumers (e.g. gate attendances and TV viewing figures) and the usual financial information on revenues, costs, profits, assets, and liabilities. But whereas sports economics could be seen as being driven by the use of sport to answer economic questions, the economics and finance of the management of sport has been driven by the use of economic and financial analysis to answer questions related to the management of sport. The emphasis in the management of sport has been much more on the specificity of sport and the practical implications of the economic and financial analysis with less concern on the general significance of the empirical findings for the development of the parent disciplines. But, of course, as the chapters in this book demonstrate, the two motivations are not mutually exclusive. Good sports economics (and finance) represents good management related to sport and vice versa, provided there is a proper understanding of the relevant economic and finance theory coupled with a sound appreciation of the specific sport context.

Much of the initial research in sports economics focused on the players' labor market. Most professional sports leagues have restricted the movement of players between teams in order to promote competitive balance (i.e. an equal distribution of playing talent between teams). But restricting the opportunity of players to bargain with potential buyers of their playing services creates monopsony power for teams, and economic theory predicts that this would lower the average level of player salaries. The obvious corollary is that the removal of these restrictions through the introduction of free agency should lead to a significant increase in player salaries as the most talented players are able to exercise their bargaining power by creating an auction for their playing services between several teams. The first systematic economic analysis of the players' labor market was provided by Rottenberg (1956) who investigated the effects of the reserve rule in major league baseball. He argued that the reserve rule would only affect the distribution of income between team owners and players but would have no long-term impact on the distribution of playing talent between teams. The so-called Rottenberg invariance proposition implies that competitive balance is unaffected by the specific labor market regime operated by a sports league. The impact of the reserve rule on baseball player salaries was first analyzed statistically by Scully (1974) who estimated that the monopsony power of the team owners resulted in players receiving only around 17–25 per cent of their economic value. Subsequent research by Zimbalist (1992) has shown that, as predicted, free agency has increased player salaries very significantly. Indeed

Zimbalist found that free agents typically earned 25–39 per cent above their economic value.

Apart from the study of players' labor markets, economic and financial analysis has been applied to a number of other aspects of sport. Demand theory has been applied extensively to the study of gate attendances starting with Noll (1974) who analyzed the principal influences on gate attendances in all four major leagues in North America. Gate attendance demand has also been researched extensively in European soccer with Hart, Hutton, and Sharot (1975), Bird (1982), and Jennett (1984) providing the first empirical studies on the subject. Jennett's study is particularly noteworthy in attempting to estimate the effects of competitive balance on gate attendances at individual matches in the top division in Scotland by including variables to capture uncertainty of outcome effects. Most gate attendance demand studies have found that the two conventional economic variables, income and price, have little statistical impact with attendances driven much more by sporting variables capturing the quality of the teams and the degree of rivalry both in regard to the current league outcomes as well as long-standing historical and/or spatial rivalries (e.g. local "derbies" between teams from the same city). Economic and financial analysis has also been applied to ownership structure of teams, the sporting and financial performance of teams, and the institutional structure of leagues. Sloane (1971) was one of the first to suggest that professional sports teams may not behave in the same way as conventional firms but rather may pursue objectives other than profit maximization. Gerrard (2005) adopts this multi-dimensional view of team-owner objectives in his analysis of the sporting and financial performance of English professional soccer teams. He finds evidence that teams with stock listed on the London Stock Exchange show significantly higher levels of financial efficiency.

Contributions from this Book

The four economics/finance chapters in Part 2 of the book demonstrate the power of formal economic analysis in sport management. The chapters by Goossens and Kesenne (Chapter 7), and Kringstad and Gerrard (Chapter 8) focus on competitive balance. A fundamental proposition of sports economics is that sports leagues are only viable if they can maintain a sufficient degree of uncertainty outcome to retain fan interest. This requires that leagues remain competitively balanced. Goossens and Kesenne approach the issue in a formal theoretical manner setting out a benchmark case and then analyzing the theoretical implications of changes in the players' labor market, the teams' product markets, and the structure of the tournaments. Kringstad and Gerrard are more empirically driven. They consider the empirical definition of competitive balance and show that even in a very simple league, competitive balance is a multidimensional concept encompassing win dispersion, performance persistence, and championship concentration. The dimensionality increases significantly once attention turns to more complex league structures that are actually observed including the regular season and postseason playoff structure favored by the North American major leagues and the promotion-and-relegation system found in most European sports leagues.

Chapter 6 by Poupaux and Andreff is more macro in orientation. It focuses on transitional economies and looks at the way changes in the overall economy affect sport organizations. The authors show that changes in the economy from a centralized to a more market economy affect the way sport organizations operate. In their chapter, Winfree, McCluskey, and Fort (Chapter 9) try to identify the economic rationale for the observed ownership structure in major league baseball, particularly the cross-ownership of minor league teams. Economists view such cross-ownership as an example of vertical integration. Winfree, McCluskey, and Fort test the conventional economic theories of vertical integration that emphasize transactions costs and demand variability as principal drivers of such ownership structures. However, their statistical evidence does not support either explanation. They find instead that vertical integration in sport is principally associated with media ownership of teams. It is yet another example of sport-specific rather than general economic factors dominating observed outcomes in the sports industry. The final economics chapter highlights the continuing importance of the players' labor market as a research site for economic analysis. Darling and Maxcy (in Chapter 10) attempt to test the implications of human capital theory using free agents in the NBA. Human capital theory distinguishes between general skills that are valued by all potential employers and firm-specific skills that are valued only by the current employer. Darling and Maxcy compare free agents retained by their current team and those that transfer to a new team. They hypothesize that the retained free agents must have more valuable team-specific skills relative to free agents who move teams. As predicted, they find that the nonmovers are characterized by significantly higher salary increases as well as more playing time on court.

Future Research

Organization theory researchers are now calling for more research on the effects of individual and collective organizations on individuals and collectives (Hinings and Greenwood, 2002), as well as more research on concepts, such as power and partnerships, which impact organizations (Parent, 2006). Other organization theories can also be used to provide a new perspective on sport organizations, such as structuration theory's (e.g., Orlikowski, 1992; Ranson, Hinings, and Greenwood, 1980) agent-structure duality and their respective roles within change, as we know that sport and sport organizations constantly change. Greater examination of governance issues, greater range of organizations and cultures, and greater balance between theory-based and sport-based research are also needed.

Future research in sports economics/finance will pursue an agenda largely set by the developments in the parent disciplines. Professional team sports will remain an attractive empirical context to test economic/finance theory because of the availability of extensive quantitative data. Labor economists in particular will continue to investigate new and existing economic theories of the labor market using players' labor markets, particularly in the North American major leagues where player salary data is more readily available.

Future research in the economics and finance of sport management is likely to be more closely aligned with developments elsewhere in the subject field. Economic and financial research will provide important insights on the drivers of organizational performance. These research findings will be "macro" in nature providing cross-sectional evidence drawn from the quantitative analysis of large samples of sporting organizations. One important theme of such macro analysis will be further applications of the economic theories underpinning recent developments in corporate strategy centered on the resource-based view and dynamic capabilities approaches. But macro studies will be required to be complemented by more detailed "micro" organization-specific case studies that give due weight to qualitative data. For example, the impact on sporting and financial objectives of ownership and governance structures in professional sports teams requires more micro-focused research. There is a pressing need for economic research on sporting performance to move beyond the predominant emphasis on the simple atomistic team sports, such as baseball, in which team performance can be more easily decomposed in individual player contributions. A better understanding of player contributions in more complex team sports with significant interdependency effects as in the various codes of football is needed and will require greater interaction with sport science. But such research has much to offer in providing important understandings of how individuals can work together effectively in teams/groups to successfully complete highly complicated tasks.

Unlike this chapter, which separated information relating to organization theory and finance/economics, the rest of the book combines these perspectives in four different topics in order to provide different views of the same topic. First, Stinson and Howard, Skille and Skirstad, Quatman and Chelladurai, Trendafilova and Chalip, and Poupaux and Andreff discuss issues relating to institutions and environments. The second section is constituted of chapters by Goossens and Kessenne; Kringstad and

Gerrard; Winfree, McCluskey, and Fort; and Darling and Maxcy discussing issues relating to the professional sports leagues. The final section examines aspects relating to event and voluntary organizations and includes contributions from Kübler and Chappelet; Parent and Slack; Thompson and Speed; Byers, Henry, and Slack; and Friederici and Heinemann.

References

Amis, J., and Slack, T. (1996). The size-structure relationship in voluntary sport organizations. *Journal of Sport Management, 10*, 76–86.

Amis, J., Slack, T., and Berrett, T. (1995). The structural antecedents of conflict in national sport organizations. *Leisure Studies, 14*, 1–16.

Bird, P.J.W.N. (1982). The demand for league football. *Applied Economics, 14*, 637–649.

Burden, J. (2000). Community building, volunteering and action research. *Loisir et Société/Society and Leisure*, 23, 353–370.

Chadwick, S. (2000). A research agenda for strategic collaboration in European club football. *European Journal for Sport Management, 7*, 6–29.

Chalip, L. (1996). Critical policy analysis: The illustrative case of New Zealand sport policy development. *Journal of Sport Management, 10*, 310–324.

Chelladurai, P., and Haggerty, T.R. (1991). Measures of organizational effectiveness in Canadian national sport organizations. *Canadian Journal of Sport Science, 16*, 126–133.

Chelladurai, P., Szyszlo, M., and Haggerty, T.R. (1987). Systems-based dimensions of effectiveness: The case of national sport organizations. *Canadian Journal of Sport Science, 12*, 111–119.

Child, J., and Faulkner, D. (1998). *Strategies of Cooperation: Managing Alliances, Networks, and Joint Ventures.* New York: Oxford University Press.

Clegg, S.R., Hardy, C., and Nord, W.R. (eds.). (1996). *Handbook of Organization Studies.* Thousand Oaks, CA: Sage Publications.

Cousens, L., and Slack, T. (1996). Emerging patterns of inter-organizational relations: A network perspective of North American professional sport leagues. *European Journal for Sport Management, 1*, 48–69.

Frisby, W., Crawford, S., and Dorer, T. (1997). Reflections on participatory action research: The case of low-income women accessing local physical activity services. *Journal of Sport Management, 11*, 8–28.

Gerrard, B. (2005). A resource-utilization model of organizational efficiency in professional team sports. *Journal of Sport Management, 19*, 143–169.

Glover, T.D. (1999). Municipal park and recreation agencies unite! A single case analysis of an intermunicipal partnership. *Journal of Park and Recreation Administration, 17*, 73–90.

Hart, R.A., Hutton, J., and Sharot, T. (1975). A statistical analysis of association football attendances. *Journal of the Royal Statistical Society (Series C), 24*, 17–27.

Harvey, J., and Saint-Germain, M. (2001). Sporting goods trade, international division of labor, and the unequal hierarchy of nations. *Sociology of Sport Journal, 18*, 231–246.

Hinings, C.R., and Greenwood, R. (2002). Disconnects and consequences in organization theory. *Administrative Science Quarterly, 47*, 411–421.

Howard, D.R., and Crompton, J.L. (2004). *Financing Sport* (2nd ed.). Morgantown, WV: Fitness Information Technology.

Hoye, R., and Cuskelly, G. (2003). Board power and performance within voluntary sport organizations. *European Sport Management Quarterly, 3*, 103–119.

Jennett, N. (1984). Attendances, uncertainty of outcome and policy in Scottish league football. *Scottish Journal of Political Economy, 31*, 176–198.

Kikulis, L., Slack, T., and Hinings, C.R. (1992). Institutionally specific design archetypes: A framework for understanding change in national sports organizations. *International Review for the Sociology of Sport, 27*, 343–370.

Kikulis, L., Slack, T., and Hinings, C.R. (1995). Does decision-making make a difference? Patterns of change within Canadian national sport organizations. *Journal of Sport Management, 9*, 273–299.

Kikulis, L., Slack, T., Hinings, C.R., and Zimmermann, A. (1989). A structural taxonomy of amateur sport organizations. *Journal of Sport Management, 3*, 129–150.

King, A. (1997). New directors, customers, and fans: The transformation of English football in the late 1990s. *Sociology of Sport Journal, 14*, 224–240.

Noll, R.G. (1974). Attendance and price setting. In R.G. Noll (ed.), *Government and the Sport Business*. Washington, DC: The Brookings Institution.

O'Brien, D., and Slack, T. (1999). Deinstitutionalizing the amateur ethic: An empirical investigation of change in a rugby union football club. *Sport Management Review, 2*, 24–42.

O'Brien, D., and Slack, T. (2003). An analysis of change in an organizational field: The professionalization of English rugby union. *Journal of Sport Management, 17*, 417–448.

O'Brien, D., and Slack, T. (2004). Strategic responses to institutional pressures for commercialization: Case study of a senior English rugby union club. In T. Slack (ed.), *The Commercialization of Sport* (pp. 164–184). London, United Kingdom, Frank Cass.

Orlikowski, W.J. (1992). The duality of technology: Rethinking the concept of technology in the organization. *Organization Science, 3,* 398–427.

Palmer, C. (2000). Spin doctors and sportsbrokers: Researching elites in contemporary sport—A research note on the Tour de France. *International Review for the Sociology of Sport, 35,* 364–377.

Parent, M.M. (2006). Organization theory in sport management. In P. Bouchet and C. Pigeassou (eds.). *Management du Sport: Actualités de la Recherche et Perspectives* (pp. 211–225). Clapiers, France: AFRAPS.

Pugh, D.S., and Hickson, D.J. (1997). *Writers on Organizations* (5th ed.). Thousand Oaks, CA: Sage Publications.

Ranson, S., Hinings, B., and Greewood, R. (1980). The structuring of organizational structures. *Administrative Science Quarterly, 25,* 1–17.

Rottenberg, S. (1956). The baseball players' labor market. *Journal of Political Economy, 64,* 242–258.

Sandy, R., Sloane, P.J., and Rosentraub, M.S. (2004). *The Economics of Sport: An International Perspective.* New York: Palgrave Macmillan.

Scully, G.W. (1974). Pay and performance in Major League Baseball. *American Economic Review, 64,* 915–930.

Silk, M., Slack, T., and Amis, J. (2000). Bread, butter and gravy: An institutional approach to televised sport production. *Culture, Sport, Society, 3,* 1–21.

Slack, T., and Hinings, C.R. (1992). Understanding change in national sport organizations: An integration of theoretical perspectives. *Journal of Sport Management, 6*(2), 114–132.

Slack, T., and Hinings, C.R. (1994). Institutional pressures and isomorphic change: An empirical test. *Organization Studies, 15*(6), 803–827.

Sloane, P.J. (1971). The economics of professional football: The football club as utility maximizer. *Scottish Journal of Political Economy, 18,* 121–146.

Smith, A. (1937, originally published in 1776). *An Inquiry into the Nature and Causes of the Wealth of Nations.* New York: Modern Library.

Sugden, J., and Tomlinson, A. (1998). Power and resistance in the governance of world football: Theorizing FIFA's transnational impact. *Journal of Sport and Social Issues, 22,* 299–316.

Thibault, L., Slack, T., and Hinings, C.R. (1991). Professionalism, structures, and systems: The impact of professional staff on voluntary organizations. *International Review for the Sociology of Sport, 26*(2), 83–99.

Thibault, L., Slack, T., and Hinings, C.R. (1993). A framework for the analysis of strategy in non-profit sport organizations. *Journal of Sport Management, 7,* 25–43.

Thibault, L., Slack, T., and Hinings, C.R. (1994). Strategic planning for nonprofit organizations: Empirical verification of a framework. *Journal of Sport Management*, *8*(3), 218–233.

Trail, G., and Chelladurai, P. (2002). Perceptions of intercollegiate athletics goals and processes: The influence of personal values. *Journal of Sport Management*, *16*, 289–310.

Zimbalist, A. (1992). Salaries and performance: Beyond the Scully model. In P.M. Sommers (ed.), *Diamonds are Forever: The Business of Baseball*. Washington, DC: The Brookings Institution.

Part I

Institutions and Environments

2

Athletic Fundraising and Institutional Development: Friend or Foe?

Jeffrey L. Stinson and Dennis R. Howard

Over the past 20 years, numerous studies have examined the impact of intercollegiate athletics on the giving patterns of donors to higher education institutions. The findings of these studies have been inconsistent and, in some cases, provide starkly different views on the ability of athletic programs to influence donor behavior. Several studies, dating back to Gaski and Etzel (1984), have concluded that athletic programs and/or the on-the-field success of athletic teams do not have any influence on donor contributions. More recently, similar findings have been reported out of the *College and Beyond* dataset, though this data is limited to academically elite, private institutions (Shulman and Bowen, 2001; Turner, Meserve, and Bowen, 2001). The NCAA has also produced a report concluding that increased operating expenditures on athletic programs are not associated with alumni giving (Litan, Orszag, and Orszag, 2003).

Other researchers have asserted that athletic programs do exert considerable influence on private giving patterns. An analysis of giving at Clemson University found a positive relationship between winning and increased donor support to the athletic department (McCormick and Tinsley, 1990). Additional empirical support was provided by a study of alumni giving at Mississippi State University. Grimes and Chressanths (1994) reported that the overall winning percentage of the football, men's basketball, and baseball teams, along with the number of televised appearances by each team, significantly influenced alumni. Additional studies have linked appearance and performance in postseason events,

17

most notably football bowl games and the NCAA basketball tournament, to increased levels of private support (Baade and Sundberg, 1996; Rhoads and Gerking, 2000). The list of studies presented here, while not exhaustive, is representative of the inconsistent conclusions offered by researchers studying the impact of athletics on institutional fundraising. Winning appears to matter at some institutions but not at others with respect to its impact on donor support for athletics.

While some evidence suggests that the successful performance of university athletic teams stimulates increased giving to athletics, very little research has examined an important implication of this giving pattern. If donors give more to winning athletic programs, are they inclined to give less support to academic programs at the same institution? Does increased support for athletics come at the expense of academics? Only a limited set of studies have examined the issue of whether competition exists between athletic and academic giving. Unfortunately, the conclusions offered by these studies are inconsistent.

Some studies asserted that athletic programs have a positive influence on both athletic and academic fundraising at the institution (McCormick and Tinsley, 1990; Toma, 1999). These researchers concluded that there is little or no competition between athletic and academic fundraising. In fact, these studies offered empirical support for a symbiotic relationship. McCormick and Tinsley (1990) estimated that a 10% increase in private support of athletic programs at Clemson University was linked to a 5% increase in donations made to academic programs.

On the other hand, some authors have refuted the existence of this kind of mutually beneficial effect, arguing that athletic fundraising often has a "crowding-out" effect on academic programs. Sperber (1990, 2000) asserted that not only do athletic donations reduce academic support by alumni, but that nonalumni making gifts to athletic programs do so with little or no interest in the academic mission of the institution. The end result is a net loss of support for university academic programs. A recent study offers empirical support for the adverse impact that athletics may have on academic giving. A study on donor giving patterns at the University of Oregon over a ten-year period indicated a significant shift toward increased athletic giving. By year ten (2003) of the study period, the shift toward athletics had become so pronounced that the overall amount given to academics actually declined (Stinson and Howard, 2004). While this finding was limited to just one institution, it raised the question of whether the profound shift discovered at the University of Oregon might also be occurring on other campuses. The following section presents a series of studies intended to examine and clarify when and how athletic programs influence donor giving patterns to both athletic and academic programs.

Research Stream Overview

The findings and discussion presented below are rooted in a series of studies we have conducted directly examining the role of athletic programs and associated fundraising efforts on the private support of academic programs. We have examined both individual giving histories and aggregated institutional giving data. Additionally, we have employed a multimethod approach including both empirical and qualitative analysis. Specifically, we have evaluated changing donor allocation patterns between athletic and academic programs. Many studies (i.e., Baade and Sundberg, 1996; Grimes and Chressanths, 1994; Rhoads and Gerking, 2000) have linked increased athletic success with increased institutional support, but have neglected to identify the primary beneficiaries of increased charitable giving. Analysis of only total institutional giving without consideration of allocation patterns (e.g., athletics versus academics) can mask fundamental changes in where donors are directing their charitable gifts. As we will discuss below, the failure to account for shifts in allocation patterns has led to inappropriate conclusions regarding the relationship between athletic and academic fundraising.

In examining the relationship between athletic and academic fundraising, we have analyzed the following data:

- Individual giving histories of all donors making annual gifts of $1000 or more to the University of Oregon from 1994–2002 (Stinson and Howard, 2004). Data were collected from the University of Oregon Foundation's database.

- In-depth interviews with a selected sample of those University of Oregon donors.

  - The annual aggregated giving to athletics and academic programs at 107 NCAA Division I-A football schools from 1998–2003. Data were extracted from the Voluntary Support of Education (VSE) database maintained by the Council for Aid to Education (Stinson and Howard, 2007).

  - The annual aggregated giving to athletics and academic programs at 118 NCAA I-AA and I-AAA institutions from 1998–2003. Data were extracted from the VSE database.

  - Individual giving histories of all donors making annual gifts of $1000 or more to five selected NCAA institutions. Data were collected from each institution's development office/foundation for the years 1990–2005. The records of more than 100,000 donors

> making more than one million gifts to the respective institutions are included in the combined dataset.

With the exception of Stinson and Howard (2004), each of the empirical studies included in our analysis used linear mixed models as the analytical tool. Given the hierarchical nature of the panel data collected for these studies, the application of linear mixed models was considered to be the most appropriate tool for analysis (Raudenbush and Bryk, 2002). Linear mixed models account for the wide amount of institutional heterogeneity (i.e., institution size, geographic location), particularly with respect to unmeasured variables (i.e., student profile, faculty size and profile, grants received). The analysis allows for the identification of the portion of variance attributable to the variables included in the study that is common to schools and/or donors (Raudenbush and Bryk, 2002). The linear mixed models approach was used as it allowed for the analysis of all data in its original form and is robust against missing data within the panel (Wolfinger and Chang, 2003). For example, an institution may have reported its giving in 8 out of 10 years. The linear mixed models approach would still allow for the inclusion of that institution in the analysis.

Combined, these studies offer the most detailed examination of the interplay between private support to athletic programs and private support to academic programs to date. The following section of this chapter will be organized around the central findings identified in these studies, and the relevance of those findings to both theoretical development and the advancement of fundraising programs.

Central Findings/Themes

This section will develop several central themes that have been evident in the results of the studies described above. Each theme will be discussed in some detail below.

Theme 1: Athletic Programs Are Increasingly the Prime, if Not Sole Beneficiaries, of Increased Institutional Giving

While colleges and universities continue to set records in terms of the number of charitable dollars raised (Council for Aid to Education, 2006), often the beneficiaries of those increased donations are not adequately identified. One of the primary objectives of this research stream has been to understand the link between private support of athletic programs and private giving directed at academic programs. Examining only total institutional support does not allow enough detail to understand why or where institutional donations are increasing. Breaking down the total institutional gift into component parts allows for much more meaningful interpretation of fund-raising increases.

Over the decade of donor records collected at the University of Oregon, there were remarkable shifts in giving behavior (Stinson and Howard, 2004). While total institutional giving grew each year from 1994–2002, nearly all of the growth was directed toward athletic programs (see Table 2–1). In fact, by 2002, more than 80% of all fund-raising growth was

TABLE 2–1
Giving to Athletics and Academics at the University of Oregon,
1994–2002*,**

Year	Alum Donors	Total Donation	% of Total Gift Allocated to Athletics	Increase from Previous Year	% of Increase Allocated to Athletics	% of Increase Allocated to Academics***
1994	508	$1,391,528	40.40			
1995	671	$1,932,050	45.18	$ 540,521	39.78	55.7
1996	731	$2,010,959	46.14	$ 78,908	63.39	41.13
1997	832	$2,318,526	47.46	$ 307,567	66.86	22.19
1998	907	$2,506,467	48.26	$ 187,941	33.22	25.07
1999	986	$2,842,499	44.81	$ 336,032	10.29	84.97
2000	1005	$2,850,159	49.36	$ 7,659	1655	−1029
2001	1198	$3,868,653	53.77	$1,018,493	55.22	39.43
2002	1385	$4,711,354	56.66	$ 842,701	81.44	8.70

Year	Nonalum Donors	Total Donation	% of Total Gift Allocated to Athletics	Increase from Previous Year	% of Increase Allocated to Athletics	% of Increase Allocated to Academics
1994	271	$ 703,787	50.48			
1995	351	$ 990,894	54.92	$287,107	52.84	39.55
1996	389	$1,012,006	56.09	$ 21,112	−250	291
1997	481	$1,313,298	58.37	$301,291	69.65	8.54
1998	507	$1,323,122	62.22	$ 9,824	1035	−1005
1999	562	$1,529,398	60.56	$206,275	6.22	70.38
2000	610	$1,586,356	62.86	$ 56,958	150.7	−29.5
2001	745	$1,912,936	68.12	$326,579	121.6	−17.2
2002	924	$2,705,804	72.07	$792,868	83.9	1.94

*Data originally reported in Stinson and Howard (2004).
**Only donors making annual gifts of $1000 or more included in analysis.
***The UO Foundation is also the fundraising arm for the Oregon Bach Festival. As a result, the percentage of increased giving to athletics and academics does not equal 100% as some increased fundraising is allocated to this affiliated program.

allocated to athletics. The trend is most noticeable by the fact that in three of the last five years of the study, total dollars donated to academic programs by nonalumni decreased despite an increase in the number of nonalumni donors making a gift to the institution. This pattern was replicated by alumni donors in only one year (fiscal year 2000). This troubling data suggests that donors are, at least in some cases, increasing their support of athletic programs at the expense of their support of academic programs.

A similar, though not as severe, trend was identified when examining the aggregated institutional data available in the VSE database (Stinson and Howard, 2007). In the study, the academic ranking of the institution (as determined by *U.S. News & World Report*) was found to moderate the effects of increased athletic fundraising on private academic support. *U.S. News & World Report* annually categorizes higher education institutions with respect to their relative academic status. While the exact *U.S. News & World Report* methodology has changed over the course of time, in general, institutions in the top category or Tier 1 include the top 50 ranked schools in the country, or the academically-elite institutions. The next or second tier of schools included those ranked from approximately 51–100, while the third tier generally includes the following 50–75 schools. The highest ranked institutions (Tier 1) were less susceptible to dramatic changes in gift allocation patterns, at least in terms of total dollars donated, than institutions ranked Tier 2 and lower. In fact, several Tier 2 and Tier 3 institutions demonstrated the same pattern as the University of Oregon, in which growth in athletic giving appeared to come at the expense of academic support. Even the Tier 1 schools were not completely immune from shifting giving patterns, though the increased allocations toward athletics were much smaller in magnitude and showed no immediate signs of leading to any reductions in academic support (see Table 2–2). Still, the vast majority of institutions appear to be susceptible to long term erosion of academic support despite continued increases in athletic giving.

Given the significant changes in giving patterns identified in these studies, it is critical to examine possible causes. Authors have noted the increased prominence of athletic programs (Goff, 2000), the use of athletic programs as a positioning mechanism (Toma, 1999), and the availability of preferred seating and parking privileges (Mahony, Gladden, and Funk, 2003) as influences on donor behavior. Little work has adequately examined how these factors have influenced the academic component of giving. Informational interviews were conducted with a small sample of selected donors to the University of Oregon to begin to understand the relationship. While many of the donors had in fact changed their gift giving behavior toward the University in recent years, most denied that any increased support of athletic programs on their part was associated with

TABLE 2–2
Average Giving Patterns to NCAA I-A Institutions, 1998–2003

All Schools

Nonalumni		Total Gift	Academic Gift	Athletic Gift	% of Gift Allocated to Athletics
	1998	$4,069,517	$3,564,448	$ 505,069	12.41
	1999	$4,019,814	$3,444,782	$ 575,031	14.30
	2000	$5,072,682	$4,436,367	$ 636,314	12.54
	2001	$5,670,842	$4,842,109	$ 828,733	14.61
	2002	$5,931,355	$5,012,866	$ 918,488	15.49
	2003	$5,469,002	$4,455,151	$1,013,851	18.54

Alumni

	1998	$5,841,124	$4,982,510	$ 858,613	14.70
	1999	$6,337,790	$5,266,509	$1,071,281	16.90
	2000	$7,330,109	$6,092,459	$1,237,649	16.88
	2001	$8,683,508	$7,140,112	$1,543,396	17.77
	2002	$7,327,726	$5,652,756	$1,674,970	22.86
	2003	$8,095,027	$5,989,239	$2,105,787	26.01

*US News &
World Report*
Unranked

Nonalumni		Total Gift	Academic Gift	Athletic Gift	% of Gift Allocated to Athletics
	1998	$1,424,583	$ 784,041	$640,542	44.96
	1999	$1,394,164	$1,029,394	$364,770	26.16
	2000	$1,995,122	$1,654,859	$340,263	17.05
	2001	$1,579,118	$ 875,309	$703,809	44.57
	2002	$1,612,036	$ 819,532	$792,504	49.16
	2003	$1,568,862	$ 902,296	$666,566	42.49

Alumni

	1998	$1,104,041	$669,879	$434,162	39.32
	1999	$ 919,668	$517,626	$402,042	43.72
	2000	$ 640,506	$495,336	$145,170	22.66
	2001	$ 891,908	$516,653	$375,255	42.07
	2002	$ 891,049	$530,903	$360,146	40.42
	2003	$ 976,424	$623,668	$352,756	36.13

TABLE 2–2
Continued

US News &
World Report
Tier 1

Nonalumni		Total Gift	Academic Gift	Athletic Gift	% of Gift Allocated to Athletics
	1998	$ 8,572,057	$ 8,048,310	$ 523,747	6.11
	1999	$ 7,640,521	$ 7,216,686	$ 423,835	5.55
	2000	$10,262,615	$ 9,620,416	$ 642,199	6.26
	2001	$12,166,394	$11,409,883	$ 756,511	6.22
	2002	$13,241,626	$12,288,381	$ 953,245	7.20
	2003	$11,411,457	$10,286,127	$1,125,330	9.86
Alumni					
	1998	$15,948,940	$14,711,517	$1,237,423	7.76
	1999	$16,869,950	$15,578,578	$1,291,372	7.65
	2000	$18,341,812	$16,567,719	$1,774,093	9.67
	2001	$22,319,110	$19,720,547	$2,598,563	11.64
	2002	$18,708,838	$15,163,452	$3,545,386	18.95
	2003	$19,908,272	$16,453,258	$3,455,014	17.35

US News &
World Report
Tier 2

Nonalumni		Total Gift	Academic Gift	Athletic Gift	% of Gift Allocated to Athletics
	1998	$4,467,503	$3,710,181	$ 757,322	16.95
	1999	$4,697,924	$3,842,755	$ 855,169	18.20
	2000	$4,952,128	$4,105,095	$ 847,033	17.10
	2001	$5,890,598	$4,727,417	$1,163,181	19.75
	2002	$6,026,017	$4,766,954	$1,259,063	20.89
	2003	$5,395,652	$4,090,200	$1,305,452	24.19
Alumni					
	1998	$6,388,074	$4,974,028	$1,414,046	22.14
	1999	$7,043,307	$5,468,831	$1,574,476	22.35
	2000	$7,299,773	$5,588,024	$1,711,749	23.45
	2001	$8,193,533	$6,250,201	$1,943,332	23.72
	2002	$7,164,917	$5,443,682	$1,721,235	24.02
	2003	$7,534,334	$5,022,673	$2,511,661	33.34

TABLE 2–2
Continued

US News &
World Report
Tier 3

Nonalumni		Total Gift	Academic Gift	Athletic Gift	% of Gift Allocated to Athletics
	1998	$2,815,608	$2,572,777	$242,831	8.62
	1999	$2,972,614	$2,442,280	$530,334	17.84
	2000	$3,717,669	$3,144,239	$573,430	15.42
	2001	$3,839,572	$3,194,961	$644,611	16.79
	2002	$3,675,048	$2,949,157	$725,891	19.75
	2003	$4,314,843	$3,327,108	$987,735	22.89

Alumni

	1998	$2,813,529	$2,392,301	$ 421,228	14.97
	1999	$3,413,462	$2,421,196	$ 992,266	29.07
	2000	$3,894,292	$3,025,835	$ 868,457	22.30
	2001	$6,003,788	$4,876,035	$1,127,753	18.78
	2002	$4,205,463	$2,998,112	$1,207,351	28.71
	2003	$5,836,203	$3,927,819	$1,908,384	32.70

US News &
World Report
Tier 4

Nonalumni		Total Gift	Academic Gift	Athletic Gift	% of Gift Allocated to Athletics
	1998	$1,930,597	$1,672,094	$258,503	13.39
	1999	$1,949,832	$1,581,875	$367,957	18.87
	2000	$2,135,969	$1,739,543	$396,426	18.56
	2001	$2,489,811	$2,027,807	$462,004	18.56
	2002	$2,424,032	$1,906,137	$517,895	21.37
	2003	$1,942,618	$1,646,144	$296,474	15.26

Alumni

	1998	$1,258,578	$1,032,603	$225,975	17.95
	1999	$1,254,674	$ 911,007	$343,667	27.39
	2000	$1,596,628	$1,195,149	$401,479	25.15
	2001	$1,554,787	$ 963,584	$591,203	38.02
	2002	$1,356,498	$ 872,543	$483,955	35.68
	2003	$1,494,753	$ 938,149	$556,604	37.24

decreased academic support. Tickets, parking, and other privileges related to their athletic support were certainly important to these donors, but only for the athletic component of their total gift, and only for the portion of the athletic gift that was "required" to secure the desired privileges. Academic giving and athletic giving, which were above the minimum "required" for a desired set of benefits, were evaluated on different criteria. The "required" giving was evaluated more consistently with a cost-benefit approach as part of the price for attending the athletic events, while the other components of the donor's total gift were likely to be evaluated more altruistically, where the outcomes associated with the academic or athletic program were the primary consideration. The distinctions donors make between the various gift components are important for institutional fundraisers to consider. It appears that donors have different motives for the component parts of their total gift. As a result, institutional fundraisers may need to address multiple forms of solicitation and cultivation to maximize the giving by any individual donor. We will return to this point below in discussing implications for organizational fundraising structure.

Theme 2: Athletic Giving and Academic Giving Are Independent Decisions, Yet Indirectly Linked

As noted previously, despite significant changes in allocation patterns, donors interviewed at the University of Oregon indicated that their charitable giving directed in support of athletic programs was independent of their giving to academic programs. In fact, donors indicated that the two gifts originated from separate areas of their personal budgets (see Heath and Soll, 1996, for a discussion of mental budgeting). Gifts directed to athletic programs as part of the "requirement" for preferred seating were more likely to originate in a discretionary entertainment budget, and were often viewed as part of the ticket purchase price. One donor reflected this sentiment by stating:

> Let me explain that I have never given a gift that was given for tax reasons because I am not that affluent. It is a little painful for me to give gifts. It is not something I can do for Uncle Sam. Yeah, it is primarily to protect six seats in Club section. I get something back for that, and I have kids, my offspring and my wife that sit in those seats.

Furthermore, donors' willingness and ability to give to athletic programs was related more to other discretionary entertainment expenses than any form of academic giving. For example, one donor noted that while some of her friends took cruises, she and her husband attended Oregon football games.

Academic giving, on the other hand, was found to be largely a function of a donor's annual charitable budget. Most donors indicate setting a finite budget for charitable gifts of all types. Any gifts allocated to the academic programs of a university come from that budget. As a result, the nature of competition for academic gifts was centered on other nonprofit/charitable agencies within the community. In this context, the donor's choice of whether to give, and how much, to higher education programs (e.g., law school building fund, endowed scholarships, etc.) is weighed against their decision to support their favorite charity (e.g., American Cancer Society, Easter Seals, etc.) or to give to their local church. The implications of these findings are quite substantial. While many athletic and academic fundraisers feel the need to "compete" for a donor's support, and institutions continue to develop and implement sophisticated pegging systems for their donor pool, the evidence here suggests that a cooperative relationship between athletic and academic fundraisers would be more likely to maximize donor support for both athletic and academic programs.

The independent nature of athletic and academic giving was explored further using the aggregated annual giving totals reported in the VSE database. The VSE analysis included broad academic (i.e., *U.S. News & World Report* Rankings, Carnegie Classification), athletic (on-the-field performance of football and men's basketball teams), and institutional characteristics (i.e., geographic location, private/public status). Analyses of these datasets revealed that annual changes in athletic and academic giving were explained by different sets of factors. Changes in academic giving were most significantly explained by the *U.S. News & World Report* rankings, suggesting that academic performance is the most crucial factor in determining a donor's level of academic support. Changes in athletic giving, on the other hand, were significantly influenced by on-the-field athletic success. This finding suggests that donors are more concerned with athletic success when making gifts to support athletic programs. While both components of giving appear to be heavily influenced by the perceived success of the respective academic and athletic programs, the results provide support for donor assertions that the two components of giving are independent.

However, analysis of the changing allocation patterns suggests a more complex relationship between athletic and academic giving. Athletic performance is a statistically significant influence on the percentage of the total gift that is allocated to support athletic programs. The necessary corollary is a reduction in the percentage of gift directed to support academic programs. As noted in the previous section, this changing allocation pattern has in some cases resulted in an actual decline in dollars allocated to support academic programs despite overall increases in giving. Thus, while the two giving components may be influenced by separate variables, they appear to be at least indirectly linked.

One possible explanation for this pattern of results may be linked to the donor's overall capacity to give. Most donors (impose a) have a financial constraint on the amount they are willing to devote to charitable activities in a given period of time. While the money donated to athletics may be part of a separate donor budget than the money allocated to academics, it is quite possible that donors easily shift between the two budgets when faced with actual solicitations. As the amount of donation required to maintain the benefits associated with athletics increases, donors may feel compelled to reduce their contributions to other programs in order to not exceed a self-imposed ceiling on total charitable giving. It is quite possible that academic programs may suffer as a result. The question of whether donors make these kinds of adjustments or trade-offs (and how those decisions are made) is deserving of further study.

Theme 3: Athletic Success Influences Athletic Giving; Academic Success Influences Academic Giving

The fact that gifts to athletics are at least somewhat independent of gifts to academic programs suggests that different factors may be considered by donors when deciding what gifts to make. With respect to athletic giving, the literature has mostly considered the effects of on-the-field athletic performance as the primary influence (i.e., Baade and Sundberg, 1996; Gaski and Etzel, 1984; Grimes and Chressanths, 1994; Rhoads and Gerking, 2000). Various measures of on-the-field success were also significant predictors of changes in athletic giving patterns in the VSE dataset discussed here. However, while statistically significant, the ability of on-the-field performance to explain practically important variations in giving is lacking. Donor interviews were again helpful in exploring this point. Donors indicated a strong desire to support a successful athletic program, and in many cases, indicated that a less than successful program might result in a reduction in support. However, donors based their conceptualization of success more broadly than short-term on-the-field performance metrics. Donors cited additional information that they believed relevant to making a judgment on the success of the athletics program, including student-athlete graduation rates, the perceived integrity of the coaches and administration, the "cleanness" of the program with respect to NCAA probation, and the long term trends of on-the-field performance. Gladden, Mahony, and Apostolopoulou (2005) identified a desire to help establish or build a successful program as a prominent motive for donors' athletic gifts. A more encompassing conceptualization and measurement of athletic success provides promise for explaining more significant variance in donor patterns.

Furthermore, the importance of on-the-field success as a determinant of giving is seemingly tied to the demand for tickets and parking. At institutions where "required" donations provide the only access to these benefits, the on-the-field success of the team may be more important, as continued success is likely to keep demand for tickets high. On the other hand, at institutions where games are routinely not sold out, and tickets are available without donations, the performance of the team may have less influence on giving patterns. Interestingly, the influence on giving appears to be largely driven by the most prominent sport on campus. Analysis of NCAA Division I-A and I-AA institutions demonstrates that only performance measures related to football are statistically significant influences on athletic giving. At institutions that do not compete in football (NCAA Division I-AAA), men's basketball team performance becomes a significant influence on giving.

Academic giving, like athletic giving, is explained in large part by the donors' judgments relative to the ability of the institution to develop and sustain successful academic programs with the assistance of the charitable donations. The most influential measure relative to academic giving in the analysis of the VSE data was the institution's *U.S. News & World Report* ranking. These results are consistent with other examinations of institutional or academic support that have also identified measures of academic prestige or quality to be the most significant determinants of charitable support (Cunningham and Conchi-Ficano, 2002; Rhoads and Gerking, 2000). Combined with the donor interviews, these results provide a strong indication of the importance of academic success to donors evaluating gift opportunities. This is especially relevant given the criticisms many administrators have with such academic rankings measures as those provided by *U.S. News & World Report*. While administrators may not weigh such rankings highly, it seems likely that donors use these and other similar measures in determining the success potential of academic programs. Both researchers and fundraisers must further explore how donors evaluate academic success, and develop metrics to communicate academic success. As one donor stated:

> And also to me, it is my feeling that my dollars are best spent there (athletics), rather than, I am trying to think of an example here, like giving to the math department or some department that I don't have a win and loss record for, because I think that is important in life.

Donors similar to this individual will increasingly look for metrics of academic success. In the absence of the ability to communicate academic success, donors may continue to place higher emphasis on external academic rankings as a primary measure of quality.

While athletics and academic giving were both influenced by separate factors, the impact of those factors on alumni and nonalumni was remarkably similar. For example, it was found that bowl (championship) appearances increased athletic support for all athletic donors (both alumni and nonalumni). While postseason bowl appearance did not influence academic giving for both groups, it was found that *U.S. News & World Report* rankings were primary indicators of changing levels of academic support for both alumni and nonalumni. Higher academic rankings were linked with higher levels of academic support on the part of both alumni and nonalumni donors. The failure to identify significant differences between alumni and nonalumni donors is counter to common assumptions and assertions that the two groups differ significantly in their giving behavior (Sperber, 1990, 2000). While there are differences in the magnitude of giving between the two groups (more alumni donors, but more making smaller gifts), the factors influencing change in the two groups are generally consistent. Both groups respond to athletic and academic success measures in essentially the same way. These findings question the need to cultivate alumni donors and nonalumni "friends" separately. Both groups of donors respond to academic rankings when making academic gifts and athletic success when allocating athletic gifts. Therefore, it would seem more efficient to target all academic donors with messages centered on the success of academic programs, and all athletic donors with messages centered on the success of athletic programs. The alumni versus nonalumni distinction need not be made.

Theme 4: Successful Athletic Programs Attract Additional Donors to the Institution, but Mostly to Support Athletics

One clear result from the studies examined for this chapter is the ability of successful athletic programs to help increase the number of donors making charitable gifts to the institution. At the University of Oregon, the number of donors making athletic gifts of more than $1000 annually grew 257% between 1994 and 2002. During the same time frame, the number of academic donors giving $1000 or more annually grew at less than half that rate (124%). Importantly, while athletics attracted many of these new donors, less than a third made an academic gift to the university during the time frame.

A similar pattern of results was revealed in the analysis of the aggregated VSE dataset when examining NCAA Division I-A institutions. Changes in on-the-field success of the football team were associated with increased numbers of donors making gifts to the institution. However, the significant shifts in allocation patterns indicated that, as for the University of Oregon, the intercollegiate athletic programs were the primary beneficiaries of these gifts. While athletic programs appear to have the ability to attract new donors to educational institutions, it is unclear that these new donors are being successfully cultivated to provide broader support to other areas of the institution. How an institution approaches the cultivation of new athletic donors may be crucial to the rate at which these donors make additional academic gifts. We will return to this point below when discussing the potential role of organizational structure.

Interestingly, this pattern of new donors supporting primarily the athletic program exists only at the top level of NCAA competition. When schools competing in NCAA Divisions I-AA and I-AAA were separated from the larger sample, not only was athletic performance associated with increased athletic giving, but it also had positive, direct effects on academic support. At these lower athletic profile schools, the nature of the athletic/academic fundraising relationship is symbiotic. While these results provide support for some of the financial benefits pursued by schools moving from NCAA Divisions II or III to the I-AA or I-AAA ranks, there are also implications for the larger I-A schools. The pattern of results suggests that the middle ground with respect to athletic profile may be the best for cultivating institutional donors. At some point, there is perhaps an overexposure or overemphasis on athletics (Goff, 2000; Toma, 1999, 2003) that makes it difficult to communicate effective academic messages to the new donors. The organizational fundraising structure may ultimately determine whether coexisting success messages (both athletic and academic) can be communicated to the donor base. Initial analysis of individual donor records from a *U.S. News & World Report* tier 1 institution with a high-profile athletic program indicates the potential for an integrated fundraising unit to mitigate the potential for overexposure of the athletic program. Contrary to the results from the VSE database discussed above, this large NCAA Division I-A institution appears to use athletic success as a tool for cultivating growth in both athletic and academic fundraising. We will return to this point in discussing the implications of organizational structure.

Theme 5: Current Models of Charitable Behavior Are Inadequate to Explain the Changing Patterns of Giving

While these studies offer important insights in the understanding of how intercollegiate athletics performance and fundraising influence the academic support of donors, it is important to recognize that large amounts of variance remain to be explained. The analysis of the VSE dataset indicated that the vast majority of the variance is still accounted for by institution-specific effects. The interaction between academic and athletic giving and how donors make decisions relative to the allocation of their gifts is more complex than any current models of donor decision making suggest. At this point, there are too many unaccounted for institution-specific and donor-specific factors to believe that a generalizable model is possible.

There are general models of donor behavior, including the Services-Philanthropic Giving Model (Brady, Noble, Utter, and Smith, 2002), the Identity Salience Model of Nonprofit Relationship Marketing Success (Arnett, German, and Hunt, 2003), and A Model of Donor Behavior (Sargeant, 1999) that begin to address the relationship between the donor and institution. Each model attempts to account for the factors connecting a donor to the institution (i.e., participation in institution–sponsored programs; previous involvement with the organization) and the precursors to charitable behavior (i.e., perceived need of the organization, previous history of charitable behavior). Nevertheless, each of the models is lacking in its ability to explain the donor decision and allocation process. Most notably, none of the models includes consideration of athletic and academic success measures. The results of our work indicate that successful outcomes that can be associated with the donor's gift are crucial in the donor decision-making process. Perceptions of success must be included in any conceptual model purporting to explain the donor decision process, especially related to private support of athletic and academic programs in higher education.

Conclusions/Implications

We conclude this chapter with a discussion of some of the primary implications of this research. Perhaps the most significant implication is the notion that donors do not consider their "required" athletic giving to be charitable, and as a result do not directly consider "required" athletic donations as part of the same budget as their charitable donations. In effect, this distinction suggests that in contrast to common sentiment that athletic programs are in competition with academic programs, the institution may more readily maximize private support by cross-cultivating and soliciting donors. Cross-solicitation strategies allow the institution to compete for both the discretionary funds the donor is willing to spend for access to tickets, parking, and other athletic-related benefits, as well as the donor's more altruistic giving that might be centered on academic programs. Our research found that major donors allocated only a small portion, approximately 20% on average, of their total annual charitable giving to educational institutions. In our view, this creates a huge opportunity for university development programs. While, at this stage of our research, we cannot offer a definitive recommendation, our preliminary analysis suggests that an optimal approach would be for institutions to implement a more integrated approach to fundraising. Under this arrangement, athletic and academic fundraisers would work together in an effort to compete for the other 80% of giving currently being directed to other charitable organizations.

A variety of structures have been used by universities and colleges to raise money for athletic programs (Howard and Crompton, 2004). The three most common organizational structures include:

- *Private Fundraising Model.* Under this organizational arrangement, fund-raising on behalf of athletics is vested in a private foundation whose sole purpose is to raise money in support of athletic department programs. These foundations operate as separate entities, often located off-campus and free of any direct institutional supervision. Clemson University's IPTAY and Fresno State University's Bulldog Foundation are successful examples of private fundraising units.

- *Independent or "In-House" model.* Under this common organization arrangement, the athletic department operates its own fundraising program, separate from the general university's development office. In this model, fund-raising staff are hired directly by the athletic department and, typically, the unit serves directly under the purview of the Athletic Director. While the athletic department's fundraising unit reports ostensibly to a senior university officer (Vice-President of External Affairs), in reality it operates with considerable autonomy, targeting and cultivating donors in support of athletic programs. The University of Oregon's Duck Athletic Fund and Louisville's Cardinal Athletic Fund are prominent examples of independent fundraising units. There is more institutional control than the private foundation model described previously, as these organizations must abide by institutional policies and pegging systems.

- *Integrated Fundraising Model.* In this organizational arrangement, athletic fundraising is housed in the university's central development or fundraising unit's office. The integrated structure has both athletic and academic fund-raisers report through the same channels, typically through a Vice-President for Institutional Advancement. Integration includes common solicitation and gift reporting systems. Consequently, this structure would seem to offer the most potential for developing the cooperation necessary to integrate a cross-cultivation strategy. The integrated structure offers the opportunity to manage donors in more of an account management system, reducing the number of contacts a donor must maintain with the institution. Furthermore, an integrated approach ideally allows for a more coordinated understanding of individual donor preferences and motives for giving. A fully coordinated structure should allow for an individual donor to be presented with a menu of funding options that include both academic and athletic opportunities tailored to the individual donor's interests. Donors have indicated in interviews that such an approach would maximize their institutional (athletic and academic combined) support.

The role of organizational structure clearly needs more research attention. Current research indicates that successful athletic programs can bring new donors to the institution. However, despite having the potential capacity to support academic programs through the charitable portion of their mental budget (Heath and Soll, 1996), these donors often do not make such gifts. A cooperative effort between athletic and academic fundraisers might offer the opportunity to develop solicitations designed to attract both athletic and academic gifts. The evidence collected from each of the studies described here indicates an important role for the organizational fundraising structure. Our impression is that integrated units are best suited to maximizing the institutional value of donors. The ability to identify, solicit, track, and cultivate donors through a common system offers the most potential for understanding the full range of a donor's charitable giving. It is noteworthy that of the five institutions included in the analysis of individual donor data, the most symbiotic relationship between athletics and academics was at a school utilizing an integrated fundraising approach. The largest crowd-out effects were at an institution utilizing a separate athletic unit under institutional control. While the interpretation of these patterns is at this point speculative, organizational structure offers a promising path for future research designed to understand donor behavior.

Success in cross-cultivation will require fundraisers to understand the motives behind each of the gift types, as donors have indicated different reasons for supporting athletic versus academic programs. However, it is clear that in both cases, the need to communicate success or potential success associated with the gifts solicited is crucial for developing long-term support. This presents particular challenges for academic programs where readily available evidence of success is often an issue. However, in the absence of fundraisers taking an interest in identifying and communicating success metrics for academic programs, fundraisers must be aware that current measures, like the *U.S. News & World Report* rankings, are considered in donor evaluations of academic programs. There are also important implications for athletic programs, particularly in communicating the program's success more globally. Restricting success to on-the-field performance is not only limiting for many programs where such performance on an annual basis is unlikely, but it is also inconsistent with other important evaluative criteria used by donors. Factors such as graduation rates, community service on the part of athletic department personnel, and the overall integrity of the department as evidenced by well-run programs all must be incorporated when communicating athletic success.

Whether athletic and academic giving are in competition or symbiotic may stem from the fundraising strategy employed by each institution. The studies included in this chapter demonstrate occurrences of apparent crowd-out effects where the vast majority of increased giving is being directed to athletic programs, in some cases even at the apparent expense of academic giving. However, qualitative results and empirical analysis of NCAA I-AA and I-AAA institutions not only suggest that symbiotic effects are possible, but that they are occurring at some institutions. Ultimately, it appears, the ability of athletic and academic fundraisers to cooperate to cross-cultivate donors may determine the influence of athletic fund-raising programs on academic support.

References

Arnett, D.B., German, S.D., and Hunt, S.D. (2003). The identity salience model of relationship marketing success: The case of nonprofit marketing. *Journal of Marketing*, 67: 89–105.

Baade, R.A., and Sundberg, J.O. (1996). Fourth down and goal to go? Assessing the link between athletics and alumni giving. *Social Science Quarterly*, 77: 789–803.

Brady, M.K., Noble, C.H., Utter, D.J., and Smith, G.E. (2002). How to give and receive: An exploratory study of charitable hybrids. *Psychology & Marketing*, 19: 919–944.

Council for Aid to Education (2006, February). *Contributions to Colleges and Universities up by 4.9% to 25.6 Billion*. Washington, DC: Author.

Cunningham, B.M., and Conchi-Ficano, C.K. (2002). The determinants of donative revenue flows from alumni of higher education. *Journal of Human Resources*, 37: 540–569.

Gaski, J.F., and Etzel, M.J. (1984). Collegiate athletic success and alumni generosity: Dispelling the myth. *Social Behavior and Personality*, 12: 29–38.

Gladden, J.M., Mahoney, D.F., and Apostolopoulou, A. (2005). Toward a better understanding of college athletic donors: What are the primary motives? *Sport Marketing Quarterly*, 14: 18–30.

Goff, B. (2000). Effects of university athletics on the university: A review and extension of empirical assessment. *Journal of Sport Management*, 14: 84–104.

Grimes, P.W., and Chressanths, G.A. (1994). Alumni contributions to academics: The role of intercollegiate sports and NCAA sanctions. *American Journal of Economics and Sociology*, 53: 27–41.

Heath, C., and Soll, J.B. (1996). Mental budgeting and consumer decisions. *Journal of Consumer Research*, 23: 40–52.

Howard, D.R., and Crompton, J.L. (2004). *Financing Sport* (2nd edition). Morgantown, WV: Fitness Information Technologies.

Litan, R.E., Orszag, J.M., and Orszag, P.R. (2003). *The Empirical Effects of Collegiate Athletics: An Interim Report*. Indianapolis: National Collegiate Athletic Association.

Mahony, D.F., Gladden, J.M., and Funk, D.C. (2003). Examining athletic donors at NCAA division I institutions. *International Sports Journal*, 7: 9–27.

McCormick, R.E., and Tinsley, M. (1990). Athletics and academics: A model of university contributions. In B.L. Goff and R.D. Tollison (Eds.), *Sportometrics* (pp. 193–206). College Station, TX: Texas A&M University Press.

Raudenbush, S.W., and Bryk, A.S. (2002). *Hierarchical Linear Models: Applications and Data Analysis methods* (2nd edition). Thousand Oaks, CA: Sage Publications.

Rhoads, T.A., and Gerking, S. (2000). Educational contributions, academic quality and athletic success. *Contemporary Economic Policy*, 18: 248–259.

Sargeant, A. (1999). Charitable giving: Towards a model of donor behaviour. *Journal of Marketing Management*, 15: 215–238.

Shulman, J.L., and Bowen, W.G. (2001). *The Game of Life*. Princeton, NJ: Princeton University Press.

Sperber, M. (1990). *College Sports Inc.* New York: Henry Holt.

Sperber, M. (2000). *Beer and Circus: The Impact of Big-time College Sports on Undergraduate Education*. New York: Henry Holt.

Stinson, J.L., and Howard, D.R. (2004). Scoreboards vs. mortarboards: Major donor behavior and intercollegiate athletics. *Sport Marketing Quarterly*, 13: 73–81.

Stinson, J.L., & Howard, D.R. (2007). Athletic success and private giving to athletic and academic programs at NCAA institutions. *Journal of Sport Management*, 21(2).

Toma, J.D. (1999). The collegiate ideal and the tools of external relations: The uses of high-profile intercollegiate athletics. *New Directions for Higher Education*, 105: 81–90.

Toma, J.D. (2003). *Football U.* Ann Arbor: The University of Michigan Press.

Turner, S.E., Meserve, L.A., and Bowen, W.G. (2001). Winning and giving: Football results and alumni giving at selective private colleges and universities. *Social Science Quarterly*, 82: 812–826.

Wolfinger, R., and Chang, M. (2003). *Comparing the SAS GLM and Mixed Procedures for Repeated Measures*. Cary, NC: SAS Institute, Inc.

3

Understanding Sport Participation— A Cross Level Analysis from the Perspectives of Neo-Institutionalism and Bourdieu

Eivind Åsrum Skille and Berit Skirstad

The central object of this chapter is to examine the possibility of combining different theoretical perspectives as a way of illuminating a particular sporting case study. The empirical data that is used covers the Norwegian Sports City Program (SCP) and its impact on adolescent (16–19 years old) sport participation. The central research question was whether more or less adolescents participate in the SCP, in comparison with conventional sport, and if they differ in gender and class group belongings. The specific case and the chosen theories make it further possible to discuss sport provision and individuals' needs as a relationship between supply and demand.

The structure of the chapter is as follows. First, Norwegian sport and the Sports City Program (SCP) are presented. Second, the theories are presented; similarities and differences are discussed. Finally, an analysis is made, applying the theoretical perspectives; and an implicit and sometimes explicit discussion of the strengths and weaknesses of the theories is included. This chapter starts with a top-down presentation of theories, and ends with a bottom-up analysis of results, where the analysis will end up by treating the levels together with a discussion about supply and demand. We want to emphasize and explain that this case study needs theory that captures both an organizational as well as an individual level.

Norwegian Sport

To understand the analysis of the SCP, it is necessary to begin with some general description or contextualization of Norwegian sport. Norwegian sport usually takes place during leisure time, and it is voluntarily conducted, mostly by parents of the participants. Participation is based on individual membership (n = 1.9 million)[1] in local sport clubs (n = 12.500), and the program is usually competitive oriented. The sport clubs are organized in the "NOC system" (Figure 3–1), with one line of district sport associations (n = 19) and one line of special sport federations (n = 55). There is one district sport association for each county, and it is responsible for "sport for all" and sport policy in its region. A special sport federation governs its specific sport(s)[2] at a national level and is the link to the international federations for its sport. Everything is federated in the Norwegian Olympic Committee and Confederation of Sports (NOC). The NOC and every organization of the NOC system are—in principle[3]— voluntary (nongovernmental and nonprofit). The relationship between the state and the voluntary sport organization(s) is an important matter in this analysis. The NOC in general and the SCP in particular get state

FIGURE 3–1. The Organization of Norwegian Sport, Under the Monopolistic Umbrella NOC

---

[1] There are many double memberships. Surveys estimate the number of members to be approximately 1.3 million (Skirstad, 2002). This is among a population of about 4.5 million inhabitants.

[2] This varies. For example, the football federation only governs football, while the ski federation governs both Nordic disciplines (cross country skiing, ski jumping, and nordic combined) as well as the alpine disciplines.

[3] The so-called voluntary and autonomous sport organization (NOC) is, of course, influenced by the market, for example, by sponsoring, by the state, and by subsidies. The latter is a main point of the subsequent analysis.

subsidies and are dependent on the state for economic support to facilities and to financing the organizational work.

The Sports City Program (SCP)

The Sports City Program (SCP) will first be described and then the main results of its impact on participation in adolescent sport will be analyzed. This study is first about whether more or less adolescents and, second whether other adolescents, participate in the SCP, in comparison with conventional sport. Third, it is about whether participation in the SCP is based on belonging to other gender and class groups than on participation in conventional sport.

The SCP was initiated by the Government's Department of Sport Policy (DSP); the Parliament resolved the actual White Paper on sport, which included these lines:

> The Ministry suggests making public funding accessible, from the main grant of the sport's gambling revenues, to programs benefiting certain groups. These groups are especially inactive children and adolescents, who in particular are a challenge for the city areas. The funding will benefit programs run by the sport organizations. It is suggested that the program be developed by local sport clubs, in cooperation with municipal authorities, with the Norwegian Confederation of Sports as the coordinating body (St. meld. nr. 41, 1991–1992, p. 136).

The aim was to get other youth into sport, than those who are usually involved. The SCP is directed and financed by the DSP and implemented by the NOC (see Figure 3–2).

During the first phase (1993–2000), the SCP comprised three cities (Oslo, Bergen, and Trondheim), and the DSP communicated directly with the SCP administrators in district sport associations. The SCP reported directly to the Ministry. Therefore, in this period, the Ministry of Cultural Affairs, to which the DSP belongs, had a very direct influence on the projects. Of course, this also represented a threat for the NOC, because this was organized outside the central umbrella organization despite the fact that it was physically established at the district sport associations. Since 2001, there has been a central SCP administrator, who is physically located in the headquarters for the NOC, and organizationally has a position on the central staff of the NOC. This positioning could be seen as a homogenization with conventional sport, with the NOC recovering power over the project. In short, central control of the SCP has shifted from the Ministry to the NOC; in the subsequent analysis we will scrutinize if and

Parliament: *White Paper on Sport* DSP: *goal steering and financing*	Norwegian Olympic Committee and Confederation for Sports (NOC) *SCP administrator (since 2001)*

District sport associations *SCP administrator*	Special sport federations

Sport clubs

Alternatives	Conventional sport

Outsiders	Members

FIGURE 3–2. The Organization of the SCP: Initiated by Public Authorities;
Implemented by the NOC. SCP Aspects are in Italics; There Are
Some New Boxes and Some New Elements in the Old Boxes

how this fact has influenced the provision of sport offers for adolescents
and the sport participation of the adolescents.

When the research started (2002), two major processes followed this
centralization of control, namely expansion and standardization. First,
after an initiation made by the central administrator of the SCP,
the program was established in several new cities, and the SCP has
since 2002 comprised eight cities and four municipalities around Oslo
(the largest city and capital of Norway). Second, after the establishment
of the program in new cities, the central administrator initiated a
process of standardization of both activities and procedures related to
applications and reports, among the SCP administrators from all over the
country.

Further, individual data were analyzed in order to determine whether
other adolescents participate in SCP activities than in conventional sport
(that is, whether one reached the outsiders that were the aim of the
project). The population of the study reported here consists of adolescents
in two areas of a Norwegian city where the Sports City Program is well
established for the 16–19 year old age group. A survey was conducted to
monitor the outcome of this program. Six (which is half) of the secondary
schools in the two areas of the city participated in the study. Both types
of Norwegian secondary schools, those that are oriented toward more
academic preparation and those that are more occupationally oriented,
were included. There were 812 questionnaires distributed, of which 566,
or 69.7%, were returned completed. The nonreplies do not skew the sample
in terms of the social characteristics of the young people themselves; hence,
the sample is representative for the adolescents of the parts of the city.
The survey procedure and sample were in agreement with the Norwegian
Data Inspectorate.

Two main dependent variables were created: one measuring participation in SCP activities, and one measuring participation in conventional sport. The different categories of status in conventional sport were based on the conventional sport participation variable, together with follow-up questions on whether respondents had participated and quit, or never participated in a sports club. The values are inactive, quitter, and active. To discover if there was any relationship between participation in SCP activities and conventional sport status (inactive, quitter, active), a one-way ANOVA analysis was conducted. Background variables were gender and class. Class in this study was indicated by choice of secondary school (vocational or academically-oriented). This approach is congruent with the argument that education transmits class-based culture (Bourdieu, 1986, p. 23). A cross-classification variable was created with categories: vocational boy, academic boy, vocational girl, and academic girl.

First, Table 3–1 depicts the number of participants in SCP and conventional sport, respectively.

Table 3–1 shows that more than half of the youth participate in conventional sport (54%) and approximately the same number (56%) in SCP. But it does not say anything about whether different people participate in the two distinct contexts. Table 3–2 identifies the partial participation

TABLE 3–1
Distribution of Participants of Sports City Program Activities and
Conventional Sport (N = 566)

Participation/arena	Sports City Program in %	Conventional sport in %
Participant	56	54
Nonparticipant	44	46
Total	100	100

TABLE 3–2
Distribution of SCP Participants Based on Categories of Conventional Sport

SCP/conventional sport	Inactives in %		Quitters in %		Actives in %		Total in %
Participant in SCP	34	4	47	32	64	64	100
Nonparticipant in SCP	66	10	53	45	36	45	100
Total	100 (n = 35)		100 (n = 207)		100 (n = 304)		(n = 546)

rate in SCP, based on the status of participation in conventional sport: active, quitted, and nonactive.

Almost two-thirds of those active in conventional sport were also active in SCP. Almost half of the quitters and one-third of the inactive were now active in SCP, and these are really the crucial groups to whom the SCP was aimed. The participants in SCP from the inactive group count only for 4% of the sample. They are the ones that belonged to the target group. But the inactive group, who never have been active in conventional sport, is small from the outset if it just counts for 6% of the total. Of the active in conventional sport, only one-third does not also participate in SCP.[4]

Table 3–3 shows the sociological characteristics of participants in SCP and conventional sport, with regard to gender and class (measured by orientation in secondary school: vocational versus academic).

More boys with academic compared to those with vocational background do conventional sport. For SCP, we find the opposite, but the difference is statistically weaker. For girls, the tendency is the same concerning conventional sport for the academic adolescents, but for participation in SCP, we find about the same for the two groups of girls. Both boys and girls with academic backgrounds are more likely to take part in both sporting contexts.[5]

These are the empirical facts we want to analyze with theory. But first, let us summarize our findings thus far. One main finding in the study of the SCP was the ongoing processes of centralization, expansion, and standardization. Another main finding, showed by the individual data,

TABLE 3–3

Participation Rates of Adolescents in "Conventional" Sport and in the Sports City Program, by (Education as Measure of) Socioeconomic Status and Gender

Educational level/ sporting setting	Academic (%)		Vocational (%)	
	Boys	Girls	Boys	Girls
Conventional sport	70.6	50.6	47.7	37.8
SCP	58.4	52.2	64.8	53.2
Both contexts	47.8	31.1	31.8	23.4
n	178	180	88	111

[4] ANOVA tests show significant differences between the groups (Skille, 2005b).

[5] Chi-square tests show significant differences, especially between genders (Skille and Waddington, 2006).

was the significant overlap of participants between the contexts. The latter could be explained by how the SCP now became organized. For this analysis, we find it helpful to use two different theories, namely Bourdieu (1977, 1990) for individuals' participation and neo-institutionalism for organizational structures (which in turn may explain participation). These theories are conceived as fitting the purpose for analyzing the presented data, because they focus on reproduction without denying change, because each of them covers one of the two levels of analysis (organizational and individual), and because they can be applied together (as will be outlined later).

Theories of Field: Neo-Institutionalism and Bourdieu

The combination of neo-institutionalism and Bourdieu is the approach we have selected to use for enhancing our understanding of this case. This part will briefly summarize these perspectives, and most important, emphasize the compatibility between the chosen theories. The presentation of neo-institutionalism will lean on the classic contributions of Meyer and Rowan (1991) and DiMaggio and Powell (1991b)[6], an early review of neo-institutionalism (Zucker, 1987), as well as a more recent overview (Tolbert and Zucker, 1996).

Both new institutionalists as well as Bourdieu discuss the dialectic between structure and agency. Bourdieu links the process of institutionalization, not (only) to organizational survival as do Tolbert and Zucker (1996), but to the reproduction of structure through the incorporated culture of individuals.

> ... it is necessary to pass from the *opus operatum* to the *modus operandi*, from statistical regularity or algebraic structure to the principle production of this observed order, and to construct the theory of practice, ... of the *dialectic of the internalization of externality and the externalization of internality*, or more simply, of incorporation and objectification (Bourdieu, 1977, p. 72, italics in original).[7]

Hence, to solve this problem (about structure and agency), or at least to have appropriate terms to speak of them, Bourdieu (1977, 1990) offers the concepts of field and habitus.

---

[6]The original articles are from 1977 and 1983, respectively. We refer to the book versions of 1991.

[7]*Opus operatum* = the results of former operations; *modus operandi* = the mode of operation.

The Field of Sport

For DiMaggio and Powell (1991b, pp. 64–65), an organizational field is "organizations that, in the aggregate, constitute a recognized area of institutional life: key suppliers, resource and product consumers, regulatory agencies, and other organizations that produce similar services or products." A field consists of organizations that share a meaning system and constitute a community, and where the organizations' participants interact frequently and fatefully (Scott, 2001). This organizational field overlaps with the social field, as Bourdieu defines it. Bourdieu's field has an internal logic that is the basis for selecting the actors that are able to or allowed to participate in the struggle for positions and power. For Bourdieu, individuals' positions in society, which he refers to as social space, structure their preferences for and access to the particular fields. Each field prescribes particular values and possesses its own regulative principles, thus it is *relatively* autonomous; on the one hand, it refers to the field as its own (atomic) world, but on the other hand, it is a part of the rest of society, influencing and influenced by other fields. The structure of a field is defined by the distribution (amount and composition) of capital, which is based on the results of previous struggles, and that directs future struggles (Bourdieu and Wacquant, 1992).

This refers to the basic forms of capital such as economic, cultural, and social, as well as symbolic and field-specific capital. Economic capital is material goods (income and fortune) and knowledge about the financial field; cultural capital is based on education, as well as competence within the field of (high) culture, that would be, for example, language or art; social capital is the sum of the resources of family relations and other social networks; and "symbolic capital, which is the form that one or another of these species [the three basic forms of capital] takes when it is grasped through categories of perception that recognize its specific logic" (Bourdieu and Wacquant, 1992, p. 119). Field specific capital here refers to what we would call "sporting capital," which includes the competence needed to be recognized and valued on the field of sport. Actors from some positions in the Norwegian society—in Bourdieu's (1986, 1991) words: social space—are more likely to appear as participants in the sports field than others. For example, people with high amounts of cultural capital, such as higher education, are more likely to participate in the sport field than people with lower education, while economic capital has a weaker explanatory value in this respect (Skille, 2005a).

Hence, while Bourdieu mainly treats the behavior of individual actors and neo-institutionalism treats the behavior of organizations, what is the link? Zucker (1987) relates the habitualized individual behavior within an organization to the confirmation of the institution of that organization. She holds: "organizational routines increase institutionalization within a given organization as a function of: (a) the degree of explicit codification in the form of work rules . . . ; (b) the length of the history of the structure/task; and (c) the degree of embeddedness in a network of structures/tasks" (Zucker, 1987, p. 456). Because of the historical process of the development of a field, its structure often has a mode of *doxa*: it is taken for granted and uncontested, and the structure is perceived as given by nature, despite being a human construction with historical and cultural origins. In this respect, the relationship between the DSP and the NOC is a typical example of an institution with organizational routines, a long history (since 1946, with the sport federation and the state's sport office established as two sides of the same coin), and embedded structures and tasks, which are reproduced through agents' habitualized practice.[8] On a field, there will always be a struggle about a silent reproduction—doxa, articulated change—heterodoxy, and preservation after fight—orthodoxy (Bourdieu, 1991).

Thus, Bourdieu and neo-institutionalism share the emphasis on the taken-for-granted, in Bourdieu's words the *doxic*, in the vocabulary of neo-institutionalism the *mythic*. According to Meyer and Rowan (1991), three processes generate such myths: while networks of actors become tight and interconnected (within a field), the number of myths increases; myths generated by specific organizational practices are spread and supposed to be effective; and myths are generated by powerful organizations forcing the environment to adapt to their structures and goals. Bourdieu calls it a *sociodicy* (Bourdieu, 1998, p. 43), a theoretical justification for a privileged position in society, which is based on the symbolic power that confers the right to define, for example, the concept of sport. Moreover, according to DiMaggio and Powell (1991a), expanding activity within a field requires standardization to obtain centralized control. The legislation of such actions is rationalization, while the "real" goals might be monopolization of one's own business. In that respect, three forms of institutional processes explain how myths spread (DiMaggio and Powell, 1991b): *coercive isomorphism* occurs when formal or informal pressure is exerted on an organization by organizations upon which they are dependent; *mimetic isomorphism* can emerge as a response to uncertainty, where organizations resemble other actors in the field that are perceived as successful; *normative isomorphism* might develop by the mechanisms of filtering personnel to do certain jobs in the field. The latter originates from professionalism; it refers not only to paid work but to an understanding of who is doing the job best, and explains the NOC's role in the

---

[8]One specific empirical element that will shed some light on this rather theoretical and abstract statement is the fact that there are, in the Norwegian field of sport and sport policy, examples of people "changing sides of the table"; that is, going from a position in the NOC to the DSP (and sometimes, but more seldom, vice versa).

Norwegian society. The NOC is the only umbrella organization for sport in Norway and has a monopoly of state subsidies to sport; it has what Bourdieu (1986, 1991) would call the hegemony on the field of sport.

Neo-institutionalists and Bourdieu share the focus on institutionalized processes as reproduction processes (Bourdieu, 1991; Scott, 2001). An institution is—according to DiMaggio and Powell (1991a, p. 21), who base themselves on Berger and Luckmann (1991)—constituted of individuals' habitualized practice (Tolbert and Zucker, 1996). If institutionalism is about reproducing established procedures, the possibilities for change seem rare. However, social institutions (such as sport) and organizations (such as the NOC), do undergo change. Following the logic of the social construction of reality, change occurs after human action (externalization), which leads us to the presentation of the theory at an individual level of analysis.

The Habitus for Sport

For Bourdieu, interests in a field can only be articulated by agents with a *habitus* that can adapt to the field and agents who have the knowledge and skills required to act in the field. Habitus is structured and structuring structures, or systems of durable and transposable dispositions that are largely implicit and developed through engagement in social practices (Bourdieu, 1977, 1990). It is a dialectical process, where practices generate habitus, and habitus generates practice. For example, what you learn during childhood makes the basis for what you do during adolescence, which in turn leads to new learning, and so on.

With habitus as an intermediary link, Bourdieu seeks to overcome the dichotomy between objective structures and subjective preferences, which constitute social practice. Habitus offers a theoretical link to institutions, and links the individual to wider social process of culture and politics (Brown and Johnson, 2000). Habitus produces individual as well as collective practices (Bourdieu, 1977, 1990), implying that individuals from similar social backgrounds—that is, coming from similar positions in the social space—create similar habituses. Thus, individuals with similar sociological characteristics, such as gender and class background, often end up in the same field.

> A particularly clear example of practical sense as a proleptic adjustment to the demands of a field is what is called, in the language of sport, a "feel for the game." This phrase . . . gives a fairly accurate idea of the almost miraculous encounter between the *habitus* and a field . . . (Bourdieu, 1990, p. 66, italics in original).

"The feel for the game" gives the activity in the field a subjective sense, a meaning. The experience of meaning depends on when and how the game on the field was learned, where, when (how often), and how it is played (Bourdieu, 1986). Broad parts of the dispositions are internalized in the early years of life, through unreflective socialization, incorporating the objective structures in the "second nature of habitus" (Bourdieu, 1977, pp. 78–79), or "quasinature of habitus" (Bourdieu, 1990, p. 56). The earlier a player enters the game, the greater is her/his ignorance of all that is taken for granted through the investment in the field. In short, early learning is doxic.[9] For example, an individual who was brought into sport during early childhood perceives sport as it is given by nature. This may explain the feeling of a high threshold for starting sport participation during late adolescence (Skille, 2005a), a threshold that the SCP aimed to lower.

Neo-institutionalism, as well as Bourdieu, has gained a number of critiques in several respects. One critique, which will be discussed here, is related to the weight that is put on reproduction, and the small possibilities for change. Within organization theory, there are other alternatives, such as resource dependence theory and theories of strategic choice (see, for example, Cunningham, 2002). In mainstream sociology, the reproductive and taken-for-granted perspectives are recently challenged by modernization theories and the concepts of *reflexivity* and *individualization*. These refer to the detachment from cultural traditions, where choices are no longer rooted in the group's customs, but in individual decision making that is based on reflexivity. Two citations from some of the most influential modernity sociologists should be enough to make the point.

> The reflexive project of the self, which consists of the sustaining of coherent, yet continuously revised, biographical narratives, takes place in the context of multiple choice. . . . The more tradition loses its hold and the more daily life is reconstituted in terms of the dialectical interplay of the local and the global, the more individuals are forced to negotiate lifestyle choices among a diversity of options (Giddens, 1991, p. 5).

> Individualization in this sense means that each person's biography is removed from given determinations and placed in his or her own hands . . . Individualization of life situations and processes thus means that biographies become self-reflexive, socially prescribed biography is transformed into biography that is self-produced and continues to be produced (Beck, 1992, p. 135).

---

[9] "Doxa is the relationship of immediate adherence that is established in practice between a habitus and the field to which it is attuned" (Bourdieu, 1990, p. 68).

In late modernity there is apparently a lack of fit between habitus and field in certain public spheres. For example, "feminine habitus has moved from private to public spheres" (Adkins, 2003, p. 21).

Before we move onto the analysis, we would like to briefly position ourselves, with regard to theoretical perspectives and other empirical studies of sport (organizations) applying neo-institutionalism. Figure 3–3 shows how we define our theory development and empirical research, quite in the middle of a diagram, with two dimensions: one axis of theory versus empirical cases; and one axis of theories of organizations versus theories of individuals. This tension between theoretical perspectives will be considered during the following analysis. With reference to Figure 3–3, we now move on from "Merging theories" to "Application of merger."

Explaining Sport Participation: Different Levels of Analysis

In explaining sport participation, the subfield of the SCP is compared to the subfield of conventional sport. It was hypothesized that objective barriers to participation, such as those associated with membership of particular class or gender groups, would be eroded for the SCP participation. The research exhibited both similarities *and* differences between the SCP participants and conventional sport participants. The case of the SCP will be discussed, first with the individual data as the basis, which seeks to explain sport participation with Bourdieu's notion of habitus. Second, neo-institutionalism, as well as Bourdieu, will be applied to discuss organizational aspects of the SCP. The point is that the organization analysis is believed to help explain the participation in sport, when comparing conventional sport with SCP activities. The discussion concludes with a note on supply and demand, with the aim of linking the levels of analysis and trying to show that/how Bourdieu is a fruitful supplement in organization—and especially cross level—analysis.

Individual Characteristics (Habitus)

There is a considerable overlap of participants between conventional sport and the SCP. Although the SCP is targeted at encouraging new groups to participate in sport, one of its consequences has been to provide new activities for adolescents who are already involved in conventional sport (64%) or at least used to be (32%) because they label themselves as quitters; thus, the SCP is benefiting primarily those who already are or have been inside the sport field (96%). The majority constitutes those who already have a habitus for sport and "a feel for the game" (Bourdieu,

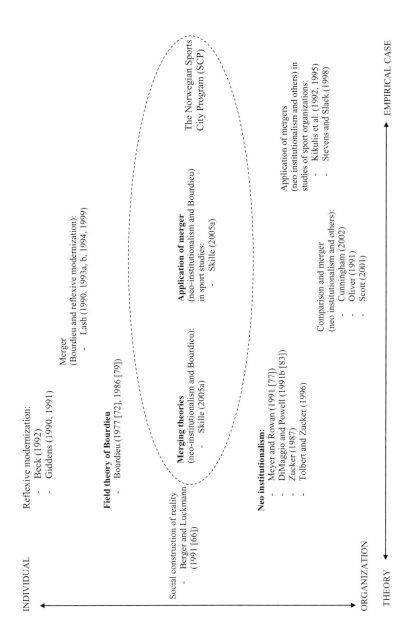

FIGURE 3–3. The Positioning of This Theory Development and Research, in Relation to Individual—Organizational Theories and Theory—Empirical Research

1990, p. 66), and they maintain the hegemony of the sport field. However, an examination of key variables, such as gender and class, suggests that the SCP does not *simply* reproduce old social patterns of sport participation; it also creates new patterns. In short, academically oriented males are most likely to take part in conventional sport, while vocationally oriented males are more likely to attend SCP activities, and the same distinction is evident for taking part in both subfields. This difference does not exist among girls, except that more girls with an academic background take part in both contexts. In addition, an important finding is that the patterns of the objective elements explaining habitus are more blurred in relation to the new subfield (Skille, 2005b).

Sport participation also has its subjective elements (Skille, 2005c). Again, there are both similarities *and* differences across subfields. On the one hand, it is evident that a key element of the habitus for conventional sport is related to competition and that the bearers of this habitus are at ease with that fact. On the other hand, SCP participants' denegation[10] of competitiveness may be interpreted as an indication that some adolescents have a habitus that requires situations where defeat is not a possible outcome. In relation to gender, boys invest more of their confidence and identity in conventional sport, indicating that sport offers an important script in the development of male identity. However, the gender issue is more nuanced than is suggested by a crude differentiation between male and female; there are at least two male routes to be taken within the field of sport, each dominating one subfield. One is the regulated and disciplined achievement script offered by conventional sport, which fits a habitus first and foremost borne by academically-oriented boys. It suggests that educational capital and competitive sporting capital are, to a high degree, found in the same habitus. The other is the detachable and self-governing script offered by alternative sport, such as the SCP, toward which vocationally-oriented boys are significantly more disposed.[11] In contrast, it appears that girls (from both classes) participating in SCP activities value the lower skill demands involved in these activities (Skille, 2005c). This suggests that most girls have a habitus that is less compatible with the subfield of conventional sport. In sum, there is a complexity of relationships between subfields and social groups that indicates that structural elements of habitus, the socially constructed reality influencing the individual's choice of practice, are linked to subjective preferences.

---

[10] The notion denegation is preferred to denial, because the latter only expresses refusal, whereas denegation points out the idea that one is objectively participating in reproducing competitiveness by affirming that it is down weighted (see Aubel and Ohl, 2004).

[11] It seems that freedom, and the here and now experience (hedonism), is in general more appreciated by the vocational-oriented adolescents (Skille, 2005c).

Organizational (Field) Considerations

The establishment of the SCP may be considered a result of "structural reflexivity" (Lash, 1994, pp. 115–116), which refers to the policy initiated by agents representing the Norwegian state, the Ministry of Cultural Affairs. The basis of this reflexivity is to be found in the logic of late modernity, where the core institutional responses of traditional modernity are no longer self-evident. The idea of the SCP would not have been included in the White Paper, which was resolved by the Parliament, if it had not been for reflexive organizational personnel. The process is due to the aspiration of the key actors and that "professionals were seen to have a voice in decision making" as Kikulis et al. (1995, p. 294) put it. Thus, theories that focus on agency and change seem fruitful, while this finding supports the reflexive modernization thesis and the organization theories that focus on strategic choice.

However, when moving from policy making to implementation, theories of reproduction seem to be more appropriate. According to neo-institutionalism, an organization's success depends on its role in society and its compliance with broader values and norms.[12] While the SCP exists partly besides and partly within the NOC, it will be of special interest in the analysis to detect to whom the SCP personnel feel loyalty and perceive pressure, and to whom they conform. The three mechanisms—coercive, mimetic, and normative—are all at work, as was shown in earlier studies of sport organizations (e.g., Cunningham and Ashley, 2001; Danylchuk and Chelladurai, 1999; Stevens and Slack, 1998). Priority will be given to the analysis of the relationship between the state and the NOC.

Coercive isomorphism is associated with formal pressures exerted on the SCP by the DSP, upon which the SCP is dependent both for financial resources (economic capital) as well as legitimacy (symbolic capital). Through coercive pressure, the DSP guides the SCP by means of defining target groups and goals, and by monitoring through reporting. To maintain their position as *the* sport implementer in Norway, the NOC implements the SCP according to the DSP's steering, at least in the initial phase. As was shown in studies of Canadian sport organizations, governmental pressure may lead to change in amateur sport organizations (Kikulis et al., 1992; Slack and Hinings, 1992, 1994). But is change necessarily the opposite of institutionalization—or de-institutionalization (Zucker, 1987)?

---

[12] The idea of how myths are constituted is not treated in depth here but is a precondition for the following discussion. See Enjolras (2003, pp. 30–31), who applies the theory on the DSP-NOC relationship in general.

Zucker (1987, p. 444) links the process of coercive isomorphism to "state legitimation in the environment-as-institution-approach, but it is explicitly considered de-institutionalizing in the organization-as-institution approach." There are three defining principles of environment institutionalization: (1) the process stems from overarching rationalization; (2) the link to the state is important to understand institutionalization; and (3) it produces task-related inefficiency. All of these were found in the case of the SCP: (1) the DSP gave the mission of implementing the SCP to the NOC for "rational" reasons; (2) the DSP may put coercive pressure on the NOC, including the SCP collegiums; and (3) it is in no way evident that this is the most efficient solution for reaching the goals of the SCP, rather that the generation of meaning inside the organization is a central process of institutionalization.

In contrast, the three defining principles of organization institutionalization are: (1) elements of institutions stem from small group processes; (2) structure and process are both highly institutionalized; and (3) it is a source for new institutionalization and it increases stability. These were also found in the SCP case: (1) the SCP collegiums' members were all, prior to the establishment of the SCP, insiders of the NOC; (2) the NOC structures, as well as the NOC functions, are historically bounded and sedimented; and (3) the stability is consequently evident. The coercive pressure from the state does not necessarily de-institutionalize the within-organization processes of the institution, as it is hypothesized by Zucker (1987). That is due to the special relationship between the state and the voluntary sport organization in Norway, and because the other isomorphic processes reproduce the institutions within the organization of the NOC. In this case, normative and mimetic processes stood against the de-institutionalization, which is expected by the coercive process.

While coercive isomorphism stems from (external) pressure, *normative isomorphism* stems from professionalization. The notion of professionalization, in relation to the voluntary-based NOC, is not so much about paid work as it is about the societal understanding of the NOC as the best and only sport implementer in Norway. Normative mechanisms emphasize that individual behavior depends on institutional definitions of what is appropriate or expected. By conforming to the norms of the NOC, the personnel of the SCP make the SCP more likely to survive within the sport field. Further, *mimetic isomorphism* refers to how organizations tend to model themselves after the activities of other, similar and successful organizations. The SCP becomes more similar to its mother organization (the NOC) because SCP personnel were NOC personnel prior to the establishment of the SCP, and people do what is familiar to them. The way individuals operate in these contexts is largely a function of how they interpret the understanding of what is taken-for-granted.

The three isomorphic processes work simultaneously but with differing strengths. Tolbert and Zucker (1996) give a description of the process of institutionalization, which gives rise to a number of implications for research. For example, which will be possible to recognize in the analysis of the SCP, "when large and more centrally linked organizations are innovators and early adopters of a given structure, that structure is more likely to become fully institutionalized than other structures" (Tolbert and Zucker, 1996, p. 185; see DiMaggio and Powell, 1991b). Institutionalization implies that organizations get additional attributes; when an organization becomes an institution, it gets "marked by a *concern for self-maintenance*" (Selznick, 1957, p. 20, italics in original). While an organization first and foremost does what it was established to do, for example providing sport, it gradually gets a value of its own. That is, it could be hypothesized that the NOC exists more because of a long history and as a sedimented institution and less because it is the most efficient sport provider. Furthermore, it can be hypothesized that the SCP implementation is more dependent on NOC norms than on DSP goals.

Supply and Demand

It is possible to argue that the evidence of a more blurred habitus explaining the social patterns of SCP participants compared to conventional sport participants suggests that there is an ongoing process of change. How can change be explained by the chosen theories? Lash (1993a, 1993b) holds that the notion of reflexive modernization, as it is developed and used by Giddens and Beck, can best be developed via Bourdieu's notion of habitus. For Lash, modernity has, in addition to a *groundless* ground, a groundless *ground* (Lash, 1999). If reflexivity is possible, it must have a point of departure; and that point varies. Although new classes are created in the late modernity, the personnel filling the different class positions are determined by ascribed characteristics, dependent on their habitus. This is in line with Ohl, who after reviewing the use of class in recent (1990s) research in the sociology of sport, holds that the postmodern thesis "has not been sufficiently proven through empirical studies" and that "Bourdieu's work helps us to understand the transformations of classifications" (Ohl, 2000, p. 154).

Moreover, organization theory will be applied to interpret and explain the results of the SCP's impact on adolescents' participation in sport. In terms of classical economic analysis, change is brought about by market mechanisms of supply and demand. However, on the one hand, the innovation of the SCP cannot be adequately understood by reducing it simply to a question of supply and demand. On the other hand, the SCP is neither purely a welfare good distributed by public authorities, nor is it purely an outcome of a voluntary organization. State subsidized sporting provision, as it has developed in Norway, is based on the historically and socially constructed tools for supply; it is not a free market but a regulated market. The SCP is a compromise that involves a governmental understanding about the need for alternative activities, and the implementation of those activities through the strongly institutionalized NOC hierarchy. Thus, the Norwegian model of state-funded sport implementation is a supply-oriented approach.

Taking a top-down perspective, there are two steps in the process of supplying sport through the SCP. The first is that the world was *interpreted* as changing and that modern youth was *perceived* as individualized; therefore, agents of the DSP in powerful positions claimed that new sport provisions were needed. The second is that implementation was done through the NOC. Although the SCP represents change, the core functions of the NOC remain: to provide sport. Taking a bottom-up perspective, the supply-oriented approach gives few possibilities for adolescents who want to attend sport to influence the decisions taken at the central levels of public policy or the NOC. The job of defining, classifying and interpreting the needs "out there" lies in the hands of the personnel initiating, goal steering, targeting, and financing the program. These interpretations may not necessarily accord with reality, as it is perceived by the adolescents.

The NOC was established to produce sport, which through history has developed a position as the conventional sport. While the SCP was established to produce alternative sport, the SCP was an opportunity for the NOC to reproduce itself as the sport implementer and thereby to conserve its role as the hegemonic actor in the sport field. In that respect, the case of the SCP-within-NOC fits with the observations made by Zucker (1987), who draws on Selznick, when holding that basic organizational objectives are deflected and not performed as well as they could be because organizations prioritize to serve legitimating functions. During the process where the SCP personnel must align themselves with the coercive requirements of the DSP, the normative and mimetic influences from the NOC seem to dominate: the provision of sport becomes a provision of conventional sport. However, "it is often extremely difficult, if not impossible, to determine whether the factors highlighted by a given theoretical perspective are actually at work in determining organizational actions" (Tolbert and Zucker, 1996, p. 186).

In sum, the supply side creates, both organizationally and symbolically, the frames where adolescents may play sport. Bourdieu conceives of symbolic systems both as structured structures and as structuring structures. In both respects, the concept of sport refers to classifications that cease to be universal or at least taken-for-granted. Symbolic forms as structured structures refers to the organizational frames within which sport takes place—the *opus operatum*—whereas symbolic forms as structuring structures refers to the instruments of the construction of the sport field or subjective knowledge of the actors in the sport field—the *modus operandi*. When the ability to define the key concept (sport) is held by one major organization (the NOC), with economic support from the other major organization (the DSP) in the field, the symbolic systems become instruments of domination. By relating the provision of alternatives to the actor with the symbolic power to define the concept of sport, symbolic violence may be imposed on actors trying to enter the Norwegian sport field.

Following the idea of a dialectic interaction between structure and agency, it is possible to argue that the evidence of a more blurred habitus explaining the social patterns of SCP participants compared to conventional sport participants suggests that there is an ongoing process of change. This is associated with a slowly changing understanding of the concept of sporting capital. However, after a—often long lasting—dialectic interplay between structure and agency, the codes for entering the sport field will change, and perhaps lead to increased participation. In sum, a major constraint of the supply approach is that the *modus operandi* of those for whom operations would make a difference is closely connected to the *opus operatum*. On the contrary, the DSP-NOC relationship can, as well as being a symbiosis, be a tension—a continual heterodoxy—that implies possibilities for change.

Concluding Remarks

With regard to the combination of neo-institutionalism and Bourdieu's theory of field, it is believed that, and showed above how, the chosen theories provide a framework with the aim of covering two broad dichotomies: first, the leap from the organizational to the individual level of analysis; second, the tension between social reproduction and social change. Habitus refers to individual dispositions, which can be indicated empirically by objective measures of, for example, gender and class, as well as by subjective preferences for social practice such as sport. The overall aim has been to remind the reader of two things:

1. The use of a multiple theory framework makes the analysis better, because, as Tolbert (1985, p.12) observes: "organizational phenomena are much too complex to be described adequately by any single theoretical approach." By interplaying between different theoretical perspectives, one gets more insight and one better overcomes what Cunningham (2002) calls "conceptual blinders," compared to relying on one single theory.

2. By challenging the chosen theories (neo-institutionalism and Bourdieu) that focus on reproduction with other theories (modernization theory), which to a higher degree includes the idea of agency, and by integrating it into the analysis as suggested by Kikulis (2000) and done by Lash (1993a, 1993b, 1994), one overcomes one of the major criticisms of institutional theory (Greenwood and Hinings, 1996; Kikulis 2000), as of Bourdieu (Alexander, 1995); namely, that they failed to recognize the contributions of agency.

Theoretically speaking, at the organizational level, neo-institutionalism was applied in the analysis, and, at the individual level, the theory of fields as outlined by Bourdieu was chosen. It is believed that this choice of theories gives meaningful interpretations; it is further believed that this chapter offers an interesting and meaningful exhibition of the theories' and the triangulation's strengths and weaknesses, by applying them/it on a specific empirical case. By doing this, opportunities, limitations, and alternatives of the combinations of the theories are implicitly and sometimes explicitly discussed.

For practitioners, this chapter may give some implications about reflecting upon the relationship between supply and demand. In that respect, the mythic or doxic power, which is executed by the supply side in the field, may be considered as a constraint for future development in relation to the demand side.

References

Adkins, L. (2003). Reflexivity freedom or habit of gender? *Theory, Culture & Society*, 20(6):21–42.

Alexander, J. (1995). *Fin de Siéle Social Theory*. London: Verso.

Aubel, O., and Ohl, F. (2004). The denegation of the economy. *International Review for the Sociology of Sport*, 39(2):123–137.

Beck, U. (1992). *The Risk Society: Towards a New Modernity*. London: Sage.

Berger, P., and Luckmann. T. (1991 [1966]). *The Social Construction of Reality*. London: Penguin Books.

Bourdieu, P. (1977). *Outline of a Theory of Practice*. Cambridge: Cambridge University Press.

Bourdieu, P. (1986). *Distinction. A Social Critique of the Judgement of Taste*. London: Routledge.

Bourdieu, P. (1990). *The Logic of Practice*. Cambridge: Polity Press.

Bourdieu, P. (1991). *Language & Symbolic Power*. Cambridge: Polity Press.

Bourdieu, P. (1998). *Act of Resistance*. Cambridge: Polity Press.

Bourdieu, P., and Wacquant, L.J.D. (1992). *An Invitation to Reflexive Sociology*. Cambridge: Polity Press.

Brown, D., and Johnson, A. (2000). The social practice of self-defense martial arts: Applications for physical education. *Quest,* 52(3):246–259.

Cunningham, G.B. (2002). Removing the blinders: Toward an integrating model of organizational change in sport and physical activity. *Quest,* 54(4):276–291.

Cunningham, G.B., and Ashley, F.B. (2001). Isomorphism in NCAA athletic departments: The use of competing theories and advancement of theory. *Sport Management Review,* 4(1):47–63.

Danylchuk, K.E., and Chelladurai, P. (1999). The nature of managerial work in Canadian intercollegiate athletics. *Journal of Sport Management,* 13(2):148–166.

DiMaggio, P., and Powell, W.W. (1991a). Introduction, in W.W. Powell and P. DiMaggio (eds), *The New Institutionalism in Organizational Analysis*. Chicago: The University of Chicago Press.

DiMaggio, P., and Powell, W.W. (1991b [1983]). The iron cage revisited: Institutional isomorphism and collective rationality, in W.W. Powell and P. DiMaggio (eds), *The New Institutionalism in Organizational Analysis*. Chicago: The University of Chicago Press.

Enjolras, B. (2003). *Statlig idrettspolitikk i Norge og Frankrike*. Oslo: ISF.

Giddens, A. (1990). *Consequenses of Modernity*. Cambridge: Polity Press.

Giddens, A. (1991). *Modernity and Self-identity. Self and Society in Late Modern Age*. Cambridge: Polity Press.

Greenwood, R., and Hinings, C.R. (1996). Understanding radical organizational change: Bringing together the old and new institutionalism. *Academy of Management Review,* 21(4):1022–1054.

Kikulis, L.M. (2000). Continuity and change in governance and decision making in national sport organizations: Institutional explanations. *Journal of Sport Management,* 14(4):293–320.

Kikulis, L.M., Slack, T., and Hinings, B. (1992). Internationally specific design archetypes: A framework for understanding change in national sport organizations. *International Review for the Sociology of Sport,* 27(4):343–370.

Kikulis, L.M., Slack, T., and Hinings, B. (1995). Does decision making make a difference? Patterns of change within Canadian national sport organizations. *Journal of Sport Management,* 9(3):273–299.

Lash, S. (1990). *Sociology of Postmodernism*. London: Routledge.

Lash, S. (1993a). Reflexive modernity: The aesthetic dimension. *Theory, Culture and Society,* 10(1):1–23.

Lash, S. (1993b). Pierre Bourdieu: Cultural economy and social change, in C. Calhoun, E. LiPuma, and M. Postone (eds), *Bourdieu: Critical Perspectives*. Chicago: The University of Chicago Press.

Lash, S. (1994). Reflexivity and its doubles: Structure, aestethics, community, in U. Beck, A. Giddens, and S. Lash: *Reflexive Modernization*. Cambridge: Polity Press.

Lash, S. (1999). *Another Modernity a Different Rationality*. Oxford: Blackell.

Meyer, J.W., and Rowan, B. (1991 [1977]). Institutionalized organisations: Formal structure as myth and ceremony, in W.W. Powell and P. DiMaggio (eds), *The New Institutionalism in Organizational Analysis*. Chicago: The University of Chicago Press.

Ohl, F. (2000). Are social class still relevant to analyse sports groupings in "postmodern" society? An analysis referring to P. Bourdieu's theory. *Scandinavian Journal of Medicine and Science in Sports*, 10(3):146–155.

Oliver, C. (1991). Strategic responses to institutional processes. *Academy of Management Review*, 16(1):145–179.

Scott, W.R. (2001). *Institutions and Organizations* (2nd edition). Thousand Oaks, CA: Sage.

Selznick, P. (1957). *Leadership in Administration*. New York: Harper & Row.

Skille, E.Å. (2005a). *Sport policy and Adolescent Sport. The Sports City Program (Storbyprosjektet)*. Oslo: Norwegian School of Sport Sciences.

Skille, E.Å. (2005b). Individuality or reproduction. *International Review for the Sociology of Sport*, 40(3):307–320.

Skille, E.Å. (2005c). Adolescents' preferences for participation— Alternative versus conventional sports. A Norwegian case. *Sport und Gesellschaft/Sport and Society*, 2(2):107–124.

Skille, E.Å., and Waddington, I. (2006). Alternative sport programmes and social inclusion in Norway. *European Physical Education Review*, 12(3):251–270.

Skirstad, B. (2002). Norske idrettslag: Oversikt og utfordringer, in Ø. Seippel: *Idrettens bevegelser*. Oslo: Novus.

Slack, T., and Hinings, B. (1992). Understanding change in national sport organizations: An integration of theoretical perspectives. *Journal of Sport Management*, 6(2):114–132.

Slack, T., and Hinings, B. (1994). Institutional pressures and isomorphic change: An empirical test. *Organization Studies*, 15(6):803–827.

St. meld (1991–1992). nr. 41: *Om idretten, folkebevegelse og folkeforlystelse*. Oslo: Kulturdepartementet.

Stevens, J., and Slack, T. (1998). Integrating social action and structural constraints. *International Review for the Sociology of Sport*, 33(2):143–154.

Tolbert, P.S. (1985). Institutional environments and resource dependence: Sources of administrative structure in institutions of higher education. *Administrative Science Quarterly*, 30(1):1–13.

Tolbert, P.S., and Zucker, L.G. (1996). The institutionalization of institutional theory, in S.R. Clegg, C. Hardy, and W.R. Nord (eds), *Handbook of Organization Studies*. London: Sage, pp. 175–190.

Zucker, L. (1987). Institutional theories of organization. *Annual Review of Sociology*, 13(1):434–464.

4

Network Perspectives on Organizations

Catherine Quatman and Packianathan Chelladurai

In today's society, whether you are a researcher, practitioner, or consumer, it is nearly impossible to escape the notion of *networks* or *networking* when talking about organizations. For example, let us say that you are about to graduate with a degree in sport management and your academic advisor suggests that you take part in an organizational internship related to the type of career in sport you would like to pursue. Your advisor stresses how important it is that you get to know the people in the organization and make a good impression on them because *networking* with the right people can serve as an important key to unlocking your dream career.

Networking to get ahead or getting to know the right people who will help you get ahead is not the only common application of networks and organizations. From a different perspective, the word *network* has become somewhat of a trendy piece of jargon used to describe such things as organizations aligning together to form *interorganizational networks* or a type of flexibly designed *network structure* (e.g., the regional businesses of Silicon Valley) that an organization should embrace in order to remain competitive in today's business markets.

Regardless of the context in which it is used, the word *network* paired with organizational settings is often rendered to a metaphorical sense and tends to refer to a form of social capital that can be utilized or even exploited by a person, department, or organization in an advantageous way. Incidentally, the metaphorical and trendy usage of the term *network* has a number of scholars lamenting that the true power and utility of the actual constructs of network and networking are more often than not overlooked. Thus, it is often argued that beneath the surface of these trendy metaphors, the term *network* can invoke much richer and more robust meanings and functions than most people realize.

In fact, an entire academic discipline related to the science, math, and application of this deeper utility and understanding of networks has emerged over the last quarter of a century or so. The practices and findings of this emergent discipline are often tied to the phrases *social network theory* and *analysis* that come together under an umbrella approach called the *network perspective* or *network paradigm*. Concurrent with the advances made in the fields of science and math, behind the network perspective, a number of disciplines have embraced the techniques and tools of social network theory and analysis as they have widespread applicability for scholars and practitioners in fields ranging from physics and sociology to organizational theory and behavior, to name a few.

One benefit of the network perspective is that it helps alleviate some of the limitations of many of the conventional approaches to research in general, as well as it integrates a unique approach toward explaining the things that go on in the world. As Nohria (1992) articulated, to employ a network perspective "means adopting a different intellectual lens and discipline, gathering different kinds of data, learning new analytical and methodological techniques, and seeking explanations that are quite different from conventional ones" (p. 8). While many of the analytical and statistical procedures related to the network perspective are rather complex, some of the rudimentary ideas and simple applications behind the approach are fairly intuitive. Moreover, they can also be quite useful for management researchers and practitioners alike.

As such, the purpose of this chapter is to provide an introduction and overview of the network perspective, discuss several of the benefits the network paradigm provides in terms of organizational theory and organizational behavior research endeavors, and describe some practical applications that can be used by a practitioner in organizational settings. The chapter is organized into four sections. The first section delves into some substantive definitions of networks and introduces the prospect of defining networks under the mathematical premises of graph theory embraced by the network perspective. The second section elaborates on the foundations and principles behind the network perspective by highlighting conventional approaches, noting the limitations of the conventional approaches, and describing how the network perspective helps overcome some of these limitations. The third section briefly considers how a network approach has been explored in organizational theory and organizational behavior studies. Finally, the chapter concludes with a section providing a few suggestions on how practitioners can integrate social network theory and analysis into their everyday management strategies.

What Are Networks?

Broadly speaking, networks are often characterized by such phrases as webs of relationships, chains of linkages or ties, and the interconnectedness of people, places, or things. In fact, substantively, the term *network* can take on a wide variety of connotations. Nonetheless, it could be argued that most people intuitively have a general understanding of what is meant by the word *network*.

Even so, let us say that you are a researcher attempting to study networks within organizations. How might you go about defining the network you plan to study and what level of analysis would you choose to employ? Are you interested in the networks of connections between people, the web of relations between departments in the organization, or perhaps the linkages of interaction between multiple organizations? Moreover, how would you go about specifying a boundary for the network you are studying? Do you consider only people within a single department, all of the departments within a branch of the organization, or all of the organizations within a single market?

Under the network paradigm, scholars have adopted a unique approach toward defining networks as a social construct. Integrating the mathematical principles of graph theory, network scholars have elected to define a network simply as the expression of a set of nodes used to represent objects or actors of interest and lines depicting the relationships between the nodes. To demonstrate, imagine the set of nodes and lines in Figure 4–1 to represent a network you are interested in understanding. The nodes (or points) can be interpreted as individual people, a collection of departments within an organization, individual organizations, or really any person,

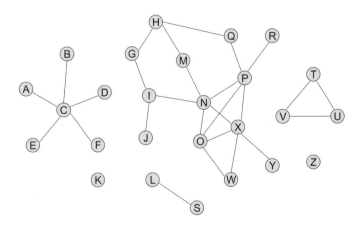

FIGURE 4–1. Visual Diagram of a Network of Actors

place, or thing you would like them to represent. The lines between them can then be defined as any sort of relationship between the actors or objects of interest, such as friendship ties, instrumental ties, or even something like the fact that their desks are located next to each other. The lines between nodes in the overall diagram thus depict how the relationships (however you want to define them) play out between all of the actors or objects in the system.

Regardless of the context in which you choose to interpret the diagram, it is apparent that the structure of the network has some unique features. For example, there are a number of nodes that are more isolated than others, several nodes which possess more ties to different nodes than others, and a few nodes that possess more central positions in the network than others. These structural features and a number of their implications will be discussed in greater depth later in the chapter. For now, it is only important to recognize the unique and concrete perspective provided by defining a network as an expression of a set of nodes and lines.

Defining networks in this regard is somewhat liberating. For one, it frees scholars from tackling debates about the wording and phrasing necessary to depict the term and imparts a universal lens for defining networks across time, space, and context. Also, the diagrams produced provide concrete visuals of the ties between the entities in a network that make for simple intuitive interpretations of the various structural properties. Furthermore, the visual diagrams can be translated into mathematical expressions for more complex analyses. The next section of the chapter delves further into some of the premises and propositions of the network perspective and describes how the network pictures, such as the diagram in Figure 4–1, can be translated into useful tools for analytical and practical purposes.

What Is the Network Perspective?

To understand the network perspective, it is useful to discuss where network methods fall into the understandings and practices of conventional research methods. As a start, simply imagine Figure 4–2 to be a population of employees for a sport organization. Pretend that you are charged with understanding how tasks are completed within the organization and what factors play into a person being promoted up the organizational hierarchy of authority.

Conventional Approaches

Traditionally, researchers usually embrace one of two approaches: (1) an individualistic, reductionist approach, or (2) a structural, holistic approach

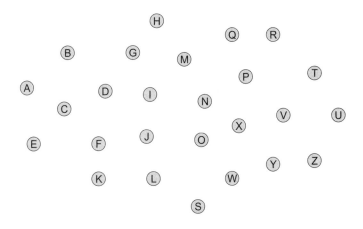

FIGURE 4–2. Visual Diagram of a Population of Actors

toward understanding social phenomena. Intrinsically, both of these approaches incur limitations that can have a huge impact on how a study is carried out and how data are analyzed and interpreted. Studies using the former approach tend to be the common quantitative-type studies that usually assume the individuality and independence of units (be they persons, groups, events, etc.). Studies of this sort often use demographic variables (sex, race, education, age, etc.) and psychological variables (personality, attitude, and affect) as explanatory variables for social behavior. In contrast, studies adopting the latter approach tend to view societal pressures and controls or deep-seated structural constraints as explanatory schema for individuals' behaviors. Studies using this second approach are often more qualitative in nature and employ the ontological premises suggested by postmodernism, critical theory, and social constructivism.

Hence, given the charge of understanding task completion and promotion within an organization, under conventional methods, you would likely adopt one of these two approaches. Using the individualistic, reductionist approach you might look for such things as employees' tenure with the organization, their education, and their personality types as variables related to their successful task completion and promotion. Conversely, under the second approach, you might adopt a feminist perspective or critical race theory as an explanatory schema for why women or minorities are more or less successful at task completion and getting promoted than others.

However, as Granovetter (1992) contended, the individualistic, reductionist approach is essentially an undersocialized view of the world. It portrays action as being controlled by individuals acting in isolation. At the other end of the spectrum, structural, holistic views can be construed as being oversocialized explanations of action. They tend to depict actions as a function of individuals conforming to social forces and norms. Consequently, both of these views fail to incorporate the fact that people do not operate in social or environmental vacuums. That is to say that people act based upon both individual properties and the properties of the group to which they belong.

To further clarify, these limitations are effectively summarized in the following quote by Allen Barton as cited by Freeman (2004):

> For the last thirty years, empirical social research has been dominated by the sample survey. But as usually practiced, using random sampling of individuals the survey is a sociological meat grinder, tearing the individual from his social context and guaranteeing that nobody in the study interacts with anyone else in it. It is a little like a biologist putting his experimental animals through a hamburger machine and looking at every hundredth cell through a microscope; anatomy and physiology get lost, structure and function disappear, and one is left with cell biology . . . If our aim is to understand people's behavior rather than simply record it, we want to know about primary groups, neighborhoods, organizations, social circles, and communities; about interaction, communication, role expectations, and social control (p. 1).

Put another way, it is almost as if in trying to understand how a bicycle functions, you were to take the bike apart and lay all of the various parts out in front of you on a table. After tinkering with all of the parts individually and coming to know how all of the parts function on their own, you claim to know how the bicycle (or all bicycles for that matter) functions as a whole. However, just because you know how all of the parts function on their own, does that necessarily mean that you know how all of those parts come together to function as a working bicycle?

In any case, whether you choose to adopt an individualistic, reductionist approach or a structural, holistic approach, you would likely be seeking to understand the population of employees very much like the way Figure 4–2 depicts this, as individuals acting in complete isolation of one another. Furthermore, the conclusions you would draw would, in a sense, assume that people are "bundles of attributes" and act in various ways based upon the attributes they possess. Hence, as Wellman and Berkowitz (1988) expressed, following these strategies can "at best only *infer* the presence of social structure when [you] discover aggregates of individuals thinking and behaving in similar ways" (p. 3). For these reasons, a number of scholars have argued for a network view of the world and approach to inquiry.

Overview of the Network Perspective

In contrast to the conventional approaches, the network perspective allows the researcher to focus on the relationships between the actors rather than the actors themselves. It is not the individual "actor" (or object) and his or her attributes that are the starting points of interest but rather the structured situation in which the "actor" or "actors" are embedded that is the foundation of analysis. A network perspective thus presents the world as sets of dynamic, unfolding relations and processes whereby the attributes and actions of actors can be amplified or suppressed by their relationships and interactions with other actors. As Brass (1995) articulated, "The difference is not a micro/macro one, nor a political/rational one. The difference is the focus on relations rather than attributes; on structure rather than isolated individual actors" (p. 41).

Some of the major benefits of using a network approach include the fact that a researcher or practitioner can holistically assess the patterns of relationships among all of the actors. For example, consider the differences in the interpretations and conclusions that can be drawn in moving from Figure 4–2 back to Figure 4–1. Going back to the scenario of studying task completion and promotion in an organization, imagine the nodes to represent employees in the organization and the lines to stand for the presence of some type of instrumental relationship between the employees. Now, in addition to the other variables you have already considered under conventional approaches, you can explore an entirely new set of variables.

For example, a reasonable explanation for employees' success in terms of task completion and promotion might be related to the people within the organization with whom they have access to for support. Under conventional approaches, it would be very difficult to quantify or systematically look for patterns that would support this proposition. However, with the network approach, a visual picture or dataset can be obtained which allows a researcher to analyze and test whether or not access to others in the organization is a significant predictor of successful task completion and promotion.

Consider this: If actors N and K in Figure 4–1 were both assigned a task outside the scope of their personal expertise and capabilities, who based on their intact instrumental relationships to others in the organization might have an easier time finding someone to ask for help or advice? Likewise, if both actors N and K were up for the same promotion and needed recommendations from their coworkers, which one would appear to have an easier time obtaining the number of necessary recommendations? Based on the network diagram presented in Figure 4–1, intuitively, you would probably answer actor N to both questions. However, under the conventional approaches, as Figure 4–2 depicts, it would be very difficult to draw the same conclusion.

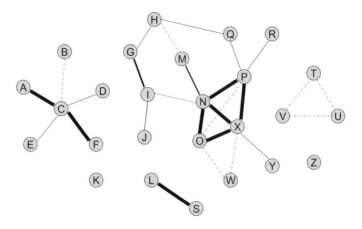

FIGURE 4–3. Network Illustration of the Intensity of Ties

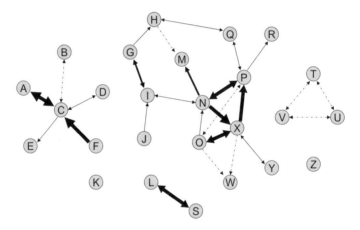

FIGURE 4–4. Network Illustration of the Directionality and Intensity of Ties

Incidentally, the network perspective can be extended to incorporate such things as the intensity and direction of ties. Thus, instead of simply considering whether or not a tie is present, you can infer additional implications from the network diagrams. Using the same example as before in which the nodes represent employees in the organization and the lines represent instrumental relationships between employees, consider what Figures 4–3 and 4–4 might hold for a network of interest. In these cases, the thickness of the lines represents how strong the ties are and the direction of the arrows indicates whether the relationship is reciprocal.

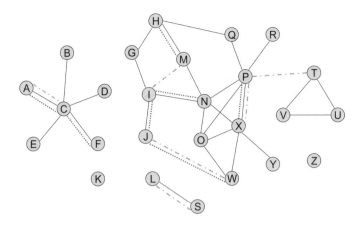

FIGURE 4–5. Network Illustration of Multiplex Ties

In addition, a single population of actors can also be used to examine the *multiplexity* of ties between actors (reference?). The multiplexity of a tie refers to the extent to which two actors are linked together by more than one relationship. For example, a network of employees in an organization can be drawn to include multiple ties at once, such as lines representing friendship ties, instrumental ties (e.g., work on projects together), and the location of desks. Figure 4–5 provides a visual depiction of the mulitplexity of a network with multiplex. You might imagine the solid lines to represent two connected actors having desks located near each other, the dotted lines to represent actors that are friends outside of work, and the dashed lines to represent the fact that two employees work together on projects on a regular basis.

One other benefit of employing the network perspective is the ability to simultaneously include multiple levels of analysis providing some fluidity between micro-, meso-, and macro-linkages. The network perspective allows for such an analysis because unlike conventional approaches that force you into categorically thinking about individuals and groups, the network paradigm assumes that the world is comprised of networks of networks.

Figures 4–6, 4–7, and 4–8 provide visual depictions of this premise of the network perspective. Imagine the larger circles in Figure 4–6 to represent various individuals within unique departments within the organization. The network perspective allows us to then interpret these groupings of individuals within departments as individual nodes that may in turn possess relationships with one another. Consequently, Figure 4–7 could be interpreted as the departments serving as nodes with relationships between one another essentially coming together to form a network within a

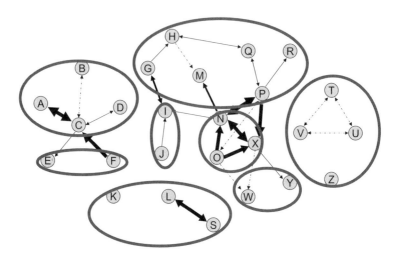

FIGURE 4–6. Illustration of an Organization Grouped into Departments

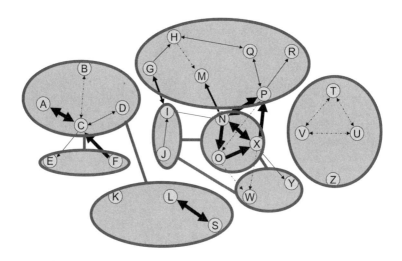

FIGURE 4–7. Illustration of a Network within a Network

network. Taking it one step further, Figure 4–8 shows how those departments can all come together to form a single organization node embedded within a network of other organizations (i.e., an example of an interorganizational network).

Interestingly, the fact that the network perspective designates the world as being comprised of networks of networks is the very tool that helps it overturn many of the limitations of the conventional approaches. It allows

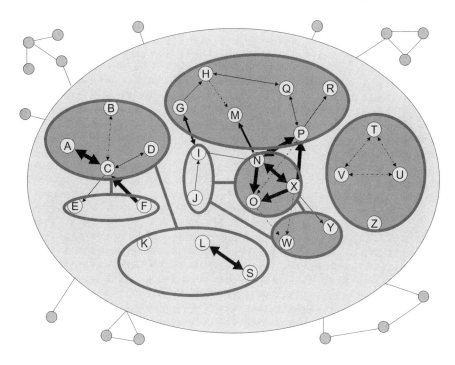

FIGURE 4–8. Illustration of a Network within a Network within a Network

one to study a network as a whole, as well as focus in on various parts
and individuals within the network. Embracing a network perspective
allows one to consider a whole new set of structural properties and their
implications for actors and the groups to which they belong. Some of these
structural properties and considerations apply only to individual actors,
others apply to only various features of parts of a network, and still others
apply to the network as a whole. Table 4–1 highlights a number of the
commonly studied network properties.

To illustrate how the implications might vary based on a certain property, Figures 4–9, 4–10, and 4–11 demonstrate that even slight structural
changes can have a huge impact on how the network properties are interpreted. Consider the role organization actor C might play given each of
the structural diagrams provided by Figures 4–9, 4–10, and 4–11. Imagine
the nodes to represent employees in a department and the directional ties
represent whether or not the employee believes he or she will take advice
from another. A node with an arrow pointing away indicates that the
directing actor respects the receiving actor enough to take advice from
him or her.

TABLE 4–1
Common Network Considerations

Individual Actor Considerations	
Degree	Number of direct links with other nodes
In-degree	Number of directional ties leading to the node from other nodes (incoming ties)
Out-degree	Number of directional ties coming from the node toward other nodes (outgoing ties)
Isolate	A node that has no links, or relatively few links to other nodes
Closeness	Extent to which a node is close to or can reach all other nodes in the network
Betweenness	Extent to which a node serves as a mediator or a necessary connector between two other nodes
Star	An node that is highly central to other nodes, which in turn are not highly connected to each other (e.g., actor C in Figure 4–1 would be a star)
Peripheral Actor	A node that is located on the outer parts of the network as compared to all other nodes
Central Actor	A node that is located in the inner parts of the network as compared to all other nodes
Partial Network Considerations	
Dyad	The relationship between two nodes in a network
Triad	The relationship(s) between three nodes in a network
Symmetry	The reciprocity and direction of ties
Component	Connected subset of network nodes and links
Subgroups	The presence of connected (and in some cases densely connected) subsets of nodes
Whole Network Considerations	
Density	Ratio of the number of present ties to the number of possible ties in the network
Size	Number of actors in the network
Connectivity or Reachability	The extent to which actors in the network are linked to one another by direct or indirect ties (the ability to reach one node from another)
Cohesion	The extent to which a network can remain connected even when various nodes are removed from the network

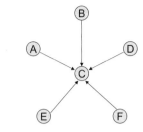

FIGURE 4–9. Ties Directed into C

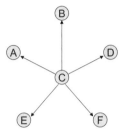

FIGURE 4–10. Ties Directed Out from C

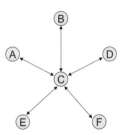

FIGURE 4–11. Reciprocal Ties

Thus, given the position of actor C in Figure 4–9, one might conclude that actor C has the potential to have a great deal of influence on all of the other actors, while the other actors may have little influence on C. As such, actor C is probably a leader of some sort and perhaps holds a position of great power relative to the other actors. In contrast, in Figure 4–10, the position of actor C might imply that he or she actually has very little power in terms of influencing the other actors, but the other actors may each possess some power to influence C. Finally, Figure 4–11 depicts actor C as being a member of a number of reciprocal relationships in

TABLE 4–2
Presence of Ties

	A	B	C	D	E	F
A	—	0	1	0	0	0
B	0	—	1	0	0	0
C	1	1	—	1	1	1
D	0	0	1	—	0	0
E	0	0	1	0	—	0
F	0	0	1	0	0	—

which actor C could potentially influence a number of others, as well as potentially be influenced by a number of others. Interestingly, both Figures 4–9 and 4–11 would indicate a unique opportunity for actor C to serve as a potential gatekeeper (of information, resources, or really anything) as he or she would be in a position of great influence to all of the other actors while all of the other actors lack the opportunity to influence each other.

As you can imagine, the more actors and ties you have in your network, the more challenging it becomes to interpret the network diagram. To complicate matters further, the attributes of the ties (i.e., directionality, intensity, and multiplexity) and the micro-, meso-, and macro-levels do not have to be considered mutually exclusive. That is, you can examine the network from any and all of these perspectives at once.

Hence, another important feature of the network perspective is that these diagrams can actually be quantified into actor-by-actor matrices for further analysis. For example, in a simple dichotomous relationship between actors, a "1" can be inserted into all of the boxes in the matrix where a relationship is present between the actors and a "0" can be inserted where there is no relationship present. Table 4–2 provides an image of this process for actors A through F from Figure 4–1. To incorporate the intensity of ties, you would follow the same procedure, only the value of the numbers would follow a continuous pattern of values. Table 4–3 depicts the matrix for this process. Likewise, to translate the network including directional ties you would follow a similar procedure such that if actor C has an instrumental tie with actor E, and the tie is not reciprocated, the box for C to E would include a value of greater than zero but the box from E to C would contain a "0." Table 4–4 illustrates the corresponding matrix for the network pertaining to the directional ties for A through F. Finally, you can incorporate both the intensity and direction for the network into a single matrix as shown in Table 4–5.

TABLE 4–3
Intensity of Ties

	A	B	C	D	E	F
A	—	0	3	0	0	0
B	0	—	1	0	0	0
C	3	1	—	2	2	3
D	0	0	2	—	0	0
E	0	0	2	0	—	0
F	0	0	3	0	0	—

TABLE 4–4
Direction of Ties

	A	B	C	D	E	F
A	—	0	1	0	0	0
B	0	—	1	0	0	0
C	1	1	—	1	1	0
D	0	0	1	—	0	0
E	0	0	0	0	—	0
F	0	0	1	0	0	—

TABLE 4–5
Intensity and Direction of Ties

	A	B	C	D	E	F
A	—	0	3	0	0	0
B	0	—	1	0	0	0
C	3	1	—	2	2	0
D	0	0	2	—	0	0
E	0	0	0	0	—	0
F	0	0	3	0	0	—

As you might imagine, converting the network diagrams into matrices can also produce quite complex and difficult data to interpret. In most cases, special computer software programs are necessary to help a person analyze and further interpret the data in these formats. Two common software programs for analyzing social networks include Pajek and Ucinet.

However, oftentimes the use of these programs necessitates special training and a great deal of practice even for a researcher experienced in conventional statistical packages. Even so, network studies have started to appear regularly in a number of management and organizational theory research journals covering a wide variety of topics. The next section of this chapter provides an overview of a number of areas in which a network perspective has been employed in organizational studies.

The Network Perspective and Organizations

Given the unique way of defining networks described above, the network perspective allows for a variety of new types of research questions and topics related to organizations to be explored. Incidentally, the use of social network theory and analysis as methodological tools has grown significantly in recent years particularly in the management and organizational behavior literatures (Brass, Galaskiewicz, Greve, and Tsai, 2004). For example, one big shift in perspective that the network literature has prompted is the recognition of the importance of studying the informal interactions that take place within an organization. As Krackhardt and Hanson (1993) noted, "If the formal organization is the skeleton of a company, the informal is the central nervous system driving the collective thought processes, actions and reactions of its business units" (p. 104). Likewise, Ibarra (1992b) expressed:

> Based on the notion that much of what occurs in organizations is only vaguely related to top management directives, the organizational chart, and the logic of vertical integration, many organizational scholars argue that it is the informal or emergent networks of relationships that account for regularities in day-to-day work . . . and generally provide key channels for the business of getting things done (p. 165).

While the network perspective has provided an important new lens for studying the activities that take place within an organization, it has also helped reinforce some of the conventional views on organizational behavior. For example, Lincoln and Miller's (1979) findings served to emphasize the extent to which the formal organizational structure both constrains and influences the patterns of interactions between individuals for both friendship and instrumental purposes. In other words, although much of what goes on within an organization does not necessarily conform to the formal hierarchy of authority, the formal hierarchy does significantly affect who is likely to interact with others based on their places in the hierarchy.

Scholars have also used the network perspective to look at such things as attributes related to a person's location (or position) within a social network. For example, Brass (1985) and Ibarra (1992a) found evidence for people's tendency to interact with others of the same gender within an organization. From a different perspective, Mehra, Kilduff, and Brass (1998) found that groupings of racial minorities were clustered on the periphery or outside the more central locations of organizational networks. In addition, various personality traits have also been linked to where people fall within social networks (e.g., Mehra, Kilduff, and Brass, 2001). These are just a few of the topics that scholars have examined thus far from the network perspective.

Aligning with the examples given in the previous sections, social structural trends, such as these, have indeed been empirically shown to have profound implications in terms of how individuals are able to successfully perform their tasks and get promoted within an organization (Brass, 1984; Brass and Burkhardt, 1993; Krackhardt, 1990). As Brass et al. (2004) noted, theoretically, people in central network positions are likely to have greater access to, and potential control over, relevant resources, such as information and influence over others. Thus, the attributes that people possess related to how they are likely to fall within an organization's social networks are important managerial considerations.

Network ideas have also been extended to other levels and contexts of networks and networking. For example, as demonstrated in Figures 4–7 and 4–8, an organization can be conceptualized as a network of networks. Thus, whole new sets of structural variables and contexts can be explored, such as interdepartmental networks and interorganizational networks. Such avenues have also been investigated in a variety of ways in the organizational theory and behavior literature. For a summary of much of the work related to these areas, see Brass et al. (2004).

While an understanding and knowledge of the literature related to social networks and organizations can be quite useful for managers in and of itself, the network perspective also provides a unique opportunity for practitioners to apply this to their own managerial strategies. As such, the next section provides a number of practical suggestions for the everyday use of social network techniques.

Practical Applications of a Network Perspective

Managers often pride themselves on their understanding of the strengths and weaknesses of their employees and sense of who works well together. Yet, the reality of their perceptions is often superficial at best. It is impossible to be everywhere at once or read people's minds. Therefore, managers' estimations of the informal structure are more often than not distorted and inaccurate.

Nevertheless, Krackhardt and Hanson (1993) suggested that by using social network analysis, managers can translate fairly accurate information about the informal networks into maps showing how work actually gets done in their organizations. They contend that valuable insight can be gained by simply diagramming three types of networks: (1) the advice network (who goes to whom for help with task-related and other problems), (2) the trust network (who shares delicate and private information with whom), and (3) the communication network (who regularly talks to whom about work-related matters). It is their belief that mapping these networks can help managers identify weaknesses and vulnerabilities of the informal structures. Consequently, managers can, in turn, adjust their human resource strategies to help remedy the weaknesses discovered and/or capitalize on the strengths.

In order to map such networks, practitioners can collect their data in a number of ways. For one, as a manager you might simply track observations of your employees—making note of such things as who spends a lot of time talking to whom at work, who goes to lunch with who, and who all seem to communicate well together. Another way of obtaining data is to distribute a questionnaire to employees asking the questions about the types of relationships you are interested in mapping. For example, ask employees to list the five people they are most likely to go to when they need work-related advice. You might also ask employees to describe their perceptions of other peoples' interactions with each other (e.g., Whom do you think John goes to for work-related advice?).

However, simply relying on your own observations can be rather limited as it is only one person's view of what is going on and does not incorporate the perspectives of the employees. The second approach can also be somewhat challenging because it requires you to ask employees personal questions. In the event that a question makes them uncomfortable, they may not answer as honestly or as completely as possible. Likewise, the third approach is only accurate to the extent that people are both honest and accurate in their perceptions. Hence, using multiple approaches as cross-checks may actually provide the most accurate picture of the social networks within your organizations.

Once you obtain the data, you can construct a visual map by using the techniques described earlier in this chapter. Points or nodes can be used to represent your employees and lines can be drawn between them to depict the patterns of relationships. You might also include such features as the direction and intensity of ties or even layer multiple networks on top of each other (e.g., layer the advice network on top of the friendship network) to provide an image of the multiplexity of ties.

How might you use this to your advantage? To give just one example, let us say that you are trying to put together an ad hoc committee for brainstorming a new policy for your organization. You might consult your social network map of who works well with each other to select the members of the committee. You might also use the map to select who would be the best person in terms of the respect their peers hold for them to lead the committee.

As you can see from these suggestions, a social network mapping of your organization could prove to be useful in a wide variety of applications. Hence, as Krackhardt and Hanson (1993) suggested, social network analysis provides managers with a great opportunity to "restructure their formal organizations to complement the informal, and 'rewire' faulty networks to work with company goals" (p. 105).

Summary and Conclusions

The ideas presented in this chapter are meant to introduce readers to the network perspective as a new lens for viewing organizational theory and organizational behavior topics. Certainly, studying organizations from a network perspective has exciting and profound implications. By studying what organizational networks concretely look like, how they emerge, and how they change and evolve over time, our understanding of organizational behavior can significantly improve. Moreover, the ideas behind the network perspective have widespread applicability for practitioner use.

This is not to say that conventional approaches to research have all been for naught. It is quite the contrary; traditional studies have been and will continue to be useful, in providing insight and a better understanding of the world in which we live. Nevertheless, if further progress is to be made, it may be time to start exploring other options. As Barabasi (2003) articulated, "Our quest to understand nature has hit a glass ceiling because we do not yet know how to fit the pieces together ... A revolution in management is in the making. It will take a new, network-oriented view of the economy and understanding of the consequences of interconnectedness to smooth the way" (p. 213).

References

Barabasi, A.L. (2003). *Linked: How Everything Is Connected to Everything Else and What It Means for Business, Science and Everyday Life.* New York: Plume.

Brass, D.J. (1984). Being in the right place: A structural analysis of individual influence in an organization. *Administrative Science Quarterly*, 26, 331–348.

Brass, D.J. (1985). Men's and women's networks: A study of interaction patterns and influence in an organization. *Academy of Management Journal*, 28, 327–343.

Brass, D.J. (1995). A social network perspective on human resources management. *Research in Personnel and Human Resources Management,* 13, 39–79.

Brass, D.J., and Burkhardt, M.E. (1993). Potential power and power uses: An investigation of structure and behavior. *Academy of Management Journal,* 36, 444–470.

Brass, D.J., Galaskiewicz, J., Greve, J., and Tsai, W. (2004). Taking stock and organizations: A multilevel perspective. *Academy of Management Journal,* 47(6):795–817.

Freeman, L. (2004). *The Development of Social Network Analysis: A Study in the Sociology of Science.* Vancouver, Canada: Empirical Press.

Granovetter, M. (1992). Problems of explanation in economic sociology. In N. Nohria and R.G. Eccles (Eds.) *Networks and Organizations: Structure, Form and Action.* Boston: Harvard Business School Press. pp. 25–56.

Ibarra, H. (1992a). Homophily and differential returns: Sex differences in network structure and access in an advertising firm. *Administrative Science Quarterly,* 45, 327–365.

Ibarra, H. (1992b). Structural alignments, individual strategies, and managerial action: Elements toward a network theory of getting things done. In N. Nohria and R.G. Eccles (Eds.), *Networks and Organizations: Structure, Form, Action.* Boston: Harvard Business School Press. pp. 143–164.

Krackhardt, D. (1990). Assessing the political landscape—Structure, cognition, and power in organizations. *Administrative Science Quarterly,* 35, 342–369.

Krackhardt, D., and Hanson, J.R. (1993). Informal networks: The company. *Harvard Business Review,* 71(4):104–111.

Lincoln, J.R., and Miller, J. (1979). Work and friendship ties in organizations: A comparative analysis of relational networks. *Administrative Science Quarterly,* 24, 181–199.

Mehra, A., Kilduff, M., and Brass, D.J. (1998). At the margins: A distinctiveness approach to the social identity and social networks of underrepresented groups. *Academy of Management Journal,* 41, 441–452.

Mehra, A., Kilduff, M., and Brass, D.J. (2001). The social networks of high and low self-monitors: Implications for workplace performance. *Administrative Science Quarterly,* 46, 121–146.

Nohria, N. (1992). Introduction. In N. Nohria and R.G. Eccles (Eds.) *Networks Organizations: Structure, Form, and Action.* Boston: Harvard Business School Press, pp. 1–22.

Wellman, B., and Berkowitz, S.D. (1988). Studying social structures. In B. Wellman and S.D. Berkowitz (Eds.) *Social Structures: A Network Approach.* New York: Cambridge University Press.

5

The Political Economy of Managing Outdoor Sport Environments

Sylvia Trendafilova and Laurence Chalip

Two trends coincide to increase the environmental risks posed by outdoor recreational sports. First, the world population explosion has increased the size of the potential market for outdoor recreational sport. Second, the percentage of the population seeking outdoor recreational sport has increased substantially in recent decades—a phenomenon fueled in part by the rapid growth in the popularity of "extreme sports" among young people (Griffin, 2002), and in part by sporting goods manufacturers and retailers seeking to develop markets for outdoor recreation equipment (Ryan, 2004). In fact, many outdoor sports are the result of new designs of recreational equipment, such as canopies for paragliding or the introduction of personal watercraft for use in coastal areas (Reynolds and Elson, 1996). Thus, the aggregate demand for outdoor recreational sports has increased dramatically in recent years.

For purposes of this chapter's discussion, we consider outdoor recreational sports to be those that take place in an open public area (with a natural setting), and for which the hedonic and/or social character of participation plays a significant motivating role. Social comparisons are often but not always present, and may be based on aesthetic rather than objective criteria. Examples include skiing, surfing, mountain biking, rock climbing, and disc-golf.

The increased demand for outdoor space and outdoor recreational sports is due not merely to an increase in the number of participants, but also to an increase in the frequency that participants engage in their chosen activity. Table 5–1 shows the change in frequent participation by

TABLE 5–1

Increased Frequent U.S. Participation in Outdoor Recreation (in thousands)

Recreation Activity	1994	2002	% increase
Fresh water fishing^	10,770	13,287	23
Overnight camping^	6,521	12,975	99
Motor/power boating^	7,624	8,526	12
Hunting with firearms^	4,355	7,152	64
Golf+	4,557	6,043	33
Hiking*	2,079	4,999	140
Saltwater fishing^	2,111	3,844	82
Wilderness camping^	1,587	3,247	105
Mountain biking off road*	1,257	2,556	103
Snowboarding#	695	2,034	193
Canoeing#	1,654	1,883	14
Alpine skiing^	948	1,152	22

The Sporting Goods Manufacturers Association defines "frequent participation" differently for different activities, as shown: #10 or more days per year; ^20 or more days per year; *30 or more days per year; +40 or more days per year.

Americans between 1994 and 2002 in twelve outdoor activities tracked by the Sporting Goods Manufacturers Association (SGMA; Sporting Goods Manufacturers Association, 2003). As examination of Table 5–1 shows, the increase in frequent participation has been substantial in only eight years (more than 53% in aggregate). Although this includes activities that are often categorized as "recreational" (e.g., camping, fishing, and hiking), we have included them here for two reasons. First, the sporting goods industry classifies these as sports. Second (and most importantly), the environmental risk results from the combined impact of these activities, so it would understate the risk to exclude activities that might popularly be classed as recreation.

Our approach is also consistent with government tracking, as the National Survey on Recreation and the Environment (NSRE) includes activities like hiking and bird watching, as well as activities traditionally classed as sports (e.g., skiing and biking). That survey shows that more than 97% of Americans participate in outdoor sport activities, with walking, bird watching, and hiking being the fastest growing activities (United States Department of Agriculture, n.d.), and the trend for higher levels of participation across most activities will continue into the foreseeable future.

Environmental concerns about outdoor recreational sport are not new. Although the problems have become increasingly salient, attention to environmental issues related to outdoor activities dates back to the early part of the 20th century, as represented by the experimental studies of Meinecke (1928) in the United States and Bates (1935, 1938) in the United Kingdom. Both scholars demonstrated negative effects of recreation and nature-based activities on vegetation and soil. More recently, Vankat and Major (1978) showed that the plant species composition in Sequoia National Park in the United States has changed as a result of increased use of the park. Similarly, the reindeer density in Finland has been reduced as a consequence of outdoor recreation activities (Helle and Sarkela, 1993). Similar environmental problems have been reported in Australia, where an increase in outdoor recreational sport has caused declines in vegetation, erosion, and stress on water resources (Hall, 1994).

The increasing saliency of environmental problems resulting from outdoor recreational sport has engendered renewed effort to improve the management of natural resources that are used by recreationists. Goeft and Alder (2001) examined problems associated with mountain biking in the southwest of Western Australia. They suggested that mountain-bike-specific trails should be established in order to sequester the environmental effects, and that sharing of trails with motorized vehicles should be avoided. Font et al. (2001) sought to develop sustainable environmental management through implementation of the specific environmental management system (EMS) for forests. The system consists of five steps: policy, site review, program, operations, and audit and review of the program. The EMS illustrates the ongoing effort to systematize environmental management of outdoor recreation environments in order to cope with the increasing stress those environments face.

Sports organizations have become increasingly involved. The concern for sustainable management of sport activities has precipitated two types of environmental initiative: to reduce the ecological footprint of sports, and to use sports as a means to raise environmental awareness (Schmidt, 2006). Recognizing that environmental degradation associated with sport could pose a threat to the industry, the International Olympic Committee (IOC) made the environment the "third pillar" of Olympism in 1995 (adding it to the two existing pillars: sport and culture). In support of that initiative, the IOC established the Sport and Environment Commission, with a global membership encompassing environmental experts, athletes, sport administrators, and IOC members to address environmental issues. The IOC has also made environmental policies an important requirement in a city's bid to host an Olympic Games.

Another significant step in the recognition of sport's relationship to the environment was the adoption of the Nagano Declaration in November, 2001, following the Fourth World Conference on Sport and the Environment. More than 350 delegates from 90 countries attended the Conference. In addition to representatives from national governments, the United

Nations, and the World Bank, 80 National Olympic Committees (NOCs) were represented as well as 24 International Federations (IFs) and 6 Organizing Committees for the Olympic Games (Nagano, Sydney, Salt Lake City, Athens, Torino and Beijing). The Nagano Declaration calls upon all participants in sport and all enterprises associated with sport to intensify their efforts to foster environmental sustainability throughout their policies and practices.

Although there is now worldwide recognition that environmental problems are increasingly associated with outdoor recreational sports, and despite efforts to control and manage those problems, progress to date has been minimal. Planning practices are often developed retrospectively rather that prospectively, with the result that planning is often overwhelmed by the rapid growth in environmental demand by sport. Further, since many of those sports take place in areas that are not patrolled, and the effects of those sports are incremental, substantial environmental damage can occur before it is even recognized that a problem is brewing. Taken together, these conditions make prevention and redress of environmental degradation associated with sport a particularly challenging undertaking. The purpose of this chapter is to address that challenge.

We begin with an overview of Hardin's classic work on the "tragedy of the commons," including its implications for understanding environmental problems associated with outdoor recreational sports. Then the Coase Theorem is used to consider whether market-based solutions could be effective. We conclude that market forces alone cannot avert a tragedy of the commons in this case, and therefore consider the challenges associated with collective action and regulatory regimes. The practical limits of collective action and regulation are considered and the need for voluntary cooperation is outlined. We argue for interventions designed to enhance environmental values among sport subcultures as a means to foster voluntary cooperation, and we conclude by considering implications for theory, research, and practice.

The Tragedy of the Commons

Hardin's (1968) exposition of the commons problem provides a particularly useful basis for understanding the root problems associated with increasing demand for outdoor recreational sport. Hardin argued that when common-pool resources are exploited collectively and without formal restriction, usage will escalate until those resources are depleted to the point of ruin. Although Hardin was particularly concerned to project the ultimate effects of population growth, he also noted that national parks and public lands are at risk of ruin because they are collectively used.

The problem is that each individual's use adds to the impact of others' use, but the individual impact is imperceptible in-and-of itself. Further, the benefits to each individual user outweigh (to them) the costs they individually impose. Studies support Hardin's description of the problem (e.g., Campbell et al., 2005; Ehrlich and Holdren, 1971; Hardin, 1985), and it is now generally agreed that proactive management of resources is required if the environment is to be used in a sustainable fashion (Goeft and Alder, 2001; Landsberg et al., 2001; Mason and Leberman, 2000; Reynolds and Elson, 1996; Sun and Walsh, 1998).

Hardin (1968, 1985) argued that the best (and possibly only) means to prevent a tragedy of the commons is to employ coercive means (e.g., regulatory supervision with sanctions). However, recent economic work has endeavored to locate bases for cooperative and sustainable use of common resources (Burger and Gochfeld, 1998). For the management of outdoor recreational sport, this mandates that a workable foundation for cooperation among users be located.

Hardin (1968, 1985) illustrated the importance of an interdisciplinary approach in the search for solutions to the commons problem, emphasizing the need to integrate social and political theory with biological data. Although there has been increased emphasis on technological advances to address the problem, technical remedies are not sufficient. There are three reasons. First, land is finite and cannot be increased. Second, there is a limit to the speed with which an ecosystem can recover and regenerate. Third, the ecosystem cannot be replaced. Thus, the effort to find solutions must draw from advances in the social sciences. Indeed, the need for a solution that draws on social knowledge is evidenced by the fact that the tragedy of the commons has its roots in social behavior.

The Coase Theorem

Although Hardin argued for a coercive solution, currently popular economic prescriptions and political rhetoric advocate free market solutions wherever possible. These prescriptions and rhetoric are supported by the Coase Theorem (Coase, 1960), which holds that clear specification of property rights will enable economically optimal free market solutions through bargaining among stakeholders. In essence, the Coase Theorem holds that commons problems would not occur if the ownership of all resources were clearly designated and bargaining among owners and users was enabled. Veljanovski (1982) advocates a slightly stronger version of the theorem, arguing that assignment of legal liability for losses caused by harmful activities is unnecessary because allocation of resources would not be improved, but the aggregate value of production could be harmed. In other words, the Coase Theorem would seem to justify leaving the solution of commons problems to a free market with well-defined property rights and an unfettered right to bargain.

The Coase Theorem rests on a number of assumptions, however, that often cannot be met (Calabresi, 1968). The theorem assumes fully rational actors, no transaction costs, and no impediments to bargaining. It is unlikely that these conditions can even be approximated in the context of outdoor recreational sports.

To begin, the rationality criterion does more than just advocate reason over emotion (itself an unlikely condition when a well-loved activity is at stake); the criterion requires that all parties have free and unfettered access to all relevant information. Several relevant pieces of information are unlikely to be available to all parties when bargaining over outdoor recreational sports environments. In the first place, the utilities (i.e., relative values) and budget constraints for each party are unlikely to be available. Further, costs are likely to be underestimated in bargaining because there are no agreed means for determining the carrying capacity of the ecosystem, and environmental processes are time-lagged such that the costs might not be apparent until years later.

Second, the transaction costs expand geometrically with the number of parties involved in the bargaining. Although bargaining could render an optimal solution when there are only a few individuals involved and when an agreement among them is easily accomplished, transaction costs exceed the benefits from bargaining when the number of parties to the bargaining is large (Daly, 1974). As the growth of participation in outdoor recreational sports illustrates, the number of persons required when bargaining about recreational land use will generally be large—so large, in fact, that transaction costs will swamp any benefits being bargained.

Third, a legal structure that allows effective attainment of an agreement requires clearly established property rights in order for bargaining to be undertaken. This is politically tricky in the case of public lands because, by definition, public lands belong to the public. The requisite property rights become all-the-more contested when it comes to resources that have always been considered free to all, such as water and air. Thus, for reasons of cultural tradition and political pragmatism, it is not likely that the requisite conditions for effective bargaining will be at hand in the foreseeable future.

As the foregoing analysis shows, a free market solution to the commons tragedy is unlikely in the case of outdoor recreational sports. The nature of environmental information, the size of the relevant stakeholder groups, and the requisite conditions for bargaining work against a market-based solution. Therefore, alternative means to address the problem are required.

Collective Action

Essentially, the tragedy of the commons is a result of failed collective action. It would seem, therefore, that one means to redress the problem would be to nurture effective collective action to solve the problem (Lubell, 2002). Specifically, those with a stake in protecting outdoor recreational sport environments would come together to formulate and implement solutions. Those solutions would include means to monitor and enforce environmentally friendly behaviors. However, as Olson's (1965) analysis shows, collective action in a case like this is unlikely to emerge, and is unlikely to be sustainable if it does emerge. The pivotal problem is that the costs of collective action are borne by those who join in the action, but the benefits accrue even to those who do not. Therefore, the logical choice is not to participate (i.e., not incur the costs), but to enjoy the benefits of any collective action (undertaken by others) that is success-ful—hence the proclivity for free-riding. Alas, this logic applies to every possible participant, with the result that most collective action groups will either not form or not endure, particularly as the size of the requisite group grows.

The pivotal result of collective action failures is that socially desirable outcomes are not attained. In the case of environmental problems, it is nonetheless essential that societies find means to balance aggregate social interests with those of individuals (Espejo and Stewart, 1998). It has, therefore, been of interest to determine if the requisite means to foster collective action could be found (Lubell, 2002). The challenge is to find a social mechanism through which to unite enough people who are socially connected and who share appropriate interests and resources. That task requires communication of shared objectives while overcoming the incen-tive to free-ride (Sally, 1995)—a task that is best accomplished when communication is face-to-face (Cardenas, 2000). However, the dispersed (and often individual) nature of outdoor recreational sport is an impedi-ment to the ongoing communication required for collective action.

Collective action can withstand free-riding if there is a sufficient number of individuals who can be incentivized to cooperate strategically (Heckathorn, 1996). The decisive factor is the availability of information to each member about the actions of other group members. This informa-tion is itself costly, particularly as the size of the group grows and its cost combines with that of the incentives for cooperation. The lower-bound on group size is the minimum number of persons required for effective col-lective action. In the case of outdoor recreational sports, this mandates sizable groups because each free-rider becomes a potential source of envi-ronmental damage, and the damage becomes more severe as the number of free-riders increases. Indeed, given the continuous increase in the number of participants in outdoor recreational sports, the conditions for free-riding are amplified, and it becomes increasingly attractive to become a free-rider. Small face-to-face groups are unlikely to intervene successfully, and large groups are costly to maintain. Although some advocacy groups, like the Sierra Club, have managed to sustain themselves, a higher degree of collective action is required to fully address the problem.

Voluntary collective action to address the environmental challenges of outdoor recreational sport therefore faces two of the same constraints as solutions based on bargaining: the information required and transaction costs militate against effective collective action. Further, the social conditions of collective action encourage free-riding, thereby reducing the likelihood that groups will form, maintain themselves, or be effective. The standard remedy has been to seek a solution based on the regulation of natural resources use through access fees, behavioral restrictions, and/or penalties.

Public Policies and Regulations

The increasing use of regulatory regimes and legal sanctions as tools for environmental management (Uphoff and Langholz, 1998) is consistent with Hardin's (1968, 1985) call for coercive means to protect the environment. There are obvious limitations though, particularly the costs to monitor and enforce the associated laws and regulations (Udehn, 1993). The effectiveness of such regimes is further compromised as participants shift to unsupervised or less-supervised locales. Efforts to drive down demand for recreation on public lands by creating or increasing user fees are politically precarious because fees are exclusionary, which is inconsistent with the public character of public land.

One increasingly widespread strategy for coping with the problem of commons overuse has been to designate natural protected areas (Carrus et al., 2005). This strategy is particularly prevalent in Europe. In effect, it removes areas from the pool of recreational land or severely curtails recreational use of that land. For that reason, it has been unpopular with local residents and communities, especially in highly populated regions, and it fails to address the underlying commons problem because it merely shifts the demand to unprotected areas.

Government agencies in Australia have sought to address these two problems by taking similar but less drastic action (Sun and Walsh, 1998). Two regulatory strategies have been employed. The first adds environmental protection clauses to land leases and licenses; the second requires that users obtain a permit. These two strategies incur the costs associated with regulatory regimes, but they permit a higher degree of recreational land use than would be available if the same areas were designated as protected. However, the efficacy with which these two strategies protect recreational environments has not been determined. Since their effectiveness relies on user willingness to comply with the terms of protection clauses and permits, efficacy depends on monitoring and enforcement conditions that are either missing or underbudgeted.

Since enforcement of recreational land use regulation depends on compliance and monitoring, the locus of regulatory control matters. Monitoring is more effective, and users are more willing to comply when regulation is locally dictated and locally managed. This is because locals can adapt and adopt rules to fit local conditions, and because they have a more intimate first-hand familiarity with the environments to be monitored. A number of field studies show that local groups of resource users have created a diverse array of institutional arrangements to manage common-pool resources (Berkes, 1989; Blomquist, 1992; Bromley and Feeny, 1992; Fortmann and Bruce, 1988; McCay and Acheson, 1987; Netting, 1993; Ostrom et al., 1993; Tang, 1992). When resources that were previously controlled by local participants were later brought under state or national authority, regulatory control has been demonstrably less effective (Ascher, 1995; Curtis, 1991; Panayotou and Ashton, 1992). For this reason, analysts of environmental policy have advocated self-regulation of environments through active citizen participation (Short and Winter, 1999). On the other hand, the increasing popularity of outdoor recreational sports makes it increasingly difficult politically for local regulatory regimes to restrict use (which is one reason that local control has sometimes been replaced by state or national control). As Ostrom et al. (1999) point out, local control is most likely to be effective if the resource is not at risk of surpassing its own carrying capacity, and there are valid and reliable systems in place to monitor the condition of the environment. Thus, outdoor recreational sport environments are not good candidates for local regulation if they are particularly at risk (i.e., most in need of regulation) or if appropriate monitoring regimes are not in place.

An alternative strategy is to manage use levels through booking systems. This was effectively applied as a means to protect the Dancing Ledge climbing area in the United Kingdom (Reynolds and Elson, 1996). Through negotiations between the National Trust and the British Mountaineering Council, a booking system was introduced that provided regulated access and charges for groups of climbers, but free access for individual climbers. This reduced the number of users by more than half, thereby decreasing the environmental impact. However, the success of applications like this is due, in part, to the small size of the recreational resource, which facilitates enforcement through monitoring. In larger areas, the prohibitive costs of monitoring increase the risk that users will fail to comply with existing rules.

Rules and regulations have become the dominant approach to management of outdoor recreational sport environments because they do seem to reduce the risk of a full-blown commons tragedy. They work only at the margins, however, because strict regulation and monitoring are too costly to apply, particularly if the region to be covered is large. Further, in democratic systems, it can be politically unfeasible to restrict or deny popular use, even when restrictions or denials are warranted on environmental grounds. These limitations are exacerbated by the time taken to pass relevant legislation or to draft new regulations. Whereas outdoor recreation demand and the environmental degradation associated with that demand are escalating geometrically, laws and regulations remain relatively stagnant. Consequently, rules and regulations are typically behind the level of need.

Although regulatory regimes are arguably necessary to protect environments for outdoor recreational sport, they are clearly insufficient. The challenge, then, is to combine regulatory practices, as a short-term strategy, with interventions designed to establish environmentally friendly norms and values among outdoor recreational sport enthusiasts. If such norms and values could be established, then participants in outdoor recreational sport would self-monitor and self-regulate.

Voluntary Cooperation

By incorporating the sociocultural domain in the search for solutions to the environmental problems associated with outdoor recreational sports, we can pursue effective tools for managing those environments—tools that do not incur the high costs associated with enforcement of rules and regulations. Indeed, research shows that common-pool resources are least likely to become overexploited and degraded if they are managed through social norms and conventions (Berkes, 1989; Bromley and Feeny, 1992; Jodha, 1992). For example, the decline in litter over the past four decades in the United States has been attributed to the creation and expansion of a social norm that proscribes littering (Haab and McConnell, 2002).

The core challenges for achieving the requisite behaviors among outdoor recreational sport participants are: (1) ensuring that those using a common-pool resource share a similar and relatively accurate view of the problem they need to solve, (2) devising simple norms with which most can comply, (3) monitoring activities sufficiently so that those who break agreements are detected and sanctioned, and (4) ensuring that trust and reciprocity are supported rather than undermined. Simply fostering awareness of environmental issues is not sufficient to generate environmentally conscious behavior, which is why increased public knowledge and information about the environment has not altered public conduct (Coppola, 1997).

In fact, contrary to popular belief, information alone is not likely to promote sensitivity to environmental degradation. Research shows that persons who are more environmentally informed are not more likely to engage in pro-environmental behavior (Allen and Weber, 1983; Lowe et al., 1980). Appropriate social norms grounded on trust, reciprocity, and the requisite social values must be created.

How? Collective action normally entails the development of a critical mass—a small segment of the population that chooses to contribute significant time and resources even though the majority do little or nothing (Oliver et al., 1985). Usually this group consists of individuals who voluntarily decide to participate and contribute, and who have considerable knowledge about the resource. The value of return expected from some specified level of contribution is not necessarily what triggers the development of the critical mass. In other words, the immediate return does not always have to be bigger than the input of the critical mass. Therefore, in most cases, the critical mass individuals are rather resourceful and financially stable. The power of the critical mass is in its ability to pay the start-up costs and induce widespread collective action. When a social solution to the collective dilemma is required, what matters most are the relationships among the possible contributors to the critical mass, not the relationships among everyone in the interest group (Oliver and Marwell, 1988).

It was argued above that collective action is not likely to be an effective means to govern or regulate outdoor recreational sport environments, because free-riding would make such governance or regulation ineffective. However, the argument here is that a smaller and, therefore, more feasible action group could be effective if the ultimate objective is to change the culture—the norms and values—of outdoor recreationists. Rather than apply collective action directly to management or lobbying to protect outdoor recreational sport environments, it would be more effective to use collective action more strategically to shift participants' values and norms. Although change of that kind is likely to take some time, as did creation of a norm proscribing littering, this strategy offers a long-term solution to complement short-term legislative and regulatory stop-gaps. The good news is that the presence of definable subcultures among sport participants establishes the necessary basis for undertaking the necessary interventions.

Subcultures and Sport

Subcultures are segments of the main culture that have their own cultural elements but still share some common characteristics with the mainstream culture. Subcultures are formed in sport because participants come to identify themselves with the values, beliefs, symbols, and norms of their sport (Amato et al., 2005; Donnelly, 1981; Donnelly and Young, 1988; Green and Chalip, 1998). Shared values, beliefs, symbols, and norms cultivate shared experiences, social interaction, and mutual affirmation and support among participants and aficionados. Thus, each sport's subculture becomes a potential lever for shaping behaviors among those who identify with the sport. Just as each sport's subculture can be leveraged to market products and services to participants and fans (Green, 2001), social marketing techniques targeted at particular sport subcultures (cf. Andreasen, 2006) and interventions designed to modify the subculture (cf. Poole and Van de Ven, 2004) can be used to create the desired norms and values.

Sport participants and spectators are socialized (to a greater or lesser degree) into the values, norms, and beliefs associated with their sport. These values, norms, and beliefs extend beyond the sport activity as they encompass matters linked to lifestyle, personal identity, and group membership. This renders the potential for sport subcultures to influence participant behaviors and enable collective action. Shared beliefs and values cultivate a common identity, which nurtures group effort (Brewer and Kramer, 1986; Kollock, 1998; Kramer and Brewer, 1984). The challenge, then, is to formulate interventions that can socialize participants (and, where appropriate, spectators) into the desired beliefs and values, and to use those beliefs and values to prompt environmentally friendly behavioral norms. The social technologies for so doing are increasingly well understood (Andreasen, 2006; Poole and Van de Ven, 2004), but the application and elaboration of those technologies for change of sport subcultures remains to be explored.

Since each sport has a distinct subculture, each sport should be targeted separately. Since subcultures reside amidst local and national cultures, the necessary interventions are likely to vary in different local and regional contexts, even for the same sport (cf. Atran and Medin, 2005; Dietz et al., 2005; Zube, 1991). Thus, although environmental management of outdoor recreational sport is a global concern, the strategies and tactics employed to foster and nurture the desired changes will vary by sport, and will be tailored to fit with local and regional customs. Tactics are likely to include (but are probably not limited to) provision of feedback about environmental consequences of the sport, demonstrations of impact, and enhancement of social relations among participants.

When the target group is relatively small and shares common norms and values, it may be unnecessary to create formal sanctions, regulations, and other enforcement rules. This has the advantage that it enables efficient management of resources without high monitoring expenditures, while at the same time developing a sense of empowerment and ownership. Local users who are members of a target subculture are capable of changing their own rules, enforcing the rules upon which they agree, and learning from experience to design better rules. Change will be incremental, beginning with one or two values and beliefs, and building further as associated behaviors become the norm. The process requires dedication and patience, but it has promise as a long-term solution.

Implications

There is clearly no simple means to solve the emerging environmental crisis in outdoor recreational sport. Although the crisis is publicly acknowledged by governments and sport organizations, it persists. Neither the free market nor governance via collective action is likely to provide an effective remedy. Regulation may slow the crisis, but it is unlikely to reverse the trend toward increasing environmental stress. On the other hand, effective voluntary action through self-regulation may be achievable by targeting interventions at sport subcultures in their local and regional contexts. Although that approach is likely to take time to show an effect (as was the case when norms about littering were changed), it is the one strategy that promises long-term sustainable results.

Hardin's (1968, 1985) advocacy of coercive interventions to protect the environment is consistent with the current reliance on law and regulation. Yet, there is a logical inconsistency in that reliance. Legislation and regulation address the problem's symptoms, but they do not attack its underlying social dynamics. As Hardin so aptly demonstrated, the tragedy of the commons derives from the social dynamics of common-resource use. If we are to enable long-term sustainable change in the ways that the commons are used, then we clearly need to change the underlying social dynamics of that use. Changing the environmental values and norms of sport subcultures is intended to achieve that goal.

This is not to argue that change of environmental values and norms is the only useful policy tool. The rapid escalation of environmental demand and stress associated with outdoor recreational sports does not permit solely a long-term strategy. There needs to be immediate action as well. Thus, regulatory regimes serve as a necessary stop-gap while subcultural interventions are being formulated and implemented. Regulation is a complement to changed values and norms, and if appropriately designed, it may even buttress the desired change.

The formulation and evaluation of interventions are likely to provide new basic knowledge about sport and environmental management. In order to formulate interventions, sport subcultures and variations among them must be better understood. Evaluation of interventions based on that knowledge can test resulting theories about subcultures in sport and the relations between subcultures and environmental consciousness, and what is learned in the sport context may have value in other settings.

Thus, the effort to change values and norms has both practical and scientific value.

References

Allen, C.T., and Weber, J.D. (1983). How presidential media use affects individual's beliefs about conservation. *Journalism Quarterly*, 60:98–104.

Amato, C.H., Peters, C.L.O., and Shao, A.T. (2005). An exploratory investigation into NASCAR fan culture. *Sport Marketing Quarterly*, 14:71–83.

Andreasen, A.R. (2006). *Social Marketing in the 21st Century*. Thousand Oaks, CA: Sage.

Ascher, W. (1995). *Communities and Sustainable Forestry in Developing Countries*. San Francisco: Institute of Contemporary Studies Press.

Atran, S., and Medin, D.L. (2005). The cultural mind: Environmental decision making and cultural modeling within and across populations. *Psychological Review*, 112:744–776.

Bates, G.H. (1935). The vegetation of footpaths, sidewalks, cart tracks and gateways. *Journal of Ecology*, 23:470–487.

Bates, G.H. (1938). Life forms of pasture plants in relation to treading. *Journal of Ecology*, 26:452–455.

Berkes, F. (1989). *Common Property Resources: Ecology and Community-based Sustainable Development*. London: Belhaven Press.

Blomquist, W. (1992). *Dividing the Waters: Governing Groundwater in Southern California*. San Francisco: Institute of Contemporary Studies Press.

Brewer, M., and Kramer, R. (1986). Choice behavior in social dilemmas: Effects of social identity, group size and decision framing. *Journal of Personality and Social Psychology*, 50:543–549.

Bromley, D.W., and Feeny, D. (1992). *Making the Commons Work: Theory, Practice and Policy*. San Francisco: Institute of Contemporary Studies Press.

Burger, J., and Gochfeld, M. (1998). The commons 30 years later. *Environment*, 40:4–27.

Calabresi, G. (1968). Transaction costs, resources allocation and liability rules—A comment. *Journal of Law and Economics*, 11:67–73.

Campbell, W.K., Bush, C.P., Brunell, A.B., and Shelton, J. (2005). Understanding the social costs of narcissism: The case of the tragedy of the commons. *Personality and Social Psychology Bulletin*, 31:1358–1368.

Cardenas, J. (2000). How do groups solve local commons dilemmas? Lessons from experimental economics in the field. *Environment, Development and Sustainability*, 2:305–322.

Carrus, G., Bonaiuto, M., and Bonnes, M. (2005). Environmental concern, regional identity, and support for protected areas in Italy. *Environment and Behavior*, 37:237–257.

Coase, R.H. (1960). The problem of social cost. *Journal of Law and Economics*, 3:1–44.

Coppola, N.W. (1997). Rhetorical analysis of stakeholders in environmental communication: A model. *Technical Communication Quarterly*, 6:9–24.

Curtis, D. (1991). *Beyond Government: Organizations for Common Benefit.* London: Macmillan.

Daly, G. (1974). The Coase theorem: Assumptions, applications and ambiguities. *Economic Inquiry*, 12:2.

Dietz, T., Fitzgerald, A., and Shwom, R. (2005). Environmental values. *Annual Review of Environment and Resources*, 30:335–372.

Donnelly, P. (1981). Subcultures, countercultures and sport. In: M. Hart and S. Birrell (Eds.), *Sport in the Sociological Process* (3rd edition). Dubuque, IA: Wm. C. Brown Company Publishers.

Donnelly, P., and Young, K. (1988). The construction and confirmation of identity in sport subcultures. *Sociology of Sport Journal*, 5:223–240.

Ehrlich, P., and Holdren, J.P. (1971). Impact of population growth. *Science*, 1:212–217.

Espejo, R., and Stewart, N.D. (1998). Systemic reflections on environmental sustainability. *Systems Research and Behavioral Science*, 15:483–496.

Font, X., Yale, K., and Tribe, J. (2001). Introducing environmental management system in forest recreation: Results from a consultation exercise. *Management Leisure*, 1(6):54–167.

Fortmann, L., and Bruce, J.W. (1998). *Whose Trees? Proprietary Dimensions of Forestry.* Boulder, CO: Westview.

Goeft, U., and Alder, J. (2001). Sustainable mountain biking: A case study from the southwest of Western Australia. *Journal of Sustainable Tourism*, 9:193–211.

Green, B.C. (2001). Leveraging subcultures and identity to promote sport events. *Sport Management Review*, 4:1–19.

Green, B.C., and Chalip, L. (1998). Sport tourism as the celebration of subculture. *Annals of Tourism Research*, 25:275–291.

Griffin, C. (2002). Defining action sports: Although the category is growing rapidly, it's not just about competition. *Sporting Goods Business*, September: 18.

Haab, T.C., and McConnell, K.E. (2002). Social norms and illicit behavior: An evolutionary model of compliance. *Journal of Environmental Management*, 66:67–76.

Hall, C.M. (1994). Ecotourism in Australia, New Zealand and the South Pacific: Appropriate tourism or a new form of ecological imperialism?

In: E. Carter and G. Lowman (Eds.), *Ecotourism: A Sustainable Option?* New York: John Wiley & Sons.

Hardin, G. (1968). The tragedy of the commons. *Science*, 162:1243–1248.

Hardin, G. (1985). *Filters against Folly.* New York: Penguin Books.

Heckathorn, D. (1996). The dynamics and dilemmas of collective action. *American Sociological Review*, 61:250–277.

Helle, T., and Sarkela, M. (1993). The effects of outdoor recreation on range use by semi-domesticated reindeer. *Scandinavian Journal of Forest Research*, 8:123–133.

Jodha, N.S. (1992). *Common Property Resources: Overlooked Needs in Underdeveloped Countries.* Washington: The World Bank.

Kollock, P. (1998). Social dilemmas: The anatomy of cooperation. *Annual Review of Sociology*, 24:183–214.

Kramer, R., and Brewer, M. (1984). Effects of group identity on resource use in a simulated commons dilemma. *Journal of Personality and Social Psychology*, 46:1044–1056.

Lansberg, J., Logan, B., and Shorthouse, D. (2001). Horse riding in urban conservational areas: Reviewing scientific evidence to guide management. *Ecological Management and Restoration*, 2:36–46.

Lowe, G.D., Pinhey, T.K., and Grimes, M.D. (1980). Public support of environmental protection: New evidence from national surveys. *Pacific Sociological Review*, 23:423–445.

Lubell, M. (2002). Environmental activism as collective action. *Environment and Behavior*, 34:431–454.

Mason, P., and Leberman, S. (2000). Local planning for recreation and tourism: A case study of mountain biking from New Zealand's Manawatu region. *Journal of Sustainable Tourism*, 8:97–115.

McCay, B.J., and Acheson, J.M. (1987). *The Question of the Commons: The Culture and Ecology of Communal Resources.* Tucson: University of Arizona Press.

Meinecke, P. (1928). *The Effects of Excessive Tourism Travel on the California Redwood Parks.* Sacramento: California Department of Natural Resources.

Netting, R.M. (1993). *Smallholders, Householders: Farm Families and the Ecology of Intensive, Sustainable Agriculture.* Stanford, CA: Stanford University Press.

Oliver, P., Marwell, G., and Teixeira, R. (1985). A theory of the critical mass, I. Interdependence, group heterogeneity, and the production of collective action. *American Journal of Sociology*, 91:522–556.

Oliver, P.E., and Marwell, G. (1988). The paradox of group size in collective action. A theory of the critical mass. II. *American Sociological Review*, 53:1–8.

Olson, M. (1965). *The Logic of Collective Action.* Cambridge, MA: Harvard University Press.

Ostrom, V., Feeny, D., and Picht, H. (1993). *Rethinking Institutional Analysis and Development: Issues, Alternatives, and Choices* (2nd edition). San Francisco: ICS Press.

Ostrom, E., Burger, J., Field, C.B., Norgaard, R.B., and Policansky, D. (1999). Revisiting the commons: Local lessons, global challenges. *Science*, 284:278–282.

Panayotou, T., and Ashton, P.S. (1992). *Not by Timber Alone: Economics and Ecology for Sustaining Tropical Forests.* Washington, DC: Island.

Poole, M.S., and Van de Ven, A.H. (Eds.) (2004). *Handbook of Organizational Change and Innovation.* New York: Oxford University Press.

Reynolds, G., and Elson, M.J. (1996). The sustainable use of sensitive countryside sites for sport and active recreation. *Journal of Environmental Planning and Management*, 39:563–576.

Ryan, T.J. (2004). Piece of cake: As sales gradually begin to increase, retailers seek growth. *Sporting Goods Business*, February: 8, 10.

Sally, D. (1995). Conversation and cooperation in social dilemmas—A metaanalysis of experiments from 1958 to 1992. *Rationality and Society*, 7:58–92.

Schmidt, C.W. (2006). Putting the earth in play. *Environmental Health Perspectives*, 114:286–294.

Short, C., and Winter, M. (1999). The problem of common land: Towards stakeholder governance. *Journal of Environmental Planning and Management*, 42:613–630.

Sporting Goods Manufacturers Association. (2003). *Outdoor recreation in America 2003.* Retrieved June 23, 2006, from http://www.sgma.com/associations/5119/files/p27–2-03-m.pdf.

Sun, D., and Walsh, D. (1998). Review of studies on environmental impacts of recreation and tourism in Australia. *Journal of Environmental Management*, 53:323–338.

Tang, S.Y. (1992). *Institutions and Collective Action: Self-Governance in Irrigation.* San Francisco: ICS Press.

Udehn, L. (1993). Twenty-five years with the logic of collective action. *Acta Sociologica*, 36:239–261.

United States Department of Agriculture. (n.d.). *National Survey on Recreation and the Environment 2000* (Chap. 2). Retrieved June 23, 2006, from http://parks.state.co.us/scorp/pdf/SCORP-Ch2.pdf.

Uphoff, N., and Langholz, J. (1998). Incentives for avoiding the tragedy of the commons. *Environmental Conservation*, 25:251–261.

Vankat, J.L., and Major, J. (1978). Vegetation changes in Sequoia National Park, California. *Journal of Biogeography*, 57:377–402.

Veljanovski, C.G. (1982). The Coase Theorem and the economic theory of markets and law. *KYKLOS*, 35:53–74.

Zube, E. (1991). Environmental psychology, global issues and local landscape research. *Journal of Environmental Psychology*, 11:321–334.

6

The Institutional Dimension of the Sport Economy in Transition Countries

Sandrine Poupaux and Wladimir Andreff

The purpose of this chapter is to highlight institutional change in the sports economy during the transition period from the former communist centrally planned system to a market economy in Eastern European countries (EECs), in a broad sense including Central Eastern European countries (CEECs) and member countries of the Commonwealth of Independent States (CIS). The whole Soviet-style system fell apart, and the break-up affected the entire economy, more precisely all sport organizations and the former institutional framework ruling both economic and sporting activities. Since the mid-1990s, economists have assessed the institutional transformation of transitional economies with an array of qualitative indicators, and checked whether the new rules are properly enforced through some governance indicators. The same methodology is carried out in this chapter to build up certain specific indicators of institutional change in the sports system and economy. Implementing these indicators results in a comparative evaluation of sports institutions' transformations among EECs over time (from 1996 to 2004). Then, comparing sports institutions' indicators to those indicators depicting institutional change in the overall economy and to governance indicators will allow for an assessment of the fit between sports institutions and the institutional framework required by a well-functioning market economy.

The Collapse of the Soviet-Style Sports Economy

The organizational model of Soviet sports, as it was developed since the first five-year plans period in the 1930s, has been covered in Western literature (Shneidman, 1979; Riordan, 1977). From an economic point of view, in the Soviet system, sports supposedly had to fuel economic growth, improve productivity in the workplace, and maintain workers' health and well-being. Sports practice was spreading from school to the army and eventually to the factory, with gymnastics exercises scheduled along the working day, the whole system continually under state supervision, as all enterprises were state-owned and state-run. Most of the latter had a stadium or some sports facility among their own assets. At a local level, Soviets and trade unions were organizing sport participation and events, while at the federal level, the Supreme Soviet for physical culture and sport and the *Goskomsport* (the state department for sports) had central tutelage and monitoring authority over all sports organizations, including sports clubs and federations. To put it in the analytical frame that is suggested below, the institutional dimension of the Soviet sports economy was characterized by: no sports *legislation*, a strong state intervention (no *privatization*), no *decentralization*, and practically no independence of sport governing bodies (i.e., no *liberalization*). It was supposed to fit with a command economy run by state mandatory planning, regulated markets, nearly no independent (private) enterprise, and no rule of (civil or common) law: one of Stalin's famous watchwords was "plan is the law."

Backed by a strong "socialism outdoing capitalism" ideology, the Soviet sport system did not perform that badly as far as high level sport is concerned: the USSR was the biggest Olympic medal winner from 1952 to 1980, except in 1968 (then the second biggest). However, this was achieved at the expense of sport for all (8% of all men and 2% of women participated in sport in the 1980s) on the one hand, and an underdevelopment of household sporting goods and services consumption on the other hand. Elite athletes, although considered as amateur, were benefiting from a state salary—twice the average wage—and bonuses in case of victory, and they were hired by state-run institutions after their sporting career (Poupaux, 2006a). The same system, though slightly alleviated, was adopted in all post-war EECs.

In the second half of the 1980s, after Gorbachev launched *perestroïka* (restructuring) and *glasnost* (transparency), the Soviet system started to break up both in terms of the economy and of sports. Reforms translated into state attempts at developing child physical education, sport for all, athletes' health care, new sport facilities, increased sporting goods production, and more autonomous and financially self-sustainable federations. More freedom was given to sport clubs in 1987 in order to compensate for cuts in state subsidies: clubs were allowed to supply the market for sport services, establish shops and restaurants, negotiate broadcasting rights, and hire new staff while freely determining supply prices and wages. The aforementioned Soviet sport system was falling apart.

However, the final kick came from sport commercialization and the emergence of a genuine sports economy. In 1988, professional sport was legalized in the USSR and in other EECs and started internationalizing (Bourg, 1995). Those top football clubs, which qualified for European competitions, were suffering a hard currency shortage. In order to match their currency needs, clubs and federations opened the door to foreign sponsors and started hosting international sport events (in cycling, tennis, motor racing, ice hockey, and track and field). Eventually the "corporatization" of professional clubs was allowed in 1992. A "muscle drain" (Andreff, 2004) of the best Soviet—and EEC—sportsmen and women toward Western professional sports emerged in the late 1980s and spread over the 1990s: on each transfer fee, a 40% share was taken over by *Goskomsport*, 20% by the state, and 40% were left to the home (nursery) club. Sponsoring contracts were heavily taxed so that, with higher wages earned abroad in hard currency, this resulted in Soviet (EEC) athletes moving away. Needless to say that Soviet sports institutions did not adapt to such a dramatic economic shake. Last but not least, outward processing of sporting goods (adidas™, Fischer skis) developed in Eastern Europe in the 1980s and was soon substituted by inward foreign direct investment at the dawn of the transition period. For instance, adidas™ opened two manufacturing plants in Moscow and Tbilisi in 1990, after one in Hungary, and Donnay started a plant in Russia in 1991. The new fashion of sport clothing and participation (and thus consumption) emerged.

Since it was not immediately intertwined with accurate institutional change (dismantling *Goskomsport* in 1991 was not enough), the swift transformation of the former sports system was not without its bad news. The low level of private funding that was prevailing in sport became a hindrance to sport development (Andreff, 1997). State investment in new sport facilities nearly vanished overnight, as well as investment in modernizing long lasting obsolete sport equipment and facilities. Many state-owned enterprises, on the brink of privatization, were in the red after meeting new market conditions. They were hit by a "transformational" recession (Kornaï, 1994) and a restructuring crisis, and they were no longer in a position to finance sport. Sport broadcasting was not yet up-to-date: an absent source of finance compared to the West. Two windfall negative effects of the "muscle drain" were a reduced investment in athlete teaching and training and a decreasing spectator interest for domestic sport events. Another source of finance (gate receipts) was also vanishing.

A last economic and social impact of the early years of transition was the rising poverty that was spreading over a large part of the population linked to increased income inequalities. This was due to initial skyrocketing inflation and emerging high unemployment rates (Andreff, 2007). People's impoverishment shortened expenditures for sport participation (now supplied at a market price, so no longer for free) and attendance at sport events. A decreased leisure time emerged from a "work-oriented" or "self-exploiting" way of life, including a second job in the second economy (Laki, 1995). The population's sport participation rate fell from 5.7% in 1989 to 4.5% in 1995 in Hungary, from 13.5% in 1989 to 1.2% in 1997 in Bulgaria, and from 10.4% in 1989 to 5.7% in 2000 in Slovakia, while it recovered and grew by the end of the last century in the Czech Republic and Poland (Poupaux, 2006a). In every EEC, most administrative and manual workers have low participation rates, whereas the new economic elite of managers, businessmen, professionals, and executives show more than 80% sport participation rates. As a result, the market for sporting goods shrunk, concentrating for a while on its richest niche.

New sources of financing, such as establishing sports lotteries (Sportlotto and Lotto-million in Russia), funding sport facilities using the construction industry (Bulgaria), athlete transportation costs covered by new private companies, and membership fees (in all EECs), were not likely to avoid the collapse of the former sport system and its economy. In the face of such a break-up, without a new institutional framework, path dependence and inertial behavior appeared to be the last resort. For example, in Hungary, state support from the central budget, state funds and foundations, and local governments, after collapsing in 1989, channeled an increased amount of money toward sports, between 1990 and 1993 (Petroczi, 1995), at least in nominal terms, even though it results in minimal or no increase in real terms. Added to the absence of appropriate sport legislation, this backlash hindered foreign investors from crowding the market for sporting goods in several transition countries during the early years of transition.

Institution Building and Economic Transformation in Transition Economies

The collapse of the Soviet-style sport system and economy occurred within a span of a short time when stabilization policies were cutting budgets in all state ministries, economic liberalization was fuelling price inflation on new markets, and privatization was creating a radical uncertainty about future property rights, not to speak of embezzlements, bribery, corruption, and so on (Andreff, 2005b). The standard stabilization-liberalization-privatization program (backed by the so-called Washington consensus) prevailed during the first years of transition, but it left unheeded the crucial issue of building those institutions that are required for a market economy to operate properly. The institutional dimension of economic transformation into a market economy started to be emphasized after the mid-1990s, namely when it was focused on by the European Bank for Reconstruction and Development (EBRD) and, later on, by the World Bank. The latter reassessed its own evaluation of the transition process (World Bank, 2002) and highlighted institution building as the cornerstone for any further progress on the path toward a market economy. We assume that institutional change is also a precondition for sport organizations to fit with a new market environment.

Institutional Economic Reforms in Eastern European Countries

In any economy, according to North (1990), institutions are comprised of a set of *formal* rules (constitution, laws, regulations, political system) and *informal* rules (transaction trust, conventional wisdom, common knowledge, social norms, routines) that determine individual and organizational behavior. This pertains to organizations such as enterprises, trade unions, nongovernmental organizations and, of course, sports organizations. The transition process toward a market economy is supposed to build up (introduce) a number of new *formal* rules into former centrally planned economies. Even though it could not be achieved overnight, this transformation was likely to be conducted at a swift pace. The problem is that changing *informal* rules requires a "learning by doing" process for each and all individuals, which is time consuming and can spread over decades (or even one or two demographic generations). Meanwhile, some informal rules inherited from the former economic system will maintain (undisclosed and biased information, bargaining, informal economic networks, and corruption) or will be used by potential winners from formal institutional change to put a brake on reforms as soon as the latter would be likely to worsen their own position. Potential losers' inertia will also rely on resisting the enforcement of new formal rules when the latter materialize into real losses, and some losers will even call for a comeback to previous formal rules. Thus, the transition period is one of political instability due to the friction between formal and informal institutions. When informal rules are too distorted compared with new formal rules of a market economy, transaction costs skyrocket and governance issues become widespread at both corporate and nationwide levels. This is exactly what occurred in some transition countries (Andreff, 2005a).

What about the basic requirements in terms of formal institution building when it comes to switching from a Soviet-style to a market economy?

Beyond liberalization and privatization, much more is needed. The corporate governance issues must be tackled with at least a new corporate law, a law on joint stock companies, a securities law, a law on insolvency of financial institutions, a law on protection of securities market investors, a land code, a corporate governance code, and a new tax code. In addition, maximizing trust and minimizing transaction costs require a new civil code, a law on restructuring of credit, a judiciary reform, and a state power strong enough to enforce all the laws and regulations (which was not the case under Yeltsin's Russia, for instance). Securing a competitive (nonmonopoly) market requires an antitrust law (free entry in the business), a bankruptcy law (for the exit of inefficient enterprises), and the prevailing rule of law to bar the way to unfair competition and illicit or illegal economic strategies (Andreff, 2007).

A strong state is also basically needed to phase out undesirable informal rules and behaviors, such as managerial entrenchment in privatized enterprises, embezzlements, financial pyramids (Ponzi schemes),[1] corruption and bribes, violent entrepreneurship (i.e., the use of naked private violence to enforce a contract or resolve a transaction), tax evasion, money laundering, all sorts of economic crimes and, of course, the state capture by private interests (either private enterprises or individual bureaucrats). Putting an end to all these undesirable informal rules takes time and has yet to be finished in many transition economies; although, among the EECs, formal and informal institutional change is far ahead in the CEECs compared with CIS countries.

Until now, no research (the exception being Poupaux, 2006b) has been undertaken to determine whether, and how much, the sports economy in EECs has evolved into the aforementioned institutional change. The purpose of this chapter is to provide a first insight into this research area, although it is limited by the paucity of information and data. Measuring formal institutional change in transition economies is not an easy task, while assessing a change in governance—taken as a proxy for a possible phasing out of undesirable informal rules—lies somewhere between expert notation and guesstimates. It is all the more so in the EEC sports economy where most information is missing or is undisclosed.

Measuring the Institutional Quality of Transition Economies

The first attempt at measuring the quality of institutional change in EECs, and today the best known set of (institutional progress) transition

---

[1] A Ponzi scheme consists of a public offering of short-term promissory notes, with an extremely high return, which is paid back to the first investors with the outcome of issuing a second wave of promissory notes, and so on and so forth. It is legally forbidden in a fully-fledged market economy.

indicators, is the one published by the EBRD since the mid-1990s. In 1994–95, the EBRD drew attention to the institutional framework as a major prerequisite for the success of economic transition in its sample of 27 countries (10 CEECs, 12 CIS countries, and 5 Balkan countries). The emphasis was placed on property rights, contract enforcement, security, bankruptcy law, corporate law, and competition policy. Eventually, the EBRD created a standardized set of eight synthetic transition indicators featuring the most important institutions to be set up in a market economy. An expert notation (countries were noted from 1 to 4+) is now published every year for each of the 27 countries. The last year available is 2004 (EBRD, 2005) when institutional change could be considered as already well advanced in some countries such as Hungary, the Czech Republic, and Estonia. We start with the 1996 notation as a situation in which institution building was only in the starting blocks in some EECs and already on the tracks in some others, but far from being completed in any of them. Aggregating all the eight EBRD indicators into a single average notation allowed us to take this benchmark as a yardstick of institutional change in the overall economy to which we would refer our own evaluation of institution building in the sports economy. On the other hand, we would take the EBRD indicators also as a methodological benchmark for elaborating on our own specific indicators of institutional change in sports.

Briefly described, the eight EBRD indicators are:

1. Large-scale privatization: the notation ranges from little private ownership (=1) to more than 50% of state-owned enterprises (SOEs) and farm assets in private ownership (=4), while typical standards of advanced market economies (more than 75% of enterprise assets in private ownership) provide the highest notation (=4+, approximated by 4.33).

2. Small-scale privatization: ranges from little progress (=1) to complete privatization of small companies (=4), and to no state-owned small enterprise and effective tradability of land (=4+).

3. Governance and enterprise restructuring: ranges from soft budget constraint in SOEs (=1) to an active corporate control market (=4), or even an effective corporate control exercised through domestic financial institutions and markets fostering market-driven restructuring (=4+).

4. Price liberalization: ranges from most prices formally controlled by the government (=1) to comprehensive price liberalization (=4) and complete price liberalization (=4+).

5. Trade and foreign exchange system: ranges from widespread import and export controls and very limited access to foreign exchange

(=1) to removal of all quantitative, administrative, and significant tariff restrictions, and full current account convertibility (=4), and up to removal of most tariff barriers and WTO membership (=4+).

6. Competition policy: ranges from no competition legislation and institutions (=1) to significant enforcement actions to reduce market power and promote competition (=4), and up to effective enforcement of competition policy and unrestricted entry to most markets (=4+).

7. Banking reform and interest rate liberalization: ranges from little progress in establishing a two-tier banking system (=1) to significant movement of banking laws and regulations towards BIS (Bank of International Settlements) standards (=4), and up to full convergence of BIS standards (=4+).

8. Securities markets and nonbank financial institutions: ranges from little progress (=1) to substantial market liquidity and capitalization, and well-functioning nonbank financial institutions (=4), and up to fully developed nonbank intermediation (=4+).

When a country reaches a 4+ (4.33) aggregated average notation, it is considered to be a full-fledged market economy in regards to all its institutions. It is a developed market economy with an average of 4 for the eight aggregated indicators. Table 6–1 exhibits that, in 1996, even the most advanced among the 22 EECs that we have selected (Hungary = 3.58) had still some way to go on the path toward a market economy. Although closer to the target in 2004, it entered the European Union still being in the transition process (Hungary = 3.87), according to EBRD notation. It is all the more so for the 21 remaining countries (from Turkmenistan = 1.33 to the Czech Republic and Estonia = 3.79) sketched in Table 6–1.

Assessing Governance Issues

Since formal institutions do not exhaust the whole institutional dimension of the economy, the EBRD indicator must be completed with some index or proxy reflecting informal rules prevailing in a given society. The World Bank started to use governance indicators, which show that, whatever the quality of formal institutional change, governance may improve or not depending on how current the laws' and formal rules' enforcement is in the EECs. Such indicators are available every second year since 1996 (until 2004 so far) and are taken from Kaufman et al. (2005). They are six indicators with a notation ranking from −2 to +2 and, respectively, stand for:

TABLE 6–1

Aggregated EBRD Economic Institutions Indicators in 22 EECs in
1996 and 2004

Country	Code	Indicators in 1996	Indicators in 2004
Armenia	ARM	2.54	3.08
Azerbaijan	AZE	1.92	2.71
Belarus	BLR	1.77	1.88
Bulgaria	BGR	2.46	3.42
Czech Republic	CZE	3.54	3.79
Estonia	EST	3.33	3.79
Georgia	GEO	2.63	3.04
Hungary	HUN	3.58	3.87
Kazakhstan	KAZ	2.75	2.96
Kyrgyz Republic	KGZ	2.92	3.08
Latvia	LVA	3.17	3.62
Lithuania	LTU	3.13	3.63
Moldova	MDA	2.71	2.88
Poland	POL	3.46	3.71
Romania	ROM	2.58	3.17
Russian Federation	RUS	2.96	3.00
Slovak Republic	SVK	3.38	3.71
Slovenia	SVN	3.17	3.42
Tajikistan	TJK	1.83	2.42
Turkmenistan	TKM	1.29	1.33
Ukraine	UKR	2.46	2.87
Uzbekistan	UZB	2.38	2.13

Source: EBRD (2005).

1. Voice and accountability: the indicator measures political, civil, and human rights (i.e., the extent to which citizens of a country are able to participate in the selection of governments).

2. Political stability: measures the likelihood of violent threats, to, or changes in, government, including terrorism (i.e., it measures perception of the likelihood that the government in power will be destabilized or overthrown by possibly unconstitutional and/or violent means).

3. Government effectiveness: measures the competence of the bureaucracy and the quality of public service delivery (i.e., it combines

perceptions of the quality of public service provision, the quality of bureaucracy, the competence of civil servants, the independence of civil service from political pressures and the credibility of the government's commitment to policies).

4. The regulatory quality: measures the incidence of market-unfriendly policies (and includes measures of the incidence of market-unfriendly policies and perceptions of the burdens imposed by excessive regulation).

5. The rule of law: it measures the quality of contract enforcement, the police and the courts, as well as the likelihood of crime and violence (i.e., it measures the extent to which agents have confidence in and abide by the rules of society).

6. Control of corruption: measures the exercise of public power for private gain, including both petty and grand corruption and state capture.

Table 6–2 shows that, in 1996, the value of the aggregated governance indicator was the lowest in Tajikistan (−1.75) and Turkmenistan (−1.33)—the two countries probably encompassing the most undesirable informal rules at that moment—while the Czech Republic exhibited the highest, though not impressive value (+0.89), followed by Slovenia (+0.79). Moreover, there is a positive relationship (Figure 6–1) between the governance index and the EBRD institutional indicator, in 1996, since they are increasing (and decreasing) together at nearly the same pace—the slope of the regression line is positive and not too far from one (+0.76). This means that the more comprehensive formal institutions, the less undesirable informal rules (and thus the better laws and regulations enforcement). The outliers for this relationship were Turkmenistan and, to a lesser extent, Azerbaijan and Belarus due to stalling institutional reforms, whereas Tajikistan had the worst governance (the country was muddling through a civil war in 1996).

In 2004, the aggregated governance notations have moved up, ranging now from −1.53 (Turkmenistan) and −1.46 (Uzbekistan) to 1.06 (Estonia) and 0.99 (Slovenia). The relationship between the governance indicator and the aggregated EBRD index (Figure 6–2), though still positive, exhibits a regression line slope (+0.69) which is slightly less steep than in 1996; i.e., a slightly smaller change in formal institutions is required in 2004 to trigger the same improvement of governance than in 1996 in EECs. Turkmenistan is still a major outlier due to both stalling reforms and bad governance while Belarus shows deteriorated governance, compared to 1996, and the second slowest pace in institutional reforms.

TABLE 6–2

Aggregated Governance Indicators in 22 EECs in 1996 and 2004

Country	Code	Indicators in 1996	Indicators in 2004
Armenia	ARM	−0.39	−0.43
Azerbaijan	AZE	−0.93	−0.96
Belarus	BLR	−0.87	−1.12
Bulgaria	BGR	−0.15	0.21
Czech Republic	CZE	0.89	0.74
Estonia	EST	0.67	1.06
Georgia	GEO	−0.72	−0.80
Hungary	HUN	0.72	0.90
Kazakhstan	KAZ	−0.62	−0.82
Kyrgyz Republic	KGZ	−0.30	−0.80
Latvia	LVA	0.25	0.71
Lithuania	LTU	0.27	0.77
Moldova	MDA	−0.19	−0.64
Poland	POL	0.60	0.54
Romania	ROM	−0.15	−0.01
Russian Federation	RUS	−0.63	−0.63
Slovak Republic	SVK	0.34	0.74
Slovenia	SVN	0.79	0.99
Tajikistan	TJK	−1.75	−1.13
Turkmenistan	TKM	−1.33	−1.53
Ukraine	UKR	−0.54	−0.63
Uzbekistan	UZB	−0.94	−1.46

Source: World Bank (2006).

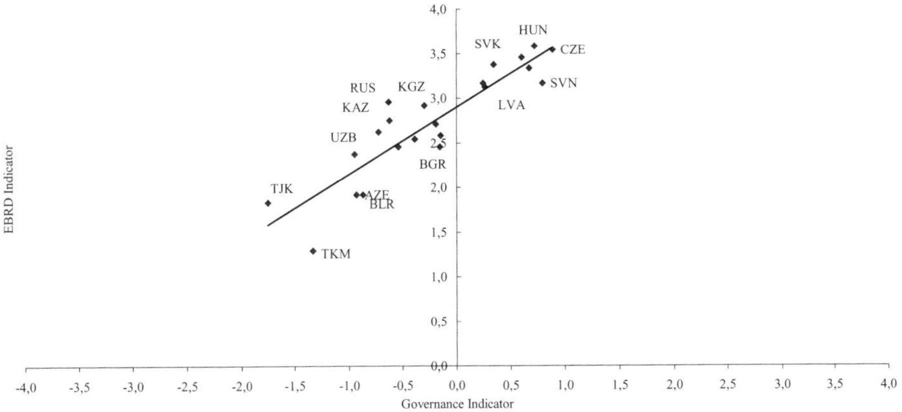

FIGURE 6–1. Governance and Institutional Change Indicators in 22 EECs in 1996

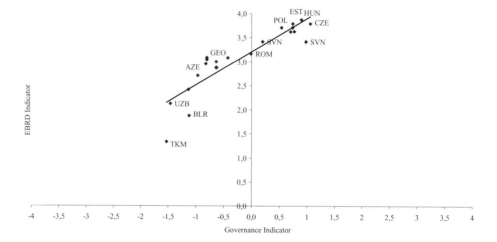

FIGURE 6–2. Governance and Institutional Change Indicators in 22 EECs in 2004

Assessing Institutional Change in Transitional Sports Economies

Just like the overall economy, the post-communist sports economy has been affected by various institutional reforms since 1990, at a different pace from one EEC to the other. We briefly sketch some drivers of institution building of a new sports system, and then we elaborate on a set of sports institutions indicators, which can be compared to the aforementioned EBRD and governance indicators.

Building Post-Soviet Sport Institutions

A global reform of sport organizations started up in the early 1990s with the restructuring of the governing bodies in each EEC. A new legislation had to be passed to ensure the proper operation of the sport system, and its economy in a new domestic market context opened to internationalizing trends. However, the former communist legislation was often maintained alongside with the newly adopted laws—an example of path dependence and institutional resilience. For instance, in 1992, after the USSR break-up, the new independent states passed their own laws ruling the physical culture and sports areas. A number of nongovernmental organizations took over sporting activities in Russia, such as trade unions (Spartak, Prosport), youth organizations (Burevestnik), and national defense (Rosto) and police (Dynamo) employee organizations (Poupaux, 2006b).

In Poland, a constitutional modification opened sports clubs, federations, and confederations to private finance, and new governing bodies were instituted. The former centralized sports administration was curtailed and lost its organizational and managerial prerogatives. This paved the way for a decentralized, autonomous, and volunteer-based sports system. Sports are increasingly relying on voluntary work in Eastern Europe. In Romania, the accountability over sports has been shared between the private sector, which handles sports for all, and the public sector heading top-level sports and high level training. In Hungary, sport organizations regained their independence on January 1, 1990, although the state remained accountable for grants, subsidies, and material resources that enable clubs to operate (Andreff, 1997). Being autonomous, sports organizations had been released from their obligation to report and supply data to the state, and they had been allowed to organize competitions, leisure, and youth sports in cooperation with the state. However, sports clubs' property rights on premises and sport facilities, that they use but do not own, were not clarified for some time, until their privatization (when transformed into foundations or limited liability companies) or their transfer to municipalities.

Institutional Indicators of a Sports Economy in Transition

Beyond the few aforementioned examples of institutional change in the sport system, if one wanted to attempt to measure the latter, it is worth elaborating more systematically some indicators pertaining to major driving forces that can help sports institutions adapt to the new market environment.

A first indicator is called a *legislation* index, and it refers to how complete is the change in the domestic sport legislation, respectively, in 1996 and 2004. Following the studies achieved for the Council of Europe by Charker (1999, 2004), we have taken three factors into consideration in building up this indicator: (1) is there any reference to sport in the constitution, (2) is there a national law specifically adopted for sport and how sophisticated is it, and (3) which type is this law (meaning that it may favor state intervention in sport or not)? The law is assumed to be "interventionist" when it exactly defines the structure and mission of sport governing bodies; the sports law is assumed to be "noninterventionist" when it only focuses on regulation and financial support to sporting activities. The target in most EECs is to harmonize the European Charter of Sport for All. The latter recommends that the state must promote sport for all, fair play, and a safe sport practice. The state must provide an access to sport participation whatever the level, promote voluntary work in sport, and facilitate an autonomous sport management while favoring well-matched relationships between the state itself and sport governing bodies.

Given the sports law content, our notation is as follows (Poupaux, 2006b):

- 1 = a Soviet-style sports law or no sports law at all;

- 1.3 = a reformed Soviet-style sports law (as in Russia in the late 1980s for instance);

- 1.7 = Governmental decisions or new laws enforceable to some particular area of sporting activities;

- 2 = a new sports law although not comprehensive;

- 3 = a new complete sports law;

- 4 = recurring emendations of the sports law.

When it comes to our *privatization* indicator, it assesses the extent of state withdrawal from sport and reflects the current governmental involvement in sport in 1996 and 2004. This indicator takes into account the actual degree of state accountability and interventionism (whatever the law says) in sport organizations, in decision making about sport finance, in supplying and maintaining sport facilities, and in providing skilled training and administrative personnel. Such an indicator also encapsulates how far the state control is spreading over national sporting activities and sport management. We have adopted the following notation:

- 1 = the state (central government) is still omnipresent in sport;

- 1.3 = the state is still omnipresent in sport, except in financing;

- 1.7 = the state formally releases a small part of its organizational and financial accountability to other sport organizations;

- 2 = the state formally delegates its organizational and financial accountability to either state decentralized bodies or nongovernmental sport organizations;

- 3 = the state cooperates and collaborates with nongovernmental sport organizations;

- 3.3 = the state cooperates and collaborates with nongovernmental sport organizations and gives substantial amounts of money to the nongovernmental sport sector;

- 4 = harmonization of the European Charter of Sport for All according to which the state is both accountable and complementary to sport governing bodies.

Then, we created a *decentralization* indicator that differentiates the institutional level where the state (the government) still intervenes in 1996 and 2004. In those EECs identified as centralized countries, sport programming and decision making, as well as sporting rules, are basically managed by the central government. In so-called decentralized countries, most decisions and actions are triggered or taken at local level. Our notation is:

- 1 = sports institutions are centralized under the central government;

- 1.3 = institutional decentralization is confined to financial domain aspects;

- 1.7 = institutional decentralization expands from the financial domain to some organizational issues;

- 2 = institutional decentralization of sport is mentioned in new laws or decrees;

- 2.3 = institutional decentralization starts materializing according to the new law;

- 3 = institutional decentralization can be observed in everyday life;

- 4 = local sport governing bodies (municipalities, counties, etc.) have a major and significant role in organizing and financing sport for all.

The *liberalization* indicator reflects how much sport governing bodies are independent from the state in 1996 and 2004, i.e., how much they retain of the released state power, how much they are socially recognized and accountable both in organizational and financial matters, and how much they are linked to the state. Our notation means:

- 1 = nongovernmental sport organizations are entirely subordinated to the state;

- 1.3 = a first stage of liberalization occurs when a number of independent clubs and sport organizations are freely created;

- 1.7 = the existence of newly created clubs and sport organizations starts to be officially recognized;

- 2 = a consulting organ gathering independent sport governing bodies is created in order to discuss and negotiate for their own sake with the central government;

- 2.3 = some written rules (decrees, etc.) recognize the existence and role of a nonstate sport sector;

- 3 = free action of clubs and sport organizations is *de facto* recognized and enshrined in a law;

- 3.3 = increase in the clubs' financial independence;

- 4 = enforcement of the European Charter of Sport for All: "voluntary sport organizations set up their autonomous decision making rules in the framework of the sports law; both the central government and sport governing bodies must recognize the need to mutually enforce their decisions."

The aggregated indicator shows that, on average, the sampled CEECs were more advanced than the sampled CIS countries in changing institutions of their sports economy, in 1996 (see Table 6–3). The same conclusion still holds true in 2004, whereas the aggregated notation exhibits an institutional improvement in sports institutions that occurred meanwhile in both country groups. Both years, the Czech Republic leads followed by Hungary, Slovakia, and Poland: these countries are front-runners in reforming sports institutions to help them adapt to a new market environment. In 2004, Hungary had harmonized the Western European sports legislation and had almost fully liberalized its sports system. The Czech Republic underperforms Hungary for the sports law but outperforms Hungary in sport privatization and decentralization.

A second country group encompasses, in 2004, the three Baltic States, Bulgaria, and Romania, in which the institutional reforms are less advanced than in the front-running group. On the other hand, Belarus, Russia, and Ukraine are lagging behind in 2004 just as they did in 1996. The main hindrance to institutional change in sports in these countries basically consists in a lack of decentralization and a limited privatization and liberalization, the only noticeable change being a new sports law passed during the first fourteen years of transition.

Thus, on the sports institutions side, transformation was slow before 1996 and it accelerated afterwards. In the CEECs, a first stage had been a state withdrawal from sport organizations and finance while passing new sports laws had come before state withdrawal in the Former Soviet Union (FSU). Until 1996, central government had been releasing only a few financing and decision-making prerogatives to decentralized authorities (municipalities, etc.) in CEECs and the Baltic States, whereas it practically did not release anything in Belarus, Russia, and Ukraine. In all EECs, independent sport organizations were increasing in number and size (after

TABLE 6–3
Sports Institutions Indicators for 12 Eastern European Countries

1996				
Code	Aggregate	Legislation	Privatization	Decentralization	Liberalization
BGR	**1.5**	1.3	1.7	1.3	1.7
ROM	**1.6**	1.7	1.7	1.7	1.3
POL	**1.775**	1.7	2	1.7	1.7
SVK	**1.925**	2	2	2	1.7
HUN	**1.925**	2	2	2	1.7
CZE	**2.325**	1.7	3	2.3	2.3
CEEC average	*1.84*	*1.73*	*2.07*	*1.83*	*1.73*
Code	Aggregate	Legislation	Privatization	Decentralization	Liberalization
BLR	**1.325**	2	1	1	1.3
RUS	**1.575**	2.7	1.3	1	1.3
UKR	**1.575**	3	1	1	1.3
EST	**1.675**	1.3	1.7	1.7	2
LVA	**1.6**	1.7	1.7	1.7	1.3
LTU	**2**	3	1.3	2	1.7
FSU average	*1.685*	*2.34*	*1.4*	*1.48*	*1.52*
2004				
Code	Aggregate	Legislation	Privatization	Decentralization	Liberalization
BGR	**2.25**	3	2	2	2
ROM	**2.35**	3	3	1.7	1.7
POL	**2.75**	3	2.7	2	3.3
SVK	**2.825**	2	3.3	3	3
HUN	**2.975**	4	2.3	2.3	3.3
CZE	**3.15**	3	3.3	3	3.3
CEEC average	*2.72*	*3.00*	*2.77*	*2.33*	*2.77*
Code	Aggregate	Legislation	Privatization	Decentralization	Liberalization
BLR	**1.5**	2.7	1	1	1.3
RUS	**1.85**	3	1.7	1	1.7
UKR	**1.85**	3	1.7	1	1.7
EST	**2.575**	3	3	2	2.3
LVA	**2.5**	3	3	2	2
LTU	**2.25**	3	2	2	2
FSU average	*2.205*	*3*	*2.28*	*1.6*	*1.94*

FSU: Former Soviet Union.
Source: Poupaux (2006b).

the initial collapse) but not in terms of decision making and capturing former state spans of control.

From 1996 to 2004, all sampled EECs have either passed a sport law in the Parliament or (in the case of Belarus and Slovakia) have adopted explicitly written rules to be enforced in sport. Liberalization has progressed in all sampled CEECs, except Bulgaria and Romania. The liberalization indicator is substantially lower in FSU countries, exhibiting an absent improvement in sport independence, in particular in Belarus. Privatization is up but remains below a 2 notation in three FSU countries, meaning a rather formal state withdrawal from sport organizations. The CEECs are in a better position. FSU countries differentiate with a still interventionist central government in sport matters in Belarus, Russia, and Ukraine on the one hand and, on the other hand, the Baltic States, which resemble the CEECs with regards to sport privatization. The same differentiation among countries applies to the observed outcome of decentralization.

Concordance between Sports and Economic Institutions in Transition Countries

Now, the last analytical step consists in comparing our numerical evaluation of sports institutions in EECs, based on the four above-defined indicators, with EBRD and governance indicators sketched in the second section. Are sport institutions ahead of economic institutions and the quality of governance in the process of transition toward a market economy? Are they exactly in tune with or lagging behind? Our specific sports institutions indicator enables us to scrutinize this issue both in 1996 and 2004.

Comparing Sports and Economic Institutions Indicators

Table 6–4 shows a *positive relationship* between the EBRD indicator of institutional change in the overall economy and the aggregate sports institutions indicator related to the sports economy. The more advanced the institution building of a market economy, the more advanced the emergence of sports institutions that fit with it, both in 1996 and 2004. Conversely, the less reformed the economic institutions, the less change in sports institutions.

The slope of the regression line is markedly below 1, which means that the improvement in sports institutions is slower than the one of economic institutions in 1996 (Figure 6–3) in the twelve EECs sample. The Czech Republic is an outlier off the regression line since its reforms of sports

TABLE 6–4

The Relationship between Sports and Economic Institutions in 12 EECs

Country	1996 EBRD economic institutions	1996 Sports institutions indicator	2004 EBRD economic institutions	2004 Sports institutions indicator
BLR	1.77	1.325	1.88	1.5
BGR	2.46	1.5	3.42	2.25
CZE	3.54	2.325	3.79	3.15
EST	3.33	1.675	3.79	2.575
HUN	3.58	1.925	3.87	2.975
LVA	3.17	1.6	3.63	2.5
LTU	3.13	2	3.62	2.25
POL	3.46	1.775	3.71	2.75
ROM	2.58	1.6	3.17	2.35
RUS	2.96	1.575	3	1.85
SVK	3.38	1.925	3.71	2.825
UKR	2.46	1.575	2.87	1.85

institutions are comparatively more advanced than in other EECs, while institutional change of its overall economy can compare with Hungary, Poland, and Slovakia. On the other hand, Poland, Estonia, and Latvia are ahead in changing their economic institutions rather than transforming their sports institutions.

In 2004, the slope of the regression line is steeper (closer to 1) than in 1996 (Figure 6–4), meaning that progress in sports institutions is now nearly in tune with institutional change in the overall economy, in most EECs. The only outlier off this regression is still the Czech Republic whose sports institutions have improved at a swifter pace than its economic institutions and in any other EEC.

The calculation of a correlation coefficient can confirm that the aforementioned relationship between economic and sports institutions is more or less significant. When a sample is very small (below 30 observations) a linear regression is not valid, and it is recommended to calculate a Spearman rank coefficient correlation (Saporta, 1978) as a way of testing the dependence or independence between two variables, because this method does not depend on the underlying distribution of variables (namely it does not depend on the assumption of a Gaussian distribution). The Spearman rank correlation is calculated as follows:

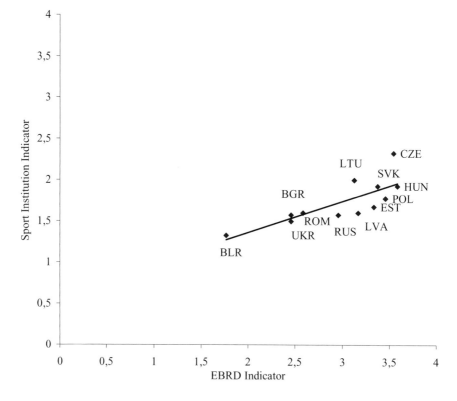

FIGURE 6–3. EBRD and Sports Institutions Indicators in 1996

$$r_s = 1 - \frac{6\sum_i d_i^2}{n(n^2 - 1)}$$

where d is the difference between the two ranks of a same country i with regards to two variable rankings, and n is the size of the sample. There is a concordance between the two variable rankings when r_s is positive and close to 1 (no relation when it is close to zero and a discordance when it is close to −1).

In 1996, the value of the Spearman coefficient (Table 6–5) is 0.86 and in 2004 it is 0.88. The concordance between economic institutions and sports institutions was already strong and significant ten years ago and still is today. This result should be interpreted as follows: those EECs that are the most involved in changing their economic institutions are

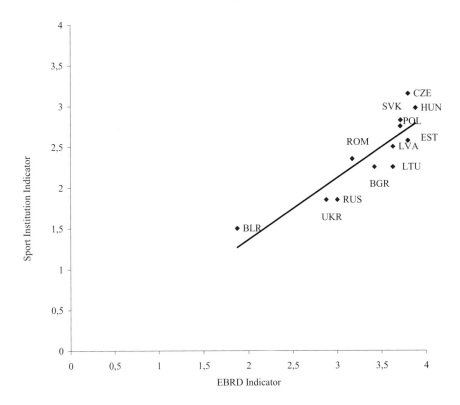

FIGURE 6–4. EBRD and Sports Institutions Indicators in 2004

TABLE 6–5
Spearman Rank Correlation

	Correlation between the EBRD indicator and sports institutions	Correlation between the governance indicator and sports institutions
1996	0.86	0.90
2004	0.88	0.64

exactly those in which the reforms of sports institutions have evolved the fastest, i.e., the Czech Republic, Hungary, Slovakia, and Poland. On the other hand, the laggards in institutional transformation of their economies exhibit stalling reforms in their sports institutions (Belarus, Russia, and Ukraine).

TABLE 6–6

The Relationship between Sports Institutions and Governance Indicators

Country	1996 Governance indicator	1996 Sports institutions indicator	2004 Governance indicator	2004 Sports institutions indicator
BLR	−0.867	1.325	−1.119	1.5
BGR	−0.155	1.5	0.207	2.25
CZE	0.888	2.325	0.745	3.15
EST	0.672	1.675	1.062	2.575
HUN	0.723	1.925	0.902	2.975
LVA	0.249	1.6	0.773	2.5
LTU	0.266	2	0.709	2.25
POL	0.602	1.775	0.542	2.75
ROM	−0.145	1.6	−0.009	2.35
RUS	−0.629	1.575	−0.634	1.85
SVK	0.630	1.925	0.74	2.825
UKR	−0.538	1.575	−0.626	1.85

Sports Institutions and the Quality of Governance

Taking the variation of governance indicators as a proxy for change in informal institutions, one can witness a *positive relationship* between the World Bank governance indicator and the aggregated sports institutions indicator related to the sports economy (see Table 6–6). The more governance improves in an EEC, the more advanced the emergence of new formal sports institutions, both in 1996 and 2004. The less improved governance, the less change in sports institutions. Of course, we cannot conclude that with better sports institutions there are decreasing informal behaviors (corruption, etc.) in sport, but we can assume that it is so since economic and political governance is now more transparent and efficient. It is the first assumption that should be tested in a further study.

In 1996, the slope of the regression line is not very steep (see Figure 6–5); a slight improvement in sports institutions is associated with a more than proportional upgrading in governance. The more advanced the strengthening of (governmental and corporate) governance structure, the more improved sports institutions fit with it. The least reformed sports institutions coincide with the weakest governance structures. Both Hungary and the Czech Republic are outliers off the regression line; the latter had the best sports institutions in 1996 with the strongest governance (a strong and popular government headed by Vaclav Klaus was still in office before the disclosure, in 1997, of embezzlements linked to enterprise privatization), and the former had the second best sports institutions and the

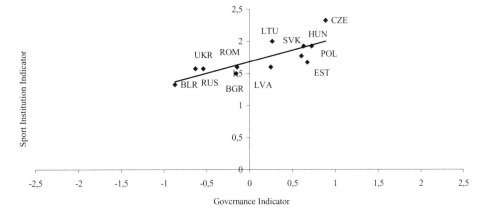

FIGURE 6–5. Governance and Sports Institutions Indicators in 1996

second ranking as regards to handling government effectiveness, the rule of law, the control of corruption, and money laundering, including in sport. Estonia was also an outlier owing to its good governance. Not surprisingly, Belarus, Ukraine, and Russia are located in the southwest corner of Figure 6–5. The notation of Russia in terms of governance might have been even worse in 1996, insofar as corruption, money laundering, economic crime, and murders were pervading its whole economy, including the sports sector (Andreff, 2000). It might be that, for political and economic reasons, experts had overvalued the governance strength (and undervalued the importance of informal rules) when President Yeltsin ranked so low in 1996 pre-electoral polls.

Eight years later, one witnesses practically the same relationship between sports institutions and governance, although it is clearly looser (Figure 6–6). Beyond the overall trend of governance improvement, compared to 1996, the governance indicator has worsened in five sampled countries: slightly in Russia; more significantly in Poland, Ukraine, and the Czech Republic; and dramatically in Belarus. Thus, even though sports institutions upgraded in all EECs, the differentiated paths followed by these countries as regards to governance structures alleviated the formerly tight relationship between the two variables. Three countries are outliers off the regression line: the Czech Republic (better sports institutions than governance), Estonia, and Latvia (better governance than sports institutions).

The variation of the Spearman rank correlation between sports institutions and governance confirms the previous conclusion (see Table 6–5). It is significant ($r_s = 0.90$) in 1996, but falls to 0.64 in 2004. The concordance between formal sports institutions and governance (supposed to contain

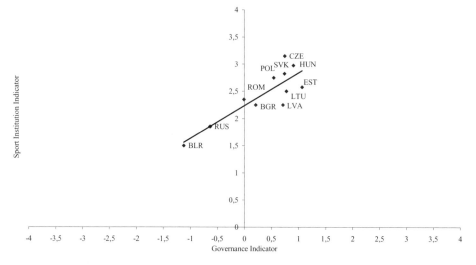

FIGURE 6–6. Governance and Sports Institutions Indicators in 2004

informal economic and political behaviors) has diminished; it was stronger ten years ago than today. A weaker concordance in 2004 than 1996 is not primarily due to a slow change in sports institutions, since the sports institutions indicator has significantly improved meanwhile in all sampled EECs, except Belarus and Romania. Thus, while EECs sports institutions have evolved in concordance with market-friendly institutions, it was less the case in regards to the concordance with upgrading governance. This is due to the five aforementioned countries (nearly half our sample) that show, contrarily to the overall trend, a deterioration of their governance indicator (i.e., resilient informal institutions) from 1996 to 2004. Although the Czech Republic and Poland are front-runners in reforming both economic and sporting institutions, they did not succeed as well in coping with voice and accountability, government effectiveness, regularity quality, the rule of law, and the control of corruption, in the last eight years. Belarus and Ukraine declined (and Russia stalled) in governance quality while they moderately improved their sports institutions.

Conclusion

Some years after the break-up of the communist centrally-planned system, Eastern European countries embarked on a deep institutional change in their economies, affecting formal and informal institutions. Then, they started more or less significant reforms regarding their sport institutions. In most sampled countries, institutional change was in tune between sports and the overall economy, except for a few outliers. Those countries, which are front-runners, perform well in both institutional areas. When it comes to informal institutions and their impact on governance, the latter's relationship with sport institutions has loosened from 1996 to 2004 because governance deteriorated, instead of improving, in five sampled countries. How did this deterioration affect sports functioning and management? What about the resilience of informal behaviors in transitional sports economies? The required information to deal with these question marks is practically undisclosed so far (Andreff, 2000). Collecting it should be of first concern in future research agendas.

References

Andreff, W. (1997). The Western economic "model" of sport and Hungarian sport in transformation: A comparison. *Journal of Comparative Physical Education and Sport*, 19(1):2–9.

Andreff, W. (2000). Financing modern sport in the face of a sporting ethic. *European Journal for Sport Management*, 7(1):5–30.

Andreff, W. (2004). The taxation of player moves from developing countries. In: R. Fort and J. Fizel (Eds.), *International Sports Economics Comparisons*, Westport, CT: Praeger, pp. 87–103.

Andreff, W. (2005a). Post-Soviet privatization in the light of the Coase Theorem: Transaction costs and governance costs. In: A.N. Oleinik (Ed.), *The Institutional Economics of Russia's Transformation*, Aldershot: Ashgate, pp. 191–212.

Andreff, W. (2005b). Russian privatization at bay: Some unresolved transaction and governance cost issues in post-Soviet economies. In: A.N. Oleinik (Ed.), *The Institutional Economics of Russia's Transformation*, Aldershot: Ashgate, pp. 213–244.

Andreff, W. (2007). *Economie de la transition. La transformation des économies planifiées en economies de marché*. Paris: Bréal.

Bourg, J.-F. (1995). Le sport dans l'ex-URSS: des ruptures aux incertitudes. *Revue Juridique et Economique du Sport*, 34, 5–18.

Charker, A.N. (1999). *Study of National Sports Legislation in Europe*. Strasbourg: Council of Europe Publishing.

Charker, A.N. (2004). *Good Governance in Sport: A European Survey*. Strasbourg: Council of Europe Publishing.

EBRD (2005). *Transition Report 2005*. London: European Bank for Reconstruction and Development.

Kaufman, D., Kraay, A. and Mastruzzi, M. (2005). Governance Matters IV: Governance Indicators for 1996–2004, draft, May.

Kornaï, J. (1994). "Transformational" recession. The main causes. *Journal of Comparative Economics*, 19(1):39–63.

Laki, L. (1995). *Economical Effects of Sport in Hungary*. Budapest, mimeo.

North, D.C. (1990). *Institutions, Institutional Change, and Economic Performance*. Cambridge: Cambridge University Press.

Petroczi, A. (1995). Financing of Sport in Hungary, 3rd EASM Congress, Budapest, September.

Poupaux, S. (2006a). Soviet and post-Soviet sport. In: W. Andreff and S. Szymanski (Eds.), *Handbook on the Economics of Sport*, Cheltenham: Edward Elgar, pp. 316–324.

Poupaux, S. (2006b). Performances économiques et transformations du secteur sportif dans les pays est-européens. Thèse, Université de Paris 1, août.

Riordan, J. (1977). *Sport in Soviet Society*. Cambridge: Cambridge University Press.

Saporta, G. (1978). *Théories et méthodes de la statistique*. Paris: Editions Technip.

Shneidman, N. (1979). *The Soviet Road to Olympus*. London: Routledge & Kegan.

World Bank (2002). *Transition—The First Ten Years: Analysis and Lessons for Eastern Europe and the Former Soviet Union*. Washington D.C., January.

World Bank (2006). http://info.worldbank.org/governance/kkz2004/tables.asp.

Part II

Professional Leagues

7

National Dominance in European Football Leagues

Kelly Goossens and Stefan Kesenne

Professional team sports generate indivisible joint-products. Neale (1964, p. 2) captures this interrelatedness in the following sentence: "pure monopoly is disaster." Or in short: teams need each other to produce games. Rottenberg (1956, p. 242) mentions that "The nature of the industry is such that competitors must be of approximate equal 'size' if any are to be successful." The notion of competitive balance is founded upon this idea: for an attractive championship, teams should not excel excessively in playing strength.

In the media and the professional sports sector, this idea of competitive balance receives significant attention and underlies many sports policy decisions. In sports economics, as well, competitive balance is at least relevant. Over the last four decades, several events occurred that can be considered to have had an impact on competitive balance. More specifically, they affect the dominance of "large-market" teams. We define such teams as those located in a large city combined with a large fan base. Such imbalance is what Kesenne (2004) calls a "bad" imbalance.

We theoretically research the impact of some major changes that caused important shifts in the revenue functions. We construct a two league—four teams model and include the market, local and national, as major determinants of the revenue functions of teams. We determine the choice of talent under both the win maximizing and the profit maximizing objectives. The difference in win percentages is used to measure the competitive imbalance. We calculate the total demand function for talent and intersect it with an elastic supply formalized into a simple linear supply function. The resulting equilibrium wage is discussed where possible.

We discuss three scenarios based on three successive periods in European football leagues. All periods are introduced by important changes generally discussed to influence dominance. We start from a benchmark scenario with a closed labor market in which ticket sales, based on the local market, are considered to constitute the main income source. The sale of broadcast rights combined with shirt sponsoring introduces the second period. In most countries, this new era began at the end of the 70s and early 80s. Both substantially increased revenues and are highly interrelated. Live matches persuaded sponsors to invest in the teams, as well as in commercial blocks on TV. Sports fans were now able to enjoy live games of teams located in another part of the country so that the market of supporters increased with a part of the national market.

The third period is marked by a combination of three events. Jean-Marc Bosman, a professional Belgian football player, changed the labor market in professional team sports in the mid 1990s. He went to court to oppose the transfer ruling. The European Court of Justice ruled that the transfer system concerning European international football players violated the free movement of workers constituted in Article 48 of the ECC treaty. Following the verdict of December 15, 1995, the European Commission abandoned the policy of transfer restrictions and abolished the rule to limit the number of foreign players fielded, giving rise to a new chapter in European football history: a more open and competitive labor market. The abolishment occurred in the middle of the season so the real impact on the acquirement of talent can be assumed to begin, at the earliest, in the 1996–1997 season.

In 1997, the Champions League (CL) changed its selection criteria and its revenue distribution. The "market pool" came into use, designating the revenue that is divided based on the national television market. Teams from countries with a larger market receive a larger share. This makes it possible that a CL champion receives a lower income than teams that ended lower in the ranking. Porto, for example, received €19 million in 2003–2004, while runners-up AS Monaco FC received €26.4 million (Uefa. com, June 8, 2004). Even though the CL, named the Champions Cup before 1992, has an extensive history of adaptations, we consider this change as the most important one to substantially influence the dominance of teams in the national competition.

With the deregulation of the television market, the competition for broadcast rights intensified. Among other things, this boosted the broadcast revenues considerably. The introduction of digital television at the end of the 90s can be assumed to be the start of a continuing boom of broadcast rights and so influences the third period as well.

We provide a first empirical verification of our results by constructing a measure that incorporates the identity of teams to focus on large market teams. Two European football leagues, England and Belgium, are briefly discussed. In our conclusion we provide an overview table and discuss some future research topics.

Theoretical Model

Following Quirk and Fort (1995), the revenue function of professional sports teams with n teams in the league should satisfy the following assumptions:

$$R_j = R(m_j, w_j) \text{ with } \frac{\partial R_j}{\partial m_j} > 0; \frac{\partial R_j}{\partial w_j} > 0 \text{ and } \frac{\partial^2 R_j}{\partial w_j^2} < 0 \text{ for } j = 1 \text{ to n} \quad (7.1)$$

The revenue function R_j of a team j depends on its local market size m_j and its winning percentage w_j. The revenues increase in the market size. A team located in a large city and, following, having a large local market is assumed to be able to attract more spectators *ceteris paribus*. The difference in local drawing power will be shown to be substantial. The revenues also increase in the winning percentage, but in a decreasing marginal matter so that the revenue function is concave in the win percentage (El Hodiri and Quirk, 1974). Fans prefer that their team wins, but appreciate that the game is exciting and the difference in fielded talent should not be too big. A game where the home team wins with a score of 2 to 1 can be assumed to be more attractive than when a team wins with a score of 7 to 0. Following this preference, a team that has already a very high win percentage will not increase their revenues by as much, or even at all, when an extra win percent is added compared to when it has a low win percentage.

A team cannot directly affect the win percentage, but we follow the main literature that the win percentage of a team is determined by the talents acquired by team j, x_j, compared to the total talent in the league, x (Quirk and Fort, 1995). Following Borghans and Groot (2005) the latter ratio forms the probability p_{jk} that team j wins against team k:

$$p_{jk} = \frac{x_j}{x_j + x_k} \quad (7.2)$$

The expected number of absolute wins for team j, $E(\text{wins}_j)$ is the sum of these probabilities for all games. In European football competitions, the teams play each other twice.

$$E(\text{wins}_j) = 2\sum_{j \neq k} p_{jk} = 2x_j \sum_{j \neq k} \frac{1}{x_j + x_k} \quad (7.3)$$

We assume that there is no home team advantage for simplicity. We can now define the win percentage of team j, w_j, as the ratio of the total number of wins divided by the total number of games:

$$w_j = \frac{E(\text{wins}_i)}{2(n-1)} = \frac{x_j}{n-1} \sum_{j \neq k} \frac{1}{x_j + x_k} \qquad (7.4)$$

We construct a basic model in which we simplify these general formulations. The first subchapter describes our benchmark scenario. A subdivision is made based on the objective function: win maximization versus profit maximization. Next, we introduce broadcasting and sponsor revenues by adding a fraction of the national market. The last scenario includes an open labor market and extra revenue from the market pool for the large team.

Benchmark: No Broadcasting/Sponsorship, Closed Labor, and Product Market

A league consists of two countries (A and B), each with two teams (1 and 2). Country A is a large market country, while country B has a smaller national market. Within each country we define team 1 as the large market team and team 2 as the small market team. We assume that the local markets of the teams sum up to the total national market. So formally:

$$m_A > m_B; \ m_{i1} > m_{i2} \text{ and } m_{i1} + m_{i2} = m_i \quad \text{for i = A, B} \qquad (7.5)$$

We combine two basic models of Kesenne (2006) to specify a revenue function for each club in each country that fulfills (1). We begin with the local market as the main source of revenues and combine this with a parameter $\beta > 0$ in such that the concavity is fulfilled.

$$R_{ij} = m_{ij} w_{ij} - \beta w_{ij}^2 \quad \text{for i = A, B and j = 1, 2} \qquad (7.6)$$

To ensure positive win percentages and positive amounts of talent, Kesenne (2007a, b) shows that the following inequalities need to be satisfied. We adapt the formula to apply to our model.

$$m_{i2} - m_{i1} < \beta < \frac{m_i}{2} \qquad (7.7)$$

With only two teams, the winning percentage (4) amounts to:

$$w_{ij} = \frac{x_{ij}}{x_{i1} + x_{i2}} = \frac{x_{ij}}{x_i} \qquad (7.8)$$

The number of playing talents of team j in country i is presented by x_{ij} and x_i is the sum of talents in country i.

On the cost side, we consider the player labor cost c_i as the sole cost of production, which is not an unreasonable assumption if a strong positive correlation between the capital cost and the number of playing talents in a club exists (see Szymanski and Smith, 1997). We assume that the teams are wage takers. With only two teams we admit that this assumption is less realistic. The following total cost function is used:

$$TC_{ij} = c_i x_{ij} \qquad (7.9)$$

The wage cost is determined endogenously. The aggregate demand function for talent is found by adding the individual demand functions horizontally. Equilibrium is found where demand intersects with the supply of talent.

We assume that the supply of talent is flexible. For computational simplicity, it is restricted to be linearly increasing in wage. This can be justified based on the following reasonable assumptions. We assume that the highest league acquires substantial training so that people are not able to have a full-time job elsewhere. Hence, people are only willing to train their innate talents to reach the necessary level if they know they will receive considerable payment. The higher this payment, the more people are willing to train and so increase the total number of supplied talents. This increase comes from the number of people entering the market as by the increase of talents within a player. Formalized, we use:

$$x_i^S = ac_i \qquad (7.10)$$

Theoretic modeling predominantly uses the objective of profit maximization. Some authors, such as Sloane (1971) and Cairns, Jennett, and Sloane (1986), mention, without algebraic formalization, that utility maximizing, where wins give utility, can be more important than maximizing profits. Following their discussion, it is often stated that American sports leagues are more profit maximizing, while European leagues maximize winning. However, even for European team sports, the profit objective remains predominant in theoretic research. We present results for both the profit maximization and the win maximization objective and start with the latter.

Professional football clubs in Europe are often considered to be mainly interested in winning as many games as possible. To achieve this, they buy as much talent as their budget constraint allows them. Reaching a certain profit can be taken up in the budget constraint because win maximization does not exclude this (Kesenne, 2006). Since calculations quickly become more complex when adding a positive or a negative profit, we assume that teams hire as much talent as allowed to break even. The following method to find equilibrium is similar for the other two periods and is only discussed here in detail.

The maximization problem for team j in league i is formulized using Eqs. (7.6) and (7.9):

$$\text{Maximize } x_{ij}$$

$$\text{Subject to: } m_{ij}w_{ij} - \beta w_{ij}^2 - c_i x_{ij} = 0 \tag{7.11}$$

We use Eq. (7.8) and find that the break even constraint holds if:

$$m_{ij}\frac{1}{x_{i1} + x_{i2}} - \beta\left(\frac{1}{x_{i1} + x_{i2}}\right)^2 x_{ij} = c_i \tag{7.12}$$

So the demand for talent is given by its average revenue function:

$$AR_{ij} = \frac{R_{ij}}{x_{ij}} = c_i \tag{7.13}$$

When the labor market is closed, the equilibrium cost of talent c_j will be determined within each country, so we added a subscript i.

The optimal number of talents (x_{i1}) of team 1 depends on the number of talents acquired by the other team (x_{i2}) and vice versa, so a game theoretic approach applies. We assume that in each country, the following simultaneous one shot game with complete information takes place. We have two players: team 1 and team 2. Each team chooses an amount of talent x_j, which lies between zero and infinity in order to maximize their win percentage given the break even constraint.

To find the Cournot-Nash equilibrium we intersect the reaction curves [Eq. (7.12)] of the two teams in a country:

$$\frac{m_{i1}}{x_i} - \beta\frac{x_{i1}}{x_i^2} = \frac{m_{i2}}{x_i} - \beta\frac{x_{i2}}{x_i^2} \tag{7.14}$$

We focus in this chapter on the dominance of large-market teams within countries. Quirk and Fort (1995) mention that the difference in winning percentages measures competitive balance. As far as we know, the present theoretic models all discuss the ratio of talents or the win percentages by themselves. We introduce the measure of dominance (D_i) by subtracting the win percentage of team 2 from the win percentage of team 1. A positive D_i reveals dominance of the large market team. After multiplying both sides of Eq. (7.14) by x_i, we can derive that:

$$D_i = w_{i1} - w_{i2} = \frac{m_{i1} - m_{i2}}{\beta} \tag{7.15}$$

which is clearly positive, so that the large-market team dominates. The larger the difference in local markets is, the larger the dominance is.

Comparison between countries needs an assumption on the differences between the local markets. Large countries have generally the same number of teams, or just a few more, in the highest league. So the dispersion over the country is much larger, and we can expect that most teams will be located in a larger local market area of their own. We believe that the differences in local markets will consequently be larger in small countries than in large countries. This will result in a more uneven balance in those smaller countries. However, more research is necessary to support or contradict this.

The demand function of talent is found by summing the individual demand functions.

$$x_i = \frac{m_i - \beta}{2c_i} \tag{7.16}$$

The equilibrium wage is found by intersecting the demand function Eq. (7.16) with the supply function of talents Eq. (7.10).

$$c_i = \sqrt{\frac{m_i - \beta}{2a}} \tag{7.17}$$

Comparing the labor costs in both countries using Eq. (7.5) enables us to derive the following inequality:

$$c_A = \sqrt{\frac{m_A - \beta}{2a}} > c_B = \sqrt{\frac{m_B - \beta}{2a}} \tag{7.18}$$

meaning that the equilibrium wage is higher in the large-market country.

When we replace c_i in Eq. (7.16) by Eq. (7.17) we find the total amount of talents purchased for each country. Because Eq. (7.5) applies we find the following inequality:

$$x_A = \sqrt{\frac{a(m_A - \beta)}{2}} > x_B = \sqrt{\frac{a(m_B - \beta)}{2}} \qquad (7.19)$$

so that the large-market country is more talented than the small-market country.

We can conclude from this analysis that, if teams that only differ in local market size maximize their win percentage, the large-market team in each country acquires more talents than the small-market team. With a linear supply curve, the large-market country has a higher equilibrium wage than the small-market country. The large-market country also acquires more talents than the small-market country.

The method of profit maximization, outlined here in detail, is similar for the next periods and is not repeated. The maximization problem of the profit function for team j in league i, using Eqs. (7.6) and (7.9), is presented as follows:

$$\underset{x_{ij}^P}{\text{Max}} \, \Pi_{ij}^P = m_{ij} w_{ij}^P - \beta w_{ij}^{P,2} - c_i^P x_{ij}^P \qquad (7.20)$$

We add a superscript P to indicate that we consider leagues with profit maximization as predominant objective.

The first order condition is:

$$MR_{ij} = \frac{\partial R_{ij}}{\partial x_{ij}} = c_i \qquad (7.21)$$

With profit maximization, the demand for talent is given by its marginal revenue function. A similar one-shot game, as with win maximization, arises but now the profit function needs to be maximized. So in this case the first order conditions are the reaction functions. Intersecting these functions leads us to the following competitive balance:

$$D_i^P = \frac{m_{i1} - m_{i2}}{m_i} \qquad (7.22)$$

which yields the well-known result that the large-market team dominates the small-market team.

The discussion concerning the differences in local markets applies here as well, and if our intuition is correct, that the differences are smaller for large-market countries, it follows that there is less large-market team domination in country A.

The demand function of talent can be derived as (see Appendix 7.1):

$$x_i^P = \frac{(m_i - 2\beta)m_{i1}m_{i2}}{c_i^P m_i^2} \tag{7.23}$$

The equilibrium wage is now simply found by intersecting this demand function with the supply of talents Eq. (7.9),

$$c_i^P = \frac{1}{m_i}\sqrt{\frac{(m_i - 2\beta)m_{i1}m_{i2}}{a}} \tag{7.24}$$

We were not able to compare the wage levels in both countries. If we calculate some examples incorporating the necessary conditions, we find a higher wage cost in country A than in country B. We have not found a contradicting example, but more research is appropriate.

The total amount of talent in country i is found by substituting Eq. (7.24) into Eq. (7.23):

$$x_i^P = \frac{\sqrt{a(m_i - 2\beta)m_{i1}m_{i2}}}{m_i} \tag{7.25}$$

When comparing profit maximization to win maximization, and referring to Eq. (7.7), the competitive balance measure shows that the large-market teams are more dominant in win maximizing leagues then they would be in profit maximizing leagues:

$$D_i = \frac{m_{i1} - m_{i2}}{\beta} > D_i^P = \frac{m_{i1} - m_{i2}}{m_i} \tag{7.26}$$

Comparing the wages we can derive the following result (see Appendix 7.2):

$$c_i > c_i^P \tag{7.27}$$

We can conclude that, if teams that only differ in local market size maximize profits, the large-market team acquires more talents and will hence dominate the small-market team.

If teams are wage takers, the large-market teams are more dominant in win maximizing leagues then they would be in profit maximizing leagues. With a linear supply of talent, the market clearing wage will be higher in win maximizing leagues then it would be when profits are maximized.

Introduction of Live Broadcasting and Shirt-Sponsorship

Broadcasting of live matches and shirt sponsoring generate extra revenue. These revenue sources are determined by the size of the national market. To include such a change, we add a fraction of the entire country to the local market of teams. We assume that large-market clubs are able to attract bigger sponsors, resulting in higher revenue. The subscript TV is added to indicate the new period of sponsoring and broadcasting.

Since each team has a different potential to attract sponsors, we multiply the total market of a country by a parameter α_{Aj}. We assume that the large-market team attracts more money and, hence, receives a larger fraction. The national market is divided over the two teams.

$$0 < \alpha_{i2} < \alpha_{i1} < 1; \; \alpha_{i2} + \alpha_{i1} = 1 \tag{7.28}$$

With these extensions to the model, all calculations are comparable to the ones from the previous section, so it can be derived that:

$$D_{Tv,i} = D_i + \frac{m_i(\alpha_{i1} - \alpha_{i2})}{\beta} \tag{7.29}$$

The dominance of the large-market club goes up if it receives a large fraction of the total market. This result follows from our assumption that the big team will be able to attract more revenue. If teams have an equal share of the total market so that $\alpha_{A1} = \alpha_{A2}$ and $\alpha_{B1} = \alpha_{B2}$ the competitive balance does not change. If the share of the total market would be used as an instrument by the league to promote competitive balance, the league could pool all the revenues of sponsoring and broadcasting. When they give a larger fraction to the small teams to compensate for the local market, a more equal talent distribution would be the result.

The demand of talent now equals:

$$x_{Tv,i} = \frac{2m_i - \beta}{2c_{Tv,i}} \tag{7.30}$$

so that the wage is larger in both countries due to the extra revenue.

$$c_{Tv,i} = \sqrt{\frac{2m_i - \beta}{2a}} > c_i \tag{7.31}$$

Under profit maximization dominance becomes:

$$D_{Tv,i}^{P} = \frac{D_i^{P}}{2} + \frac{(\alpha_{i1} - \alpha_{i2})}{2} \qquad (7.32)$$

The broadcast and sponsor revenues can change the dominance of large-market teams. If in a profit maximization league, the small team receives a larger broadcast share than its local market share, and the difference in winning percentages decreases so the national competitive balance improves. Therefore, the impact of the extra revenue depends on the dispersion of the revenues compared to the spread of the market shares. This is shown in Appendix 7.3.

$$D_{Tv,i}^{P} > D_i^{P} \Leftrightarrow \alpha_{c1} - \alpha_{c2} > \frac{m_{c1}}{m_c} - \frac{m_{c2}}{m_c} \qquad (7.33)$$

It is obvious that the total demand for talent in each country is now higher given the extra revenue, so that, with the same supply curve, the equilibrium wage also will be substantially higher. See Appendix 7.4 for algebraic notation.

When comparing profit and win maximization, we find equal numerators of the dominance measure. Using Eq. (7.7) it is obvious that:

$$D_{Tv,i} > D_{Tv,i}^{P} \qquad (7.34)$$

so that the concentration of talents remains higher in win maximization leagues than it would be with profit maximization, independent of the difference in shares.

We can conclude for this section that the broadcast and sponsor revenues increase the dominance of large-market teams when these teams receive a larger fraction of the total market. This result applies for a league that maximizes wins. With profit maximization, the dominance can already be lowered if the small team receives a higher percentage than its local market share. That percentage can still be lower than what the large team acquires. For both objectives, the wages go up in both countries, and the win maximization league remains most dominated.

Introduction of the Champions League with an Open Labor Market and Large Increase in Broadcast Rights

The Champions League joins the best national teams and gives them the opportunity to play each other. Broadcasting and sponsoring, merchandizing and licensing revenues increase because the market enlarges to the

European market. We assume that the big market team of a country reaches the Champions League, as a representative for the European football leagues.

We consider the changes in 1997/1998 as the most influential on the dominance of large-market teams. Teams, besides the champions of the national leagues, were taken up in the league and extra revenue is rewarded, called the "market pool," based on the national TV market. The larger the national TV audience is, the more revenue teams receive. We focus on the market pool alone and add a parameter d to the national market. So we assume that this enlargement can be presented as an increase in the fraction of the national market and that it is equal for all teams and countries. Teams that enter the Champions League also receive a lump sum independent of their market or number of games played. Playing in the Champions League introduces, however, extra costs, such as investments in the playing grounds to receive international teams, in extra security, in transportation costs for away games, in extra medical costs, etc. We assume that the lump sum covers these extra costs.

We assume that the teams do not take the talent of other countries into account when deciding on their own talent. The fact that a team like Real Madrid bought star players is assumed not to have an effect on the talent of other teams playing in the Champions League if they do not play in the Spanish Primera División.

At the end of the 90s, the deregulation of the television market boosted broadcast revenues. The increases have not yet stabilized, but the impact is comparable to the second scenario. We do not explicitly include this in our model, but it is possible to multiply α_{Aj} by a factor larger than one. If the increases in broadcast revenues are equally divided over all teams, no changes in dominance occur. If the biggest increase is noted for the biggest teams, dominance increases under win maximizing. Under profit maximizing, the new broadcast shares need to be compared to the local market shares.

The opening of the labor market after the Bosman arrest introduces a European labor cost. Hence, we no longer use the subscript i. We assume that the European supply function can be represented by the horizontal summation of the supply functions of each individual country. Football players are indeed traveling all over Europe, so this is a plausible simplification.

If only the large-market teams enter the CL, and teams are win maximizers, the maximization problem is formulated including the parameter d and adding the subscript Cl as indicator of this last period:

$$\text{Maximize } x_{Cl,il}$$

$$\text{Subject to } (m_{il} + (\alpha_{il} + d)m_i)w_{Cl,1} - \beta w_{Cl,1}^2 - c_{Cl}x_{Cl,il} = 0 \quad (7.35)$$

The smaller team does not receive any extra income since it does not enter the Champions League.

$$\text{Maximize } x_{Cl,i2}$$

$$\text{Subject to } (m_{i2} + \alpha_{i2} m_i) w_{Cl,2} - \beta w_{Cl,2}^2 - c_{Cl} x_{Cl,i2} = 0 \qquad (7.36)$$

For both teams, the budget constraints need to be fulfilled and, hence, act as reaction functions. Intersecting these functions shows that the increase of the revenue results in the following dominance measure:

$$D_{Cl,i} = D_{Tv,i} + \frac{dm_i}{\beta} \qquad (7.37)$$

which yields the obvious result that the dominance of large-market teams increases under win maximization when these teams alone receive extra income.

Because of the opening of the labor market the wage is now determined on the world market. The world demand for talent is derived by adding $x_{Cl,A}$ to $x_{Cl,B}$, so that:

$$X_{Cl}^D = \frac{m_A(2+d) + m_B(2+d) - 2\beta}{c} \qquad (7.38)$$

We find the market wage cost by intersecting the demand and supply function. We need to adapt the supply function since all talents can now play in other countries. The aggregate world supply function is found by adding the two individual country supply functions so that:

$$X_{Cl}^S = 2ac \qquad (7.39)$$

Equilibrium is found by the intersection of Eqs. (7.38) and (7.39) and the wage is now:

$$c = \sqrt{\frac{m_A + m_B + \dfrac{d}{2}(m_A + m_B) - \beta}{a}} \qquad (7.40)$$

This again shows an increase compared to the second period. The proof is given in Appendix 7.5.

If the large teams in both countries maximize their profits, including their share of the market pool represented by the parameter d, and the small teams have the same maximization problem as in the second period, we find the new competitive balance:

$$D^P_{Cl,i} = D^P_{Tv,i} + \frac{d}{2} \tag{7.41}$$

so that the market pool increases the dominance of the large teams.

As in both previous periods, the win maximizing leagues are more dominated by their large-market teams (see Appendix 7.6):

$$D^P_{Cl,i} < D_{Cl,i} \tag{7.42}$$

We can conclude for this third period that the dominance of the large-market teams further increases in both the profit and the win maximization cases. It is also obvious that the extra revenue further increases demand and the equilibrium wage level in both countries for the win maximizing league. When teams maximize profits we are not able to derive the latter result algebraically. Again, the dominance of the large-market teams is less extreme in the profit maximization leagues than it would be in win maximization leagues.

We summarize the results for all periods in a table in the last section. In the following section, we provide a first empirical verification.

A First Empirical Verification

We add a first empirical analysis to verify some results. We did not find a measure in the literature that focuses on the identity of a team so we introduce a new dominance measure. This dominance measure focuses on large-market teams and ranges between 0 and 1. We choose England as our large-market country with 49 million inhabitants and Belgium as the small-market country with 10 million inhabitants. We consider a period of 30 seasons beginning with 1975 up to 2004.

Only three teams remained in the highest league in Belgium during the 30 seasons: RSC Anderlecht, Club Brugge, and Standard de Liège. All three are located in a large local market and enjoy a large fan base, so they are defined as large-market teams. In England, four teams stayed in the highest league: Arsenal, Everton, Liverpool, and Manchester United. To have as many teams as in Belgium, three teams are needed. The time frame was chosen to include Manchester United. Everton is excluded.

We focus on the sum of the win percentages of the chosen three large-market teams. To range between 0 and 1 we compare the actual sum of win percentages to its minimum and its maximum. It is theoretically possible that the three large teams finish at the bottom of the ranking. The minimal sum of win percentages is attained when the last team has won no games, the second to last won the two games against the last and the third won against the other two, so four games. Combined, they won 6 games out of 42 when there are 22 teams and out of 34 when there are 18 teams. Formulized for n teams and K large-market teams you have the following minimal sum:

$$\text{Minsum} = \frac{K(K-1)}{2(n-1)} \qquad (7.43)$$

When the K teams are dominant, they fill the top K. If they are perfectly dominant, the first team wins all of its games, the second all except against the first, the third all except against the first two, and so on. The maximal sum of win percentages is then reached (see Appendix 7.7):

$$\text{Maxsum} = \frac{K[2n-(K-1)]}{2(n-1)} \qquad (7.44)$$

The dominance of K Large Teams measure for country i (DoKLaT$_i$-measure) is the ratio of the actual range of the sum of win percentages to the maximal range. It is modeled as follows:

$$DoKLaT_i = \frac{\sum_{i=1}^{K} w_i - \text{Min Sum}}{\text{Max Sum} - \text{Min Sum}} = \frac{2(n-1)\sum_{i=1}^{K} w_i - K(K-1)}{2K[n-K]} \qquad (7.45)$$

So when the measure equals 1 the teams are perfectly dominant in the competition. If the measure equals 0 a good imbalance (Kesenne, 2004) occurs, and the large-market teams end up at the bottom of the ranking dominated by the small-market teams. Figure 7–1 shows our calculated time series for our two countries.

Descriptive analysis shows that in the beginning of the period, Belgium is more dominated by its three large-market teams than England is. With the introduction of extra revenue for all teams in the early 80s, the dominance of England's large teams increases. This follows our theoretic model: when, at the benchmark model, the large country is less dominated than the small, both suffer in the next period from an increase in dominance, but the large-market teams of the large country increase their win percentage with a larger fraction. Consequently the imbalance measures come closer to each other. For Belgium, no real increase is present. From season 1996 onwards, both countries show an increase in dominance. The large country, again England, increases with a larger fraction than Belgium, now with an almost equal evolution as a consequence. For

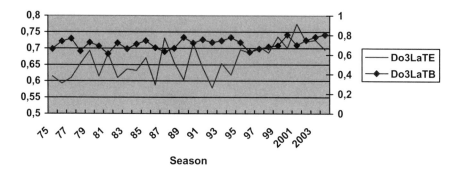

FIGURE 7–1. Do3LaT$_B$ and Do3LaT$_E$

these two countries, the descriptive analysis supports our theoretic model very well.

Conclusions

Table 7–1 summarizes our theoretical results: 7–1a discusses the win maximizing leagues and 7–1b the profit maximizing ones. The three periods are placed in the columns and each period is split up into two subcolumns. The first shows the derived algebraic expression. The second column of the first period compares the begin situation of the two countries. For the other two periods we show when an increase is present, compared to the previous period. A simple arrow without further specification shows an unconditional increase. In the first row we place our dominance measure, in the second the wage cost.

Large-market teams are more dominant in a win maximizing league than in a profit maximizing one. Important increases in revenues, as the football leagues have encountered over the last decades, increase talent demand and consequently increase wage costs. The distribution of extra revenue can improve competitive balance in a country. Our alfa-parameter is a possible revenue sharing instrument. Revenue sharing models mostly include shares of total revenue of other teams. Our model may be a more realistic alternative and invites further research. The extension of the model to n teams is not expected to alter our results significantly but deserves attention.

A balanced competition is only shown to be present when local markets are either equal or are compensated for. Extra revenue that is limited to only one or a few teams, such as the market pool, is shown to increase

TABLE 7–1
Summary of the Theoretical Model

7–1a: Win Maximization.

	1: Benchmark		2 = 1 + National market	3 = 2 + open + market pool
D	$\dfrac{m_{i1} - m_{i2}}{\beta}$	Imb.	$D_i + \dfrac{m_i(\alpha_{i1} - \alpha_{i2})}{\beta}$ $\uparrow \Leftrightarrow \uparrow$ $\alpha_{i1} > \alpha_{i2}$	$D_{Tv,t} + \dfrac{dm_i}{\beta}$ $\uparrow$
c	$\sqrt{\dfrac{m_i - \beta}{2a}}$	$c_A > c_B$	$\sqrt{\dfrac{2m_i - \beta}{2a}}$ $\uparrow$	$\sqrt{\dfrac{m_A + m_B + \dfrac{d}{2}(m_A + m_B) - \beta}{a}}$ $\uparrow$

7–1b: Profit Maximization.

	1		2	3
D	$\dfrac{m_{i1} - m_{i2}}{m_i}$	Imb.	$\dfrac{D_i^P + (\alpha_{i1} - \alpha_{i2})}{2}$ $\uparrow \Leftrightarrow \uparrow$ $\alpha_{c1} - \alpha_{c2} > \dfrac{m_{c1}}{m_c} - \dfrac{m_{c2}}{m_c}$	$D_{Tv,i}^P + \dfrac{d}{2}$ $\uparrow$
c	$\sqrt{\dfrac{(m_i - 2\beta)m_{i1}m_{i2}}{am_i^2}}$	?$c_A > c_B$ calc!	$\sqrt{\dfrac{2(m_i - \beta)}{am_i^2}} * \dfrac{\sqrt{(m_{i1} + \alpha_{i1}m_i)}}{\sqrt{(m_{i2} + \alpha_{i2}m_i)}}$ $\uparrow$	No interpretable algebraic solution found

the demand of talent of these teams. When the large teams enjoy these extra revenues their dominance increases even more. Concerns expressed in the media with the introduction of the market pool seem justified. A first empirical verification shows that although our theoretical model is a simplification it is not contradicted by the actual evolution of three large teams in Belgium and England. An adaptation of the market pool seems appropriate when the national balance is of major concern. Researching the consequences on the international competition levels is an interesting extension of this study.

References

Borghans, L., and Groot, L. (2005). The competitive balance based on team quality. Working paper, Utrecht University.

Cairns, J., Jennett, N., and Sloane, P.J. (1986). The economics of professional team sports: A survey of theory and evidence. *Journal of Economic Studies*, 13(1):1–80.

El-Hodiri, M., and Quirk, J. (1974). The economic theory of professional sports league. In: R.G. Noll (Ed.), *Government and the Sports Business*. Washington, DC: The Brookings Institution, pp. 33–80.

Kesenne, S. (2004). Competitive balance and revenue sharing: When rich clubs have poor teams. *Journal of Sports Economics*, 5(2):206–212.

Kesenne, S. (2006). The win maximization model reconsidered: Flexible talent supply and efficiency wages. *Journal of Sports Economics*, 7(4):416–427.

Kesenne, S. (2007a). The peculiar international economics of professional football in Europe. *Scottish Journal of Political Economy*, forthcoming.

Kesenne, S. (2007b). *Economic Theory of Professional Team Sports: An Analytical Treatment*. Forthcoming with E. Elgar.

Neale, W.C. (1964). The peculiar economics of professional sports: A contribution to the theory of the firm in sporting competition and in market competition. *Quarterly Journal of Economics*, 78(1):1–14.

Quirk, J., and Fort, R.D. (1995). Cross-subsidization, incentives, and outcomes in professional team sports leagues. *Journal of Economic Literature*, 33(3):1265–1299.

Rottenberg, S. (1956). The baseball players' labor market. *Journal of Political Economy*, 64(3):242–258.

Sloane, P.J. (1971). The economics of professional football: The football club as a utility maximizer. *Scottish Journal of Political Economy*, 18(2):121–146.

Szymanski, S., and Smith, R. (1997). The English football industry profit, performance and industrial structure. *International Review of Applied Economics*, 11(1):135–153.

Appendix 7.1

Total Demand for Talent in Profit Maximizing Benchmark Scenario

Intersection of the first order conditions:

$$m_{i1}\left(\frac{1}{x_i^P} - \frac{x_{i1}^P}{(x_i^P)^2}\right) - \beta\left(\frac{2x_{i1}^P}{(x_i^P)^2} - \frac{2(x_{i1}^P)^2}{(x_i^P)^3}\right)$$
$$= m_{i2}\left(\frac{1}{x_i^P} - \frac{x_{i2}^P}{(x_i^P)^2}\right) - \beta\left(\frac{2x_{i2}^P}{(x_i^P)^2} - \frac{2(x_{i2}^P)^2}{(x_i^P)^3}\right)$$

Reduce to a common denominator and simplify:

$$x_{i1}^P = x_{i2}^P \frac{m_{i1}}{m_{i2}} \qquad (*)$$

Use the latter expression to replace x_{i1}^P in the following rewritten FOC of team 2:

$$m_{i2}x_{i1}^P(x_{i1}^P + x_{i2}^P) - 2\beta x_{i1}^P x_{i2}^P = c_i^P(x_{i1}^P + x_{i2}^P)^3$$

Reduce to a common denominator, simplify and single out x_{i2}^P:

$$x_{i2}^P = \frac{m_{i2}^2 m_{i1}(m_i - 2\beta)}{c_i^P m_i^3}$$

We can use the latter expression in (*) to find x_{i1}^P:

$$x_{i1}^P = \frac{m_{i2}m_{i1}^2(m_i - 2\beta)}{c_i^P m_i^3}$$

Total demand for talent is the sum of the individual demands:

$$x_i^P = \frac{(m_i - 2\beta)m_{i1}m_{i2}}{c_i^P m_i^2}$$

Appendix 7.2

Comparison of Wages in a Profit Maximizing League versus a Win Maximizing League

$$c_A^P = \sqrt{(m_A - 2\beta)\frac{m_{A1}m_{A2}}{am_A^2}} < c_A = \sqrt{(m_A - \beta)\frac{1}{2a}} \Leftrightarrow$$

$$(m_A - \beta)\frac{m_{A1}m_{A2}}{m_A^2} - \beta\frac{m_{A1}m_{A2}}{m_A^2} < (m_A - \beta)\frac{1}{2} \Leftrightarrow$$

$$(m_A - \beta)(m_{A1}m_{A2} - m_A^2) < 2\beta m_{A1}m_{A2} \Leftrightarrow$$

This inequality is always fulfilled because $m_A - \beta > 0$ (7) and $m_{A1}m_{A2} - m_A^2 < 0$. So the wage cost in a win maximizing country is higher than in a profit maximizing league. The same applies to country B.

Appendix 7.3

Comparison of Competitive Balance under Profit Maximization between the First Two Periods

$$D_{Tv,i}^P = \frac{(m_{i1} - m_{i2}) + m_i(\alpha_{i1} - \alpha_{i2})}{2m_i} > D_i^P = \frac{m_{i1} - m_{i2}}{m_i} \Leftrightarrow$$

$$\frac{m_i(\alpha_{i1} - \alpha_{i2})}{2m_i} > \frac{1}{2}\left(\frac{m_{i1} - m_{i2}}{m_i}\right) \Leftrightarrow$$

$$\alpha_{i1} - \alpha_{i2} > \frac{m_{i1}}{m_i} - \frac{m_{i2}}{m_i}$$

Appendix 7.4

Algebraic Representation Demand Function and Wage Cost

$$x_{Tv,i}^P = \frac{2(m_i - \beta)(m_{i1} + \alpha_{i1}m_i)(m_{i2} + \alpha_{i2}m_i)}{c_{Tv,i}^P m_i^2}$$

$$c_{Tv,i}^{P} = \sqrt{\frac{2(m_i - \beta)(m_{i1} + \alpha_{i1}m_i)(m_{i2} + \alpha_{i2}m_i)}{am_i^2}}$$

Appendix 7.5

Comparison of the Wage Cost for Win Maximizing Leagues when Transition to Third Period

$$c = \sqrt{\frac{m_A + m_B + \dfrac{d}{2}(m_A + m_B) - \beta}{a}} > c_{Tv,A} = \sqrt{\frac{2m_A - \beta}{2a}} \Leftrightarrow$$

$$m_A + m_B + \frac{d}{2}(m_A + m_B) - \beta > \frac{2m_A - \beta}{2} \Leftrightarrow$$

$$2m_B + d(m_A + m_B) > \beta \Leftrightarrow$$

Since $2m_B > \beta$ [see Eq. (7.7)] the wage cost in the third period is necessarily larger than the one from the second period. This applies to country B as well because $2m_A > \beta$ [see Eq. (7.7)].

Appendix 7.6

Comparison of Dominance in Win versus Profit Maximizing Leagues When the Market Pool Is Introduced

$$D_{Cl,i}^{P} = \frac{m_{i1} - m_{i2} + m_i(\alpha_{i1} + d - \alpha_{i2})}{2m_i} < D_{Cl,i} = \frac{m_{i1} - m_{i2} + m_i(\alpha_{i1} + d - \alpha_{i2})}{\beta} \Leftrightarrow$$

$$2m_i > \beta$$

This inequality is always fulfilled given Eq. (7.7).

Appendix 7.7

Maximal Sum of Win Percentages

When we start from K = 3 the sum of the three win percentages is:

$$\text{MaxSum} = \frac{2(n-1)}{2(n-1)} + \frac{2(n-1)-2}{2(n-1)} + \frac{2(n-1)-4}{2(n-1)}$$

So,

$$\text{MaxSum} = \frac{3*2(n-1) - 2\left(\sum_{i=1}^{2} i\right)}{2(n-1)}$$

For K teams:

$$\text{MaxSum} = \frac{k*2(n-1) - 2\left(\sum_{i=1}^{k-1} i\right)}{2(n-1)}$$

Solving the arithmetic series and further simplifying shows:

$$\text{MaxSum} = \frac{k[2n-1-k]}{2(n-1)}$$

8

Beyond Competitive Balance

Morten Kringstad and Bill Gerrard

The importance of competitive balance for the well-being of a professional sports league is one of the most fundamental and long-standing propositions in sports economics. But the concept of competitive balance is ill-defined both theoretically and empirically. It is a "catch-all" term widely used by academic researchers, industry practitioners, and sports fans. There is an ever-increasing range of statistical measures to be found in the sports economics literature, all purporting to provide an essential metric to capture and quantify the degree of competitive balance in a professional sports league. The diversity of these measures often appears bewildering, particularly to practitioners and fans, and leaves one wondering whether or not after 50 years of academic research on the subject there has been much in the way of cumulative progress toward a better understanding of how changes in the relative competitiveness of athletes and teams in a specific sporting contest or tournament affects its economic value.

The objective of this chapter is to propose a more systematic approach to the definition and measurement of competitive balance in professional sports leagues. The focus is on professional team sports, particularly the North American major leagues and European club football. However, much of the discussion is easily transferable to more individualistic professional sports, such as golf, athletics, and motor racing. The possible negative impact of competitive dominance by, say, Tiger Woods in golf or Michael Schumacher in F1 motor racing, may be as much a concern in those sports as the financial extravagance of extremely wealthy team owners prepared to spend whatever it takes to acquire the best talent for their teams. In addition, the chapter focuses only on professional team sports that employ a round-robin (i.e., league) tournament structure in some form or other with teams playing a series of matches against the other teams in the league to determine tournament success. (In the case of a full round-robin tournament, each team plays every other team an equal number of times home and away.) Again, some of the discussion is easily transferable to professional sports that mainly employ elimination (i.e., knockout or cup) tournament structures.

The principal argument advanced in this chapter is that the existing literature on competitive balance is rooted in the context of a simple league structure, but even in that context there is a diversity of dimensions constituting competitive balance and, as a consequence, it is necessary to employ a range of alternative statistical measures to represent the relative competitiveness of teams in the league. The need to use a range of alternative measures of competitive balance becomes even more imperative once you move toward consideration of more complex league structures actually observed in professional team sports. A key conclusion of the chapter is that an appreciation of the richness of tournament structures, particularly the recognition that many leagues offer multiple prizes rather than single-prize, "winner-takes-all" structures, implies that it may be more appropriate to conceptualize the problem in terms of the competitive intensity of leagues encompassing both traditional concerns with competitive balance, but also recognizing the impact of tournament structures on the distribution of team competitiveness and fan interest (Kringstad and Gerrard, 2004).

The chapter is organized as follows. The next section provides a brief literature review on why competitive balance is considered to be so important, what are the existing definitions and measurements, and what are the main determinants of competitive balance in a sports league. The following section considers the nature of competitive balance in the simplest form of league context with a closed, pure round-robin tournament structure and a single championship prize. We then focus on more complex league structures, including hybrid tournament structures consisting of both round-robin and knockout components and open merit-hierarchy leagues with promotion and relegation. The subsequent section reports empirical evidence on the degree of competitive balance in the North American major leagues and European club football using the various measures discussed in previous sections. The last section offers some concluding thoughts on the need for a more general notion of competitive intensity and the importance of tournament and prize structures in affecting the economic value of professional sports leagues.

Uncertainty of Outcome, Competitive Balance, and the Theory of Professional Sports Leagues

An essential characteristic of sport is the uncertainty of outcome. Unlike other forms of drama entertainment, sporting contests are unscripted and require no suspension of belief on the part of the audience. The ending has not been written in advance. Uncertainty of outcome has long been seen by many as a crucial driver of the economic value of sporting contests (i.e., individual match ups between athletes and teams) and tournaments (i.e., the overall contest between a group of athletes and teams). However, sports economists disagree over the strength of the uncertainty of outcome hypothesis, and empirical gate attendance demand studies have provided mixed results on the impact of uncertainty of outcome on match attendance behavior (Szymanski and Kuypers, 1999; Szymanski, 2003). If, as is believed, sports fans consider uncertainty of outcome as one of the valuable attributes offered by professional team sports, it necessarily follows that the financial well-being of a professional sports league is enhanced by a relative equality across teams in their degree of competitiveness. Hence, a fundamental proposition of sports economics is that competitive balance is a necessary requirement for a professional sports league to be financially viable. It is one of the peculiar features of the economics of the professional sports industry compared to other industries that profitability is likely to be reduced by monopolization (i.e., competitive dominance) (Neale, 1964). Variously referred to as the Yankee or Louis-Schmelling paradox, it has been long recognized that sports leagues benefit from greater competition between teams. This creates a basic economic dilemma for sports leagues arising from the inevitable conflict between individual and collective interests. Individual teams striving for sporting success seek to dominate their competitors but, as a collective entity, teams require to be relatively equally balanced in order to ensure the financial viability of the league as a whole. Individual sporting dominance can undermine fan interest if the league loses its uncertainty of outcome and becomes merely a coronation rather than a competition.

The terms "uncertainty of outcome" and "competitive balance" tend to be used interchangeably by many sports economists. However, despite being closely interrelated, it is our contention that the two concepts are not exactly equivalent and can be usefully differentiated. It is proposed that uncertainty of outcome should be defined quite narrowly as the probability distribution for the alternative outcomes of a specified sporting contest. Uncertainty of outcome is, therefore, an *ex ante* concept. It can encompass both relative-frequency and rational-degrees-of-belief (or logical) interpretations of probability. It can also encompass Knight's distinction between situations of risk in which there exists a well-defined probability distribution and situations of uncertainty in which the probability distribution is ill-defined in some sense (Knight, 1921). The Knightian risk-uncertainty dichotomy turns crucially on what Keynes (1921) called "weight of argument" representing the degree of knowledge and ignorance on which any probability distribution is based. Probability statements are always conditional on the available information. If the currently available information is augmented by "news" (i.e., new, unexpected, and previously unpredictable information), then the weight of argument is likely to increase (unless the news increases the perception of our degree of ignorance). But increased weight of argument need not necessarily change the probability distribution in the sense of the relative degrees of belief in alternative outcomes, but it may lead to a greater propensity to act on the probabilities if the absolute degree of belief (what Gerrard, 1994, calls "credence") increases. For example, if teams draft a high number of rookies with uncertain ability as well as engage in extensive player trading, fans may consider there is considerably greater uncertainty of outcome although they may be unable to quantify the precise effects on the *ex ante* probability of any specific team's chances of winning the tournament.

By contrast, it is proposed that competitive balance be considered as a more general concept that refers to not only the *ex ante* probability distribution of sporting outcomes but also the underlying *ex ante* determinants of the probability distribution and the *ex post* distribution of actual sporting outcomes. The focus of this chapter is on the appropriate set of metrics to employ to capture the different dimensions of competitive balance in its *ex post* sense as the actual distribution of sporting outcomes.

An important consideration in defining uncertainty of outcome and competitive balance in any specific context is determining the relevant outcome or set of outcomes. The unit of analysis may be an individual match between two teams, the tournament as a whole consisting of a set of matches between the competing teams, or the series of outcomes of a tournament played regularly (i.e., a repeated tournament). In addition, uncertainty of outcome and (*ex ante*) competitive balance can be evaluated continuously over time as a tournament progresses and new information becomes available. It is useful to differentiate existing empirical studies between those concerned with within-season (i.e., *ex ante*) and those focusing on end-of-season (i.e., *ex post*) competitive balance. In this chapter the concern is with empirical measures of end-of-season competitive balance.

The principal proximate determinant of competitive balance in a professional sports league is the distribution of playing talent between teams. The distribution of playing talent depends, in turn, primarily on the relative economic power of teams. The distribution of economic power across the league is the principal fundamental determinant of competitive balance. The economic size of a team ultimately depends on history and geography, although some argue that in the modern global, media-integrated economy, geographical factors have less weighting now than in the past (see, for example, Szymanski and Kuypers, 1999, p. 263). A team's potential market size depends on the size of its fan base. Fan allegiance to teams is driven by local and/or family affinities, and/or sporting success. Big-market teams tend to be located in large metropolitan areas and have a history of sporting success. The financial value of playing talent to a big-market team as measured by a player's marginal revenue product (i.e., a player's incremental contribution to team revenues due to both sporting and marketing performance) is higher, *ceteris paribus*, due to the bigger revenue-earning potential of the player's contribution. As a consequence, big-market teams can offer higher salaries to attract the most talented players. This creates a potentially virtuous circle of success in which current sporting success by big-market teams helps generate the revenues needed to attract the playing talent necessary for future sporting success. In such circumstances, a professional sports league can inevitably become split into the "haves" and "have-nots" with the big-market teams establishing successful sporting dynasties and the smaller-market teams becoming merely doormats to make up the numbers and fill out the match schedule. Such leagues may face severe problems in retaining fan interest.

The fear of the detrimental effects of financial determinism in professional team sports has been one of the main reasons why professional sports leagues have introduced a variety of regulatory mechanisms to mitigate the impact of unequal distribution of economic size between teams (Quirk and Fort, 1992). Professional sports leagues have used a variety of product-market mechanisms, such as sharing gate receipts and collective selling of media and other image rights to try to equalize team revenues. Professional sports leagues have also used a number of labor-market restrictions to prevent, or at least hinder, the free movement of the best players to the big-market teams or reduce the financial incentives for player movement between teams. These labor-market restrictions have included setting a maximum wage, salary caps (i.e., a limit on total player wage expenditure), luxury taxes (i.e., financial penalties for spending beyond a stipulated maximum player wage budget), a drafting system in which rookies (i.e., new entrants) are allocated between teams in a centrally-administered scheme (usually giving advantages to poorly-performing teams), and a player reservation system (such as the reserve clause in Major League Baseball and the retain-and-transfer system in association football in which teams have the right to retain their current players subject to offering a new employment contract at least as good as the player's previous contract).

The effectiveness of labor-market and product-market regulations in preserving competitive balance remains a matter of considerable debate both theoretically and empirically. The starting point remains for these debates Rottenberg's invariance proposition (Rottenberg, 1956) that argues that the equilibrium distribution of playing talent is unaffected by whether or not the players' labor market operates as a player reservation system or a free agency system (i.e., players are free to move to any team on completion of their employment contract with no transfer fee payable). Rottenberg's argument turns on the assumption that both team-owners and players are wealth-maximizers and so, irrespective of whether team-owners or players possess the rights to initiate player movements between teams, players will gravitate toward those teams that maximize their financial value. According to Rottenberg, the impact of player reservation and free agency systems is on the distribution of income between team-owners and players, not the distribution of playing talent between teams. Rottenberg's invariance proposition is an example of a fundamental economic proposition known as the Coase theorem that holds that the changes in the distribution of property rights affects only monetary outcomes, not real economic activity (Coase, 1960). A similar argument can be employed to show theoretically that the distribution of playing talent in a professional sports league is invariant to product-market restrictions.

Theoretically, the impact of product and labor market regulations on the distribution of playing talent depends crucially on the assumptions about the objectives of team owners and the supply conditions of playing talent although there is considerable debate over the effects of different ownership objectives and changes in players' labor supply (see, for example, Késenne, 1996). With respect to the optimal method of league regulation, Fort and Quirk (1995) conclude that theoretically the most effective regulatory mechanism is a hard (i.e., no significant exemption clauses), enforceable salary cap, but in practice salary caps can be difficult and expensive to police. Empirically the evidence on the impact of league restrictions on the distribution of playing talent is inconclusive. However, there is extensive empirical support on the impact of player reservation systems and free agency on player remuneration.

Although most of the focus on the determinants of competitive balance has been with the distribution of playing talent between teams and the possible impact of league regulations, it should be remembered that competitive balance also depends on other factors, including the relative effectiveness of coaches, the structure of the game and the scoring system, the tournament structure, and the prize structure. The impact of tournament and prize structures on competitive balance is a central concern of this chapter.

Competitive Balance in the Simple League Context

What are the appropriate *ex post* measures of end-of-season competitive balance? From the outset it should be clear that we consider competitive balance to be a multidimensional concept requiring multiple metrics to capture its different dimensions. There is no single optimal measure of competitive balance even though it often seems as if sports economists still search for the Holy Grail of the definitive summary statistic. In order to appreciate the need for a set of measures, it is useful to consider the nature of competitive balance in the simple league context and to realize that even in this context competitive balance has many different aspects.

A league can be defined as simple if it has the following five characteristics:

1. It is a closed league with the same set of teams competing in the league every season. There is no promotion and relegation as in a merit hierarchy league structure.

2. The league tournament has a unitary structure in which the tournament outcome depends on the equally-weighted results from all matches played. In a unitary structure there is only a regular season with no play-offs.

3. The league tournament consists of a full round-robin set of matches with all teams playing each other an equal number of times home and away. This excludes league structures with unequal (or partial) round-robins in which teams may not play every other team or may not do so an equal number of times. In a simple league structure there are no elimination matches as in a cup knockout competition.

4. All individual matches result in a win for one team and a loss for the opposing team. There are no tied matches and no differentiation in the weighting of results between matches won in regular time and matches won in overtime. A win is a win is a win.

5. There is a single prize with the championship winner determined by the best win-loss record.

Even in the simple league context there are three different dimensions of competitive balance in the sense of the *ex post* distribution of league outcomes. The three dimensions of competitive balance are: win dispersion, performance persistence, and prize concentration. Win dispersion is the distribution of wins between teams in a single league tournament. Performance persistence refers to the relationship between the win-loss records of teams across seasons (i.e., a series of regular repeated league tournaments). Prize concentration represents the distribution of prizes between teams across seasons. Performance persistence and prize concentration are both concerned with the time-dependence of tournament outcomes across a number of seasons and the possible emergence of a dynasty-doormat segmentation of teams (or what industrial organization theorists would describe as "strategic groups") (Caves and Porter, 1977). Win dispersion, on the other hand, is concerned with a more limited form of time-dependent performance between matches in a single season.

Before considering specific metrics to report these three dimensions of competitive balance as summary statistics, it is instructive to consider the two polar cases of perfect competitive balance and perfect competitive dominance in the simple league context. In the case of perfect competitive balance every team would have an equal chance of winning every match in every season. This does not imply that we would observe teams with identical win-loss records in any single season as well as across seasons. It also does not imply that we would observe teams having an equal share of championship wins. Perfect competitive balance means equality of outcome probabilities, not equality of observed outcomes. The equality exists *ex ante*, not *ex post*. Equality of outcome probabilities implies a random distribution of observed outcomes that only in the limit (i.e., as the number of repetitions tends toward infinity) tends toward an observed equality of relative frequencies. Observed outcomes should exhibit a binomial (and tending toward a normal, bell-shaped) relative frequency distribution in which the probability of success equals the probability of failure for any individual event. In other words, the statistical properties of win dispersion, performance persistence, and prize concentration should be akin to the distribution of outcomes that would emerge if wins and losses are decided by the toss of a fair coin. In the case of perfect competitive balance there is no time-dependency of match outcomes. The probability of winning a match is unaffected by the outcome of all previous matches. The probability of winning a match in any season is unaffected by the team's performance in previous seasons. The probability of winning the league championship is unaffected by the number of previous championship titles.

The polar opposite case of perfect competitive balance is perfect competitive dominance. Perfect competitive dominance exists if two conditions are met. First, the probability of victory for one of the teams in any individual match is unity. Second, there is perfect time dependence with a team's probability of victory in any match correlated perfectly with its past performances against the opposing team. Perfect competitive dominance implies that the strongest team wins every match, the next strongest team wins every match except the matches against the strongest team, and so on. In a perfectly competitive dominated league teams always win their matches against the weaker teams. And this pattern is repeated across seasons with the same rankings year after year and only the dominant team ever winning the league championship.

So, in short, the two polar cases are randomly distributed win dispersion with zero time dependence for wins and prizes (i.e., perfect competitive balance) and deterministic (i.e., nonstochastic) win dispersion with perfect time dependence (i.e., perfect competitive dominance). These two polar cases provide benchmarks for comparison of actual observed outcomes. These are also suggestive of the appropriate summary statistics.

What then are the appropriate summary statistics of win dispersion, performance persistence, and prize concentration? Turning first to win dispersion, in statistical terms, this implies measurement of the second moment of a distribution. There are several widely used summary statistical measures of dispersion, such as the range (i.e., the difference between the observed maximum and minimum values) and the interquartile range (i.e., the difference between the first and third quartiles). These measures are limited in the sense that they do not use all of the information provided by the distribution of outcomes. The most commonly used measure of dispersion is the variance, but usually reported by its square root known as the standard deviation. The variance is defined as the sum of the squared deviations from the mean. Equation (8.1) provides the formal definition of the standard deviation in the case of win dispersion.

$$\sigma = \sqrt{\sum_i (w_i - .5)^2} \tag{8.1}$$

where w_i is the win ratio for the ith team (defined as the number of wins divided by the number of matches played). By definition, the mean win ratio is .500.

The problem with standard deviation and common with many other summary statistics is that the value obtained is unit-dependent as well as being affected by the number of observations in the specific situation. Hence, many summary statistics are not immediately comparable. In the case of win dispersion the standard deviation is not comparable across leagues with different numbers of teams and/or different numbers of matches played. Hence, it is always useful to standardize the summary statistic using a specified benchmark so that the observed summary statistic is reported as a ratio relative to the benchmark. In the case of competitive balance, the most commonly used benchmark is the polar case of perfect competitive balance. The Quirk and Fort (QF) ratio (as proposed by Quirk and Fort, 1992) reports the standard deviation of the win distribution across teams relative to the theoretical standard deviation of a binomial distribution with an independent success probability of .5 for each event. The QF ratio is formally defined in Eq. (8.2).

$$\text{QF ratio} = \sigma/(.5/\sqrt{N}) \tag{8.2}$$

where N is the number of matches played by each team. The theoretical standard deviation of the win ratios in a league with perfect competitive balance is $.5/\sqrt{N}$. Hence, the QF ratio provides a standardization that allows comparisons to be drawn for win dispersion across leagues in which the number of matches played by teams differs. The QF ratio is the most widely used measure of win dispersion. In a league with perfect competitive balance, the QF ratio should be unity, although it is possible for leagues to exhibit a win-ratio standard deviation less than the theoretical ideal implying a QF ratio less than unity. The QF ratio increases above unity as the observed win-ratio standard deviation increases beyond the theoretical ideal. Recently, however, it has been suggested by Goossens (2006) that perfect competitive dominance may provide a better benchmark to derive a standardized ratio for the win-ratio standard deviation. The Goossens national measure of seasonal imbalance (NAMSI) index takes values between zero and unity with unity representing perfect competitive dominance. Improved competitive balance implies a Goossens index less than unity and tending toward zero.

An alternative approach to measuring win dispersion is to focus on only part of the win-ratio distribution and compare the properties of a specific area of observed distribution with those of the corresponding area of the theoretical ideal distribution. For example, Quirk and Fort (1992) consider the excess tail frequency defined as the difference between the actual percentage of teams with win ratios more than two ideal standard deviations away from .500 (i.e., the mean win ratio) and the theoretical percentage if there is perfect competitive balance. Gerrard (2004) focuses on the top team's win ratio relative to both the mean win ratio as well as the win ratio of the second-placed team. The latter is a crude measure of the extent to which there has been a "championship race" with at least two teams competing closely to win the league.

Rather than using statistical measures of dispersion (i.e., the degree to which observations are spread out), win dispersion can also be measured using measures of inequality that focus of the degree of difference between observations. This is the approach adopted by Michie and Oughton (2004). Michie and Oughton use three alternative measures of inequality as indicators of the degree of competitive balance in leading European domestic football leagues: the C5 Index of Competitive Balance (C5ICB), the Herfindahl Index of Competitive Balance (HICB), and the Lorenz Seasonal Balance Curve. Michie and Oughton define their indicators in terms of the points won by teams (i.e., three points for a win and one point for a tied match), but it is straightforward to transform their definitions for use in a simple league context with only wins and losses. The C5ICB is the concentration ratio of the top five teams (CR5) measured by their total number of wins as a proportion of the total number of matches in the league schedule and then standardized as a ratio using the benchmark of a league in which there is *ex post* equality of outcome with all teams winning exactly the same number of games. CR5 and C5ICB are defined in Eqs. (8.3) and (8.4).

$$CR5 = (W_1 + W_2 + W_3 + W_4 + W_5)/M \qquad (8.3)$$

$$C5ICB = CR5/(5/N) \qquad (8.4)$$

where W_1 is the total number of wins by the top team, W_2 is the total number of wins by the second-placed team, and so on. M is the total number of matches played during the league tournament. N is the number of teams in the league.

The choice of the five-team concentration ratio by Michie and Oughton is arbitrary. The C5ICB can be generalized to the CnICB with the choice of n (i.e., the number of top teams) depending on the total number of teams in the league and the pattern of dominance. It may be useful to report several CnICB indices using different n-team concentration ratios.

One limitation of the CnICB indicator is that it only uses information on the win records of the top n teams. The HICB overcomes this limitation by using the Herfindahl (H) index defined as the sum of the squared shares over the whole membership of the specified set. In the case of win dispersion, the H-index is measured as the sum of the squared win share (i.e., number of wins as a proportion of the total matches played in the league) of every team in the league as set out in Eq. (8.5).

$$\text{H-index} = \sum_i (W_i/M)^2 \qquad (8.5)$$

where W_i is the number of wins by the ith team and M is the total number of matches in the league. Again, Michie and Oughton propose that the H-index should be standardized relative to the H-index for a league with a perfectly equal *ex post* distribution of wins between teams. It is easy to show algebraically that the H index for a perfect equal distribution is $1/N$. Michie and Oughton also prefer to rebase their index to set perfect competitive balance equal to 100 rather than unity. Hence, the HICB is defined as follows:

$$\text{HICB} = 100[H/(1/N)] \qquad (8.6)$$

Michie and Oughton also use the Lorenz curve as a graphical indicator of win dispersion. The Lorenz curve shows the relationship between cumulative percentage shares and the percentage of members of a specified set ranked in either ascending or descending order (i.e., the member with the smallest or largest share ranked first, then the next smallest or largest, and so on). In the case of perfect equality with every member having an equal share, the Lorenz curve would be the diagonal line. The Lorenz curve can be reduced to a summary statistic known as the Gini coefficient in which the area under the Lorenz curve is divided by the area under the diagonal (i.e., the perfect competitive balance outcome).

The three basic measures of inequality—the concentration ratio, the Herfindahl index, and Gini coefficient—can also be used to measure prize concentration. In this case instead of measuring the degree of inequality in the distribution of match wins, the focus is on the distribution of championship titles between teams over a number of seasons. Gerrard (2004), for example, uses CR2, CR3, and the H-index to measure the concentration of championship titles in 16 leading football leagues in Western Europe. One possible refinement to show trends over time is to compute prize concentration as a moving-average over a specified number of seasons, for example, a 10-year moving-average.

The final dimension of competitive balance to consider is performance persistence. One measure of performance persistence is the Spearman rank correlation coefficient (SRCC), which measures the correlation between team rankings in two consecutive seasons (Daly and Moore, 1981; Maxcy, 2002; Maxcy and Mondello, 2006).

$$\text{SRCC} = 1 - \left[6\sum_i D_i^2 \right] / [N(N^2 - 1)] \tag{8.7}$$

where D_i is the difference between the ith team's rank in the two seasons, and N is the number of teams in the league. If there is perfect performance persistence with teams finishing in the same order in consecutive seasons, SRCC has a value of unity. If SRCC is close to zero, this indicates no relationship between team rankings in consecutive seasons. SRCC can also take negative values indicating an inverse relationship between team rankings between seasons. If the SRCC equals −1 this signifies a complete reversal in team rankings, i.e., the top team finishes last next season, the second-placed team finishes second to last, and so on. Maxcy and Mondello (2006) use the SRCC as one of their two indicators (the other being the QF ratio) of competitive balance in their study of the impact of changes in labor market regulations on the North American major leagues.

Performance persistence can also be measured using mobility measures employed in the study of strategic groups and mobility barriers in industrial organization. For example, Feigenbaum and Primeaux (1983) propose the M-index as a measure of the frequency of change in the membership of strategic groups.

$$\text{M-index} = 1 - \left(\sum_i p_i\right) / G \qquad (8.8)$$

where p_i is the relative frequency of remaining in the same strategic group in the next period, and G is the number of strategic groups. Gerrard (1998) has applied the M-index to competitive balance in English professional football using win ratios with strategic groups defined by distance from the mean win ratio.

Another mobility measure is the D-index developed by Cable (1983), which measures the degree of change in market shares over time. Gerrard (1998) calculates the D-index for the top league in English professional football using the following formula:

$$\text{D-index} = \left(\sum_i |\Delta w_i|\right) / 2 \qquad (8.9)$$

where $|\Delta w_i|$ is the absolute change in the win ratio of the ith team from the previous season.

All of these measures of competitive balance are simple one-dimensional metrics in the sense that they provide alternative summary statistics for measuring win dispersion, prize concentration, or persistence. Some authors have suggested more complex, composite measures that combine more than one dimension of competitive balance, such as, for example, Humphreys (2002), who proposes the competitive balance ratio (CBR) that combines both win dispersion and performance persistence (see also Eckard, 1998). While useful for reporting changes in competitive balance over time in a single summary statistic, these complex measures are of limited analytical value, requiring to be decomposed into their constituent dimensions in order to identify the nature of any underlying changes in the competitive balance. For this reason reporting a set of simple one-dimensional measures seems preferable.

Competitive Balance in More Complex League Structures

In the simple league context, there is a fixed set of teams competing in a pure round-robin tournament with rankings based on matches won and a single championship prize awarded to the team with the highest number of wins. However, the actual league structures observed in professional team sports are more complex. There are four main types of complication to be considered: (1) rankings not based solely on matches won; (2) unequal/partial round-robin tournaments; (3) multistage tournaments; and (4) promotion and relegation. These real-world complications require modifications of the standard measures of competitive balance, as well as the development of further measures to capture additional aspects of competitive balance.

Considering first tournaments in which final league standings are not based solely on matches won, one particular complication is that created by sports that allow tied (or drawn) matches as, for example, in association football and most other codes of football, with the exception of American (i.e., gridiron) football. If leagues allow tied matches, this inevitably requires a decision on how to weight tied matches relative to wins. Leagues allowing tied matches have to use a points system to determine league rankings. Points systems differ between leagues. For example, historically association football awarded teams two points for a win, one point for a draw, and no points for a loss. This system effectively treated a draw as the equivalent of a half-win. However, association football from the early 1980s onward, partly as a reaction to falling attendances and the perception that the fans could be attracted back by teams adopting a more attacking style of play, began to change the points system to give relative greater weighting to wins compared to draws by awarding three points for a win. Some leagues award additional points if a team achieves a certain level of scores in its match. There are also differences in how leagues with odd numbers of teams treat byes (i.e., a team with no scheduled opponent in a set of matches). Some leagues, for example, the National Rugby League in Australia, award two points for a bye, the same as for a win. All teams have two byes in the season so that the rankings are unaffected, but clearly the total points awarded is greater than an equivalent league in which no points are awarded for a bye, creating comparability issues.

Measuring win dispersion becomes more complicated in the case of leagues with rankings based on a points system. The simplest approach is to use the points ratio as the equivalent of the win ratio where the points ratio is the actual points achieved as a proportion of the maximum attainable. An alternative approach is to treat tied matches as a half-win and calculate the win ratio on this basis. Either approach allows the standard measures of win dispersion, such as the QF ratio, to be calculated. The major problem is that of comparability between different leagues with different points systems. For example, leagues that allow tied matches are likely to exhibit lower levels of win dispersion, *ceteris paribus*, compared to leagues that have a match-decider mechanism to determine a winner and loser in every match. Recalculating the win dispersion excluding tied matches can give a rough indication as to the extent of the tied-match effect on win dispersion.

A second source of complication for competitive balance measures is created by unequal (or incomplete) round-robin tournaments. This is particularly a feature of North American major leagues where teams do not play each other the same number of times during the season. European club football, with only a few exceptions, such as the Scottish Premier League, has a full round-robin structure. Unequal round-robin structures create comparability issues between leagues, affecting the degree of win dispersion rather than the method of calculation. The standard deviation for theoretical ideal of perfect competitive balance as used in the QF ratio depends only on the total number of matches played by each team, not the precise structure of the match schedule. However, the Goossens index, which uses perfect competitive dominance as the benchmark, is sensitive to the structure of the match schedule. The standard deviation of the theoretical polar case of perfect competitive dominance tends to decrease if there is an unequal round-robin tournament with the stronger teams playing each other more often than playing the weaker teams.

The third source of complication is the move away from a unitary league structure. In many league structures, particularly in North America and Australia but in recent years becoming increasingly prevalent in European professional team sports, there is a two-stage tournament structure with a regular season (full or partial) round-robin tournament acting as a qualifying process for a postseason elimination play-off tournament. This is the tournament structure adopted by the North American major leagues, as well as the National Rugby League and the Australian Football League (i.e., Australian rules football). But association football in Europe also has a two-stage structure with the domestic round-robin leagues acting as a qualifier for two pan-European tournaments—the UEFA Champions League and the UEFA Cup—to be played in the following season. In addition, some domestic leagues in association football have relegation play-offs. Effectively the two-stage (or, more generally, the multistage) tournament structure requires an extension of the measures of prize concentration. Rather than a single championship prize, there is now a set of prizes, namely, the qualification to the next stage of the tournament. Thus, for example, in the case of the North American major leagues, as well as measuring win dispersion in the regular season, performance persistence between regular seasons, and the prize concentration on the overall major-league champion, it is also important to measure the concentration of play-off qualification. Under conditions of perfect competitive balance, every team should have an equal probability of play-off qualification with observed outcomes displaying a random binomial distribution. This can be used for benchmark comparisons of actual observed distributions of play-off qualification across teams. An alternative approach is to compare the win ratios of the play-off qualifiers with the mean win ratio and/or the win ratio of the highest ranking nonplay-off qualifier.

The final major real-world complexity in measuring competitive balance is the impact of promotion and relegation systems common in European professional team sports. The North America major leagues are closed leagues with a fixed membership that is only changed by agreement of the current teams. The major leagues represent the highest level in a fixed hierarchy. By contrast, European team sports tend to be organized as an open league structure with a merit hierarchy in which teams move up and down based on sporting performance (although in exceptional cases teams may be moved down a merit hierarchy as an administrative punishment for serious rule infringements).

A promotion-and-relegation system has two broad implications for the measurement of competitive balance. First, there are definitional and calculation issues since promotion and relegation implies that there is no fixed membership of a specific league tournament across time. Teams move up and down the various tiers of the merit hierarchy. This complicates the calculation of both performance persistence and prize concentration, and creates obvious comparability issues. It is no surprise that empirical research on competitive balance in leagues with promotion and relegation has tended to focus almost exclusively on the top-tier league. It is not clear, for example, what is the appropriate definition of prize concentration for a lower-tier league given that the ultimate prize is to exit that league by winning promotion.

The second broad implication of promotion and relegation for the measurement of competitive balance is the need to augment the standard set of measures of win dispersion, performance persistence, and prize concentration, with measures specifically intended to report the performance of promoted and relegated teams. For example, a key concern in European domestic football leagues in recent years has been the widening financial gap between the top-tier league and the lower-tier leagues, creating a situation in which teams promoted to the top-tier league find it increasingly very difficult to be competitive and, as a consequence, tend to be relegated back to the lower-tier league within one or two years of being promoted. This has created the phenomenon of the "yo-yo" teams bouncing between the top two tiers of the domestic league structure, too strong to remain in the lower-tier league for long, but not strong enough to become established in the top-tier league.

In the theoretical polar case of perfect competitive balance with promotion and relegation, all teams in any tier of the league structure would have equal probabilities of promotion (equal to the number of promotion places as a proportion of the total number of teams), and equal probabilities of relegation (equal to the number of relegation places as a proportion of the total number of teams). These theoretical probabilities can be used to predict the expected relative frequencies of different performances by promoted and relegated teams. For example, in a top-tier league with N teams and R relegated teams replaced by promoted teams every season, the relegation probability for any team is R/N if all teams have an equal chance of relegation. It is straightforward to show algebraically that under these conditions the expected number of promoted teams are relegated within a specified number of seasons. After two seasons, it can be shown that the expected number of the promoted teams to be relegated is (R/N)[2R − (R²/N)]. In the case of a league with 20 teams and three relegation places, it is expected that 0.8325 promoted teams (i.e., less than one team) would be relegated within two years. This provides a benchmark against which to compare the actual survival rates of newly promoted teams.

Measuring Competitive Balance in the North American Major Leagues and European Club Football

In order to illustrate some of the alternative measures of competitive balance, we shall compare and contrast the trends in competitive balance over the last 40 years in both the North American major leagues and the top divisions of the "Big 5" European domestic football leagues (i.e., England, France, Germany, Italy, and Spain). We will consider win dispersion as measured by the QF ratio, performance persistence as measured by the SRCC, and prize concentration measured in three different ways— the H-index of championship winners, the H-index of play-off qualifications in the North American major leagues, and the actual-to-expected ratio of promoted teams relegated within two years in the Big 5 European football leagues. All of the measures are reported as 10-year averages (with exceptions due to missing data indicated, e.g., strike years).

Table 8–1 shows the win dispersion in the North American major leagues and the Big 5 European football leagues. Win dispersion has been calculated using the QF ratio. In the case of the European football leagues, the calculations have been based on wins, not points with tied matches treated as half-wins. The NFL has the highest degree of competitive balance (i.e., lowest QF ratio) in the North American major leagues in all four 10-year periods. The NFL has also exhibited a trend toward greater competitive balance apart from the final 10-year period. The NHL is the only other major league with a continuous trend toward greater competitive balance. Both the MLB and NBA have shown a tendency toward less competitive balance. The Big 5 European football leagues have generally had greater competitive balance than all of the North American major leagues until the most recent 10-year period when both the English and Italian top divisions had higher QF ratios than the NFL. The other

TABLE 8–1
Win Dispersion in the North American Major Leagues
and European Football, 1966/67–2005/06, QF Ratio

League	1966/67–1975/76	1976/77–1985/86	1986/87–1995/96	1996/67–2005/06
North American Major Leagues				
NFL[a]	1.70	1.51	1.48	1.54
MLB	1.78	1.81	1.62	1.90
NBA	2.71	2.43	2.96	2.77
NHL[b]	2.42	2.32	1.82	1.74
Big 5 European Football Leagues				
England	1.44	1.46	1.44	1.61
France	1.22	1.45	1.30	1.30
Germany	1.26	1.45	1.35	1.46
Italy	1.46	1.39	1.54	1.67
Spain	1.21	1.33	1.47	1.38

[a]Data for the NFL and AFL has been merged for the seasons prior to their full amalgamation in 1970.
[b]Tied games in the NHL treated as half wins as in the Big 5 European football leagues.

three European football leagues have shown no consistent trend in either direction although all three had greater competitive balance in the first 10-year period compared to the most recent period. It is no surprise that win dispersion should be lower in the European football leagues given the occurrence of tied games with no tie-break procedure.

Table 8–2 shows the degree of performance persistence between successive seasons using the SRCC. The patterns are much less clear compared to those for win dispersion. The NFL has the lowest degree of performance persistence in the most recent period with a consistent trend toward lower persistence over time. Again the NHL appears to be improving over time. There is no clear trend over time in performance persistence in either the MLB or the NBA. The MLB has had one of the lower degrees of persistence over the whole 40-year period. The European football leagues have not tended to have more or less persistence than the North American major leagues, particularly in the latter 10-year periods. There has also been no evidence of any clear trend in either direction.

Championship prize concentration is summarized in Table 8–3. In general the North American major leagues have had a greater spread of championship winners than the Big 5 European football leagues, which

TABLE 8–2

Performance Persistence in the North American Major Leagues
and European Football, 1966/67–2005/06, SRCC

League	1966/67– 1975/76	1976/77– 1985/86	1986/87– 1995/96	1996/67– 2005/06
North American Major Leagues[a]				
NFL	0.59	0.51	0.41	0.29
MLB	0.54	0.54	0.26	0.53
NBA	0.65	0.57	0.71	0.62
NHL	0.72	0.75	0.55	0.55
Big 5 European Football Leagues				
England	0.51	0.48	0.44	0.62
France	0.39	0.47	0.49	0.47
Germany	0.41	0.62	0.58	0.53
Italy	0.70	0.59	0.66	0.64
Spain	0.56	0.67	0.55	0.59

[a]Expansion teams are treated as having the lowest rank in the preceding season; franchise movements are treated as the same team moving to a new location.

TABLE 8–3

Championship Prize Concentration in the North American Major Leagues
and European Football, 1966/67–2005/06, H-Index

League	1966/67– 1975/76	1976/77– 1985/86	1986/87– 1995/96	1996/67– 2005/06
North American Major Leagues				
NFL (Super Bowl)	0.16	0.16	0.22	0.18
MLB (World Series)	0.18	0.12	0.14[a]	0.24
NBA (Play-offs)	0.24	0.22	0.28	0.24
NHL (Stanley Cup)	0.34	0.36	0.18	0.19[a]
Big 5 European Football Leagues				
England	0.16	0.52	0.20	0.38
France	0.54	0.20	0.30	0.32
Germany	0.34	0.28	0.26	0.52
Italy	0.22	0.40	0.32	0.42
Spain	0.42	0.26	0.42	0.30

[a]Adjusted by a factor of 0.9 for comparability in cases in which the championship prize was only awarded in nine of the ten seasons due to industrial action.

TABLE 8–4

Play-off Qualification in the North American Major Leagues,
1966/67–2005/06, H Index

Major League[a]	1966/67–1975/76	1976/77–1985/86	1986/87–1995/96	1996/67–2005/06
NFL	0.071	0.049	0.046	0.041
MLB	0.111	0.087	0.065	0.068
NBA	0.080	0.055	0.047	0.041
NHL	0.082	0.055	0.048	0.044

[a]Franchise movements are treated as the same team moving to a new location with the exception of the Cleveland Browns and Baltimore Ravens in the NFL.

have been more prone to a winning dynasty persisting over a number of seasons as, for example, Liverpool in England that won 11 league championships over an 18-year period between 1973 and 1990.

A key prize in the North American major leagues beyond the championship prize is qualification for the postseason play-offs. Table 8–4 provides the unadjusted H-Index for the 10-year periods for the play-off places. Two features stand out. First, all of the major leagues exhibit a downward trend in the concentration of play-off qualification reflecting the expansion of both the number of teams in the leagues and the number of play-off places. Second, the MLB has the highest concentration of play-off qualification, whereas the other three leagues tend to have broadly similar concentration levels. This is due in part to the lower number of play-off places in the MLB, currently eight play-off places for 30 MLB teams, compared to 12 play-off places for 32 NFL teams and 16 play-off places for 30 teams in both the NBA and NHL. Indeed, after correcting for differences in the number of teams and number of play-off places, the current level of concentration of play-off qualification in the MLB is on a par with that of the NHL and only slightly higher than the NBA. The NFL has the highest adjusted degree of dispersion of play-off qualification.

Table 8–5 reports the average number of newly promoted teams to the top division that are relegated within two seasons as a ratio of the theoretical ideal if newly promoted teams had an equal probability of relegation as incumbent teams. As can be seen, the top divisions of the Big 5 European football leagues show very different patterns. The German and Italian top divisions had the lowest survival rate of newly promoted teams (i.e., the highest ratio of actual relegations of newly promoted teams relative to the theoretical ideal) in the first time period, but both these leagues have exhibited a trend toward improved survival rates. By contrast, the English top division initially had a very high survival rate.

TABLE 8–5
The Survival of Promoted Clubs in European Football, 1966/67–2005/06,
Ratio of Actual to Expected Number of Newly Promoted Teams Relegated
within Two Seasons

League	1966/67– 1975/76	1976/77– 1985/86	1986/87– 1995/96	1996/67– 2005/06
England	1.301	1.049	1.563	2.042
France	1.108	1.866	1.361	1.622
Germany	2.169	2.181	1.816	1.636
Italy	2.298	1.962	1.306	1.534
Spain	1.722	1.964	1.521	1.912

Indeed in the period 1976/77–1985/86, the number of newly promoted teams relegated within two years was very close to the theoretical ideal. However, the survival rate has fallen in the last 20 years and is now the highest of all five leagues. The French top division has also shown a trend toward lower survival rates. The Spanish top division has tended to have one of the lower survival rates over the whole sample period with some tendency toward further deterioration, although there was an improvement in the late 1980s and early 1990s.

Overall the Big 5 European football leagues do not appear to be markedly less competitively balanced than the North American major leagues, despite significantly less regulatory intervention by the leagues in the product and labor markets. Win dispersion tends to be lower in European football as a consequence of tied matches and the incentive effects of the promotion and relegation systems. Performance persistence is broadly similar on both sides of the Atlantic. European football has tended to be more prone to higher levels of championship prize concentration, probably because of the reliance on a pure round-robin tournament structure that reduces the probability of surprise outcomes compared to the elimination format of the postseason play-offs in the major leagues. One area in which European football does appear to face an increasing problem of competitive dominance is the low survival rates of newly promoted teams as a consequence of the increasing financial gap between the top division and the lower divisions.

Some Concluding Thoughts

The focus of this chapter has been the concept of competitive balance. It has been argued that even in a simple league context competitive balance is a multifaceted concept. In particular, competitive balance is concerned with win dispersion, performance persistence, and prize concentration. There are a variety of summary statistics capable of measuring each of these aspects of competitive balance. It has also been argued that real-world league structures are much more complex requiring modifications to the standard measures, as well as the development of new measures, particularly in the case of leagues with a promotion-and-relegation system. It is also important to recognize the comparability problems when attempting to draw conclusions about the relative degrees of competitive balance across leagues with very different structures.

Traditionally, empirical studies of competitive balance tended to focus almost exclusively on win dispersion and championship prize concentration. The literature has moved beyond this limited conception of competitive balance to encompass a greater concern with the time dependency of team performance. However, it is our firm belief that there needs to be further expansion of the notion of competitive balance. The emphasis on win dispersion and championship prize concentration is a product of focusing on league structures characterized by a single "winner-takes-all" prize. Although this was a common prize structure for leagues historically, most modern league structures have developed a more complex prize structure including play-off (or another postseason tournament) qualification and retention of league status in promotion-and-relegation system. The emergence of complex tournament and prize structures with multiple prizes has been motivated largely by the desire of leagues to maximize fan interest by providing as many meaningful competitive matches as possible. In these more complex tournament and prize structures, there may be less concern with the competition for one specific prize being dominated by a few teams if there are sufficient levels of competition for other prizes in the league. Thus, for example, although there is evidence that the competition in European football for domestic championship titles has become more dominated, gate attendances and TV viewing figures show little loss of fan interest. This may be partly due to the effects of the competition for European tournament qualification, as well as the competition to avoid relegation. Fan interest may depend not just on competitive balance *per se* but on the overall degree of competitive intensity in a league as determined by the degree of competition for each of the prizes. This in turn requires the development of better summary statistics of the dynamics of competitive intensity to measure the extent to which teams remain in contention for the various prizes throughout the season. It is in this sense that we believe that there is an urgent need to move beyond competitive balance.

References

Cable, J.R. (1983). On the measurement of market share mobility and entry. Working Paper No. 230, Department of Economics, University of Warwick.

Caves, R.E., and Porter, M.E. (1977). From entry barriers to mobility barriers: Conjectural decisions and contrived deterrence to new competition. *Quarterly Journal of Economics*, 91: 241–261.

Coase, R. (1960). The problem of social choice. *Journal of Law and Economics*, 3: 1–44.

Daly, G., and Moore, W.J. (1981). Externalities, property rights and the allocation of resources in Major League Baseball. *Economic Inquiry*, 19: 77–95.

Eckard, E.W. (1998). The NCAA cartel and competitive balance in college football. *Review of Industrial Organization*, 13: 347–369.

Feigenbaum, A., and Primeaux, W.J., Jr. (1983). Strategic groups and mobility barriers: The level of struggle in an industry. Working Paper No. 984, University of Illinois.

Fort, R.M., and Quirk, J. (1995). Cross-subsidization, incentives, and outcomes in professional team sports leagues. *Journal of Economic Literature*, 33: 1265–1299.

Gerrard, B. (1994). Beyond rational expectations: A constructive interpretation of Keynes's analysis of behavior under uncertainty. *Economic Journal*, 104: 327–337.

Gerrard, B. (1998). Competitive balance in the F.A. Premier League, unpublished mimeo, Leeds University Business School.

Gerrard, B. (2004). Still up for grabs? Maintaining the sporting and financial viability of European club soccer. In: R. Fort and J. Fizel (Eds.), *International Sports Economics Comparisons*. Westport, CT: Praeger.

Goossens, K. (2006). Descriptive analysis of competitive balance within and between European football leagues. IASE Conference, Bochum, Germany.

Humphreys, B.R. (2002). Alternative measures of competitive balance in sports leagues. *Journal of Sports Economics*, 3: 33–148.

Késenne, S. (1996). League management in professional team sports with win maximising clubs. *European Journal of Sport Management*, 2: 14–22.

Keynes, J.M. (1921). *A Treatise on Probability*. London: Macmillan.

Knight, F.M. (1921). *Risk, Uncertainty and Profit*. New York: Houghton Mifflin.

Kringstad, M., and Gerrard, B. (2004). The concepts competitive balance and uncertainty of outcome. In: G.T. Papanikos (Ed.), *The Economics and Management of Mega Athletic Events: Olympic Games, Professional Sports and Other Essays*. Athens, Greece: ATINER.

Maxcy, J. (2002). Rethinking restrictions on player mobility in Major League Baseball. *Contemporary Economic Policy*, 20: 145–159.

Maxcy, M., and Mondello, M. (2006). The impact of free agency on competitive balance in North American professional team sports leagues. *Journal of Sport Management*, 20(3): 345–365.

Michie, J., and Oughton, C. (2004). *Competitive Balance in Football: Trends and Effects*. London: The Sports Nexus.

Neale, W.C. (1964). The peculiar economics of professional sports. *Quarterly Journal of Economics*, 78: 1–14.

Quirk, J., and Fort, R.D. (1992). *Pay Dirt: The Business of Professional Team Sports*. Princeton, NJ: Princeton University Press.

Rottenberg, S. (1956). The baseball players' labour market. *Journal of Political Economy*, 64: 242–258.

Szymanski, S. (2003). The economic design of sporting contests. *Journal of Economic Literature*, 41: 1137–1187.

Szymanski, S., and Kuypers, T. (1999). *Winners and Losers: The Business Strategy of Football*. London: Viking.

9

Transactions Cost Variation and Vertical Integration: Major League Baseball's Minor League Affiliates

Jason A. Winfree, Jill J. McCluskey, and Rodney Fort

If profits after vertical integration, less the costs of doing so, exceed pre-integration profits, then basic economic intuition suggests the firm will integrate. Reasons why profits might be higher fall under the two general headings of reduced transactions costs and demand variation. Lieberman (1991), summarizing the work from Coase (1937) and Stigler (1951) on through Williamson (1988) and Perry (1989), provides a comprehensive classification along these lines and fully seven well-specified hypotheses. Consequently, any variation in vertical integration among firms should be explained by variation in these two categories.

We do so for the vertical relationships between Major League Baseball (MLB) and so-called minor league teams of the National Association of Professional Baseball Leagues (NAPBL). There is significant observed variation in MLB team ownership of, and affiliation with, NAPBL teams over time, and we pursue "the seven hypotheses" for an explanation of this variation. Interestingly, "the seven hypotheses" explain nearly none of the observed variation. However, adding team-specific fixed effects to the model suggests that variation in the form of ownership of MLB teams explains NAPBL ownership and affiliation. In particular, we distinguish MLB teams owned by media providers, companies or owners where the baseball team is the primary holding, and others.

Following this inference, we pursue a much simpler and more direct hypothesis about transaction costs from Coase (1937), Alchian and Demsetz (1972), and Klein et al. (1978) and posit that, since media provider owners already deal with many upstream and downstream firms, the net of organizing vertical relationships might be greater for them. However, owners that have their team as their primary livelihood have no experience in vertical relationships and may do so less frequently. Profit analysis supports this idea. This type of result corresponds with the interface between economics and management.

The chapter proceeds as follows. In the second section, we document the variation in MLB ownership and affiliation with NAPBL teams. The third section presents "the seven hypotheses" as they apply to the MLB example. The results of the hypothesis tests are in the fourth section, along with our subsequent inference on team-specific fixed effects. The fifth section presents an econometric investigation of that subsequent inference based on ownership structure of MLB teams. Conclusions round out the chapter in the sixth section.

Vertical Integration in MLB

MLB provides a unique setting to analyze vertical integration. Most talent enters MLB one of two ways. Signed foreign-born players (there is no draft of foreign-born players) typically move up to the major league level after seasoning on NAPBL teams that are affiliated with or owned by major league teams. The National Agreement governs this relationship between MLB and NAPBL teams, specifying territorial jurisdictions, financial responsibilities, and playing field quality. Talent development is accomplished either by MLB-employed managers at NAPBL teams wholly owned by MLB owners or at independently owned minor league teams with a contractual affiliation with MLB team owners. The latter are referred to as player development contracts.

Players that join the majors without seasoning on NAPBL teams are few and far between. A very few have entered MLB directly out of high school. And some players take a nontraditional route through "independent leagues" (not officially recognized by the NAPBL). Drafted domestic players can refuse and take the independent league route and that is the only route for nondrafted domestic players.

Figure 9–1 presents data on how this vertical relationship between MLB and NAPBL teams has changed over a sample period where some data on all relationships for both the American League (AL) and National League (NL) of MLB are available. Figure 9–1 shows variation in the number of NAPBL and independent league teams, the number of affiliated NAPBL teams, and the actual outright ownership of NAPBL teams by MLB teams. The total number of NAPBL teams rose dramatically through the late 1930s, fell just as dramatically into the war years, and reached unprecedented levels from the postwar years to the early 1950s. From 1950 to the mid-1960s, the number of teams declined to a low level not observed

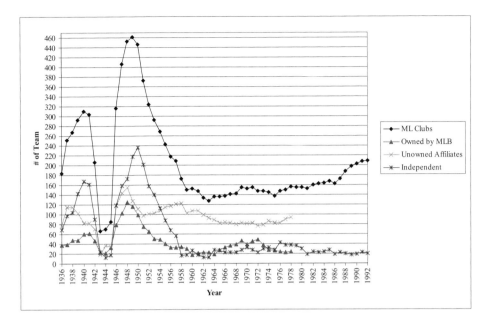

FIGURE 9–1. MLB/NAPBL Relationships, 1936–1992
        Source: Hoie (1993)

since before the war. There have been some minor ups and downs since then, and it appears that there has been a gradual resurgence since the early 1980s and on through the 1990s.

The pattern of minor league team ownership by MLB owners roughly followed the pattern of the number of teams. Except for the war years, MLB owners have primarily made use of affiliations rather than ownership. Interestingly, until the mid-1950s, there were more teams in independent leagues than either MLB-owned or affiliated NAPBL teams. All that began to change around 1950, when the number of teams in independent leagues began a dramatic plunge to the end of the 1950s. By the end of that decade, the number of teams in independent leagues and MLB-owned teams was approximately the same. Affiliation (as opposed to outright ownership) was at its peak shortly after World War II. It also took off beginning in the late 1950s but returned to its prewar level and hovered there through the 1970s.

Unfortunately, data limitations allow the closest look at affiliation and ownership only for the NL, and only for 1955–2004, shown in Figure 9–2. There was interesting convergence between owned and affiliated teams that occurred from about 1965–1970. However, this convergence subsequently reversed itself. Further, the number of NL-owned NAPBL teams

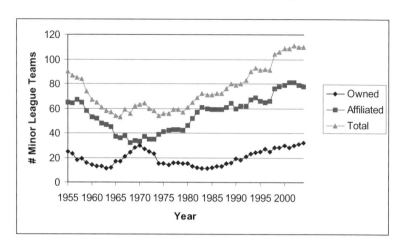

FIGURE 9–2. NL/NAPBL Relationships, 1955–2004
          Source: *National League Green Book,* for years depicted.
          Thanks to *The Sporting News* archive for supplying
          copies for some years

increased coincident with the MLB expansions of 1969, 1993, and 1998 but not for earlier expansions before 1969. Finally, ownership by NL teams gradually increased as a percent of all relationships with NAPBL teams since the mid-1980s. However, affiliation dominated ownership in the relationship between NL owners and NAPBL teams. This variation, both for MLB in general (Fig. 9–1) and for the NL more recently (Fig. 9–2), leads us to the following empirical investigation of vertical integration.

Transaction Costs and Demand Variation: Specification

Lieberman (1991) categorizes the backward integration literature into transactions cost hypotheses and demand variation hypotheses, providing a convenient point of departure for empirical analyses. We list the hypotheses and how they enter our empirical specification for MLB in this section, beginning with the three transactions cost hypotheses.

  H_1: Downstream producers are more likely to integrate backward when the upstream market contains only a smaller number of suppliers.

While data limitations preclude our ability to explicitly capture H_1, we will follow its intent with dummy variables intended to separate transactions cost regimes based on changes in the number of NAPBL teams related to MLB expansion. The remaining transactions cost hypotheses are:

H_2: Backward integration is more likely when the downstream firm must commit to large sunk investments in (transaction-specific) assets.

H_3: Backward integration is more likely when the input in question accounts for a large proportion of total cost.

Large sunk investments characterize MLB investment in talent, and clearly talent is the dominant total cost element for MLB teams. But there is no variation along these dimensions across teams or over time, so there is no need for tests of H_2 and H_3.

There are four demand variation hypotheses:

H_4: A firm is more likely to integrate when the other buyers of the input have high variability in demand.

When other demanders have high variability, their impact on input prices is unpredictable. This would lead to backward integration as a protection against input price uncertainty. At the individual MLB team level, H_4 suggests that vertical integration should increase when the remaining teams have higher variability in demand. We can measure this with attendance and include it in the empirical analysis. The second demand variability hypothesis is:

H_5: A firm that accounts for a large fraction of total demand for the input is more likely to integrate.

Backward integration is more likely in this case because of gains from risk pooling with upstream suppliers. In our baseball case, this suggests two possibilities. Again, suppose teams are the unit of observation. Larger revenue teams should be more likely to backward integrate than smaller revenue teams since they buy more of the talent produced by NAPBL teams. In terms of units of talent (not players), larger revenue market teams account for the larger fraction of total demand.

The third demand variability hypothesis from Lieberman is:

H_6: The likelihood of backward integration is diminished by the presence of demand fluctuations in the input market that are correlated with fluctuations in the firm's downstream market.

The idea here is risk-averse firms find backward integration less attractive when quantity disturbances to the buying and selling industries are positively correlated over time. Citing the difference between H_4 and H_6, Lieberman notes that upstream output variability needs to be decomposed into components correlated with downstream output and components uncorrelated with downstream outputs. In our baseball example, in the short run, downstream output can be measured by attendance. Upstream output measurement must capture the quality of that output, that is, units of talent produced by NAPBL teams for purchase by MLB.

The final demand variability hypothesis is:

H$_7$: Firms are less likely to integrate backward when they face large fluctuations in downstream demand.

Vertical integration in volatile settings reduces the degree of internal transfer, lowers ownership stakes, and reduces vertical integration. In our baseball case, again, the short run measure is attendance.

We note that Perry (1989) offers other reasons why firm owners should vertically integrate, including assuring inputs, internalizing externalities, avoiding government restrictions, creating market power, and eliminating competitors' market power. The external competitive environment is also important in Stigler (1951). These other factors seem to us not to apply to MLB. Since contracts are with players, assured through the draft, the first idea of assuring inputs does not pertain to the relationship between MLB teams and NAPBL teams; the NAPBL teams do not procure for MLB teams. Further, we can think of no government restrictions that can be avoided by backward integration (especially since MLB enjoys its anti-trust exemption under the *Federal Baseball* ruling of 1922). Similarly, since MLB operates as a group decision-making body, there is really not much more market power to create through vertical integration.

Data limitations that shorten our empirical horizon to 1977–2004 render changes in the competitive environment moot. There have been seven rival leagues situations at the major league level (Fort, 2006, p. 151) and two during the period covered in Tables 9–1 and 9–2. The African American leagues played in 1923–1950, and the Pacific Coast League (mid-1950s) actually sought official recognition as a third major league in the mid-1950s. However, these are not relevant since we will only be analyzing a later period.

The "seven hypotheses" as they pertain to MLB relations with the NAPBL suggest the following specification. Suppose we have data at the individual team level for i = 1, . . . , n teams over t = 1, . . . , T years. The choice to vertically integrate can be captured by:

$$\ln\left(\frac{O}{A}\right)_{it} = a_{it} + b_{it}W_{it} + g_{it}X_{it} + k_{it}Z_{it} + e_{it} \qquad (9.1)$$

In Eq. (9.1), O is the number of owned NAPBL teams and A is the number of affiliations with NAPBL teams that are not owned. The vector

TABLE 9–1
NL Descriptive Statistics and Sources

Year	#MLB Teams	Ave. Payroll ($000 nominal)	Ave. Attendance (000)	S.D. W%
1977	12	1,549	1,589	0.081
1978	12	2,414	1,671	0.063
1979	12	2,953	1,769	0.072
1980	12	3,819	1,760	0.062
1981	12	4,609	1,024	0.085
1982	12	5,910	1,792	0.062
1983	12	8,010	1,792	0.045
1984	12	8,357	1,732	0.054
1985	12	10,906	1,858	0.087
1986	12	12,501	1,861	0.074
1987	12	11,376	2,063	0.059
1988	12	12,467	2,039	0.076
1989	12	14,689	2,107	0.059
1990	12	16,502	2,041	0.057
1991	12	24,514	2,058	0.061
1992	12	29,514	2,056	0.066
1993	14	27,182	2,532	0.091
1994	14	30,079	1,843	0.072
1995	14	31,042	1,793	0.060
1996	14	33,197	2,170	0.056
1997	14	37,811	2,259	0.058
1998	16	39,918	2,402	0.088
1999	16	47,952	2,395	0.079
2000	16	55,665	2,480	0.069
2001	16	62,661	2,483	0.065
2002	16	65,741	2,312	0.081
2003	16	73,054	2,295	0.070
2004	16	67,065	2,514	0.086

Source: Rodney Fort's website, Sports Business Data Area (www.rodneyfort.com/SportsBusiness/BizFrame.htm).

W includes independent variables representing the transaction cost hypotheses, X includes independent variables representing the demand variability hypotheses, and Z includes any remaining explanatory variables. Since we can observe the choices by all teams, there is neither a truncation nor censoring problem for a regression specification of Eq. (9.1).

Lieberman (1991, p. 461) employs the following approach for testing H_4, H_6, and H_7 that hinges on ascertaining correlated and uncorrelated elements in upstream (NAPBL) and downstream (MLB) outputs. First,

TABLE 9–2
The Winning Percent and Lieberman Technique Regressions

Variable	Model (4)	Model (5)	Model (6)	Model (7)
Constant	0.2967*	0.1153*	18,310*	1.392*
	(0.0239)	(0.0209)	(1996)	(0.1007)
W_{it-1}	0.3816*			
	(0.0485)			
E_{it}	6.68e–7*			
	(2.39e–7)			
t		0.00035	216.8	−0.00376
		(0.00333)	(317.3)	(0.00773)
t^2		−0.00044*	22.01**	−0.00051***
		(0.00011)	(10.62)	(0.00028)
M_t				−6.34e–6
				(4.83e–6)
R^2	0.184	0.909	0.838	0.879
DF	371	25	25	25

*Significant at 99%; **significant at 95%; ***significant at 90%.

we remove the trend in NAPBL output by regressing time and time-squared on total minor league output. Then we similarly remove the trend in MLB output by regressing time and time-squared on total MLB output. Let RSS_{NAPBL} and RSS_{MLB} be the residual sum of squares from these two regressions, respectively. Then we regress time, time-squared, and total MLB output on total NAPBL output. Let RSS'_{NAPBL} be the residual sum of squares from that regression. RSS'_{NAPBL} is now the variance of total NAPBL output independent of fluctuations in total MLB output. The correlated component is:

$$RSS''_{NAPBL} = RSS'_{NAPBL} - RSS_{NAPBL} \tag{9.2}$$

This approach yields the following regarding the demand variability hypotheses: for H_4, a positive relation between backward integration and RSS'_{NAPBL}; for H_6, a negative relation between backward integration and RSS''_{NAPBL}; for H_7, a negative relation between backward integration and RSS_{MLB}.

Given this development and the limitations in the data, we adopt the following specification of Eq. (9.1) for $i = 1, \ldots, n$, NL teams and $t = 1977, \ldots, 2004$:

$$L_{it} = a_{it} + d_1 D_{93-97} + d_2 D_{98-04} + b_4 RSS'_{NAPBLt} + b_5 F_{it} +$$
$$b_6 RSS''_{NAPBLt} + b_7 RSS_{MLBt} + e_{it} \tag{9.3}$$

On the left-hand side of Eq. (9.3), $L_{it} = \ln\left(\dfrac{O_{it} + 0.5}{A_{it} + 0.5}\right)$, the logistic ratio of owned to otherwise affiliated teams (the 0.5 is the usual adjustment for efficiency). The variables $D_{93\text{-}97}$ and $D_{98\text{-}04}$ are dummy variables to separate the data into three transaction costs regimes in order to capture H_1. In our case, $D_1 = 1$ if $t = 1993\text{--}1997$ and $D_2 = 1$ if $t = 1998\text{--}2004$. We would expect that league expansion would increase the number of NAPBL teams and MLB teams would reduce vertical integration according to H_1. This means that, relative to the omitted category years (from 1977–1992), we would expect these expansion periods to have less vertical integration.

The rest of the variables require a bit of development. Since we approach H_4, H_6, and H_7 with Lieberman's (1991) technique, we turn first to the development of the F_{it} variable and H_5. The idea is that we need to capture the fraction of total input demanded by team i at time t. Using the convention from Quirk and Fort (1992), we conceptualize the talent input measured in units that generate one more winning percent point. This means that talent and winning percent are interchangeable. We capture the minor league contribution to winning percent as follows. Let $F_{it} = \exp(\hat{e}_{it})$, where $\hat{e}_{it}$ is determined from the following regression:

$$\ln(W_{it}) = c_{it} + g_{it}\ln(W_{it-1}) + h_{it}E_{it} + e_{it} \tag{9.4}$$

In Eq. (9.4), $W_{it} = $ winning percent of MLB team i at time t so that $W_{it-1} = $ winning percent of MLB team i lagged one period. $E_{it} = $ total expenditure (payroll adjusted for inflation) for MLB players by MLB team i at time t. So, $\hat{e}_{it}$ includes the part of talent purchased (one-to-one with winning percent) that was *not* MLB talent, i.e., it had to be NAPBL talent-generated winning percent. Finally, $F_{it} = \exp(\hat{e}_{it})$ undoes the logarithmic outcome from Eq. (9.4).

The rest of the right-hand-side variables in Eq. (9.4) come from our version of the Lieberman (1991) technique. First, RSS_{NAPBL} is derived from an NAPBL industry output regression. We already have the quantity of NAPBL industry output demanded by each MLB team, so the total in any year would just be $\ln(m_t) = \sum_{i=1}^{n} \hat{e}_{it}$ (where the summation is over the n teams in the league at time t, and remember that the residuals are in logarithmic form since the regression in Eq. (9.4) is in logs of the dependent variable). RSS_{NAPBL} is the residual sum of squares from:

$$\ln(m_t) = k_1 t + k_2 t^2 + e_{it} \tag{9.5}$$

In a given year, in the short run, MLB output for the second Lieberman regression can be measured as league attendance (in thousands), M. RSS_{MLB} is the residual sum of squares from:

$$M_t = \gamma_1 t + \gamma_2 t^2 + e_{it} \qquad (9.6)$$

Finally, following Lieberman's last step, RSS''_{NAPBL} is the residual sum of squares from:

$$m_t = G_1 M_t + G_2 t + G_3 t^2 + e_{it} \qquad (9.7)$$

Given Eqs. (9.4–9.7), we test the demand variation hypotheses as follows for the coefficient estimates in Eq. (9.3)—H_4: $\hat{b}_4 > 0$; H_5: $\hat{b}_5 > 0$; H_6: $\hat{b}_6 < 0$; and H_7: $\hat{b}_7 < 0$.

Ownership and affiliation data for all but the National League (NL) end in 1978. As a result, we focus on the NL; and data for the NL were obtained from the *National League Green Book* since then (the similar *American League Red Book* does not contain the same detail about ownership versus affiliation). The data required to capture the hypotheses tests are MLB payrolls, MLB winning percentages, and MLB attendance. Finally, individual team payroll data (in thousands of dollars) are only available for the period from 1977–2004.

"The Seven Hypotheses": Results and Further Evaluation

Table 9–2 summarizes the underlying regressions in expressions Eqs. (9.4) through (9.7). There is not much of interest to interpret since these regressions generate statistical outcomes that are used to calculate our versions of the demand variation independent variables in Eq. (9.3). However, it is interesting that payroll and lagged log of winning percent only explained about 18.4% of the variation in the log of winning percent in a given year. In addition, we estimated the model in Eq. (9.7) with the sum of gate revenue and local TV revenues in place of attendance. The results were nearly identical to those reported for attendance.

We estimated model Eq. (9.3) using weighted least squares to correct for autocorrelation, and the results are presented in Table 9–3. With a Durbin-Watson statistic of 0.162, severe autocorrelation was present. The R^2 statistic is a paltry 0.008, and no estimated coefficients were significant. There is literally no explanation offered by either the transactions cost regime indicator variables or the demand variability variables. Since this is not at all expected, we turn to an inferential approach for further insight.

TABLE 9–3

Weighted Least Squares Logit Regressions Dependent Variable: L_{it} in Eq. (9.3)

Variable	Model (3)	With Fixed Effects	With Ownership Structure
Constant	−2.166**	−1.287*	−2.057**
	(1.102)	(0.3427)	(0.8083)
Transaction Cost Dummies			
D93-97 (−)	1.400	−0.00659	0.4063
	(1.308)	(0.3995)	(1.068)
D98-04 (−)	2.037	0.2365	0.7379
	(1.564)	(0.3487)	(1.162)
Demand Variablility			
RSS′$_{NAPBL}$ (+)	30.04	−1.982	14.41
	(28.51)	(12.90)	(25.24)
F (+)	0.1446	−0.2834	0.3107
	(0.3817)	(0.2340)	(0.3547)
RSS″$_{NAPBL}$ (−)	−6.929	−6.569	−9.951
	(37.21)	(18.32)	(33.77)
RSS$_{MLB}$ (−)	−1.10e–8	1.955e–10	−4.930e–9
	(1.24e–8)	(5.645e–9)	(1.091e–8)
Team Fixed Effects			
Arizona		0.0905	
		(0.2386)	
Atlanta		2.457*	
		(0.1576)	
Chicago		0.1972	
		(0.1980)	
Cincinnati		−0.4517*	
		(0.2204)	
Colorado		−0.8540*	
		(0.2820)	
Florida		1.064*	
		(0.2865)	
Houston		0.7420*	
		(0.2381)	
Los Angeles		0.7864*	
		(0.2443)	
Milwaukee		−0.3726	
		(0.3182)	
Montreal		0.6141**	
		(0.2455)	
New York		0.4823**	
		(0.2422)	

TABLE 9–3
Continued

Variable	Model (3)	With Fixed Effects	With Ownership Structure
Philadelphia		0.6976*	
		(0.2331)	
Pittsburgh		0.3756***	
		(0.2176)	
San Diego		−0.8498*	
		(0.1917)	
San Francisco		−0.7089*	
		(0.1464)	
Media			0.9192*
			(0.1264)
Syndicates			0.1403
			(0.1174)
DF	367	352	352
R²	0.008	0.659	0.155

*Significant at 99% level; **significant at 95% level; ***significant at 90% level.

The second column in Table 9–3 adds team-specific fixed effects using indicator variables to indicate individual teams (the omitted team, St. Louis, was randomly chosen). Again, a weighted least squares approach was used due to autocorrelation. The inclusion of fixed effects clearly reveals something since R^2 is now a more respectable 0.659. Adding fixed effects still leaves the rest of the specification in Eq. (9.3) without any explanatory power. None of the demand variation variables is significant at even the 90% level.

We infer the following from the fixed effects estimates. Relative to St. Louis (the omitted team), Atlanta, Florida, Houston, Los Angeles, Montreal, New York, and Philadelphia had greater vertical integration, while Cincinnati, Colorado, Milwaukee, San Diego, and San Francisco had less. Those with positive fixed effects all had a more complicated ownership structure (see Table 9–4 for owners and structure). Media providers (or individuals directing media providers associated with teams) own Atlanta (Time Warner) and New York. The owner of the Marlins until 1999, Wayne Huizenga, also owned its regional media provider, and the owner of the Los Angeles Dodgers was NewsCorp until 2004. Finally, Drayton McLane's holding company owned the Houston team since 1992.

However, there also are some exceptions to this idea. Philadelphia (owned by Bill Giles and David Montgomery) and Montreal have significantly positive fixed effects but not complicated ownership arrangements.

TABLE 9–4
National League Owners, 2000

Team	Owner	Business Interests
Arizona	Jerry Colangelo/others	Sports Team
Atlanta	Time Warner	Media
Chicago	Tribune Company	Media
Cincinnati	Carl Lindner	Various
Colorado	Jerry McMorris/others	Various
Florida	John Henry (Wayne Huizenga to 1999)	Various (Various including Media)
Houston	Drayton McLane/others	Various; Holding company
Los Angeles	NewsCorp	Media
Milwaukee	Selig Trust (Wendy Selig-Prieb)	Sports Team
Montreal	Jeffrey Loria	Art Buyer/Sports Team
New York	Nelson Doubleday/Fred Wilpon	Various including Media
Philadelphia	Bill Giles	Various
Pittsburgh	Kevin McClatchy	Print Media
San Diego	John Moores	Computers
San Francisco	Peter McGowan/others	Safeway
St. Louis	William Dewitt/Fred Hanser /Andrew Baur	Various

Chicago, owned by the media Tribune Corporation (since 1981), has no significant fixed effect. This begs the question of why it would be the case that the less complex ownership structures of the teams with negative fixed effects make them different than St. Louis, another uncomplicated structure. Finally, these effects are *very* team specific since we created a dummy variable equal to 1 for teams with complicated ownership and ran an interacted version of Eq. (9.3) with little difference from the other reports in Table 9–3.

We also tried to control for a variety of other changes in the time series tied primarily to labor-management relations. However, indicator variables for the lockout of 1990, collusion episodes from 1985–1987, the strike of 1994–1995, and the alteration in the local revenue sharing after 1995 had no statistically detectable effects on the results.

Consequently, our inference from this exercise is to pursue the model of vertical integration along the lines of ownership variation in the next section. Although we should note some caveats. First, it could be that our attempt to mimic Lieberman's technique, although faithful, fails due to the limited nature of our data. We have only one industry (and only the NL) where he had many, and our data are limited to only one input where he had many. In addition, the data only go back to 1977 (missing the potentially important imposition of the draft in 1965 and free agency in 1975). There simply may not be enough variation. This suggests that efforts to structurally capture the transaction cost and demand variation hypotheses, rather than using the residual sum of squares decomposition approach, might prove more enlightening.

Ownership Structure and Vertical Integration

Since "the seven hypotheses" do not seem to explain vertical integration variation across MLB teams, we follow the inference from the fixed effects in the last section and go back to basics. Coase (1937) argued that vertical integration depends on the costs of organizing transactions within the firm or outside of the firm relative to profit gains. Alchain and Demsetz (1972) argue that some of those costs come in the form of monitoring by the owners as residual claimants. The amount and form of organizational relationships outside the firm depends on the net benefits involved. Some will be in the form of more ownership and some will be affiliations by contract. For example, Monteverde and Teece (1982) show that transaction costs dealing with human capital are very important in determining vertical integration in the automobile industry.

Therefore, if some MLB owners vertically integrate more than others, whether the heterogeneity among teams is on the cost side or the benefit side, surely there is variation in net benefits. Following the inference from the last section, where more complicated ownership structures coincide with greater vertical integration, we posit that variation in experience with vertical relationships in other aspects of business increases the net benefits of vertical integration.

For example, MLB teams that also own NAPBL teams would also own many types of businesses and have experience expanding into other areas. As stated earlier, many media providers currently own or at one time have owned MLB teams. Most media companies are experienced in dealing with vertical relations, which may help efficiency with MLB teams airing on television. Other media providers, such as newspapers, own MLB teams. These types of vertical integration should also give owners more experience in vertically integrating and doing so efficiently.

Consequently, our hypothesis is that media provider owners of MLB teams will own more of their NAPBL teams than other owners. We recognize that we do not explain the original decision to vertically integrate. However, we do allow that variation in net benefit determines the ongoing decision on how much to vertically integrate. This part of our study is different from most vertical integration studies because the decision for each owner is presumably the same; however, the owners are different.

Searching for explanations from ownership structure has its place in related literature on competition and mergers in the media industry (Waterman and Weiss, 1996; Yoo, 2002) and in the beer industry (Slade, 1998).

To test this hypothesis, we again estimate model Eq. (9.3) without the fixed effects, but with two indicator variables dealing with ownership structure. Although ownership structures can be complicated in professional sports, making categorization subjective, we are able to put owners into three groups. The first ownership variable is a media variable indicating that the MLB owner offers some sort of media. The five examples of media companies owning MLB teams in the sample include NewsCorp (Los Angeles Dodgers 1998–2003), Tribune Company (Chicago Cubs 1981–2004), Time Warner/Ted Turner (Atlanta Braves 1977–2004), Nelson Doubleday/Fred Wilpon (New York Mets 1980–2004), and Kevin McClatchy (Pittsburgh Pirates 1996–2004). Media providers owned 26.2% of the sample. As stated earlier, we expect these owners to own more of their minor league teams owing to their experience and possible gains in efficiency. The second ownership variable is ownership groups or syndicates. Syndicates represent owners that come together specifically to own the team. These owners represented 28.2% of the sample. The omitted group of owners is conglomerate or single owners. Although it may seem counterintuitive to group single owners with conglomerates, most single owners also own other corporations. It is ambiguous whether syndicates will own more or less of their minor league teams than corporations.

The results of the estimation are also found in Table 9–3. After correcting for autocorrelation, the R^2 is 0.155. This model does show that media owned teams do tend to own more of their minor league teams, but there is no statistically significant difference between syndicates and conglomerates. Still, none of the transactions costs or demand variability variables is significant.

Conclusions

What causes vertical integration in professional baseball is an open research question. Is baseball really different from other industries, and if so, why? Examining the data on the relationship over time between MLB owners and NAPBL teams shows significant variation in both ownership and affiliation. This is a natural area for an investigation of backward vertical integration. Utilizing transactions cost and demand variation hypotheses from the economic literature on vertical integration, we estimated a logit model of that choice by NL teams over the period 1977–2004. The results offer no support for either type of explanation.

Seeking guidance through inference, we added team fixed effects to the estimation. The pattern of significance suggested to us that differences in ownership structure of MLB teams might explain the decision to integrate vertically. Experience with vertical relationships in other areas of business might translate into greater net value in vertical relationships with NAPBL teams. We posit that media providers that own MLB teams were the most likely candidates. Further estimation of the panel data supports this hypothesis.

Our work also suggests a few paths for future analysis of MLB vertical integration with NAPBL teams. As we note, we do not address Stigler's (1951) idea that vertical integration should increase if competition is brisk. For example, Fort and Maxcy (2001) notice that MLB ownership of NAPBL teams was nearly complete at the time of integration and claim it contributed to the demise of the African–American baseball leagues. If data can be found that predate ours, then the impact of rival leagues on vertical integration choices can be investigated more thoroughly and estimated.

There are other topics of interest, such as the impact of the decision to vertically integrate. Blair and Kaserman (1983) show that hiring should increase and wages should fall in the upstream market with backward integration when the downstream firm is a monopsonist. This makes their specification especially relevant since MLB is nearly the only buyer of NAPBL talent. However, once again, this pursuit will require more data than we were able to muster.

References

Alchian, A., and Demsetz, H. (1972). Production, information costs and economic organization. *American Economic Review*, 62:777–795.

Blair, R.D., and Kaserman, D.L. (1983). *Law and Economics of Vertical Integration and Control.* New York: Academic Press.

Coase, R. (1937). The nature of the firm. *Economica*, 4:386–405.

Fort, R. (2006). *Sports Economics* (2nd ed.). Upper Saddle River, NJ: Prentice Hall.

Fort, R., and Maxcy, J. (2001). The demise of African-American baseball leagues: A rival league explanation. *Journal of Sports Economics*, 2:35–49.

Hoie, B. (1993). The minor leagues. In: J. Thorn and P. Palmer (Eds.) *Total Baseball.* New York: HarperPerennial, pp. 502–517.

Klein, B., Crawford, R., and Alchian, A. (1978). Vertical integration, appropriable rents, and the competitive contracting process. *Journal of Law and Economics*, 21:297–326.

Lieberman, M.B. (1991). Determinants of vertical integration: An empirical test. *Journal of Industrial Economics*, XXXIX:451–466.

Monteverde, K., and Teece, D. (1982). Supplier switching costs and vertical integration in the automobile industry. *Bell Journal of Economics*, 13:206–213.

Perry, M.K. (1989). Vertical integration: Determinants and effects. In: R. Schmalensee and R.D. Willig (Eds.) *The Handbook of Industrial Organization*. Amsterdam: North-Holland.

Quirk, J., and Fort, R.D. (1992). *Pay Dirt: The Business of Professional Team Sports*. Princeton, NJ: Princeton University Press.

Slade, M.E. (1998). Beer and the tie: Did divestiture of brewer-owned public houses lead to higher beer prices? *The Economic Journal*, 108:565–602.

Stigler, G. (1951). The division of labor is limited by the extent of the market. *Journal of Political Economy*, 59:185–193.

Waterman, D., and Weiss, A. (1996). The effects of vertical integration between cable television systems and pay cable networks. *Journal of Econometrics*, 76:357–395.

Williamson, O.E. (1988). Transaction cost economics. In: R. Schmalensee and R.D. Willig (Eds.) *Handbook of Industrial Organization* (5th ed.). Amsterdam: Elsevier Science.

Yoo, C.S. (2002). Vertical integration and media regulation in the new economy. *Yale Journal of Regulation*, July.

10

Organization Specific Training and Player Salaries: Evidence from the National Basketball Association

Joshua Darling and Joel Maxcy

Professional basketball players in the National Basketball Association (NBA) have the right to freely offer their services to the highest bidder through the process of free agency. This is a process by which a player qualifies for the option to pursue more lucrative or appealing opportunities with another league franchise. Since the 1984–1985 season, NBA franchises have been restricted by a league imposed salary cap limiting the total monetary value of their player payroll. The NBA employs a "soft" payroll cap that allows organizations to surpass the league mandated payroll maximum. With the inception of the Bird exception in 1991, named for Boston Celtics legend Larry Bird, NBA teams are allowed to re-sign their own free agents to maximum value contracts and surpass what other prospective league organizations are able to offer. The Bird exception increases the likelihood that free agents sign again with their original team rather than transfer to a new team because the original team is in a position to offer a higher salary. Nonetheless, numerous free agents transfer to new teams each season, and a primary reason to change teams is the offer of a more lucrative contract. The purpose of this study is to draw a comparison between the free agent players that transfer to other teams and those that do not. Free agent players that receive better offers and sign again with their own teams may be presumed to have some team specific capacity that is of less value, or is not known, to rival teams. Individual and team factors assumed to determine player compensation are examined for the purpose of determining differences between these two groups of free agents.

Human capital theory, as developed by Becker (1975), distinguishes between training that develops general and specific skills. General skills are those that are of use to many potential employers, while specific skills only improve productivity for the current employer. Becker's theory implies that workers with firm specific skills earn more than workers without specific training, but less than their actual marginal revenue product (MRP) as there is no competition for their firm specific expertise. Generally speaking, the skills of professional team sport athletes would be considered highly general as they are easily transferable regardless of which franchise employs the player. In basketball, shooting, passing, rebounding, and defensive proficiency are all examples of general skills. Notwithstanding, these skills are often functions of innate talent and are often developed through training (coaching) received prior to a player's entering the NBA. Actual coaching at the NBA level may involve some general training, but the focus of coaching is often more team specific, such as the implementation of the coach's system and learning team applications including offensive plays and defensive sets.

Firm specific training in team sport leagues also may be assumed to include the player's ability to respond to a specific style of coaching and instruction, as well as adherence to established organizational values. Team specific skills may also include intangible issues that include the player's behavioral traits and his role in team chemistry and leadership. If free agents who remain with their original team earn more on average than those that transfer, all else being constant, the implication according to human capital theory is that those who don't transfer possess a higher level of team-specific skills.

Due largely to readily available salary information, there has been extensive research conducted in the area of human capital compensation in the North American professional team sport leagues. Much of the economic literature on team sport salary differentials has focused on race and discrimination. Kahn and Sherer (1988), Kahn (1991), and Kahn and Shah's (2005) explorations of the racial aspects of player compensation in the NBA papers are representative. Additionally, Kahn (1992) examined the effects of race and free agency on player compensation in the National Football League. Jones and Walsh (1988) explore the competitive factors of financial compensation of players in the National Hockey League. They focused on salary differentials based on player skill difference and positional discrimination and examine if salary discrimination exists against French Canadians. Studies addressing other aspects of compensation differentiation include Kahn (1993) and Maxcy (2004a), who address contract length and compensation for both free agents and nonfree agents in Major League Baseball. Berri (1999) determined a method by which certain players are valued above others within team sports. He devised a measurement scale designed to calculate an individual NBA player's contributions to team wins based on their statistical performance. Berri and Jewell (2004) examined the contract values of NBA players following the 1998–99 labor dispute and lockout in relation to wage inequality and team production.

Accurate and current salary data on NBA players, particularly length of previous contract, are not readily available, and as a result, there has been very little research attempted to determine if there is a statistical correlation between player movement and human capital compensation in the NBA. This study focuses on an underrepresented area of sport economics research by an examination of what factors determine the decision of free agent players to remain with their team or to sign with another club. As stated by Kahn (2000), "professional sports offers a unique opportunity for labor market research . . . [and] there is no research setting other than sports where we know the name, face, and life history of every production worker and supervisor in the industry." Sport presents an excellent opportunity to examine labor economics in relation to human capital and compensation with very specific information not otherwise available.

This chapter proceeds as follows. The next section will describe the data and their collection and explain the empirical model. The third section will present and discuss the empirical results as they pertain to the model. This chapter concludes with discussion and suggestions for avenues of further research.

Data and Models

The NBA, its players, coaches, general managers, and owners are all heavily and mutually invested in each other at both a financial and competitive level. With the high levels of compensation and investment involved, it is reasonable to assume that these parties find it useful to have a system in place that helps them in gauging a potential free agent's salary and contract terms. A player about to reach free agency would be expected to be able to learn the salary and contract terms that they could anticipate receiving with a free agent contract, and could then determine if it may be more lucrative to re-sign with their current team or test the open market. From the standpoint of the organization, it would be beneficial to have information at their disposal when they are generating a financial plan for free agency as they will more accurately be able to estimate the value of a player, and whether it is wiser to re-sign that player or allow them to leave for another organization and sign another player in their place. This would also serve a function when an organization is deciding whether or not to offer a contract extension to a star player before they are eligible for free agency, thus enabling them to retain the player's services without direct market competition that may increase the price. The decision to enter a contract is by mutual agreement. For the club, the decision to pursue alternative free agents means sacrificing an informational benefit. Though much information, statistical and otherwise, is readily available for all NBA players, the team is forgoing a known quantity in terms of personal factors, such as how the player responds to coaching, interacts with teammates, and so forth. Likewise, players who transfer are also sacrificing by moving to a more uncertain situation.

The process by which a player becomes a free agent occurs in several ways; most often, a player's current contract expires before an extension is signed with the player's current team. Second, veteran players may be "released." This occurs when an organization makes the decision that a player's services are no longer required or beneficial to the team based on their salary or other tangible criteria. The release of a player removes the individual from their current team and they are free to sign elsewhere, while their previous club is sometimes obligated to pay them a portion of their salary. Rookie players that have entered the league's draft process without being selected are also classified as free agents. The latter two groups typically represent marginal players, who may or may not earn an NBA roster spot. The players in the first category comprise the group that is of the greatest interest to this study and comprise the majority of the dataset. The sample also contains many of the players that gained free agency by release, as there is no clear way to differentiate between these groups. Rookie free agents are excluded from the data.

Given these parameters, it is the goal of this research to compare players that change teams via free agency to those the sign again with their current team, and to determine whether changing teams significantly impacts the salary when an NBA player obtains a new contract. To these ends, this study has focused on answering questions concerning which factors play a major role in an NBA player obtaining a more profitable contract as a free agent. Primary among these questions is whether or not changing teams as a free agent significantly impacts a player's ability to maximize his earning potential in their next NBA contract. Theoretically, a player who possesses a team-specific skill set that is highly valued by his current team would be more likely to garner a greater salary from that team, because they are a known quantity to that organization, than they would be if they chose to offer their services to one of the other 29 teams in the league.

Description of the Data

The primary data collected in this study are salary data for the 122 players for whom full data could be obtained, encompassing the 2005 class of

NBA veteran free agents. Included in this data are the total value and contract length for all new contracts that were signed following the 2004–05 season, and the player's contract value from his immediately previous contract. The length of the contract, in years, is used to produce the average annual salary for both the new and old contracts, and the difference is calculated along with the percentage change. The dependent variable becomes the percentage change in average annual salary for each player observation, facilitating a fixed effects regression model.

Several independent variables are used to gauge the impact on changes in a free agent player's salary. The key variable for the purpose of testing human capital theory is the transfer status of the player. Players who switched teams are designated by a dummy variable of value one. In theory, if the coefficient estimate is positive, then players transferring earn more, all else being constant. Moreover, if the coefficient is negative, players remaining with their original team earn more; and the hypothesis that firm specific human capital is rewarded is supported.

Independent variables that distinguish player productivity and characteristics are included. The NBA has guaranteed minimum salaries and operates these on a graduated scale, based on the player's tenure in the league (years of experience), elevating their minimum base pay for each additional year of service. This same scale also governs the maximum amount that a player can earn based on his tenure and, in part, dictates when a player is eligible for free agency. Years of experience is also closely correlated with the player's age. Professional athletes reach their peaks early and skills typically decline more rapidly with age, in comparison to other occupations. For these reasons, it is hypothesized that years of experience in the league would be a significant factor in determining salary change relative to free agency. The usual labor market formation includes variables measuring both experience and experience squared, as the relationship between experience and earnings is expected to be nonlinear.

Expected performance is highly correlated to compensation in team sports. Variables representing productivity are critical indications of the likelihood for salary variation. For this study, data measuring each player's average minutes played per game are utilized. With the fixed effects dependent variable measuring change in salary from the pervious contract, the issue here is to document the effect of a change in the player's production during his contract year—the last year of the player's contract; 2004–05 in this case. Many statistical methods of production available by which to evaluate NBA players exist. But, the individual's contribution to team production is crucial. For example, the NBA calculates a summary statistical measure for each player, the player efficiency rating (PER)—a simple difference between a player's positive statistical contributions and his negative statistics. Other researchers, including Berri (1999), have constructed linear weighting statistics using regression analysis to calculate the magnitude of specific individual statistics to team wins. The choice here is to evaluate production based on the club's, and coach's, evaluation of the player's production. Given the assumption that the coach's objective is to win, it can be assumed that the most productive players receive more playing time. Coefficients of correlation reveal that average minutes per game are in fact closely related to other summary statistics. For example, the coefficient of correlation for average minutes per game and the NBA's PER in the sample of 2005 free agents is 0.92. Notwithstanding, playing time is also an excellent proxy to determine if intangible factors not captured by statistical methods have a significant effect on the relationship between salary change and team changes.

Overall, the quality of a player's team is also theoretically important. Players employed by higher quality teams can be assumed to be in part responsible for team production. A low winning percentage would indicate a higher average minutes played per game, while a higher winning percentage would indicate fewer minutes per game for a similar player, all else being constant. In the case of high quality players, this is less likely to be significant as they would likely play significant minutes regardless of the quality of their team due to their skill level.

Contract length may also influence players' annual salaries; therefore, the term of the new contract is included as an explanatory variable. Traditional compensating wage differential theory implies that players would trade income for job security and accept a lower annual salary for additional years of guaranteed salary. Notwithstanding, Maxcy (2004b) suggested an alternative theory that firms and workers share market risk for uniquely skilled workers and higher annual salaries for athletes with multiyear contracts as firms are as willing as workers to absorb a risk premium. Kahn (1993) and Maxcy (2004a) found that Major League Baseball players with long-term contracts received higher annual compensation, all else being constant, suggesting that players who receive long-term contracts receive a salary premium.

As explained above, NBA teams are subject to a payroll cap each season. It may be expected that the willingness to make an offer to a free agent is influenced by a team's total payroll and relationship to the cap. In order to determine the effects of team payroll on player salary variation, data were also collected on each individual team's total spending on player salaries for the 2004–05 season. These data were then coded into three categories by which teams were labeled as low spenders ($20,000,000–$50,000,000), medium spenders ($50,000,001–$65,000,000), and high spenders ($65,000,001–$110,000,000). Low spenders comprise nine teams, while medium spenders markets register the middle twelve teams, and high spenders include the highest spending nine teams.

Due to the fractured nature of some of this information, particularly the salary data and length of contract, data are garnered from a number of different sources in order to compile the necessary information. The list of the free agents for the summer of 2005 is collected from ESPN.com's *2005 NBA Player Movement* chart, which lists each team's eligible free agents, where they had signed, as well as which players had signed with the listed organization. For confirmation, the data were cross-referenced with the unofficial *NBA Reporter* website (2005). NBA.com, the NBA's official site, is utilized to obtain 2004–05 team winning percentages, the player's previous and current teams, average minutes played per game in the 2003–04 and 2004–05 season, and each player's years of experience in the league directly prior to the start of the 2005–06 season. Storyteller's Salary website (2006) compiles the length of the players' 2006 contracts and their salaries. This information was cross-referenced with the data available at HoopsHype.com (2006). The corresponding data for the player's previous contract length and yearly salary were taken from *Patricia's Various Basketball Stuff* (Bender, 2006) and confirmed with NBA.com (2006) and Insidehoops.com (2006). The raw data were used to compile the total value of the contract through the yearly salary records. These data facilitated construction of a complete dataset for each player's previous and current contract length, and the total value was then used to construct the data that would serve as the dependent variable for this study—the percentage difference between the average annual salary of the previous and current contracts.

Empirical Model

The regression analysis of human capital compensation in the NBA employs a fixed effects model using ordinary least squares regression. The model is formulated as follows, and is tested for the full sample and each subsample omitting the transfer variable.

$$\text{DSALARY}_i = a_0 + a_1\text{EXPERIENCE}_i + a_2\text{EXPERIENCE}_i^2 + \\ a_3\text{DMPG}_i + a_4\text{WPCT}_i + a_5\text{TRANSFER}_i + \\ a_6\text{TERM}_i + a_7\text{TEAMSPENDi} + e \qquad (10.1)$$

$$\text{DSALARY}_i = a_0 + a_1\text{EXPERIENCE}_i + a_2\text{EXPERIENCE}_i^2 + \\ a_3\text{DMPG}_i + a_4\text{WPCT}_i + a_5\text{TERM}_i + \\ a_6\text{TEAMSPENDi} + e \qquad (10.2)$$

The variables are defined as in Table 10–1. Equation (10.1) represents the full sample model. Equation (10.2) is used to test separately the group of players that did and did not transfer, respectively.

TABLE 10–1
Variable Definitions

DSALARY$_i$: Percentage difference between the player i's previous year's
    average annual average salary (2004–05) year t-1 and new annual average
    salary based on the 2005–2006 contract
EXPERIENCE$_i$: Player i's years of experience in NBA prior to 2005–06
    season
EXPERIENCE$_i^2$: Player i's years of experience squared in NBA prior to 2005–
    06 season
DMPG$_i$: The percent change player i's average minutes played per game from
    the 2003–04 season to the contract year, the 2004–05 season.
WPCT$_i$: Regular season winning percentage of player's primary 2004–05 team
TRANSFER$_i$: Dummy variable coded 1 if player i moved to another team as
    a free agent following 2004–05 season; coded 0 otherwise
TERM$_i$: Player i's contract term signed in 2005 measured in guaranteed years
TEAMSPEND$_i$: 2005–06 franchise spending category 1, 2, or 3 based on
    coding of 2004–05 player payroll

e: disturbance term $E(e) = 0$ and $\text{Var}(e) = \sigma_e^2$.

Discussion of Results

The summary statistics are shown in Table 10–2 and include the subgroupings for transfers and nontransfers. Sixty percent (73 players) of the free agents transferred to new teams, and 40% (49 players) remained with their current team. The dependent variable, percent change in average annual salary, showed a mean increase of 127% for free agents (an average increase of more than $0.5 million) from 2004–05 to 2005–06. It is clear that the greatest increase came for free agents remaining with their teams. Percentage increases in salary increases for transfers were, on average, only about half of the increase for nontransfers—85% compared to 190%, respectively. Average contract length for the free agent class was slightly more than 2.5 years, and slightly more on average for those players not transferring teams, indicating that overall, those players returning to their current teams received more favorable contract terms that those who transferred. The free agents increased their playing time by an average of 25% over the previous season in 2004–05, before signing their new contracts. The increase in playing time was slightly less overall by players who transferred. The summary statistics imply that players not changing teams incur some financial advantage. The regression results provide substantiating evidence.

Regression results for the models are presented in Tables 10–3A to 10–3C. Durbin-Watson statistics revealed no significant autocorrelation in

TABLE 10–2
Summary Statistics

Variable	Mean	Standard Deviation	Minimum	Maximum
Full Sample				
122 Players				
TRANSFER	0.60	0.04	1.00	0.00
DSALARY	1.27	0.22	−0.89	11.84
EXPERIENCE	5.79	0.34	1.00	16.00
EXPERIENCE^2	47.51	5.05	1.00	256.00
DMPG	0.25	0.06	−0.80	3.12
WPCT	0.50	0.01	0.16	0.76
TERM	2.54	0.15	1.00	6.00
TEAM SPEND	1.88	0.76	1.00	3.00
Nontransfers				
49 Players				
DSAL	1.92	0.41	−0.55	11.26
EXP	5.69	0.57	1.00	16.00
EXPERIENCE^2	47.86	8.71	1.00	256.00
DMPG	0.30	0.10	−0.80	2.91
WIN	0.51	0.02	0.16	0.72
TERM	2.71	0.24	1.00	6.00
TEAM SPEND	1.84	0.10	1.00	3.00
Transfers				
73 Players				
DSAL	0.84	0.24	−0.89	11.84
EXP	5.85	0.43	1.00	15.00
EXPERIENCE^2	47.27	6.14	1.00	225.00
DMPG	0.21	0.08	−0.72	3.12
WIN	0.50	0.02	0.16	0.76
TERM	2.42	0.18	1.00	6.00
TEAM SPEND	1.90	0.09	1.00	3.00

any of the models. Coefficient estimates for the full sample (Table 10–3A) show the theoretically expected effect. The signs of the estimates for experience and its square indicate that while the rate of salary increase slows over a player's career, it does so at a declining rate, yielding the theoretical quadratic relationship. Increased playing time during the contract year has a positive and significant relationship to increase in salary. Notwithstanding, the quality of a player's team, as measured by win percent, also shows a positive effect, but it is not statistically significant.

TABLE 10–3
Fixed Effects Model OLS Results

10–3A. Full Sample N = 122
Dependent Variable DSALARY Mean = 1.27
$R^2 = 0.533$; Adj. $R^2 = 0.504$

	Coefficient Estimates	t-ratio	Probability Value
Constant	1.438	1.51	0.13
EXPERIENCE	−0.578[a]	−3.10	0.00
EXPERIENCE^2	0.025[b]	2.07	0.04
DMPG	0.522[c]	1.95	0.05
WPCT	1.137	1.07	0.29
TRANSFER	−0.669[b]	−2.05	0.04
TERM	0.807[a]	8.06	0.00
TEAM SPEND	−0.202	−0.93	0.35

10–3B. Nontransfers N = 49
Dependent Variable DSALARY Mean = 1.92
$R^2 = 0.576$; Adj. $R^2 = 0.515$

	Coefficient Estimates	t-ratio	Probability Value
Constant	0.945	0.51	0.61
EXPERIENCE	−0.708[b]	−2.11	0.04
EXPERIENCE^2	0.030	1.45	0.16
DMPG	0.489	0.88	0.38
WPCT	1.890	0.91	0.37
TERM	0.940[a]	5.21	0.00
TEAM SPEND	−0.048	−0.10	0.92

10–3C. Transfers N = 73
Dependent Variable DSALARY Mean = 0.84
$R^2 = 0.470$; Adj. $R^2 = 0.422$

	Coefficient Estimates	t-ratio	Probability Value
Constant	0.939	0.87	0.39
EXPERIENCE	−0.424[c]	−1.77	0.08
EXPERIENCE^2	0.018	1.07	0.29
DMPG	0.559[c]	1.89	0.06
WPCT	0.956	0.76	0.45
TERM	0.670[a]	5.36	0.00
TEAM SPEND	−0.351	−1.50	0.14

[a]Significant at the .01 level; [b]significant at the .05 level; [c]significant at the .1 level.

Consistent with the findings of Kahn (1993) and Maxcy (2004b), players signing a long term contract receive a premium, indicating that, like their Major League Baseball counterparts, NBA owners pay the risk premium when signing players to a long term contract. Team payroll has no discernable effect on player salaries.

Most notably, the negative coefficient estimate for player transfers is significant and consistent with human capital theory. Players who sign with their current teams receive a salary premium with raises 67% larger (approximately $1.3 million on average) than their like counterparts that change teams. This implies that such players are rewarded for firm (team) specific human capital. As stated, this may include traits such as demonstrated adherence to established organizational values, the player's personality, and its role in team chemistry and leadership skills.

Comparison of the two subsamples reveals additional differences between transfers and nontransfers. Those players that transfer are a more diverse group. The R^2 values indicate that the regression variables do not fit this sample nearly as well despite the larger number of observations. Additionally, with one exception, the coefficient estimates are weaker and less significant than is the case for nontransfers, indicating that players who switch are a less homogeneous group. The only one case where the coefficient estimate is stronger for transfers is increased playing time in the contract year. Free agent players with increased playing time in their contract year earn slightly larger raises when transferring teams. We assert that this supports the theory as increased playing time is an indicator of the intangible benefits a team desires when signing a free agent away from another franchise.

Conclusions and Suggestions for Further Research

Nine of the 122 players in the sample received salary increases in excess of 600%. None of these players had more than four years of experience and most were becoming free agents for the first time in their careers—seven fitting the category of rookie scale players. All nine of these players were productive in terms of minutes played, as four averaged more than thirty minutes per game and three more had more than twenty minutes per game. Most importantly, seven of these nine players re-signed with their previous club while an eighth, Joe Johnson, was acquired by the Atlanta Hawks in a sign-and-trade with his previous club, the Phoenix Suns. Conversely, ten of the twelve players included in the category of greatest reduction of annual salary, a decrease of 70% or more from their previous contract average, had a minimum of eight years of experience. Only three of these players averaged more than 30 minutes per game, and all twelve players changed teams.

The above illustrates a common pattern in professional sport; young players with the potential for many more productive years are rewarded with lucrative new contracts in terms of both salary and contract length. In the NBA, the Bird exception nearly always allows the player's current team to make the most lucrative offer, so these players are not likely to transfer. Players near the end of their careers accept pay cuts in order to maintain a roster spot with any team willing to take a chance on them. Nonetheless, giving consideration to the full set of players comprising this sample, a broad cross-section of players at various stages of their careers is represented. Controlling for both experience and productivity, it is seen that players who stay with their current team earn a significant salary premium. This is consistent with Becker's theory, and these players are earning a return on intangible team specific skills.

The present findings open the door for further research. The NBA's player labor market is now exceedingly international, but coaches and team management remain almost exclusively North American. As stated earlier, economic research on salary differentials in the NBA have typically focused on racial discrimination. It would be interesting to determine if the transfer and compensation patterns are different for foreign born or nonnative English speaking, free agent players. If such traits as leadership, response to coaching, and effect on team chemistry are important factors in the determination of team specific human capital, we should like to know if language and cultural background are influential.

References

Becker, G. (1975). *Human Capital* (2nd ed.). New York: National Bureau of Economic Research.

Bender, P. (2004). *Patricia's Various Basketball Stuff 2004–05 NBA Salaries.* Retrieved from http://www.dfw.net/~patricia/misc/salaries05.txt.

Bender, P. (2005). *Patricia's Various Basketball Stuff Detailed Contract Information.* Retrieved from http://www.dfw.net/%7Epatricia/contracts.

Bender, P. (2006). *Patricia's Various Basketball Stuff* General Site. Retrieved from http://www.dfw.net/~patricia/.

Berri, D.J. (1999). Who is most Valuable? Measuring the player's production of wins in the National Basketball Association. *Managerial and Decision Economics*, 20(8):411–427.

Berri, D.J., and Jewel, T. (2004). Wage inequality and firm performance: Examining a natural experiment from professional basketball. *Atlantic Economic Journal*, 32(2):130–139.

ESPN.com (2005). *2005 NBA Player Movement.* Retrieved from http://sports.espn.go.com/nba/news/story?id=2128722.

HoopsHype.com (2006). *2005–06 Salaries*. Retrieved from http://www. hoopshype.com/salaries.htm.

InsideHoops.com (2006). *NBA Salaries*. Retrieved from http://www. insidehoops.com/nbasalaries.shtml.

Jones, J.C.H. and Wlliams, D. (1988). Salary determination in the National Hockey League: The effects of skills, franchise characteristics, and discrimination. *Industrial and Labor Relations Review*, 41(4): 592–604.

Kahn, L.M. (1991). Discrimination in professional sports: A survey of the literature. *Industrial & Labor Relations Review*, 44(3):395–418.

Kahn, L.M. (1992). The effects of race on professional football players' compensation. *Industrial and Labor Relations Review*, 45(2):295–310.

Kahn, L.M. (1993). Free agency, long term contracts and compensation in Major League Baseball: Estimates from panel data. *The Review of Economics and Statistics*, 75(1):157–164.

Kahn, L.M. (2000). The sports business as a labor market laboratory. *Journal of Economic Perspectives*, 14(3):75–94.

Kahn, L.M. and Shah, M. (2005). Race, compensation and contract length in the NBA: 2001–02. *Industrial Relations*, 44(3):444–462.

Kahn, L.M. and Sherer, P.D. (1988). Racial differences in professional basketball players' compensation. *Journal of Labor Economics*, 6(1): 40–61.

Maxcy, J.G. (2004a). Motivating long-term employment contracts: Risk management in Major League Baseball. *Managerial and Decision Economics*, 25(2):109–120.

Maxcy, J.G. (2004b). Contract length as risk management when labor is not homogeneous. *Labour*, 18(2):177–189.

National Basketball Association (2006). Retrieved from http://www. nba.com.

NBAReporter.com (2005). 2004–05 NBA Salaries. Retrieved from http://users.pandora.be/nbareporter/freeagents20042005. htm#freeagentshuidig.htm.

Storytellers' Salary website (2006). Spreadsheet of Individual Player Salary Figures for 2005–06. Retrieved from http://home.earthlink.net/ ~jtkramer65/05-06salaries.htm.

Part III

Event and Voluntary Organizations

11

The Governance of the International Olympic Committee

Brenda Kübler and Jean-Loup Chappelet

For more than a century, international sport has mainly been governed by a network of nonprofit associations centered on the Olympic Games and the World Championships in various sports. This network has adopted the name of "The Olympic Movement," and its leading actor is the International Olympic Committee (IOC): a club of individuals that co-opts its own members and that was founded in 1894 by Pierre de Coubertin. Since the IOC's founding, the main task of the members has been to perpetuate the Modern Games. Despite the considerable evolution of sport during the 20th century and the increasing scale of the Summer and Winter Games, the IOC has continued to exist without major changes to its structure throughout what, in fact, proved to be a century that brought with it a great deal of upheaval. It was only in 1999 that the very foundations of the IOC suddenly trembled, as a result of around 20 of its members being involved in a corruption scandal related to the awarding of the Olympic Winter Games to Salt Lake City. It was also around this time that doping in, and violence during, sports events began to constitute a serious concern for governments, who realized that the Olympic Movement was unable to keep these issues under any real control. And so, at the end of the last century—and thanks to the media—the IOC suddenly found itself confronted with doubts regarding its legitimacy on the part of the public and the authorities (Chappelet, 2001).

We can situate the emergence of the term "governance" within Olympic circles around this same period, notably thanks to the influence of American journalists and sponsors. It was officially introduced within the

Olympic Charter in 2004 (IOC, 2004, Rule 19.3.2). This focus on governance is a result of the dysfunctions mentioned above but also, as of the 1980s, of the growing professionalism within Olympic organizations, and the increasing interest on the part of the various stakeholders—and in particular, nation states, the European Union, and the sponsors—in how the Olympic system functions (Chappelet, 1991). Although this system was one of the oldest ways of self-government by means of a network, with consensual, horizontal coordination mechanisms, its fragile equilibrium became threatened at the end of the century as a result of new types of public or commercial actors who wished to take part in its governance.

The question of the functioning of the IOC remained central within the new organization of world sport that saw the day at the dawning of the 21st century. This chapter is thus devoted to the governance of the IOC, and more precisely the governance of the enterprise that has become the IOC. As a nonprofit association the IOC is not, of course, a commercial enterprise in the usual sense, but it nevertheless owns several limited companies (see The IOC's Management below) and regularly deals with multinationals that are in turn subject to the rules of *corporate governance.* The IOC has no shareholders but is responsible for numerous contracted parties and, above all, it is accountable for its management of the Olympic ideal in the eyes of the public. Today, then, the IOC must draw inspiration from the rules of good governance: rules that are to an increasing extent required by those national or supranational governments with which it must cooperate in order to organize the Olympic Games, and more generally in order to promote a certain philosophy of sport, known under the name of "Olympism."

There are a number of approaches regarding the governance of an enterprise, and some specific research has been carried out on its application to sport organizations (Caiger and Gardiner, 2000; Chaker, 2004; EOC and FIA, 2001; Hums and MacLean, 2004; Katwala, 2000; Zölch, 2004). The work of Pérez (2003) will be used to structure this chapter. Pérez identifies five successive levels of governance—from the management of an organization to the legal and societal framework in which it operates—and these can also be applied to describe and analyze the current governance of the IOC (see Fig. 11–1). The specific organizational characteristics of the IOC and other entities related to its governance will be presented as needed. A conclusion will summarize the evolution of the IOC's governance in accordance with four well known criteria for good governance.

The IOC's Management

The IOC's daily management is carried out by its Administration (formerly termed the Secretariat), which unites all of the organization's

FIGURE 11–1. The IOC's 5 levels of governance

salaried staff and has been located in Lausanne (Switzerland) since 1915. Somewhat embryonic until the 1960s, it developed during the 1970s thanks to the boost provided by a director, Frenchwoman Monique Berlioux, and following the arrival of income from television broadcasting rights for the Olympic Games. That development gained impetus under Juan Antonio Samaranch's presidency of the IOC from 1980 until 2001, since its Administration grew from a staff of around thirty to around one hundred, with the arrival of specialists in various fields. From a managerial point of view, however, the most important development was Samaranch's decision to live and work in Lausanne and use the Administration as a base for his work and thus to become a full-time, executive president—which was not the case for his predecessors (with the exception, perhaps, of Coubertin). That decision led to the departure of Berlioux in 1985. The President nevertheless remained a nonremunerated official, even though all the expenses related to carrying out his mission and his residence costs in Lausanne (notably his hotel suite and taxes) were borne by the IOC. That arrangement continued with the election of Jacques Rogge to the presidency in 2001, since the idea of a salary for the future President—discussed in 2000—had been abandoned. In 2004, the presidential residence costs amounted to USD 397,000 and those for the Honorary President for Life (as Samaranch became in 2001) totaled USD 174,000 (IOC, 2005, p. 109).

With the arrival of Rogge, the quantitative and qualitative growth of the administration continued and in 2006 reached approximately 325 persons from about 30 countries. The average age of staff members is 37.5, and women represent 62% of the total (IOC, 2005, p. 20). This spectacular growth is partly due to incorporating the salaries of the Olympic Museum staff and those of other entities, which were previously not included, in order to remain below the arbitrary threshold of 100 employees laid down for the Administration by Samaranch.

Following several internal and external audits that were commissioned by Rogge over several years, the administration has today been restructured into 15 departments (here listed in the order as published in the Olympic Movement Directory (IOC, 2006)): Executive Office of the President, Office of the Director General, Olympic Games, International Cooperation and Development, Finance and Administration, Sports, Relations with the National Olympic Committees (NOCs), Technology, Communications, Information Management, Marketing, Legal Affairs, Medicine and Science, Olympic Solidarity, and Olympic Museum. A director heads each department; only one is a woman.

On a hierarchical level, the directors report to a director general, who in turn reports to the President. Two directors, however, occupy particularly key positions: the Chief of Staff, who handles all political questions and relations with the IOC members, and the Executive Director (the only director to have such a title) of the Olympic Games, who is in charge of the IOC's principal "product." These two directors and the Director General attend the meetings of the IOC's Executive Board (see the next section), while all the others are called upon to present their reports as and when needed. (Under Samaranch, they all attended the entire meetings scheduled.) The Director of Communication also plays an important role as the President's spokesperson. No organization chart of the Administration is published officially, but that shown in Figure 11–2 below is at times presented in public.

The Director General is appointed by the IOC Executive Board, and the other directors are appointed by the IOC President, who informs the Executive Board accordingly. The current Director General was appointed in 2003. Most of his directors had already been in place for some time. The directors hold a monthly Management Committee meeting, at times with the President, and have regular external one-day management seminars. Otherwise, they run their departments in a fairly autonomous manner. Staff units are, however, attached to the Director General for Human Resources and Corporate Development. The directors of the Olympic Museum and of Olympic Solidarity (the department that redistributes the sums due to the NOCs) have a greater degree of autonomy because they are geographically located outside the main headquarters in Vidy, and because of the nature of their activities. The Director of Olympic Solidarity also heads the NOC Relations Department.

In 2004, the operating costs for the IOC and its administration amounted to approximately USD 91 million (IOC, 2005, p. 87). For a detailed analysis of how the IOC is financed (expenditure, income, and assets), see

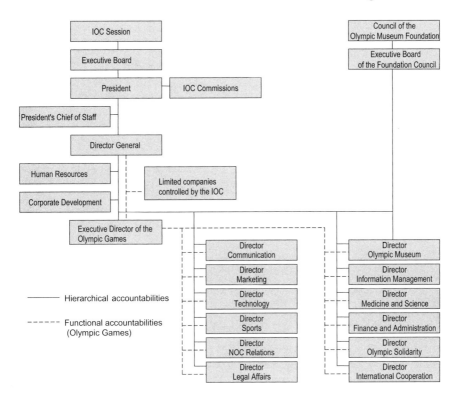

FIGURE 11–2. Organization Chart of the IOC

Chappelet (2006). The great majority of the IOC's assets are shared between two foundations subject to Swiss law that the IOC controls: the Olympic Foundation and the Olympic Museum Foundation. They are managed by the IOC administration. The latter owns the Olympic Museum, which is located in Lausanne and houses two of the IOC's departments: that of the Museum and that of Information Management. The Olympic Foundation accumulates the IOC's financial assets and owns several limited companies that are subject to Swiss law, of which two have a large number of employees: IOC Television and Marketing Services (formerly Meridian Management SA) and Olympic Broadcasting Services. The former, which provides services contractually promised to the IOC's sponsors, is managed by the IOC's Marketing Director and the second, in charge of producing the basic televised images of the Games, is headed by a former executive of the European Broadcasting Union. The two companies have Boards of Directors that are chaired by members of the IOC (respectively, the Chairmen of the Marketing Commission and the

Commission for the Coordination of the 2008 Games). The foundation boards (the supreme governing bodies) of the IOC's two foundations consist of members of the IOC Executive Board and are chaired by the IOC President (for the Olympic Foundation) and the Honorary President for Life (Museum Foundation). All these legal entities (foundations and limited companies) under the aegis of the association that is the IOC are known internally by the term "IOC Group."

There can be no doubt that the arrival of Jacque Rogge as the IOC President constituted a major turning point for the IOC on a management level, with the introduction of more solid structures and procedures and, above all, a change to a more technocratic style of management that is far more sensitive to questions of governance and risk management, yet less entrepreneurial and paternalist than that of the former President. A consolidation phase followed a strong period of expansion. At the same time, the role of the Director General became far less political in order to focus on operational issues and the management of the structure. The former Director General was, in fact, flanked by a Secretary General who handled administrative issues; that post was not filled when the last holder resigned in 2002.

Managing the IOC's Management

The second level of the governance of an enterprise according to Pérez (2003) begins with reflection on the managing of management. At the IOC, this level is handled by the institutional authorities elected by the members of the IOC association. These authorities are, in order of importance, the Session (i.e., the Annual General Assembly of the members, or the legislative body); the Executive Board (a kind of committee or sub-entity of the Session that plays an executive role); and the IOC President, who is the IOC's permanent representative.

These structures and their functions are laid down in the Olympic Charter. This document recalls the principles and values and also the rights and obligations of the components of the Olympic Movement. At the same time, it serves as the statutes of the IOC (notably its Chapter 2). The Charter is drawn up and modified according to the wishes of the IOC, meaning by its session and based on proposals by the Executive Board. It is made up of the fundamental principles of Olympism and 61 rules, at times accompanied by by-laws. Modifying a rule requires a two-thirds majority vote by the members, while a simple majority is sufficient for the by-laws. The text of the Charter was entirely reviewed and refined in 2004, as had already been the case in 1986. The rules concerning the members and the election of the Olympic Cities had been considerably revisited in 1999 (see the next section).

The IOC members assemble once a year for their session. During Olympic years, the meeting is held just prior to the Games in the Olympic city. Its decisions are sovereign regarding all issues concerning the running of the IOC and of the Olympic Movement that are brought to its attention by the Executive Board. The members' decisions include, notably, the attribution of the Host Cities for the Games. They also elect, from among their number, a President, four Vice Presidents and ten other members of the Executive Board, i.e., a total of 15 people. Four seats on the Executive Board are, in principle, reserved for the Presidents of the ANOC (Worldwide association of the NOCs), of the Athletes Commission, of the Association of the IFs whose sport is on the program of the Summer Games (ASOIF) and of its counterpart for the Winter Games (AIOWF). The terms of office are of four years, except for the President who is elected for eight years and who can be reelected for a further four (i.e., maximum 12 years). Samaranch remained in office as the President for 21 years; this was a major criticism against the IOC in 1999. The elections do not all take place simultaneously, meaning that the IOC members are constantly occupied with election campaigns within their numbers. Since 1999, with a view to transparency, the proceedings of the Session are broadcast by closed circuit television to interested journalists.

Below the sovereignty of the session, the Executive Board nevertheless enjoys extensive powers. "[It] assumes the general overall responsibility for the administration of the IOC and the management of its affairs. [. . .] it approves all internal governance regulations relating to its organization" (Article 19.3 of the Olympic Charter). It also controls the boards of the Olympic Foundation and the Olympic Museum Foundation, since these boards mainly consist of its members. It has a strategic function compared to that of the Administration, which is mainly responsible for operational issues, even though it is extremely difficult to separate the two dimensions and many board members are jealous of the considerable power of certain directors. The Executive Board is thus at the heart of the IOC's "management of the management," since it meets far more regularly than the session (held annually): usually four times a year or if specially convened by the President or by a majority of its members. In 2006, only one woman (a Vice-President) was a member of the Executive Board.

According to the Olympic Charter, the IOC President has far fewer powers than the Executive Committee. The 1999 reform enhanced this characteristic, which constitutes a strong difference between the IOC and a classical enterprise. Thanks to his presence in Lausanne and his daily involvement in management issues, however, he is able to make all kinds of decisions, and not only those that are urgent, as the Charter states. He must, however, in principle submit such decisions to the Executive Board or to the session as rapidly as possible. His main autonomous power is that of appointing the directors of the administration and the individuals who make up the various IOC Commissions (except for the Executive Board and the Athletes Commission, whose members are elected). He may also create commissions or dissolve nonstatutory ones. The role of nonstatutory commissions is to make recommendations to the Executive Board and the session. Each is assisted by an IOC director and serves, in a sense, as that director's supervisory board for his department. Some commissions, consisting of IOC members and external experts, form an official part of the governance authorities (those that are statutory, mentioned as such by the Charter and designated below by the letter "S"); the others play roles of varying importance within the management of the IOC management.

In 2006, the IOC had some 24 commissions for the following areas, uniting over 350 individuals (IOC, 2006): Culture and Olympic Education, Athletes (S), Ethics (S), Nominations (S), Women and Sport, Finance, Juridical, Marketing, Medical, Press, Olympic Program, Radio and Television, Olympic Solidarity (S), Sport and Law, Sport and Environment, Coordination of the Games in Preparation (3 or 4 commissions depending on the year), Olympic Congress, Philately and Memorabilia, International Relations, Television Rights, and New Media. When taking office as President in 2001, Rogge attempted to reduce the number of commissions that had existed at the time of his predecessor, but without real success. The commissions in fact permit their chairmen, who are all IOC members, to focus on a topic of interest to them. Rogge did, however, significantly reduce the number of their meetings, which today in principle take place in Lausanne and only once per year.

Certain commissions are nevertheless far more important than others: the Ethics, Candidature, Athletes, Finance, Television, and Solidarity Commissions. The first three will be presented in the following section since they relate to the IOC's regulatory processes or the management of its governance. The others are presented below.

The Finance Commission is a long-standing one, and its chairmanship is one of the most prestigious offices. It supervises the IOC's accounts and the management of its financial assets. It is assisted by professional auditors (PricewaterhouseCoopers for nearly 20 years, as a result of several renewed mandates). The Chairman cosigns the contracts with the elected Host Cities. Following the 1999 reforms, the IOC has published two reports covering four years of activity (with the somewhat strange name of "Final Reports")—for the periods 1997–2000 (IOC, 2001) and 2001–2004 (IOC, 2005). These public documents contain relatively detailed financials (balance sheet and accounts) that contribute toward a certain degree of transparency from the institution. The most recent report provides, for the first time, consolidated figures for the "IOC Group." We note, in particular, that the IOC under Rogge has adopted a policy of constituting financial reserves and of risk management thanks to insurance taken out against the cancellation of the Games: a policy clearly inspired by good governance practices for an enterprise.

Since 2006, the Finance Commission has been completed by an Audit Committee that has the same Chairman but whose secretariat is provided by the IOC President's Chief of Staff (and not the Director of Finance). This Committee functions as an internal control unit. A small group devoted to the issue of remuneration also existed from 2001 until 2005. Like their President, the IOC members are not remunerated for their work, but the expenses involved in accomplishing their mission are reimbursed and—at times—a fee is paid to them for a particular task. This group had been set up following the discovery by the new President that large amounts had been paid as remuneration under Samaranch's presidency, notably to the Chairman of the Marketing Commission. Since 2005, each member receives a lump sum of USD 5000 per year for office expenses, and the special remunerations appear to have disappeared.

Jacques Rogge has chaired the TV and New Media Commission since his election, thus demonstrating its importance. Today, it negotiates the broadcasting rights based on public tenders for two consecutive editions of the Games (Winter and Summer). This practice differs considerably from that under the previous President, who proceeded in a far less transparent manner and also granted rights spanning several Olympiads. A description of the former and current approaches, and of the IOC's managerial practices relating to marketing, is provided by Payne (2006, pp. 49–74), a former IOC Marketing Director.

The Olympic Solidarity Commission is also extremely important because of the budget it controls, i.e., USD 244 million for the period 2005–2008. This amount represents the portion due to the NOCs from the IOC's various revenues (mainly from television rights and from the marketing of the Games). The funds are used to assist the NOCs to accomplish their missions, and in particular those whose needs are the greatest. The eminence of this statutory Commission was reinforced by the Olympic Charter, which until its revision in 2004 specified that its Chairman should be the IOC President (Article 8.2). Perhaps to avoid any potential conflict of interest, Jacques Rogge preferred, from the outset of his period in office, that the responsibility be borne by the President of the ACNO (Worldwide association of the NOCs): first as "Acting Chairman," and then as Chairman as of 2005. Olympic Solidarity publishes full annual and quadrennial reports on how the funds are allocated, but the main question that remains open is that of how the expenses are accounted for at the sites receiving them. Controlling that aspect is extremely difficult from an Administration located in Lausanne and that does not have an army of individuals available to carry out checks.

We thus note that, with its Session and its Executive Board assisted by other Commissions, the IOC has mechanisms that permit it to manage its management, i.e., level two governance as described by Pérez (2003). These mechanisms have been strengthened since 1999, and to a large extent, are based on the IOC members. But who appoints and monitors the IOC members, and how? This central question for the governance of the institution is the subject of the following section.

The IOC's Regulatory Mechanisms

The main reforms implemented by the IOC in 1999, following the crisis that arose as a result of the Salt Lake City scandal, concerned its members. Until that point, few rules applied regarding their recruitment and their behavior. That state of affairs was severely criticized by the media, the sponsors, and the governments. Many of them saw it as being the very source of the IOC's governance problems, since the guardians of the Olympic temple were not guarded by anyone. To use the formula by Pérez (2003), what "management of governance" or what regulatory mechanisms could be proposed for the IOC in the new century?

Under pressure from the media, Samaranch created an ad hoc commission by the name of "IOC 2000" to reflect on the issue. It consisted of around 50 members, with IOC members and individuals from outside the Olympic Movement (such as Henry Kissinger and Giovanni Agnelli) in equal proportions. It worked at a rapid pace from March to December 1999, and its conclusions, symbolically united in the form of 50 recommendations, were all adopted by the IOC's (extraordinary) session held in Lausanne in mid-December 1999 (IOC, 1999). Those relating to the composition, structure and the organization of the IOC (numbered 1–12) and to the designation of the Host City of the Olympic Games (49–50) have been fully implemented. Recommendations 13–48, concerning the role of the IOC, have only been partially put in place. We shall now describe those that are directly related to regulatory mechanisms for the IOC members.

First of all, the number of members was fixed at a maximum of 115. The number had risen from around 15 to around 100 between the IOC's foundation and its centenary in 1994, but then rose to 130. In 2006, following the Turin Winter Games, the IOC had exactly 115 members, of which 15 were women. (The IOC suggested that, for the end of 2005, there should be a quota of 20% of women in all the decision-making structures of the Olympic Movement—a suggestion that is not being respected by the IOC itself.)

Of these 115 members, 15 hold executive offices (usually as President) of an International Sports Federation (IF) and 15 within a National Olympic Committee (NOC). The members admitted to these "reserved seats" lose their membership if they leave the corresponding office. A further 15 members are "active" athletes, i.e., having taken part in the Olympic Games less than eight years previously. For the other 70 members not subject to such a quota, it was decided that there could not, in the long term, be more than one per country as opposed to two per country until 1999. Many countries, in fact, have no members; in 2006, Italy and Switzerland had five (a record!). It is because no such restriction regarding nationality exists for members who are athletes or come from the IFs or NOCs. There has also been a case where an IOC member for his country (Un Yong Kim) was also the President of an IF (taekwondo) and of his NOC (South Korea).

The IOC stresses that its members do not represent their country, IF, or NOC at the IOC, but on the contrary, represent the IOC within their country and the institutions from which they came. This stance sometimes puts IFs and NOCs presidents in difficult positions. The Olympic Charter stipulates, moreover—but only since 1999—that the members do not take part in votes concerning their countries or one of its citizens (By-Law to Rule 18). For the rest, "Rules relating to conflicts of interest" were adopted in 2002 after difficult discussions during the Session held in Salt Lake City.

Each member is now elected for eight years, and membership is renewable. S/he ceases office at age 70, and if s/he has served for at least ten years, becomes an honorary member but with no right to vote. In the past, a member was elected on a permanent basis until age 80. Moreover, a seven-member Nominations Commission was created in 1999 to examine the quality of potential candidates, who may be proposed by an existing member or by an organization recognized by the IOC (including the IFs and the NOCs). This Commission recommends several individuals to the IOC Executive Board each year, and the Executive Board may propose them for individual election at the session. Elections are now held by secret ballot and by simple majority. One candidate proposed was in fact not elected in 2001. Prior to 1999, the IOC President proposed a list of names, and a genuine vote at the session rarely took place.

Twelve active athletes from the quota of 15 are subject to an election by their peers, by secret ballot at the Olympic Village (4 at the Summer Games and 2 at the Winter Games, over two Olympiads). The remaining three are proposed among members of the Athletes Commission, to guarantee a certain degree of balance regarding gender and geographical distribution and to include types of members who would not necessarily be elected. Candidate athletes are presented by their NOC (maximum one per country) if they are taking part at the current Games or if they took part in those preceding them, and if they have never been found guilty of doping. There were 15 candidates in Turin for two places, and 70.4% of the Olympic athletes voted. The elected athletes form part of the

Athletes Commission, which comprises 19 members, with the others being appointed by the IOC President. The elected athletes are confirmed as members by the session, at the end of the Games, and then presented to the public at the Closing Ceremony.

The IOC members have a series of rights and obligations that are laid down in the Olympic Charter. They must take an oath whereby they make a commitment to serve the Olympic Movement, to respect the Charter, to comply with the Code of Ethics, to remain free from any political or commercial influence, and to refrain from appealing IOC decisions (Rule 16.1.3). Apart from voting for a colleague wishing to become a member of the Executive Board, the main power of a member resides in his/her vote for a candidate city for the organization of the Games. In 1999, a few members wished to reduce this power drastically by entrusting the IOC Executive Board with this designation, or by imposing a single round of voting with relative majority. In the end, however, the members retained their main prerogative. The reforms relating to the designation process for the Olympic city in 1999 nevertheless led to a reduction in the number of finalists thanks to a preselection by the Executive Board. Members were also prohibited from visiting the cities concerned, and representatives of the cities were prohibited from visiting members in their countries. In principle, the only contact now authorized is at predesignated Olympic meetings.

The IOC's Ethics Commission is tasked with investigating whether the members and the cities respect these clauses. More generally, it is responsible for evaluating ethical behavior (with the exception of doping) on the part of the staff and members of the IOC, of athletes and officials taking part in the Games, of the NOCs, of the organizing committees, and of candidature committees for the Games. To do so, it edicts and applies a Code of Ethics that was adopted in 1999. Several members have already been excluded upon its recommendations, or have tendered their resignation. The Commission was created in March 1999, even before the other reforms relating to governance were set in motion, and was in response to enormous pressure on the IOC by the media and the American sponsors at the time. It consists of seven individuals, of whom a maximum of three are IOC members. The Ethics Commission has taken on considerable importance since its creation, notably since the election of Jacques Rogge in 2001. For a study of its first six years of existence, see Chappelet (2005). To summarize, one could say that the Ethics Commission has improved the governance of the IOC, but that there is still room for progress to be made with respect to its independence from the IOC and in particular from its President, and to its involvement in the selection process of the Host City (de Rendinger 2006, p. 244). Its role in the election of the IOC President in 2001 has also been criticized by a senior member (Pound, 2004).

The 1999 reforms made it possible to guarantee that a certain number of IOC members come from the main stakeholders of the Olympic Movement, i.e., the athletes, the IFs, and the NOCs. It would be possible to go even further on a level of representation, by imagining that all Olympians (those who have taken part in the Games at least once) or fans of Olympism—for example, via the Internet—could vote. (In 2002, the IOC did in fact launch an online system for finding ideas with a view to reducing the gigantism of the Games.) A World Olympian Association was founded in 1995 but has so far no particular role in IOC governance. In order for their voices to be better heard within the IOC's reform process, Canadian athletes founded OATH (Olympic Advocates Together Honorably) in 1999. The organization, financed by the Magna Corporation, has since disappeared. An organization along the lines of UN Watch, which has taken it upon itself to systematically check whether the United Nations Charter is applied by the UN system, could be envisaged for the IOC.

Certain authors, moreover, believe that the Olympic sponsors and the media that broadcast the Games should have a say regarding how the IOC is regulated. Based on agency theory, Mason et al. (2006) even propose incorporating all these stakeholders within a board that would supervise the session. The IOC members could not, of course, be in agreement with such a proposal, which would reduce their personal interests in being agents of the IOC. Having said that, however, the President of Samsung (an Olympic sponsor) and a Vice-President of NBC Sports (the broadcaster of the Games in the United States for twenty years) have been IOC members for many years. Other members are also closely connected with sponsors.

Harmonizing the Regulatory Mechanisms

As we have just seen, the Ethics Commission is, with the Nominations Commission, the IOC's main mechanism for managing its governance. But its authority goes well beyond the IOC members and staff, since the Code of Ethics is also applied to the NOCs, the organizing committees, and the candidature committees for the Games. Curiously, the IFs are not officially among the "Olympic parties" (sic) subjected to the Code of Ethics. Moreover, the sanctions stipulated by the Olympic Charter only relate to the participation of individuals or organizations in the Games. They do not affect other areas of sport. Several IFs and NOCs do, in fact, have their own ethics commissions and codes of ethics, or regulations concerning conflicts of interest, or even rules of good governance. This is the case, for example, of the IFs for cycling, football, wrestling, and volleyball (Chappelet, 2005) and the NOCs of the United States, The Netherlands, Italy, Slovenia, and Switzerland (Chaker, 2004, p. 29). Some national governing bodies also have their own regulatory bodies, such as the French Football Federation's National Ethics Council.

We could thus imagine, for example, that an IF or NOC President who is a member of the IOC would be sanctioned with regard to ethics by the IOC, but not by his IF or NOC—as a result of the disparities between the various regulatory texts or simply because of different interpretations among the regulatory entities concerned. Such a case almost arose with the International Volleyball Federation (FIVB) in 2004 (Chappelet, 2005). Here, the problem is one of harmonizing the regulatory mechanisms, or the "governance of the governance" to use Pérez's expression (Pérez, 2003).

This type of problem has already been encountered by international sport, in connection with doping. In 1999, it led to the creation of the World Anti-Doping Agency (WADA), a private foundation subject to Swiss law, controlled in equal parts by the Olympic Movement and the public authorities (Chappelet, 2002). One of the main objectives of the Agency is to harmonize the various sport and legislative mechanisms related to doping. At the time, the case of a cyclist from Sydney was frequently cited: he took part in the Tour de France cycling race that started in Gand, Belgium, and was thus subject to four or five different sets of regulations: Australian, French, Belgian (and Flemish), as well as those of the International Cycling Union. The beginning of a solution to this problem was reached, in 2003, with the adoption of the World Anti-Doping Code, signed by the IOC and all the IFs. This Code is in the process of being accepted by the various Member States, within their respective national legislation via the signature of an International Anti-Doping Convention adopted by the United Nations Educational, Scientific, and Cultural Organization (UNESCO) in 2005. WADA is considered to be an organization that is independent from the IOC, despite half its budget coming from the television broadcasting rights for the Games and the fact that its Chairman has, since 1999, been an IOC member. It therefore provides a private form of regulating the IOC's governance for the cases of doping it handles, i.e., those identified at the Games. On a more global level, WADA constitutes an international public–private partnership that symbolizes a new and better sport governance for the 21st century.

Citing WADA as a good example, Bourg and Gouguet (2004) believe that beyond codes and specialized agencies, a "supranational organization" that would be called, for instance, the United Nations Sport Program, could be tasked with protecting and regulating international sport, including the Olympic Games as a "global public good".

In addition to the divergences that can exist within the sport movement, we also note a harmonization problem between the IOC's governance rules and the national laws of the states where it operates and where its members live. On several occasions, the IOC Ethics Commission was forced to suspend its recommendations until state courts made decisions. This was the case, for example, for Guy Drut. In 2004, Drut, a French IOC member and Olympic gold medal winner, was found guilty of abusing public funds in an affair that was not related to Olympism and took place before he was elected to the IOC. He appealed against the court's decision and was finally granted a pardon by the French President. Subsequently the Ethics Commission recommended a reprimand for having tarnished the reputation of the Olympic Movement and an interdiction to chair IOC commissions for five years. Until a final decision is taken by the competent court, the Ethics Commission prefers not to make a final decision, for fear of reaching opposing conclusions. It simply proposes that the member be provisionally suspended. All that is legal is not, however, necessarily ethical. The Commission could thus, in theory, sanction a member who is judged to be innocent.

Contradictions between the IOC's rules of governance and Swiss law—under which it mainly operates—can also occur. Many IFs also operate under Swiss law. Two cases can be cited in this connection. The first dates from 1979 and concerns the problem of the "two Chinas." The Taiwanese IOC member at the time lodged a complaint before a court in the Canton of Vaud (whose capital is Lausanne) against the decision by the IOC's Executive Board to impose a change of name and of emblem on the NOC of his country in order to be allowed to continue taking part in the Games. The plaintiff also took advantage of his legal prerogatives as a member of a Swiss association to contest a decision that had not been voted upon by the General Assembly. The problem resolved itself two years later when the complaint was withdrawn. Following the incident, the members' oath was modified to indicate that they considered the IOC's decisions as being without appeal on their part. This clause is probably not valid before a Swiss court, but for the time being has avoided other complaints being filed by members against "their" IOC.

The second affair dates from 2003, and has not yet been resolved in the courts of Vaud. It concerns an Association by the name of "Gibraltar National Olympic Committee," which has been requesting recognition by the IOC as an NOC in its own right since the end of the 1980s. The Association fulfils the conditions that were required at the time of its application, notably before the IOC demanded that the territory concerned be "recognized by the International Community" (Rule 31 of the Olympic Charter). It criticizes the fact that the decision by the IOC has been so slow in coming; the IOC does not want to take a positive decision (which would not be accepted in Spain) or a negative one (which risks a negative outcome in a Vaud court because of the Charter that was in force at the time).

In its Olympic Charter, the IOC states that its decisions "are final." Any dispute relating to their application or interpretation may only be resolved by the IOC Executive Board, and in certain cases by arbitration, before the Court of Arbitration for Sport (CAS) (Rule 15.4). Since arbitration before the CAS is, however, subject to agreement by both parties concerned, it is clear that this clause by no means prevents the case from being brought before the Vaud courts and, if necessary, to the Federal Court (Switzerland's highest court) if the party opposing the IOC does not wish to resort to the CAS or if the IOC does not wish to do so.

Nonetheless, the CAS has in the past provided the IOC—and more widely sport organizations and athletes—with the possibility of avoiding state courts in Switzerland and elsewhere (Blackshaw et al., 2006). It has frequently been seized by athletes who contest decisions by the IOC or the IFs in relation to doping. (The World Anti-Doping Code has, moreover, declared it the supreme court once all internal appeal mechanisms have been exhausted.) The IOC, on the other hand, has rarely been able to impose recourse to the CAS within the contracts it signs with its commercial partners.

The CAS judges are appointed by an international council of sport arbitration, which itself is a foundation subject to Swiss law, and of which the IOC only designates one-fifth of the members. The structure functions within the framework of Swiss public order, and in particular the Swiss Federal Private International Law, which regulates questions of arbitration even though the parties can decide, jointly, to apply another national law. The CAS' independence has been acknowledged on two occasions by the Swiss Federal Court, which may nevertheless be seized in the case of an alleged procedural error (or, surprisingly, the Vaud Courts if both parties reside in this canton, as it was recently discovered following a doping case). During its activity, over more than 20 years, the CAS has incontestably contributed toward aligning sport regulations with natural law, and toward a certain degree of harmonization of the Rules of the Olympic sports organizations, which use it regularly and designate it as the supreme court for sport. Even FIFA, which wished to create its own court of arbitration, has recently accepted the role of the CAS. In this sense, the CAS indeed constitutes a mechanism for the governance of the IOC's governance (and that of the IFs).

The Metagovernance of the IOC

The IOC receives no subsidies from public authorities, which protects it from governmental pressure—unlike many NOCs. As already stressed, however, the IOC functions within the framework of Swiss legislation as an Association in accordance with Article 60 et. seq. of the Civil Code, or through its foundations and limited companies that are also subject to Swiss law. Admittedly, it was granted a special agreement with the Federal

Council (Swiss Government) in 2000 regarding its status, which, according to Latty (2001), makes it a subject (and not only an object) under international law. The fact remains, however, that the IOC—even if it benefits from certain privileges concerning its direct taxes and the recruitment of its staff—is not a fully-fledged international organization and does not benefit from a Headquarters Agreement that would provide it with the classical diplomatic privileges.

This situation could change with the vote on a new Federal Law on the Host State (Department of Foreign Affairs, DFAE, 2006), which the Parliament began examining in 2006. The law would permit the Swiss Government, without referring to its Parliament as it does at present, to grant certain "other international entities" (Article 2.1m of the draft) privileges, immunities, and other special waivers of Swiss law. From a governance point of view, this could permit the IOC to avoid any cases being filed against it in Swiss courts.

The IOC enjoys no specific protection in other countries and under other national legislations. It is mentioned every two years, within the Resolutions of the General Assembly of the UNO, with reference to the Olympic Truce; it has been mentioned in UNESCO resolutions concerning doping. It is recognized by the Treaty of Nairobi (1981) as being the owner of the Olympic symbol (interlaced rings). All that, however, does not give the Olympic Charter any legal power. There are even other, lesser-known texts that have greater legal scope: for example, the International Charter for Physical Education and Sport (adopted by UNESCO in 1978) or the European Charter for Sport and the Code of Ethics for Sport (adopted by the Council of Europe in 1992), or even the Declaration on Sport (adopted by the Council of the European Union in Nice, in 2000). The aforementioned texts are considered to be recommendations for the Member States. It should be noted that the European Code of Ethics for Sport has virtually nothing in common with the Olympic Code of Ethics; the problem is one of harmonization. Recently, the Court of Justice of the European Communities has declared that the IOC's rules on doping control fall within the scope of the Community competition law (CJEC, 2006). This prompted the IOC and IFs to organize a brainstorming meeting in September 2006 on the autonomy of sports organizations.

Sport is moreover mentioned within numerous national constitutions and in the draft European Constitution (not yet adopted). Such texts constitute the fundamental framework for the life of a nation's citizens, from which neither sport nor the IOC can be excluded. The IOC states, moreover, in the preamble to the Olympic Charter, several principles that can be found in constitutional texts and the recommendations of inter-governmental organizations: for instance, respect for "universal fundamental ethical principles," the preservation of human dignity, the right to practice sport being a human right, solidarity, nondiscrimination, the education value of sport, etc. This highly general framework remains at the base of the IOC's metagovernance.

Conclusions

As we have highlighted, the IOC's governance has evolved considerably since the end of the 20th century. This is partly thanks to the influence of the media and of public opinion that, in 1999, forced the IOC to carry out drastic reforms, but also to the determination of the new President who, as of 2001, introduced classical principles of corporate governance that had previously been virtually ignored on the part of the hundred-year-old organization.

It is possible to summarize that evolution by referring to the four pillars of governance that are well known and frequently cited in literature, notably regarding their application to the world of nongovernmental organizations: transparency, democracy, accountability, and predictability (see, for example, Schiavo-Campo, 1999). The first three concepts were, moreover, used by Jacques Rogge in his speech at the opening of a conference on the governance of sport in January 2001, a few months prior to his election as IOC President: "Since sport is based on ethics and competition on fair play, the governance of sport must comply with the highest standards in terms of transparency, democracy and accountability" (Rogge, 2001).

Regarding transparency, the IOC has made considerable progress over recent years. Despite being at the head of a massively mediatized event, the IOC remained—until the Salt Lake City scandal—an organization whose work was not widely known, and whose methods of functioning were somewhat secretive. As of 1999, the IOC authorized journalists to follow the proceedings of its annual session (although by means of a televised broadcast). For the last two Olympiads, the IOC has been publishing a report on its activities, including precise financial information. The Olympic Solidarity Department, which distributes the NOC's share of the funds, does the same. An extremely comprehensive institutional Internet site (www.olympic.org), totally reorganized in 2002 and equipped with a powerful search engine, makes it possible to find numerous official IOC documents (reports, press releases, statements, etc.). The meetings of the Executive Board nevertheless remain confidential, and the minutes of the various Olympic meetings are only accessible following an embargo of several decades.

Regarding democracy and, more generally, participation in the decision-making process, the IOC has worked in two main directions. First, it improved the representation of the main components of the Olympic Movement by means of reserved places for athletes and the executives of the NOCs and IFs (15 for each group). It has not gone so far as institutionalizing the Olympians' representation, or that of the sponsors of media. Secondly, it has implemented secret ballot procedures for all major decisions, notably for coopting new members. The duration of a member's period in office is now limited to eight years (which is already long for an NGO), although it can be renewed and the Presidents of the IFs and NOCs, who are IOC members in that capacity, tend to remain in office longer. We shall see, over coming years, whether a genuine rotation process takes hold within the IOC, or whether its members will cling to their functions. It is, in fact, as of 2007 that the members—who were all "re-coopted" in 1999—can be reelected after their first period in office of eight years, a period bestowed automatically in accordance with the new statutes.

The most striking changes accomplished have been those related to accountability, because that ground had not even been broken in the past. The "Olympic actors," and in particular the IOC members, are now accountable before the Ethics Commission in case of questionable behavior. The Ethics Commission has taken on considerable importance since 2001, under the direct aegis of the new President. It remains for the Commission to be exemplary in its functioning, to concentrate on the essential, to be more independent, and to proceed to a harmonization of ethic standards throughout the Olympic Movement.

Finally, the IOC's predictability and professionalism have been improving over several Olympiads, although certain decisions concerning the candidate cities for the Olympic Games are at times surprising. This process of professionalization, which began under Samaranch, has accelerated under Rogge. It is indispensable in order to maintain the IOC's independence toward its stakeholders (sponsors and the media) and toward governments. It is linked to managing the organization's performance, i.e., the achievement of strategic objectives defined by the IOC and its President and that go beyond the "simple" organization of the Olympic Games—even if this, the IOC's main responsibility, has become a far more complex affair.

The question that can thus be raised is why better governance would be advisable. It would appear, in fact, that the current focus of the organization's management is more on the form than the substance of the decisions taken. The example of the difficult and yet essential reform of the sports in the Olympic program is a striking one in this connection. (Baseball and softball were dropped in 2005 without being replaced.) Paradoxically, a better governance of the IOC would lead to worse leadership of it.

References

Blackshaw, I.S., Siekmann, R.C.M., and Janwillem, S. (Eds.) (2006). *The Court of Arbitration for Sport, 1984–2004.* Cambridge: University Press.

Bourg, J.-F., and Gouguet, J.-J. (2004). L'économie des Jeux olympiques. *Revue juridique et économique du sport,* no. 72, Septembre, pp. 107–126.

Caiger, A., and Gardiner, S. (Eds.) (2000). *Professional Sport in the European Union: Regulation and Re-regulation.* The Hague: Time Asser.

Chaker, A.-N. (2004). *Good Governance in Sport: A European Survey.* Strasbourg: Council of Europe. Also exists in French.

Chappelet, J.-L. (1991). *Le Système olympique.* Grenoble: Presses universitaires. Collection Sport en questions.

Chappelet, J.-L. (2001). Le Système olympique et les pouvoirs publics face au dopage et à la corruption: partenariat ou confrontation? In: *Sport et ordre public* (J.-C. Basson, Ed.). Paris: La documentation française, collection. IHESI—La sécurité aujourd'hui, pp. 215–234.

Chappelet, J.-L. (2002). L'Agence mondiale antidopage, un nouveau régulateur des relations internationales sportives. *Relations Internationales,* no. 111, pp. 381–401.

Chappelet, J.-L. (2005). Une commission d'éthique pour la gouvernance du mouvement olympique. In: *Ethique publique,* 7(2):132–143.

Chappelet, J.-L. (2006). The economics of the International Olympic Committee. In: W. Andreff and S. Szymanski (Eds.) *Handbook on the Economics of Sport.* London: Edward Elgar, Chapter 22.

CJEC (2006). *The International Olympic Committee's rules on doping control fall within the scope of Community competition law.* Press Release 65/06, Luxembourg, July 18.

de Rendinger, A. (2006). *Jeux Perdus. Paris 2012, pari gâché.* Paris: Fayard.

DFAE (2006). *Projet de loi fédérale sur les privilèges, les immunités et les facilités, ainsi que sur les aides financières accordés par la Suisse en tant qu'État hôte. Rapport explicatif.* Berne: Department of Foreign Affairs (DFAE).

EOC and FIA (2001). *The Rules of the Game. Conference Report & Conclusions.* Available at www.governance-in-sport.com.

Hums, M.A., and MacLean, J.C. (2004). *Governance and Policy in Sport Organizations.* Scottsdale, AZ: Holcomb Hathaway.

IOC (1999). *Report by the IOC 2000 Commission to the 110th IOC Session.* Lausanne, December 11 and 12.

IOC (2001). *IOC Final Report 1997–2000.* Lausanne: IOC.

IOC (2004). *Olympic Charter. Version in force as from 1 September 2004.* Lausanne: IOC.

IOC (2005). *IOC Final Report 2001–2004.* Lausanne: IOC Communication Department.

IOC (2006). *Olympic Movement Directory.* Lausanne: IOC Communication Department.

Katwala, S. (2000). *Democratising Global Sport.* London: The Foreign Policy Centre.

Latty, F. (2001). *Le Comité international olympique et le droit international.* Paris: Montchrestien.

Mason, D.S., Thibault, L., and Misener, L. (2006). An agency theory perspective on corruption in sport: The case of the International Olympic Committee. *Journal of Sport Management,* 20(1):52–73.

Payne, M. (2006). *Olympic Turnaround.* London: Business Press Limited.

Pérez, R. (2003). *La gouvernance de l'entreprise.* Paris: La Découverte. Collection Repères.

Pound, R. (2004). *Inside the Olympics.* Montreal, Canada: Wiley.

Rogge, J. (2001). Governance in sports: A challenge for the future. In: EOC and FIA (Eds.), *The Rules of the Game. Conference Report & Conclusions.*

Schiavo-Campo, S. (Ed.) (1999). *Governance, Corruption and Public Financial Management.* Manilla: ADB Press.

Zölch, F.A. (2004). Corporate governance in sport. In: U. Scherrer and F.A. Zölch (Hrsg.), *Sportveranstaltungen—im Fokus von Recht und Wirtschaft.* Zürich: Orell Füssli, pp. 93–112.

12

Structural Factors Influencing the Volunteer-Professional Staff Relationship in Large-Scale Sporting Events

Milena M. Parent and Trevor Slack

Most of the literature on volunteers and their involvement in sporting events has focused on issues of motivation and/or commitment. For example, Farrell, Johnston, and Twynam (1998), in a study of volunteers at the Scott Tournament of Hearts (a women's national curling championship), found that motivation could be grouped into four factors: purposive, solidary (sic), external traditions, and commitments. Caldwell and Andereck (1994), in a study of a recreational organization, described three categories of motivations or incentives for volunteering. These were (1) purposive incentives related to doing something useful and contributing to society; (2) solidary incentives based on social interaction, group identification, and networking; and (3) material incentives including tangible rewards, such as perks and memorabilia. Andrew (1996) talked of volunteer recruitment and employment guidelines to determine volunteers' effectiveness. Results identified autonomy, just wanting to be involved, and effective communications as components of motivations and expectations. Green and Chalip (1998) argued that the recruitment and retention of sport event volunteers is a marketing problem: the volunteer opportunity has to be presented in a positive light to recruit and retain sport volunteers.

In a novel approach, Solberg (2003) tried to put a value on volunteers' work at sporting events using the Opportunity Cost Approach (OCA) and the Market Price of Equivalency model (MPE). Results indicated a low displacement of other goods and services in both the formal and informal economic sectors. He found that a large number of volunteers enjoy volunteering and therefore get psychological rewards. Buying parallel services to volunteers, i.e., hiring staff, is suggested to be expensive.

Strigas and Jackson, Jr. (2003) explored the demographics and motivational factors in sport volunteerism. They found a five-factor model to explain volunteer motivation in marathon running events: purposive, leisure, external influences, material, and egoistic. Their study stands somewhat in contrast to those mentioned above in that it draws on organization theory, as opposed to organizational behavior, to focus on the way in which volunteers affect the organization and are affected by it. Instead of focusing only on individuals—as does the organizational behavior approach—organization theory allows the researcher to explore how a given aspect of the organization works, such as its design or what processes are present.

Most research on sport event volunteers (such as the papers presented above) has focused on volunteers working only during the actual Games. Other research involving sport volunteers looks at volunteer boards and volunteer organizational structures. For example, Kikulis, Slack, and Hinings (1992) described three design archetypes for sport organizations (kitchen table, boardroom, and executive office) based partly on the ratio of volunteers to paid professional staff in the organization's structure.

Nevertheless, rare is the research article that discusses the volunteer's relationship with paid professional staff or professionals. Two notable exceptions exist. Amis, Slack, and Berret (1995) examined conflict found between volunteers and paid professional staff in Canadian national sport organizations. They found conflict to be partly a consequence of structural characteristics of the organization. The second exception is Colyer (2000), who finds evidence of tensions between volunteers and professional staff in sport organizations, suggesting the presence of subcultures. The author does, however, acknowledge that the findings only touch the tip of the iceberg relating to the study of culture and sport organizations.

We take up the organizational theory approach used by Strigas and Jackson, Jr. (2003) and the works of Amis et al. (1995) and Colyer (2000) on the volunteer-professional staff relationship, but in organizing committees of large-scale sporting events. As such, the purpose of this chapter is to determine structural factors influencing the volunteer-professional staff relationship in large-scale sporting events. The findings in this chapter offer organizational- and individual-level structural factors, thus linking organizational theory and behavior. By virtue of the exploratory nature of the study, we first describe the setting, data collection, and data analysis techniques. Results are then presented and discussed.

Methodology

To explore the structural factors influencing the volunteer-professional staff relationship in large-scale sporting events, an exploratory case study approach was used (Eisenhardt, 1989; Yin, 2003). This approach allows for a greater understanding of a context in order to allow issues to emerge (cf. Glaser and Strauss, 1967). First, a description of the setting used is provided, followed by a description of the data collection and analysis techniques.

Setting

The 1999 Pan American Games were held in Winnipeg, Manitoba, Canada from July 23 to August 8, 1999. The Games were organized by the Pan American Games Society, or PAGS, which was created in 1994. There were 4949 athletes from 42 countries across the Americas participating in 35 Olympic sports and six non-Olympic sports across 22 venues. There were 2266 technical officials and technical support officials, more than 20,000 volunteers, 2000 media, and 500,000 spectators also taking part (PAGS, 1999). These Games were the third largest in North America after the Los Angeles and Atlanta Olympics.

Data Collection

Building the case study was done through the use of archival material and interviews. This allowed for richer data as well as results triangulation for increased construct validity (cf. Miles and Huberman, 1994; Yin, 2003). Archival material included organizational websites, organizational documents (e.g., meeting minutes, final reports, and a volunteer daily diary), commemorative documents, and media reports. A total of 99 documents were collected. Field notes were developed throughout the data collection phase and were included in the archival material as they are a part of the case study's database (Miles and Huberman, 1994; Yin, 2003).

Semi-structured interviews were conducted with 17 organizing committee members distributed in the following way: nine volunteers and eight professional staff representing three different hierarchical levels. Eight stakeholder interviews were also conducted with representatives of the Canadian governments, the community, the media, delegations, and sport organizations. A combination of purposive and snowball sampling was used for the interviews and for obtaining the archival material (Miles and Huberman, 1994).

Fifteen interviews were conducted face-to-face but ten interviews had to be conducted by telephone because of time and geographical constraints. Interviewees provided their informed consent prior to interviews. They were notified ahead of time of the nature of the research. This allowed them to refer to documentation they had in order to refresh their memory since interviews were conducted four years after the event (cf. Golden, 1992, 1997; Miller, Cardinal, and Glick, 1997).

Interviewees were asked to describe the organizing committee and their role within or in relation to the organization. They were also asked to describe issues they had to face. Particular attention was paid to the mention of the volunteer-professional staff relationship: how they described it and what issues (if any) were raised. Prompts were used to elaborate on this relationship.

All interviews were transcribed verbatim (cf. Arksey and Knight, 1999; Denscombe, 1998). Verbal emphasis by interviewees was transcribed with the emphasized word(s) typed in capital letters. Archival material was transformed into electronic format if need be. Texts were formatted into Rich Text Format in preparation for data analysis. A preliminary description of the case was written to develop an understanding of the setting and actors before data analysis started.

Data Analysis

A total of 324,677 words were analyzed using ATLAS.ti 5.0 through pattern-matching and inductive content analysis (cf. Henderson, 1991; Silk, 1999; Yin, 2003). Data were coded for all references to volunteers and professional staff. A list of issues related to the volunteer-professional staff relationship was established. Next, issues were grouped into related areas dictated by the data.

Throughout the whole data analysis process, we let the data indicate the issues/areas to discuss by determining those that were recurring and therefore significant (cf. Eisenhardt, 1989; Yin, 2003). From the 324,677 words, data related to volunteers and professional staff comprised 346 pages. This was then distilled down to key volunteer-professional staff relationship issues and management areas. The areas and issues managed could then be grouped into categories, as they related to structural factors, specifically organizational design and personal (individual) resources.

Results and Discussion

For large-scale sporting events, such as the Pan American Games, both volunteers and professional staff were needed to plan and deliver them. The data indicated that the volunteer-professional staff relationship was impacted by a number of structural factors. Each structural factor is described below as it was presented during interviews and in the archival material.

Organizational Design

A factor that influences both professional staff and volunteers is the organizational design. Careful thought must be given when determining the design of the organization and of each division, as divisions have different needs and, thus, will need different ratios of volunteers and professional staff to be more effective. For example, the division dedicated to recruiting volunteers will naturally be more inclined to organize itself using a majority of volunteers, whereas the division dedicated to operations will be more inclined to organize itself using a majority of professional staff by virtue of the nature of the work. However, it is essential to create links between the different divisions so as to coordinate activities (cf. Lawrence and Lorsch, 1967). Coordination is further described in a subsequent subsection. As respondents noted:

> There's not one particular model that fits every division of the Games. There are certain areas where volunteers will take a bigger leading role and there are certain divisions where staff will take a bigger leadership role (PAGS Volunteer).
>
> If I was going to sit down and invent a Games and structure things, first of all, I'd get my own internal act in gear. I'd get my system of coordination of staff and those functions (and that relationship). I would get that in place . . . You really need to have good working relationships internally or else it just falls apart (PAGS Staff).

Clear definitions of volunteer and professional staff roles and responsibilities must be established from the outset to avoid duplication, frustration, and confusion. "As a group, [the division] could have been developing the policies and procedures, selecting the sites and operating the sites. This would reduce any duplication of tasks, functions, and communication gaps" (PAGS Documentation). Volunteers and professional staff must have equal standing in the organizing committee by virtue of the mutually supportive roles. This allows work to be delivered and timelines to be followed. As one volunteer noted:

> ONE of the things that I think we struggled with in the early part, was a CLEAR definition of what staff would do and what volunteers would do. As it turned out, and as we worked our way through it, we managed to get that kind of sorted out, at least in the division I was responsible for. My suggestion to ANYBODY organizing these things is that they take a GOODLY amount of time and sort out the relationship between the organizing committee, the volunteers, the staff (PAGS Volunteer).

Clarity of structures and of volunteer/professional staff roles and responsibilities may balance differences in commitment and motivation between volunteers and professional staff (cf. Caldwell and Andereck, 1994; Chang and Chelladurai, 2003; Farrell et al., 1998; Slack and Hinings, 1992; Strigas and Jackson, Jr., 2003) and avoid potential structurally-related conflicts (cf. Amis et al., 1995). Such clarity relates to differentiation and coordination within the organization's design (cf. Lawrence and Lorsch, 1967) and formalization of roles and responsibilities, which therefore become control mechanisms (cf. Braveman, 1974; Clegg and Dunkerley, 1980). These mechanisms can therefore save event managers critical time and resources, which should be dedicated to hosting the event and not to solving internal problems. As such, clarity is a strategy for conflict management in large-scale sporting events.

While professional staff have control over the day-to-day issues, volunteers must also have positive control or operational responsibilities so as to ensure the Games time implementation of the plans established by the professional staff and to ensure equal standing of the volunteers and professional staff, i.e., to not let the control over decision making result in increased power for one group or another (cf. Macintosh and Whitson, 1990; Slack and Parent, 2006). As respondents noted:

> As a staff member, I was more the day-to-day in dealing with that kind of stuff. [The top volunteers] were dealing more with directing the volunteer team for the venue. I would deal more with them and then they would filter to their volunteer team (PAGS Staff).
>
> I wanted to make sure that, at the end of the day, that on a POSITIVE basis, the volunteers in the community who were going to organize the Games had control over the exercise, not negative control but positive. I wanted to make sure that, at the end of the day, that if the event was going to proceed forward and a decision had to be taken, the decision had to be taken by the volunteers who were going to make the Games work (PAGS Volunteer).

This control, however, is difficult to manage. More precisely, once the bid is successful, the first structure to be established is the (volunteer) Board of Directors, which sets out the general, overall direction for the organizing committee and the Games. Then the professional staff take over to translate those broad plans into operational plans. Finally, the volunteers once again take over to deliver the actual Games. These transitions mean changes in who has control. Understanding that these changes will occur helps the organizing committee balance the work and avoid control struggles. As one volunteer noted:

> At the beginning it's all about volunteers, right, and then it goes to a level where the staff start to take it over because they're working with it, [spending] more and more time. Then at the end of this, it has to be delivered by the volunteers; and staff have to let go. So it's

a real slippery slope trying to manage all that and [the] transition from one phase to another. And each part of the organization happens at a different rate; you've got some at different times. It can go back and forth. So it's a real balancing act (PAGS Staff).

Managing the transitions means managing not only potential conflict but also changes. What the preceding quotes indicate is that within this organizing committee, there are two types of changes occurring simultaneously: structural/systemic changes and people (human resources) changes. These changes are inevitable—the organizing committee must be ready to host the world by the opening ceremonies. Moreover, unlike enduring organizations, the pace of change in organizing committees continually increases, thereby being ever more revolutionary in nature, as compared to evolutionary (cf. Greenwood and Hinings, 1996). Therefore, managing change is essential. Resistance to change must be minimized through such strategies as participation and involvement, communication and education, idea champions (leadership), and facilitation and support (cf. Burgelman, 1983). The organizing committee did, in fact, use such change management strategies.

Both professional staff and volunteers must be held accountable for their actions and for the success of the event, a task more difficult in regards to volunteers as they are not paid organizational members. "It was impossible to hold volunteer committees accountable for missed deadlines" (PAGS Documentation). Yet, "ultimately the volunteers are accountable but the staff have to deliver" for them (PAGS Staff). This accountability therefore balanced the involvement and participation of both volunteers and professional staff.

Moreover, having volunteers and professional staff means that both are impacted by policies, rules, and procedures instituted in the organization. Bureaucracy is inevitable. So, too, is the need for both to control their budgets, separating the needs and wants. However, by virtue of the professional staff being responsible for the day-to-day aspects, they should also be responsible for the overall resource management during the planning stages. As noted by interviewees:

We continually had to do a 180-day goal, an operational review, and a budget review, the accountability of the Games. I know that that was really IMPORTANT in order to make sure that we were sticking to budgets and protocols and policies etc. But it was just A LOT of paper pushing and A LOT of work . . . So if I were ever chair in a Games—or staffing, being the head staff person—I would want to make sure that we minimized the bureaucracy. You need to keep the accountabilities but just minimize them, yet be true to them, be honorable to them (PAGS Volunteer).

Staff were responsible for developing the standard levels of service and resource allocation within existing budgets, which comprise the overall divisional plan. Staff were responsible for ensuring that the plan to deliver the Games was created, resourced, and fully delivered by the volunteers (PAGS Documentation).

Strong leadership must also be built into the organizing committee structure. It must include a strong leader for the volunteers, the Chairman of the Board of Directors, for example, and a strong leader for the professional staff, the Chief Operating Officer (COO), for example, in order to coordinate professional staff, volunteers, and the professional staff-volunteer relationship, another structural coordination technique. As volunteers noted:

The Chair of the Games was absolutely infectious. That I would say is NUMBER ONE ABOVE ALL: to have the volunteer chair of the Games be a man or a woman who has the CHARISMA to DARE TO DREAM. And dare to dream so damn big that it ASTOUNDS the community, and then just NOT STOP until it happens. [The Chairman] had credibility from both the sport and the corporate angle; and the volunteer community. But whenever I saw him—and we happened to be friends anyway—but whenever I saw him, the amount of stroking he would do of just REASSURING me that I was ABSOLUTELY critical to the Games, which is not true, I was not critical, but I mean he just had that ability to make you feel like you were that linchpin to make the whole thing successful. So I would say, above all, number one, you've got to have somebody at the top who first of all has charisma and can bring a whole table together under that vision and who has the smarts to hire the best people for the job (PAGS Volunteer).

Originally, we were set up as 10 separate divisions and there was [the] President and the Vice-President [who] left early on and we never filled that position 'til [the COO]. To me, I remember several times talking with [the Chairman] and [the President] about it "we need someone coordinating the 2 sides" ... When [the COO] came, it made a big difference, he really took that position because he was on early [as the Chief Financial Officer] but with the reorganization, THAT made a huge difference (PAGS Volunteer).

Finally, the organizing committee must determine who has ultimate authority to resolve conflicts between volunteers, professional staff, and volunteer-professional staff. As noted in the PAGS documentation:

Conflict between senior staff and volunteers did arise in some cases where personnel decisions were involved. If future Games were to operate on a similar basis it should be clear who is ultimately responsible for hiring and firing staff . . . Another area of conflict related to differing recommendations coming forth from different committees or divisions. Both volunteers and staff should be clear on who has ultimate authority in resolving such conflicts. Flexibility and a tolerance for ambiguity are requirements of all staff and volunteers and should be taken into consideration when making appointments and defining roles (PAGS Documentation).

Although Schriesheim, Von Glinow, and Kerr (1977) are writing about professionals in bureaucracies, their arguments could equally well apply to the organizational design of sporting events. They suggested that rather than the dual hierarchy that is used here where two groups (e.g., professional staff and volunteers) are vying for control of an organization's design, triple hierarchies (where a person is liaising between the two hierarchies that exist in the current design) are a more effective option. Despite the fact that respondents did not refer to this type of design, it is an option for those who run sporting events.

Even though communication and coordination are both a part of an organization's design and are influenced by it, we treat each separately as respondents referred to each when talking about the relationship between professional staff and volunteers.

Communication. Communication is an essential aspect of the volunteer-professional staff relationship. A large part of communication is the information flow between professional staff and volunteers. As one PAGS volunteer noted:

> I felt there were bad or ineffectual communications [in PAGS, so] you really need to have good working relationships internally or else it just falls apart. You need information to flow. I just think that was a HUGE difficulty with the '99 Games: not knowing certain key things and that would affect what you were doing, but you wouldn't have known about it. Information didn't flow very well. It was protected by certain people (PAGS Volunteer).

Therefore, communication flow patterns must be built into the organizational design for it to be effective. As well, it is easier to communicate volunteer-to-volunteer and professional staff-to-professional staff than volunteer-to-professional staff: "especially [when] dealing with volunteers because it's easier [for] a volunteer talking to a volunteer than it is for a professional staff person telling a volunteer what to do" (PAGS Staff). As one senior professional staff member mentioned:

> As Senior Vice-President, I would deal more with [top volunteers] and then they would filter to their volunteer team. You know, volunteer-to-volunteer works so much better than staff-to-volunteer. And having a volunteer at the lead level that you can work with who understands "this is what we have to achieve, and we have to convey this to the volunteers, we want them to do this, we don't want them to do this or whatever" is paramount and just makes life really an awful lot easier (PAGS Staff).

Communication is not only essential before and during the Games but also after the Games. A post-event evaluation by both volunteers and professional staff at all levels is an often forgotten task; yet, it is often stated as an essential task for knowledge transfer to future organizing committees. As one professional staff noted:

> My biggest BEEF on behalf of myself as a staff person AND on behalf of some key volunteers who were involved prior to Games time is that we weren't ever asked afterwards our opinion or to submit in any way to a discussion forum or a written evaluation or anything but we were in fact pretty much dropped like a hot potato. A lot of staff people had a very bad taste in their mouth when the Games were over because they felt that part of the problems we experienced leading up to and during Games time with poor organization and communication management was because certain people were trying to keep the information for themselves so that they would have a job following the Games (PAGS Staff).

Highlighting the importance of communication (information, pattern, and time) allows us to extend and combine the literature relating to volunteer-professional staff relationships and event management. More precisely, while Amis et al. (1995) suggested that structural interdependence and lack of influence in the decision-making process lead to conflict between volunteers and paid professional staff, we add that these structural aspects must be managed through relationship building, thus through good communication patterns. We also support the suggestions in the event management literature relating to the proposed importance of post-event communication (e.g., Getz, 1997), with an emphasis on post-event evaluation by all organizing committee members. In so doing, we strengthen the event management literature by bringing in organizational theory concepts, and we extend organization theory's applicability to large-scale sporting events.

However, our organization theory approach to the volunteer-professional staff relationship also allows us to see similarities between volunteers and professional staff, instead of just differences, as much of the research using an organizational behavior approach has done. More precisely, previous research using a largely organizational behavior approach has shown that volunteers and staff differ in their needs (e.g., Inglis, 1994), values (e.g., Schultz, 1996), and organizational commitment (e.g., Cuskelly et al., 1999). Yet, our findings indicate that in at least one area, communication, volunteers and professional staff are similar. Both volunteers and professional staff see communication as essential for effective and efficient event management.

Coordination. Structure and communication allow coordination and cooperation to occur, but it must consciously be done at each level. In order for the Games to happen, a spirit of compromise and good faith must be in place; a team approach is essential. As noted:

> Because the Games are put on by volunteers, the Host Society [PAGS] must find ways to insure that everyone is engaged—in a meaningful way—thus, compromise and negotiation are critical to keeping everything on track. If the Games were a corporate entity, one might deal in a different manner; but they are not (PAGS Volunteer).
>
> The reality is that you are building a major enterprise from scratch within a set time frame and it cannot succeed without the staff and volunteers approaching the task in a spirit of compromise and with a healthy measure of good faith. An event of this magnitude is no place for inflexible or overly "principled" people. Neither does it sufficiently or fairly represent the hundreds of thousands of hours of work put in by the staff and volunteers, nor could it ever (PAGS Documentation).

The presence of a coordination factor influencing volunteer-professional staff relationships supports previous research such as Amis et al. (1995) who found interdependence to be a source of conflict and Auld (1997) who found reciprocity as existing in the volunteer-professional staff relationship in relation to decision making. We extend these findings to the large-scale sporting event setting. However, the present findings add that coordination, interdependence, or integration mechanisms are also a way to decrease volunteer-professional staff conflicts.

The presence of the communication and coordination issues also supports Colyer's (2000) evidence of tensions between volunteers and professional staff in sport organizations. Part of the tensions found in the present study stem from the lack of time spent on determining an appropriate design and role definition for both volunteers and professional staff. We therefore extend Colyer's findings by proposing that design, communication, and coordination may influence the formation of subcultures.

The approach suggested in the present study also supports findings in other areas using volunteers and professional staff. For example, Wandersman and Alderman's (1993) study on the American Cancer Society indicated the need for negotiation and diplomacy to have a good relationship between volunteers and professional staff. Addington-Hall and Karlsen's (2005) study on staff and volunteers in voluntary hospices also pointed to the need for mutual support and motivation, components of good coordination.

Personal Resources

Not only do organizational design, communication, and coordination impact volunteer-professional staff relationships, so too do the individuals' resources that they bring with them to an organizing committee. Personal resources include competencies, abilities, contacts, and knowledge. As one volunteer noted: "We certainly had the skills, management, proven ability to execute, and knowledge to access resources (public or private) to get the necessities done. Winnipeg is a small community with a successful Pan Am history" (PAGS Volunteer).

For top volunteers, personal resources must also include their community networks and connections. As professional staff members noted: "Some of the volunteers were extraordinarily supportive. They were really good. Lots of good advice and connections and networking and whatever called upon, they always came through" (PAGS Staff). "The volunteers from within are one of the best systems for sharing info and getting the word out and building community connections" (PAGS Staff).

While the tendency for organizing committees is to recognize the work of Games time volunteers, pre-Games time volunteers and professional staff also wish to be recognized for their work. As respondents noted:

Recognizing your volunteers EVERY STEP of the way. And one of [the Volunteer Chair's] committees was recognition and their whole job was to make sure that the volunteers were stroked all along the way; setting up a system to recognize them. And it sounds ridiculous but I mean if you're going to ask people to spend 5 years or 2 weeks of their time, you have to make them feel that they're very valuable (PAGS Volunteer).

Here's another tip on the recognition side of things. I don't feel [pre-Games] people were ever really properly recognized for the ENORMOUS efforts that they put in because the focus on recognition became for Games time volunteers . . . These [pre-Games time] people were never OFFICIALLY really recognized in my opinion, even to the extent that some of them (laugh) will still say one of their pet peeves was they could never get business cards for presenting themselves in the role they played for the Games (PAGS Staff).

The presence of personal resources as influencing volunteer-professional staff relationships allows the previous research using an organizational behavior approach—mainly the sport volunteers' commitment and motivation literature (e.g., Cuskelly et al., 1999)—to be tied into organizational theory factors. More precisely, individuals' reasons for volunteering or the reasons individuals are recruited to do so, such as an individual's specific skills or network of contacts, may not only have an impact on whether the individual has a positive experience and stays with the organizing committee until the end of the Games (cf. Andrew, 1996; Caldwell and Andereck, 1994; Farrell et al., 1998; Strigas and Jackson, 2003), but may also have an impact on how that individual works with other volunteers and professional staff members. As Hickson et al. (1971) noted, this access to personal resources makes volunteers nonsubstitutable and, hence, able to manage uncertainty.

The findings in this chapter therefore bring an organization theory perspective to the examination of the volunteer-professional staff relationship in large-scale sporting events, highlighting both organizational- and individual-level structural factors and their impact on the volunteer-professional staff relationship.

Conclusions

When preparing and hosting large-scale sporting events, both volunteers and paid professional staff are essential in order to balance work load/complexity and cost of human resources. Having both volunteers and professional staff drive the preparations for the event creates a dynamic that may be unique to this particular setting. This chapter set out to explore the structural factors influencing the volunteer-professional staff relationship in large-scale sporting events.

This relationship in large-scale sporting events is impacted by a number of structural factors (the organizing committee's design, communication, coordination, and members' personal resources). We explored each of these factors as they pertain to large-scale sporting events. While design is the largest component of these factors, it works in tandem with communication and coordination. Communication involves the flow of information between professional staff and volunteers. It is easier to communicate volunteer-to-volunteer than professional staff-to-volunteer. Top volunteers must therefore support the professional staff's efforts and communicate those efforts (and any other messages) down to lower-level volunteers. Communication does not stop with the closing ceremonies of the Games.

A post-Games evaluation, which includes all levels of volunteers and professional staff, is important to these individuals (they have a voice) and may help future organizing committees avoid making the same mistakes. The coordination component relates to cooperation, compromise, and good faith on both sides of the volunteer-professional staff relationship. A team approach must be used so as to not waste important resources, such as time and money, through intergroup competition.

Another type of factor is the volunteers' and professional staff members' personal resources. This includes their skills, abilities, and knowledge. Volunteers are also recruited and placed in high positions within the organizing committee because of their network of contacts and their abilities to get to key individuals/organizations within the community in order to access necessary resources for the Games. Regardless of whether individuals are volunteers (pre-Games or Games time) or professional staff, they want to, and must be, recognized for their efforts in preparing and delivering the Games.

Individuals who are part of an organizing committee choose their type of involvement (volunteer or paid staff) based on different reasons. However, this study shows that certain individuals are recruited or become involved because of certain personal resources they may have (i.e., skill-set or network of contacts). This, therefore, creates an inelastic demand (imperfect substitution) (cf. Duncombe and Brudney, 1995) between Games volunteers and professional staff. Future organizing committees must be careful when hiring individuals; they must determine whether their job situation, skill-set, and network of contacts are better served as volunteers or as professional staff.

In sum, this chapter, unlike previous research, has explored those structural factors that may impact a volunteer-professional staff relationship. Future research now needs to further examine the various structural factors identified in this chapter, as well as other organization theory components, such as power/politics, organizational culture, and organizational environment, in order to understand in greater depth the factors influencing the volunteer-professional staff relationship.

References

Addington-Hall, J.M., and Karlsen, S. (2005). A national survey of health professionals and volunteers working in voluntary hospices in the UK. II. Staff and volunteers' experiences of working in hospices. *Palliative Medicine,* 19: 49–57.

Amis, J., Slack, T., and Berrett, T. (1995). The structural antecedents of conflict in voluntary sport organizations. *Leisure Studies,* 14: 1–16.

Andrew, J. (1996). Motivation and expectations of volunteers involved in a large scale sports event—a pilot study. *Australian Leisure,* 7: 21–24.

Arksey, H., and Knight, P. (1999). *Interviewing for Social Scientists. An Introductory Resource with Examples.* London: Sage Publications.

Auld, C.J. (1997). Professionalisation of Australian sport administration: The effects on organisational decision making. *European Journal for Sport Management,* 4: 17–39.

Braveman, H. (1974). *Labor and Monopoly Capital.* New York: Monthly Review Press.

Burgelman, R.A. (1983). A model of interaction of strategic behavior, corporate context, and the concept of strategy. *Academy of Management Review,* 8: 61–70.

Caldwell, L.L., and Andereck, K.L. (1994). Motives for initiating and continuing membership in a recreation-related voluntary association. *Leisure Science,* 16: 33–44.

Chang, K., and Chelladurai, P. (2003). Comparisons of part-time workers and full-time workers: Commitment and citizenship behaviors in Korean Sport Organizations. *Journal of Sport Management,* 17: 394–416.

Clegg, S., and Dunkerley, D. (1980). *Organization, Class, and Control.* London, UK: Routledge & Kegan Paul.

Colyer, S. (2000). Organizational culture in selected Western Australian sport organizations. *Journal of Sport Management,* 14: 321–341.

Cuskelly, G., Boag, A., and McIntyre, N. (1999). Differences in organisational commitment between paid and volunteer administrators in sport. *European Journal for Sport Management,* 6: 39–61.

Denscombe, M. (1998). *The Good Research Guide for Small-Scale Social Research Projects.* Buckingham, UK: Open University Press.

Duncombe, W.D., and Brudney, J.L. (1995). The optimal mix of volunteer and paid staff in local governments. *Public Finance Quarterly,* 23: 356–384.

Eisenhardt, K.M. (1989). Building theories from case study research. *Academy of Management Review,* 14: 532–550.

Farrell, J.M., Johnston, M.E., and Twynam, G.D. (1998). Volunteer motivation, satisfaction, and management at an elite sporting competition. *Journal of Sport Management,* 12: 288–300.

Getz, D. (1997). *Event Management & Event Tourism.* Elmsford, NY: Cognizant Communication Corporation.

Glaser, B., and Strauss, A.M. (1967). *The Discovery of Grounded Theory: Strategies for Qualitative Research.* New York: De Gruyter.

Golden, B.R. (1992). The past is the past—or is it? The use of retrospective accounts as indicators of past strategy. *Academy of Management Journal,* 35: 848–860.

Golden, B.R. (1997). Further remarks on retrospective accounts in organizational and strategic management research. *Academy of Management Journal,* 40: 1243–1252.

Green, B.C., and Chalip, L. (1998). Sport volunteers: Research agenda and application. *Sport Marketing Quarterly,* 7: 14–23.

Greenwood, R., and Hinings, C.R. (1996). Understanding radical organizational change: Bringing together the old and the new institutionalism. *Academy of Management Review,* 21: 1022–1054.

Henderson, K. (1991). *Dimensions of Choice: A Qualitative Approach to Recreation, Parks and Leisure Research.* State College, PA: Venture.

Hickson, D.J., Hinings, C.R., Lee, C.A., Schneck, R.E., and Pennings, J.M. (1971) A strategic contingencies' theory of intraorganizational power. *Administrative Science Quarterly,* 16: 216–229.

Inglis, S. (1994). Exploring volunteer board member and executive director needs: Importance and fulfillment. *Journal of Applied Recreation Research,* 19: 171–189.

Kikulis, L., Slack, T., and Hinings, C.R. (1992). Institutionally specific design archetypes: A framework for understanding change in national sport organizations. *International Review for the Sociology of Sport,* 27: 343–370.

Lawrence, P.R., and Lorsch, J. (1967). *Organization and Environment.* Boston: Harvard Graduate School of Business Administration.

Macintosh, D., and Whitson, D.J. (1990). *The Game Planners: Transforming Canada's Sport System.* Montreal and Kinston, Canada: McGill-Queen's University Press.

Miles, M.B., and Huberman, A.M. (1994). *Qualitative Data Analysis: An Expanded Sourcebook* (2nd ed.). Thousand Oaks, CA: Sage Publications.

Miller, C.C., Cardinal, L.B., and Glick, W.H. (1997). Retrospective reports in organizational research: A reexamination of recent evidence. *Academy of Management Journal,* 40: 189 204.

PAGS (1999). *XIII Pan American Games: PASO Report.* Winnipeg, Canada: PAGS.

Schriesheim, J., Von Glinow, M.A., and Kerr, S. (1977). Professional in bureaucracies: A structural alternative. *TIMS Studies in the Management Sciences,* 5: 55–69.

Schultz, J.B. (1996). An investigation of the beliefs and expectations that lead to role conflict and role ambiguity amongst volunteers and staff in volunteer organizations. Unpublished research report. Brisbane, Australia: Griffith University.

Silk, M. (1999). Local/global flows and altered production practices: Narrative construction at the 1995 Canada Cup of Soccer. *International Review for the Sociology of Sport,* 34: 113–123.

Slack, T., and Hinings, C.R. (1992). Understanding change in national sport organizations: An integration of theoretical perspectives. *Journal of Sport Management,* 6: 114–132.

Slack, T., and Parent, M.M. (2006). *Understanding Sport Organizations: The Application of Organization Theory* (2nd ed.). Champaign, IL: Human Kinetics.

Solberg, H.A. (2003). Major sporting events: Assessing the value of volunteers' work. *Managing Leisure,* 8: 17–27.

Strigas, A.D., and Jackson, E.N., Jr. (2003). Motivating volunteers to serve and succeed: Design and results of a pilot study that explores demographics and motivational factors in sport volunteerism. *International Sports Journal,* Winter: 111–123.

Wandersman, A., and Alderman, J. (1993). Incentives, costs, and barriers for volunteers: A staff perspective on volunteers in one state. *Review of Public Personnel Administration,* 13: 67–76.

Yin, R.K. (2003). *Case Study Research: Design and Methods* (3rd ed.). Thousand Oaks, CA: Sage Publications.

13

A Typology of Sponsorship Activity

Peter Thompson and Richard Speed

Sponsorship is attracting increasing academic research interest outside the confines of specialist sport and sponsorship journals. A number of mainstream journals have published special issues examining sponsorship-related topics [*Asia-Australia Marketing Journal* (1997), *International Marketing Review* (1997), *Psychology and Marketing* (1998, 2001), *International Journal of Advertising* (1998), *European Journal of Marketing* (1991, 1999), and *Journal of Advertising Research* (2001)]. In addition, papers examining sponsorship-related topics have appeared in a number of regular issues of mainstream journals (Clark, Cornwell, and Pruitt, 2002; Cornwell, Weeks, and Roy, 2005; Johar and Pham, 1999; Klincewicz, 1998; McDaniel, 1999; Speed and Thompson, 2000).

This academic interest is in part a reflection of the increasingly significant role of sponsorship in the marketing activities of firms. Sponsorship spending has increased significantly around the world, and although reported figures of sponsorship expenditure must be viewed with some care given the confidentiality of most contracts, there can be no doubt that global expenditure on sponsorships and associated activities constitutes a significant proportion of corporate communications budgets.

Marketing activities are being subject to scrutiny over the ability to deliver commercial outcomes; and as pressure is increasing for the marketing discipline to provide meaningful metrics, the sponsorship industry retains a strong focus on the importance of evaluating its effectiveness in delivering sponsors' objectives. As research into how sponsorship has an effect continues (Cornwell, Weeks, and Roy, 2005) and the combinations of sponsorship resources and objectives grow in complexity and variety, the ability to accurately compare sponsorship opportunities in different circumstances becomes increasingly important to researchers and organizations involved in sponsorship planning and implementation.

This chapter will propose a typology of sponsorship activities, the purpose of which is to describe "ideal types" of sponsorships that provide the most efficient combination of sponsorship resources for achieving particular sponsorship objectives. This typology should serve as a research tool for the comparison of sponsorship activities; it should provide an impetus to further sponsorship research and it should provide an important strategic tool for sport organizations in their planning, development, and packaging of sponsorship rights.

We define sponsorship as the exchange of resources between sponsor and sponsipient for mutual benefit; the benefit to the sponsor being the receipt of rights of association, which give access to resources that will assist in the achievement of commercial corporate objectives. We offer the term sponsipient as an alternative to "sponsee" or "property" and define sponsipient as the recipient of sponsorship.

If we consider the observation that expertise in sponsorship implementation can become a resource-based competitive advantage for sponsors (Amis, Pant, and Slack, 1997; Amis, Slack, and Berrett, 1999; Fahy, Farrelly, and Quester, 2004) in conjunction with the idea that sponsorship can be characterized as a business-to-business relationship (Farrelly and Quester, 2003), it can be argued that competence in development and packaging of sponsorship resources can become a source of competitive advantage for sponsipients as well. It is advantageous from the point of view of both sponsor and sponsipient to share a common understanding of the ideal set of sponsorship resources required to serve any particular corporate objective when negotiating and jointly implementing resource-based sponsorships.

From the sport organizations' perspective, their dependence on sponsorship revenue requires them to be adept at satisfying sponsors and delivering on their objectives. To aid this, the language of interaction between sponsor and sponsipient needs to be precise, and an understanding of the most efficient use of sponsorship resources to achieve objectives needs to be shared. This allows sponsors to be efficient in their choice of sponsorship resources and encourages sponsipients to be parsimonious and appropriate in their construction of sponsorship packages.

Observing the activities of sponsors from the marketplace, we do not know the strategies upon which their practices are based, nor do we know how well companies integrate these activities into an overall communications strategy [see Cornwell and Maignan (1998) for a review of sponsorship research]. Through the media, we know that event sponsors vary widely in the rights they seek and the activities they undertake in attempting to extract maximum benefits from these resources; however, we have no tools that identify where comparison between sponsorships is appropriate and where it is not. Researchers have made explicit calls for such tools (Cornwell and Maignan, 1998).

In answer to such calls, we offer a typology of sponsorship activity that provides a basis to explain the differences we see between sponsorships. Our objective is to create a framework to ensure greater generalizability of sponsorship research in the future and to articulate an explicit connection between the resources offered by the sponsipient and the objectives of the sponsor.

Taxonomy and Typologies

The objective of taxonomic approaches is to identify a "natural" (or at least defensible) grouping of cases as a mechanism to aid research. It is rarely an end in itself [see Tiryakian (1968) for discussion of the development and history of taxonomic approaches in the social sciences]. Once cases are successfully classified, researchers may use the classification for prediction, for instance as an independent variable in prediction, or as moderator of the relationship between two other variables. The classificatory process can be carried out in two ways—either *post hoc*, by measuring similarities and differences within a sample, or *a priori*, by using a classification scheme derived from some conceptual framework.

An *a priori* classification scheme consists of explicit decision rules that create a mutually exclusive and exhaustive set of groups of empirical cases. The term "typology" is reserved for *a priori* classification schemes that create a mutually exclusive and exhaustive set of ideal types. The existence of ideal types has particular implications in the use of typologies. First, they are extreme, abstract cases that might conceivably exist in real cases but should not be expected. Hence, they do not represent categories, since all empirical examples are expected to deviate from the ideal. We, therefore, do not propose that this typology should be used to generate classifications of cases. What is significant is the degree to which a case is similar or dissimilar to an ideal case. Thus, we propose that this typology be used to generate a measure of deviation from each ideal type.

Typologies highlight the relationship between the internal consistency among the constructs used in their development within an ideal type and the dependent variable (Doty and Glick, 1994). Ideal types represent cases where a particular configuration among these constructs is achieved, and so a particular effect on the dependent variable is hypothesized. Failure to achieve a configuration conforming to an ideal type represents a degree of dissimilarity to that ideal type. Hence, the same effect on the dependent variable is no longer hypothesized to occur.

With these observations in mind, we seek to propose a typology of sport sponsorship activity. We believe this is an important step in assisting researchers and managers to identify more clearly best practices in sport sponsorship, and to allow systematic examination and testing of alternative methods of sponsorship implementation. Doty and Glick (1994, p. 232) define a typology as "a conceptually derived interrelated set of ideal types . . . each of which represents a unique combination of the . . . attributes that are believed to determine the relevant outcomes." In this case, the relevant outcome is the performance of the sponsorship. In the following sections, we seek to identify the attributes of sponsorships that might be utilized in defining a set of ideal types, and identify the implications of this typology for both empirical and conceptual research. We also discuss the implications for sponsorship practitioners.

Sponsorship Characteristics

The term "sponsorship" is used to cover a wide range of activity. Our definition: "the exchange of resources between sponsor and sponsipient for mutual benefit; the benefit to the sponsor being the receipt of rights of association that give access to resources that will assist in the achievement of commercial corporate objectives" emphasizes that sponsorship is a resource-based activity that centers upon the concept of value exchange. It illustrates that sponsorship is not altruism, nor is it philanthropy. It implies that sponsors need to engage in activity in addition to entering into a sponsorship in order to achieve their objectives.

If sponsorship decisions are the outcomes of a deliberate, strategic process intended to achieve some rational objective, then sponsorship activities that are observed in the marketplace represent the implementation of this sponsorship. Hence, the sponsorship activities undertaken should be determined by the objectives set.

The resources available will also limit the activities undertaken. Any strategic decision process seeks to achieve the objective given the constraints imposed by the resource availability. Hence, in understanding the actions of sponsors, it is important to recognize that the resource base for any sponsorship campaign are the rights that are granted to the sponsor by the sponsipient.

In the interests of parsimony, we have concentrated this typology on the sponsorship of events, although many of the principles outlined are applicable to other forms of sport sponsorship.

Targets and Objectives

Various authors (e.g., Abratt, Clayton, and Pitt, 1987; Thwaites, 1995; Apostolopoulou, 2004; Tomasini, 2004) have investigated the possible

TABLE 13–1
Sponsorship Targets and Objectives

Target	Objective
Consumers	Raise awareness, impact brand attitudes and perceptions, stimulate trial and sales
Channel Members	Raise awareness, impact brand attitudes and perceptions, garner distribution commitment, develop trade relationships
Employees and Management	Impact brand attitudes, motivation, improved internal relationships
Community and Government	Raise awareness, impact brand attitudes and perceptions, demonstrate involvement in community, enhance relationships
Competitors	Exclude from opportunity

commercial objectives set for sponsorships. We have categorized objectives on the basis of targets in Table 13–1. In general, targets for sponsorships can be classified as consumer or nonconsumer. When the target of the sponsorship is consumers, the objectives are brand-related or sales-related. Typically, consumer-based objectives are to increase brand awareness, to have some impact upon brand attitudes and perceptions, to stimulate trial or to win sales.

Nonconsumer targets of sponsorship are channel members, the employees and management of the sponsor and the government or community with which the sponsor interacts. A third subdivision of targets is that containing competitors, in that a competitor becomes a target of the sponsorship if the objective of the sponsorship is to block a competitor from having the opportunity to sponsor the event.

Resources

Sponsorship contracts can provide a wide variety of resources that may be used in pursuit of a corporate objective. These resources are summarized in Table 13–2.

A primary sponsorship resource is one that achieves its effect as a result of the event occurring, and where no further investment by the sponsor is required. A secondary sponsorship resource is a resource provided to the sponsor that requires additional investment to achieve its effect. Some resources have an impact at the event because they can be seen by those

TABLE 13–2

Primary and Secondary Sponsorship Resources

Primary Resources	Definition
Naming right	Brand name becomes part of event name
Signage	On-ground and on-broadcast exposure of sponsor name through signs at venue
Equipment logos	On-ground and on-broadcast exposure of sponsor name through signs on equipment
Equipment used	Use of sponsor's equipment in the event
Speech	The right to make presentations/speeches at the event

Secondary Resources	Definiton
Sponsor status	Association of brand name with event in event promotion, publicity and media coverage
Event identifiers	The right to use event identifiers
Hospitality	Access to hospitality at the event
Seating	Access to seating at the event
Unique opportunity	Access to participants during event
Exclusive sale	The sole right to sell product through event outlets
Samples	The right to distribute product samples at the event
Product info	The right to distribute product information at the event
Merchandising	The right to develop event related products
TV ads	The right to advertising slots during event telecast
TV footage	The right to use event footage in subsequent advertising
Endorsement	The right to use the event or participants as product endorsers
Player visit	The right to use participants for in-house motivation/ presentations/coaching
Player appearance	The right to use participants for in-store appearances

attending the event. Media coverage of an event increases the audience of the event and, thus, the size of the target audience of primary resources. Some primary resources can be leveraged by added investment, but as these resources will have an effect without such leveraging, they remain primary resources.

Sponsors can build these sponsorship resources into their own promotional activity either as the basis of sponsorship-themed marketing communications or to engage in what Cornwell (1995) calls "sponsorship-linked marketing" (p. 15). Both these sets of activities are described as sponsorship "leveraging." Such activities are intended to increase the benefits obtained through the sponsorship association. It is the resources that are being leveraged, and we define those resources that require leveraging to have an effect as secondary resources.

Conceptual Framework

We see the role of this typology as explaining the performance of sponsorships as a consequence of the consistency among the constructs used in their development. We propose that the performance of a sponsorship is conditional upon the consistency between the objectives set for the sponsorship and the resources available to implement the sponsorship. The typology we propose is a set of ideal types, and these ideal types represent situations where such consistency is achieved. There is a fundamental assumption that the ideal type describes the achievement of the objective with the least use of resources.

The managerial decision-making literature has long recognized the implications for performance arising from the relationship between a firm's objectives and resources. We know that managers must employ their resources to best assist them to achieve their objectives. We also know that managers must set objectives that can be realistically achieved using their available resource base. The achievement of consistency between objectives and resources is a fundamental element in the strategy-making process. The "resource view" of the firm proposes that it is the deployment of resources that is the basis of sustainable competitive advantage. We define sponsorships as exchanges of resources, and successful sponsorships occur because firms treat them as such and develop strategic competencies around specific sponsorships (Amis, Slack, and Berrett, 1999). As providers of these resources, sport organizations have a critical role in developing the bundle of resources offered to firms, and it is critical for the mutual achievement of objectives that sport organizations develop a parallel competence in understanding the strategic value to the sponsor of the resources being exchanged.

In sponsorship, as in any aspect of marketing strategy, consistency between objectives and resources creates greater effectiveness and efficiency, and so impacts on sponsorship performance. For any given objective, there are resources that enhance our ability to achieve that objective, so improving effectiveness. There are also resources that do not affect our ability to achieve that objective, but if these resources must be paid for, then efficiency declines. Similarly, a given resource set might be better suited to the pursuit of one particular objective rather than another. Pursuing the wrong objective using that resource set reduces effectiveness. A given resource set might contain resources that are well suited to the pursuit of one particular objective along with resources that are not suited to the pursuit of that objective. In this case, the additional resources are redundant and efficiency is reduced.

The Dimensions of Classification: Targets and Objectives

The resources that are available to sponsors have different values depending on the objectives sought. In identifying consistency between objectives and resources, we classify resources on the basis of two dimensions. The first dimension is the target of the sponsorship; that is, whether those resources relate to event attendees, or whether they relate to a wider audience of nonattendees. This classification is relevant whether targets are consumers or not. The second dimension is the nature of the objectives sought. For consumers we assume a hierarchy of effects model for the impact of sponsorship [although Cornwell, Weeks, and Roy (2005) suggest a number of alternatives], and as such, the objectives can be to change awareness, to have an impact upon brand image, or to stimulate trial or purchase.

   With regard to nonconsumer targets, it is legitimate for sponsors to have brand awareness and image impact objectives for channel members and members of the community and government. These objectives will be satisfied using the same resources as for consumer targets. For channel members, the two other objectives of a sponsorship are to garner channel distribution commitment for the sponsor's products and to improve trade relationships. For community and government targets, additional objectives for sponsors are to demonstrate involvement in the community and to enhance relationships with the community and with government. Objectives for sponsorships targeting employees and management can be to improve brand image, to motivate, and to improve internal employee relations.

Sponsorship Target

Resources located at the event have greater value when the target for the sponsorship is attendees rather than nonattendees. These resources include rights to sales and information outlets. Signage rights, logos on equipment, and product use in the event are effectively rights to advertising media at the event. Presentations and speeches made by executives of the sponsor company are also seen at the event. These rights will only have value for a sponsor pursuing objectives relating to nonattendees if the event and the signage, logos, and speeches receive media coverage. This media coverage my be a result of telecast (television coverage of the event), broadcast (radio coverage of the event), or broadband coverage (Internet or mobile phone streaming). Media coverage may also be a product of news coverage of the event on any news medium. These two forms of media coverage can be classified as "direct" or "news" coverage.

The naming right resource, that is where the sponsor's name becomes part of the name of the event, has value when the target for the sponsorship is attendees. Attendees can be exposed to the event name association through event materials, such as tickets, programs, and announcements. The value when the target for the sponsorship are nonattendees depends on the extent to which the event is promoted, the name association with it, and the extent to which the event receives publicity and media coverage that exposes the name association.

Resources that can be utilized away from the event have greater value when the target for the sponsorship is nonattendees rather than attendees. These rights include the right of sponsor status, where the sponsor has the right to have its brand name or logo on promotional material associated with the event; rights to TV advertising during event coverage; the right to use event identifiers in promotional activity and product packaging; the right to use event footage or images; and the right to use the event or participants as product endorsers in subsequent promotions, in-store appearances, or as sponsor workplace visitors. Merchandising rights, being the right to use event identifiers to develop event-related products, have evolved from being an activity that was directed primarily at attendees seeking souvenirs to an activity targeted at the general public.

Nature of the Objectives

In addition to the target for the sponsorship, the other variable that affects the value of a sponsorship resource is the nature of the objectives sought. Resources that have particular value when a sponsor has a behavioral objective, such as sales, are those that give direct access to the consumer at the point of sale. An exclusive pouring right is one of the few situations that allow for the artificial restriction of the consideration set. These pouring rights allow exclusive sales outlets at the event.

The right to use event identifiers (event logos or images) on product packaging provides a resource to differentiate a product to the consumer while they are considering purchase.

Seating and hospitality rights also present good opportunities to pursue sales-based objectives because they can be used as part of incentive or reward programs for employees and channel members, or they can be used as prizes in sales promotions.

Another behavioral objective is product trial, which can be aided by the distribution of free samples to attendees.

Resources that are well suited to pursuing image objectives and affecting attitudes to the sponsoring brand are those where the links between the event and sponsor are clear to the consumer. Sponsorship research has repeatedly shown that, where consumers see a fit between the sponsor and the event, there is a greater impact from the sponsorship (Crimmins and Horn, 1996). The basis of this image affect is the transfer of event attributes and meanings to the brand of the sponsor (Cornwell, Weeks, and Roy, 2005; Dean, 2002; Gwinner and Eaton, 1999; Speed and Thompson, 2000).

Equipment usage, where the sponsor's brand is used within the event as sporting equipment, provides an endorsement for the product in terms of its quality. The use of footwear, racquets in tennis, balls in many sports, and oil and tires in motor sports are all examples of equipment usage. The provision by sponsors of timing equipment and computer services are examples of equipment usage within an event that are not directly used by the participants in the event, but are nevertheless opportunities to demonstrate performance attributes of the sponsor's brand.

Television advertising slots, event identifiers, event footage, and endorsements all provide opportunities to highlight the nature of the fit, and affect the image of the sponsoring brand. Since it is necessary to establish a link with the event to affect the image of the sponsor, the ability to provide information and samples to potential customers through the event is useful in pursuing image objectives only if such a link is made. Hence, resources that provide inputs into the sponsor's own promotion provide an opportunity to affect brand image.

Sponsorship-linked marketing is "the orchestration and implementation of marketing activities for the purpose of building and communicating an association to a sponsorship" (Cornwell, 1995, p. 15). The objective of this form of sponsorship leveraging is to communicate the association between the sponsor and the event. Sponsorship-themed marketing communication is the use of event-linked attributes, images, or resources to communicate directly about the sponsoring brand. Sponsorship-themed marketing can link attributes of the sponsored event to the brand without having to establish a link between the event and the brand.

An example of sponsorship-themed marketing communications was seen leading up to the 2006 Commonwealth Games. National Australia Bank (NAB), one of Australia's oldest and largest banks, was a major sponsor of the Games and was simultaneously engaged in a brand-building communications program after a corporate scandal. NAB used an unknown discus thrower in a television commercial and showed him receiving coaching from a middle-aged ballet teacher. The voice-over said, "Sometimes, to get what you want, you need some words of experience. Which is where we come in." The advertising sought to use sponsorship-sourced imagery to say something about the brand. As the sponsorship-themed marketing communications objectives are brand-focused rather than sponsorship-focused, these objectives are likely to have a greater scope than the sponsorship objectives.

Where the target of the sponsorship is a nonconsumer, the importance of the event to the community as well as a clear link between the event and the sponsor are important (Speed and Thompson, 2000).

Resources that are well suited to pursuing brand awareness objectives are those that deliver high levels of brand name exposure. It is in this area where name association, signage, and logos can provide value. In addition, the ability to provide information and samples to potential customers through the event can also serve to create awareness for a product.

Sponsorship Typology

Identifying the sponsorship resources that are consistent with alternative objectives provides a conceptual framework for the construction of a typology of sponsorship activity.

Consumer-Targeted Sponsorships

For consumer-targeted sponsorships, the typology consists of six ideal types. They are distinguished from each other by their objectives in terms of communication (brand awareness, image or use) and their target audience (attendees and nonattendees), and by the ideal set of sponsorship resources for pursuit of this objective. The ideal set of sponsorship resources is subdivided into primary and secondary resources. The ideal types are summarized in Table 13–3.

Because the relationship between objectives and resources has been previously discussed, Table 13–3 is largely self-explanatory. A few clarifying notes on each ideal type are provided below.

Attendee-Awareness Sponsorship (AAS) and Nonattendee-Awareness Sponsorship (NAS)

Creating brand awareness involves enabling consumers to link the brand to its category (recall) and/or to its brand identifiers (recognition). Hence, sponsorship to achieve brand awareness should generate exposure of the brand name, its category and/or its identifiers. Whether such exposure is to the attending audience or to nonattendees depends on the extent to which the event is televised or reported by the media. The primary resources used to satisfy the awareness objective is the same in each case.

TABLE 13–3
Consumer-Targeted Sponsorships

Target	Resource	Objectives		
		Awareness	Image	Use
Attendee	Primary	Naming right Signage	Naming right Signage and message and/or dominance	
		Equipment logo Equipment use Speeches	Equipment logos Equipment use Speeches	
	Secondary	Samples	Event identifier and samples	Exclusive sale
		Product info	Event identifier and product info	Samples
				Event identifier at event POS
Nonattendees	Primary	Naming right and media coverage Naming right and event promotion Signage and telecast	Naming right and media coverage Naming right and event promotion Signage and message and/or dominance and telecast	
		Equipment logos and telecast Equipment use and telecast Speeches and telecast/ broadcast	Equipment logos and telecast Equipment use and telecast Speeches and telecast/ broadcast	
	Secondary	Sponsor status and publicity and advertising Event identifier and advertising	Sponsor status and publicity and advertising Event identifier and advertising Film/photo and advertising	Merchandising Event identifier and POS Hospitality and sales promotion
			Endorsement and advertising	Seating and sales promotion
			Advertising purchase	Event identifier and packaging

Secondary resources for an attendee-awareness sponsorship are rights to distribute samples and product information. These resources require further investment by the sponsor to provide and distribute the material. For a nonattendee-awareness sponsorship, secondary resources are those that can be leveraged to generate additional publicity for the brand name.

Brand awareness can exist without any opinion or image of the brand being held by the consumer. If a consumer can recall a brand name given a category cue, their ability to recall that brand name is unaffected by their knowledge of where they were exposed to that brand name. Hence, for a sponsorship to create brand awareness, creating a link between the brand and the event is not necessary. For this type of sponsorship, leveraging is limited to seeking additional exposure for the brand name through publicity. In this type of sponsorship, the sponsor is effectively using the sponsorship as the advertising medium.

Attendee-Image Sponsorship (AIS)

Attendee-image sponsorships are those where the objective is to change the image of the sponsoring brand among attendees. Hence, the key resources for such a sponsorship are resources that allow a message about product attributes to be delivered at the event.

If the impact on the image of the brand is to be achieved by attaching an attribute associated with the event to the brand, then a connection between the event and the brand needs to be established. In this circumstance, the communications message is more complicated than in the case for awareness building sponsorships. This reduces the value of relatively simple resources, such as signage at an event. Signage that simply exposes the brand name does not necessarily establish a link of association between the event and the brand. Hence, it is not *per se* an image building resource. Its value in image building depends on the extent to which, through message, location or dominance, a valuable association can be made. Other valuable resources include naming rights, use of the product in the event, and mention of the association between the product and the event during announcements and presentation speeches.

Secondary resources for an attendee-image sponsorship are rights to distribute samples and product information through which a message about product attributes can be delivered. These resources require further investment by the sponsor to provide and distribute material that assists in creating an image change.

Nonattendee-Image Sponsorship (NIS)

The key primary resources for nonattendee-image sponsorships are the same resources that allow a message about product attributes to be delivered at the event, coupled with television and media coverage. Secondary resources that require further investment are more extensive, and these would include media advertising access, endorsements, and access to event footage, which can all be leveraged through further advertising.

It is worth noting that some of these secondary resources, or close substitutes for them, can be acquired without undertaking sponsorship. For instance, a celebrity endorsement can be obtained directly from the individual participant, and footage that appears to be of the event can be acquired from other sources. It is the use of such promotions in the hope that consumers perceive them to be the use of secondary sponsorship resources by the actual sponsor that is the key strategy of sponsorship ambushers.

Attendee-Use Sponsorship (AUS)

Attendee-use sponsorships seek to change behavior toward the product on-site through stimulating product trial. The key resources for such a sponsorship are resources that give access to potential consumers. These would include rights such as exclusive sale, the distribution of product sample, and product information. As each of these rights requires additional investment in the form of establishment and staffing of sales outlets at the event and distribution efforts for samples, they are classified as secondary resources. An additional secondary resource is the right to use event identifiers in point of sale material on-site.

Nonattendee-Use Sponsorship (NUS)

Nonattendee-use sponsorships seek to change behavior toward the product off-site. All the resources in this case are secondary and require additional investment. Such a sponsorship may target consumers who view the opportunity to attend the event as an incentive to purchase a product. In these circumstances, seating and hospitality are valuable resources since they can be used as incentives for consumers.

Merchandising, where the sponsor creates products directly linked to the event (such as special edition cars or clothing), can be considered a secondary resource which will stimulate purchase. Other key resources for such a sponsorship are resources that allow the sponsor the ability to cue potential customers about their sponsorship while they are considering their purchase. Such resources would include permission to use event identifiers on the sponsor's packaging and point of sale material.

Channel Member-Targeted Sponsorships

Awareness and brand attitude effects will occur for members of the distribution channel in the same way that they occur for consumers, so the sponsorship ideals for these objectives are the same as those for AAS, NAS, AIS, and NIS ideals. If a channel member happens to attend an event as a spectator, they will be targeted in the same fashion as consumers.

In a similar vein, channel commitment may come as a product of use of the product by channel members. As a result, a sponsorship that encourages channel members to use or trial the product will increase the likelihood of channel commitment. The resources for such a sponsorship are the same as the AUS. These resources are summarized in Table 13–4.

Nonattendee–Distribution Commitment Sponsorship (NDCS)

Distribution channel members are more likely to support a product if they can be persuaded that the product will have high turnover, will have some distinguishing display feature, and will be profitable. The resources that deliver this ideal sponsorship are the same as those that will deliver increased use in consumer targeted sponsorships for nonattendees (NUS), with the addition of the right to player appearances. These in-store appearances if made available to distribution partners will generate traffic and aid turnover of the sponsor's product.

Attendee Improved Relationship Sponsorship (AIRS)

If a sponsor wishes to improve channel relationships, channel member impacts will occur when the targets are recipients of invitations to attend the event. When the sponsors can spend a day at an event in a corporate box or at an exclusive corporate dinner, intra-channel relationships will be improved. If the sponsor is able to take the channel member into the coach's prematch address to the players, what we call a "unique opportunity," levels of trust within the channel are likely to increase.

Nonattendee Improved Relationship Sponsorship (NIRS)

One resource that may improve relationships with channel members, which can be deployed away from the event, is the player visit. If a participant in the event is made available by the sponsor to visit the workplace of the channel member to address channel member organizations' employees, the relationship between sponsor and channel member must be improved.

Employee and Management-Targeted Sponsorships

As employees and managers are already aware of the brand, objectives for sponsorships targeted at them are image impact, internal relationship

TABLE 13–4
Channel Member-Targeted Sponsorships

Target	Resource	Objectives			
		Awareness	Image	Distribution Commitment	Improved Relationships
Attendee	Primary	Signage Equipment logos Naming right Equipment use Speeches	Signage Equipment logos Naming right Equipment use Speeches		Unique opportunity Hospitality Seating
Attendee	Secondary	Samples Product info	Event identifier and samples Event identifier and product info	Exclusive sale Samples Event identifiers at event POS	
Nonattendees	Primary	Naming right and media coverage Naming right and event promotion Signage and telecast Equipment logos and telecast Equipment use and telecast Speeches and telecast/broadcast	Naming right and media coverage Naming right and event promotion Signage and telecast Equipment logos and telecast Equipment use and telecast Speeches and telecast/broadcast		
Nonattendees	Secondary	Sponsor status and publicity and advertising Event identifier and advertising	Sponsor status and publicity and advertising Event identifier and advertising Film/photo and advertising Endorsement and advertising Advertising purchase	Merchandising Event identifier and POS Event identifier and cause-related marketing Seating and sales promotion Event identifier and packaging Player appearance	Player visit

building, and rewards. Image impact is delivered to employees and managers as they are for consumers, through AIS and NIS sponsorships.

Employee/Management Motivation Sponsorships (EMMS)

When a sponsor wishes to use its sponsorship for the purposes of motivation of employees and managers, incentives that link performance to the receipt of special privileges of attendance at the sponsored event can only be delivered to attendees.

Employee/Management Relationship Sponsorships (EMRS)

Internal relationships can be improved by the social interaction of employees and managers at sporting events. This improvement can be delivered by the use of sponsorship resources, such as unique opportunities, hospitality, and seating at the event. Nonattendees can be targeted by the use of player visits to the sponsor's workplace to improve internal employee relations. Employee/management targeted sponsorships are summarized in Table 13–5.

Community and Government-Targeted Sponsorships

For communities and government, the objectives are to impact brand image, to demonstrate involvement with the community, and to enhance government relationships. Image impact will be achieved, as it is for consumer-targeted sponsorships, by the use of AIS and NIS sponsorships.

Nonattendee Community Involvement Sponsorship (NCIS)

Involvement with the community will be achieved by using the same set of resources as consumer-targeted image objectives, because there would

TABLE 13–5
Employee/Management Targeted Sponsorships

Targets	Resources	Objectives	
		Motivation	Improved internal relationships
Attendee	**Primary**	Unique opportunity	Unique opportunity
		Hospitality	Hospitality
		Seating	Seating
Nonattendee	**Secondary**		Player visits

need to be a link between the event and the sponsor in the minds of the target, and so this is a more exacting communications objective than that of brand awareness. These objectives are delivered to attendees by the same set of resources as in AIS sponsorships.

The set of resources to deliver the evidence of community involvement objective to nonattendees is the same as the NIS sponsorship, but with the added opportunity of using player visit rights to target specific groups within the community. Improved government relationships would be achieved through IGR sponsorships. Community/government targeted sponsorships are summarized in Table 13–6.

Empirical Use of the Typology

As noted previously, the value of a typology of ideal types does not lie in classification, but in benchmarking. Distance from an ideal type is hypothesized to be negatively associated with sponsorship performance. In using a typology of this type empirically, it is necessary to measure the distance of each case from each ideal type. The techniques for doing this are well developed (see Doty and Glick, 1994, for a review). It is worth noting that because the types presented are ideal types, there is no necessity for an actual case to resemble only one of the types. Hybrid types may exist. These are sponsorships where two objectives are being pursued. A typical example might be a sponsorship by a drinks company. Drinks firms will almost always pursue sales objectives at the event, alongside any awareness or image objectives they may hold. A hybrid sponsorship, such as this, is hypothesized to generate the required performance outcomes on both objectives, so long as the resource set that is consistent with each objective is present.

Theoretical Use of the Typology

Since typologies are research tools, it is also important to examine what additional research directions a typology may open up. The typology proposed here has implications for the implementation of sponsorships. The objectives sought and resources available form the basis for sponsorship activity, but the mechanism by which the sponsorship is implemented does not follow automatically from this base. However, the implementation mechanisms likely to be well suited to that type of sponsorship can be hypothesized. Table 13–3 summarizes potential extensions of the typology of consumer-targeted sponsorships to implementation and evaluation activities. All the cells in this table can be treated as hypotheses about the implementation and evaluation activities associated with an ideal type.

TABLE 13–6
Community/Government Targeted Sponsorships

| Targets | Resources | Objectives | |
		Evidence of Community Involvement	Improved Government Relationships
Attendees	**Primary**	Naming right	Unique opportunity
		Signage and message and/or dominance	Hospitality
		Equipment logos	Seating
		Equipment use	
		Speeches	
	Secondary	Event identifier and samples	
		Event identifier and product info	
Nonattendees	**Primary**	Naming right and media coverage	Player visits
		Naming right and event promotion	
		Signage and message and/or dominance and telecast	
		Equipment logos and telecast	
		Equipment use and telecast	
		Speeches and telecast/broadcast	
	Secondary	Sponsor status and publicity and advertising	
		Event identifier and advertising	
		Film/photo and advertising	
		Endorsement and advertising	
		Advertising purchase	
		Player visits	

The hypotheses should be stated in terms of closeness to the ideal type.

The typology proposed in this chapter draws on the role of objectives and resources in managerial decision making. Hence, the results of managerial decision making in sponsorship are codified in terms of objectives sought and resources available.

The usefulness of the typology lies in the predictions that arise about how sponsorships will be implemented, how they will be integrated into a broader communications program, and how they will be evaluated. These predictions require empirical examination, and the typology proposed appears no more difficult to operationalize than any other application of typologies (Doty and Glick, 1994). Sponsorship researchers have frequently pointed out the weakness of existing research into sponsorship practices and the difficulty of comparison of cases. We propose this typology as a tool for future investigations, and invite researchers to test its appropriateness.

References

Abratt, R., Clayton, B.C., and Pitt, L.F. (1987). Corporate objectives in sponsorship. *International Journal of Advertising*, 6(4): 299–311.

Amis, J., Pant, N., and Slack, T. (1997). Achieving a sustainable competitive advantage; A resource-based view of sport sponsorship. *Journal of Sport Management*, 11: 80–96.

Amis, J., Slack, T., and Berrett, T. (1999). Sport sponsorship as distinctive competence. *European Journal of Marketing*, 33: 250–272.

Apostolopoulou, A., and Papadimitriou, D. (2004). "Welcome home": Motivations and objectives of the 2004 Grand National Olympic Sponsors. *Sport Marketing Quarterly*, 13(4): 180–192.

Clark, J.M., Cornwell, T.B., and Pruitt, S.W. (2002). Corporate stadium sponsorship, signaling theory, agency conflicts and shareholder wealth. *Journal of Advertising Research*, 42: 16–32.

Cornwell, B. (1995). Sponsorship-linked marketing development. *Sport Marketing Quarterly*, 4: 13–24.

Cornwell, T.B., and Maignan, I. (1998). An international review of sponsorship research. *Journal of Advertising*, 27: 1–21.

Cornwell, T.B., Weeks, C.S., and Roy, D.P. (2005). Sponsorship-linked marketing: Opening the black box. *Journal of Advertising*, 34(2): 21–42.

Crimmins, J., and Horn, M. (1996). Sponsorship: From managerial ego trip to marketing success. *Journal of Advertising Research*, 36(4): 11–21.

Dean, D.H. (2002). Associating the corporation with a charitable event through sponsorship: Measuring the effects on corporate community relations. *Journal of Advertising*, 31(4): 77–87.

Doty, D.H., and Glick, W.H. (1994). Typologies as a unique form of theory building: Towards improved understanding and modelling. *Academy of Management Review*, 19(2): 230–251.

Fahy, J., Farrelly, F., and Quester, P. (2004). Competitive advantage through sponsorship: A conceptual model and research propositions. *European Journal of Marketing*, 38(8): 1013.

Farrelly, F., and Quester, P. (2003). The effects of market orientation on trust and commitment: The case of the sponsorship business-to-business relationship. *European Journal of Marketing*, 37(3/4): 530.

Gwinner, K.P., and Eaton, J. (1999). Building brand image through event sponsorship: The role of image transfer. *Journal of Advertising*, 28: 47–57.

Johar, G.V., and Pham, M.T. (1999). Relatedness, prominence, and constructive sponsor identification. *Journal of Marketing Research*, 36: 299–312.

Klincewicz, K. (1998). Ethical aspects of sponsorship. *Journal of Business Ethics*, 17(9/10): 1103–1110.

McDaniel, S.R. (1999). An investigation of match-up effects in sport sponsorship advertising: The implications of consumer advertising schemas. *Psychology and Marketing*, 16(2): 163–184.

Speed, R., and Thompson, P. (2000). Determinants of sports sponsorship response. *Journal of the Academy of Marketing Science*, 28(2): 226–238.

Tiryakian, E.A. (1968). Typological classification. In: D. Sills (Ed.), *International Encyclopaedia of the Social Sciences* (Vol. 16, pp. 177–186). New York: Macmillan Company / Free Press.

Tomasini, N., Frye, C., and Stotlar, D. (2004). National Collegiate Athletic Association corporate sponsor objectives: Are there differences between divisions I-A, I-AA, and I-AAA? *Sport Marketing Quarterly*, 13(4): 216–226.

Thwaites, D. (1995). Professional football sponsorship—Profitable or profligate? *International Journal of Advertising*, 14: 149–163.

14

Understanding Control in Voluntary Sport Organizations

Terri Byers, Ian Henry, and Trevor Slack

Control lies at the heart of organization theory.
Delbridge and Ezzamel (2005, p. 603)

Researchers from a wide variety of disciplines, such as engineering, accounting, cybernetics, sociology, and psychology, have made explicit attempts to examine the concept of control in organizations (e.g., Anthony, 1965; Ashby, 1956; Chua, Lowe, and Puxty, 1989; Gertosio, Mebarki, and Dussauchoy, 2000; Johnson and Gill, 1993; Salaman and Thompson, 1985). The result has been a fascinating yet complex diversity of discussions on the origins, definitions, mechanisms, and processes of control, in a variety of organizational settings. However, much of the "control" literature is preoccupied with the concept of control as the "prized model" (Oliga, 1996, p. 3), something to be sought after for the purpose of optimal organizational efficiency and effectiveness.

These conceptualizations of control are underpinned by the notion that organizations and people are rational entities. Yet the notion of "rationality" has been strongly contested in the literature first by scholars, such as Simon (1957, 1976) and Weick (1979), and more recently in the work of Fineman and Sturdy (1999), for example. Writers such as these have suggested that control is not a neutral process directed toward legitimate goals, such as efficiency, but is an emotional and continuous process of negotiation between all organizational members. Furthermore, much of the past research on organization control has been conducted in the context of private and public sector organizations (e.g., Agarwal, 1999; Cohen, 1995; Gupta and Govindarajan, 1991; Tankersley, 2000) and neglects

269

voluntary sector organizations. This is an important gap in the literature on organization control, given the social and economic significance of the voluntary sector (Kendall, 2003; NCVO, 2000).

Voluntary organizations are potentially different from work organizations given that there may be little or no economic necessity to join or remain a member of such organizations. As a consequence, formal, hierarchical, and/or structural controls might be expected to be less effective/relevant than in a work organization (Johnson and Gill, 1993). Likewise, given the different contextual demands placed upon the voluntary sector, it is possible that the more subtle forms of control play a more pivotal role in the control process. And finally, small organizations often place less importance on administrative devices; their decisions are often constrained by personal motivations/social situation, emotions, limited cognitive capacity, and individual personalities (Byers and Slack, 2001; Simon, 1976).

As reported by the Leisure Industries Research Centre (2003), the voluntary sector in sport is composed of more than 106,400 affiliated clubs in England, containing more than 8 million members. In addition, nearly 15% of the population (5,821,400) volunteer in the administration of sport and sports events. The report highlighted that volunteers contribute a significant 1.2 billion hours per year to sport and represent an estimated value of more than £14 billion. Voluntary sports clubs therefore represent a significant population that has had relatively little formal research to understand how they operate. In particular, Nichols (2001) suggested a need to understand the existence of control in these organizations.

The purpose of this chapter is first to introduce a holistic conceptualization of organization control, to enable an investigation that examines what control mechanisms exist within voluntary organizations, and articulates how these mechanisms operate. Our intention, therefore, is to provide a more dynamic theory of how control exists, specifically within voluntary organizations. To do this, the chapter briefly discusses the literature on control in organizations and suggests a theoretical framework that serves to address our criticisms of this literature and defines our central research questions. Following this, we suggest an appropriate methodology to satisfy the requirements of a holistic view of control. Finally, we report some initial findings from our three year study of control in three small voluntary sport organizations in England. Some conclusions are presented with suggestions for future research.

Past Research

In examining the literature on control in organizations, it is evident that control has clear intuitive links with the notion of power (Otley, 1996),

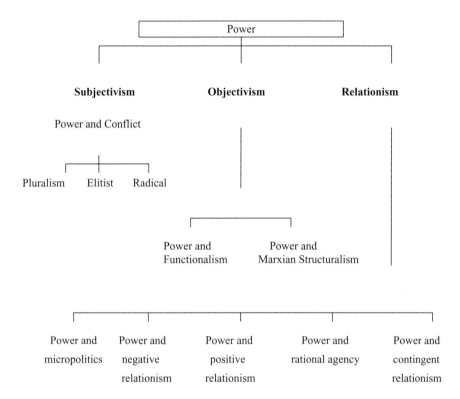

FIGURE 14–1. Conceptions of Power [Adapted from Oliga (1996, p. 72)]

and both concepts have been viewed from a variety of perspectives, with their meanings contested throughout the literature. It is useful to differentiate between these concepts in order to continue with our focus on organization control. Oliga (1996) provides a useful categorization of the different conceptions of power in the literature (see Fig. 14–1), and the resultant implications these conceptions have on different researchers' use of the term in organization studies.

Essentially, the subjective view of power indicates that power is essentially negative and exists when there are conflicts of interest between individuals or groups. The objective view sees power as positive and legitimate (Robson and Cooper, 1989). This view has been commended for its recognition that power is an expandable property of social systems within which members of society interact (Giddens, 1984), yet it has been criticized for its similarity to subjectivist views, which intrinsically relate power to interests (congruent interests in functionalism and conflictual interests in subjectivism) (Oliga, 1996). There are several relational perspectives of power that theorize about the nature of forces thought to be essential (structures and agents) in the relations of power, which is seen as having potentially both positive and negative effects, and so can be exploitative and oppressive or can be empowering, transformative, and synergistic (Oliga, 1996). However, the approach is critical of situations characterized by structures of domination and denies that power is inherently positive nor inherently oppressive. The structural forces of power are grounded in and constituted by the understandings of agents (Oliga, 1996), highlighting that power can take different forms, in different situations, and is subject to (and a catalyst of) change. We can now turn our attention to the various interpretations of control found within the literature and note the relationship of the concept with the notions of power.

A significant portion of the early research on control was underpinned by positivist ontology. Therefore, researchers have tended to focus on either administrative control mechanisms such as operating procedures, job descriptions, or disciplinary policy (see, for example, Agarwal, 1999; Anthony and Dearden, 1989; Fortado, 1994; Kirsch, 2004), management control as a function of an organization (see Anthony and Young, 1988), or contextual controls, such as structure, size, and the external environment (see Burns and Stalker, 1961; Lawrence and Lorsch, 1967; Slack, 1997). These mechanisms as objects of analysis are directly observable and tangible to a researcher and, of course, attractive to those employing a positivistic investigation.

Das (1989) referred to a growing body of literature questioning the logic of research that focuses on organization control as objective evaluation and correction of performance. More recently, a critical perspective of control acknowledges the value of these control processes, functions and, for example, hierarchical structures but conceives that contemporary mechanisms of control are quite often far less obtrusive than the formal, administrative mechanisms described above (see Jermier, 1998). A positivistic and/or "management" centered approach does not consider the different types of controls that operate in organizations (see Barker, 1993; Hopwood, 1974; Ouchi, 1980; Perrow, 1995).

Hopwood (1974) and later Manz and Simms (1989) pointed out that management controls alone do not significantly influence employee behavior if the standards and policies advocated by the external control mechanisms are not internalized by employees. This strongly suggests that the anticipated results of external control mechanisms are open to the active interpretation of those members. Ferner (2000) provided evidence for this in his examination of the relationship between "bureaucratic" control systems and social control mechanisms. We can see then that some research on organization control has made attempts to recognize that subordinates, as well as managers, endeavor to control their actions, and the actions and values of others (Ashforth and Saks, 2000; Oliga, 1996).

On the important relationship between power and control, we can make some suggestions as a result of this review of the literature. Control can be seen as a process engaged in by managers and organization members and/or as an organizational system designed by managers (e.g., Ouchi and Johnson, 1978; Pennings and Woiceshyn, 1987) but influenced by the desires and actions of organization stakeholders. Power is not a process or a system in itself but is likely to be present within the design of a control system or throughout the process of organization control where agents interact, perhaps in competition for resources (e.g., Green and Welsh, 1988), for example. Power can take different forms within the control process, exercised by an individual (Giddens, 1984), held by a group (Oliga, 1996), or present in a structural sense through institutional practices (Meyer and Rowan, 1977; Poulantzas, 1973). We would argue that power is not a mechanism of control but an important force that facilitates or inhibits the effectiveness of a control mechanism.

Das (1989) argued that there is rarely one homogeneous mechanism of control that operates across an entire organization. Therefore, it is possible that different types of control will be more prevalent in different organizational settings, yet there is still a distinct lack of investigation into voluntary sector organizations. For instance, voluntary sport, cultural, leisure, and charitable organizations often exhibit systems of control that are more informal and normatively constructed than the corporate entities on which much of the research on control has been conducted. The lack of focus on voluntary organizations is an unfortunate omission given the important role these organizations play in the modern world (Kendall, 2003). As such, given the importance of context and the significance of voluntary organizations, the focus of this research is to examine what control mechanisms exist in small voluntary sport organizations, and to describe how these mechanisms operate in order to provide a more dynamic theory of organization control.

Underpinnings of a New Conception of Control

A focus on control as an external phenomenon constrains our understanding of control in different contexts, where "it is difficult to arrange for extrinsically motivated control systems to operate functionally" (Johnson and Gill, 1993, p. 123). In an attempt to understand control in voluntary organizations, we adopt a framework that allows for different types of control and does not focus simply on those mechanisms designed or initiated by hierarchical superiors. Hopwood (1974) suggested there are various mechanisms of control that operate in organizations, interdependently and simultaneously. He refers to these mechanisms as administrative (e.g., job description, operating, and disciplinary procedures), social (e.g., norms developed through socialization or identification), and self-controls (e.g., internalization of norms leading to "self" regulation).

Administrative controls include formal rules and procedures, found in, for example, plans, budgets, operating manuals, formal patterns of organizational relationships, and recruitment policies. These are designed to provide structure to decision-making processes in complex organizations by "specifying and limiting alternatives," thereby guiding subordinate managers and employees to appropriate courses of action (Hopwood, 1974, p. 24). Administrative control mechanisms are closely related to the formal structure of power within large organizations and are often used in an attempt to ensure that subordinates' goals are compliant and respectful of more senior management interests. Rules and procedures are therefore a "necessary means to a wider end" but their intended effect depends considerably on the social pressures and personal motivations/desires that exist among employers and employees simultaneously (Hopwood, 1974, p. 21).

Social controls, according to Hopwood (1974), emerge from the shared values, norms and commitments of organizational actors. These develop through two forms of socialization: formal, planned strategies designed by management to "regulate systems of beliefs and meaning" (administrative control), and through spontaneous social interaction (Johnson and Gill, 1993, p. 30). As such, administrative controls may have an influence on shaping social controls. Thus, while a variety of similar administrative controls may exist in organizations (i.e., training programs, rules and procedures, recruitment policies), how managers choose to implement the controls and how employees respond to the controls are strongly influenced by the pressure of social interaction within an organization.

People are heavily influenced by social interaction with certain individuals and/or groups, which they consider significant (Johnson and Gill, 1993), whereby that individual or group may serve as a "reference" (and acts as a control) for what constitutes appropriate behavior. Reed (2001) suggested that shared moral values and norms can lead to a social mechanism known as "trust"; Spreitzer and Mishra (1999) also described trust as an alternative to formal control mechanisms.

Self-controls, the third category in Hopwood's (1974) typology, are constituted by the personal motives of individual members. Hopwood (1974) suggested that in order for administrative and social controls to be effective, they must operate as "self-controls." Important here is the internalization (directly or indirectly) of the norms embodied in the administrative and social controls. However, Kelman (1961) suggested that "internalization" is only one type of conformity to social and administrative controls. He suggested that "identification" is also a powerful force for conformity, as it involves emotional gratification and attachment to "significant" organizational members. Therefore, identification is a significant form of self-control in organizations.

Hopwood (1974) believed that in order for administrative control mechanisms to be effective, they must become social, and ideally, self-control mechanisms. However, this scenario cannot describe how control is achieved in all organizational contexts. This is especially the case in, for example, voluntary organizations where there are likely to be few and sometimes even no administrative control mechanisms, such as formal rules and procedures. It is conceivable that in the voluntary organizational context, social and self–control mechanisms would be more powerful than the administrative mechanisms. Therefore, to understand what control mechanisms exist in a given organization, and to understand how and why those mechanisms operate, a theoretical approach is needed that values context and allows for a holistic investigation. We believe Hopwood's (1974) framework provides such an approach. We now turn to the methods adopted for this study that enable an investigation into control in voluntary sport organizations.

Methods

The purpose of this research is to suggest that a more holistic understanding of the concept of organization control is needed, taking into consideration small voluntary organizations. In order to achieve such an understanding, the research poses two principal questions: What are the control mechanisms that operate in small voluntary organizations and how do they operate? Throughout this study, data were recorded through participant observation, interviews, and historical documentation (newsletters, past minutes of meetings, newspaper articles, etc.). Jorgensen (1989) recommended the use of multiple sources of data to aid the process of understanding a phenomenon or process.

Eight small voluntary sports clubs, of a similar nature, size (same sport), and geographic location were contacted and informed of the study via a letter. Three clubs responded positively and were consequently included in the study. Initially, participation in discussions and decision making by the principal researcher was limited. Gradually, involvement in the clubs increased, and relationships and roles/responsibilities were unique to each individual club. Participant observation data came from committee meetings, competitions, club events (e.g., annual general meetings), and general social interactions around club related activity.

For approximately three years, this type of data has been collected during participant observation and personal interviews in three small horse–riding clubs. Garfinkel (1967) and later Holy (1984) suggested that validity of research data from fieldwork is attained by getting so closely involved in the research setting to "describe the world as they [subjects] see it" (Fortado, 1994, p. 255). However, even once the formal fieldwork was complete, due to the relationships and involvement with the clubs, contact with individuals continued, and therefore insight into the club and individuals within the committee continued to develop. Historical material has also been obtained, such as past minutes and newsletters, histories of clubs, and past versions of club constitutions. Therefore, any formal written document designed to direct the club's operations or indicate how the club currently operated was collected as evidence of administrative control mechanisms. Unfortunately, availability of documents varied between clubs. For example, while all clubs had some minutes and news-letters, the filing and storage of these documents were not centrally kept or monitored. From one club, research identified a founding member of the club who held a scrapbook and early records of accounts, newsletters, and minutes, so this member was interviewed. However, even these items were not systematically or rigorously archived and some information is missing.

A variety of documents were used to enable what Altheide (1996) called an emergence of meaning, in which he refers to the gradual shaping of meaning through the interpretation of documents, where themes and categories of data/documents are constantly distilled and revised. This method of analysis allows for reflexive movement between concept development, document sampling, data collection, coding, and analysis/interpretation. It also allows for controlled but interactive and flexible methods of developing understanding of a concept. Inductive and deductive reasoning are used attempting to avoid the positivist contention that predefined theoretical categories can be forced from data.

Results and Discussion

This section describes some preliminary results from our investigation of three small voluntary sport organizations in England. Using Hopwood's (1974) framework, we suggest that there are a wide variety of administrative, social, and self-control mechanisms operating in small voluntary sport organizations. Administrative mechanisms found to operate included agendas, minutes of meetings, club Constitution, National Governing Body rules, and some club-specific procedures (although these were rarely present in a formal, written format). Social control mechanisms identified included emotion, organization history, avoidance, social/cultural and economic capital, shouting, and social hierarchy. Self-control mechanisms included identification with club, personal identity, emotion, avoidance, and cultural capital.

Hopwood (1974) suggested that organization control is a complex and dynamic process where a diversity of administrative, social, and self-control mechanisms operate simultaneously. However, we would argue that this is too simplistic to describe how control mechanisms operate and how control exists, particularly within the organizations examined in this study. Indeed, all of the control mechanisms mentioned above operated at some time throughout the study and held some significance to understanding control in these organizations. However, to suggest they were all operating simultaneously throughout the entire study is inaccurate. Rather, we suggest that important to understanding organizational control and concurrent with the work of Cardinal, Sitkin, and Long (2004) is the historical development of these mechanisms over time. That is, organization control in each of the three committees in this study, as it was observed during participant observation and the specific mechanisms used by committee members, was deeply rooted in the history of the club/committee development.

The three case studies presented in this study indicate that control is not only dynamic in the founding years (Cardinal, Sitkin, and Long, 2004), but continues to evolve and change in response to changes mainly in the internal environment of the organization. The pace and sequence of change in relation to control mechanisms, however, differed in each organization. For example, change in control mechanisms occurred as organization members attempted to balance formal and informal controls. The suggestion of "balance" needed between formal and informal controls is recommended by Johnson and Gill (1993) as essential to organization operations. Club A became more effective and efficient in its operations when the Chairwoman made a successful effort to increase the importance of administrative mechanisms to balance the overuse of social mechanisms of control that had dominated club operations for a considerable period, approximately two decades. This change was made in response to an influx of "new blood" and new ideas when, in 2002, four new committee members were nominated and elected to the committee at the AGM. The committee then contained only 6 long standing members among a committee of 12 people.

One of the most significant details about the influx of new members was that it was not planned by the Co-Chairwoman. As the balance of new individuals versus long standing members changed, so too did the control mechanisms employed. As new members came onto the committee and did not possess the historical knowledge of how the club had always operated, they naturally imposed pressures for change. In order to cope with the unplanned change in the group, the Chair moved from informal friendly meetings to meetings led by a "specific" agenda, created by her, and according to the Chair, "to discuss the issues I thought needed to be discussed" (interview the Chair, 01/09/03). There was never any input from the committee as to what should or could go on the agenda. Previously, a generic agenda was used, with little effect as the committee often seemed to discuss items in a haphazard manner. The Chair also enforced any "rules" that were initiated/created by herself, but ignored rules that were not derived from herself, such as National Governing Body rules (likewise, the club Constitution was never referred to). For example, a rule was created in relation to nonattendance by a committee member whereby if anyone missed more than three meetings without informing the co-chair that person could be removed from the committee. The Chair also admittedly "tried to chair the meetings more formally" (interview The Chair, 1/9/03) after the influx of several new members of the committee.

The pace of development of control in Club B was more continuous (and stagnant) than in Club A. There were several members of Club B who had no previous committee experience and, therefore, lacked the knowledge of how to keep administrative records. Then there were people like William (Vice President) who just did not want to even have a meeting, therefore records were not considered. In his opinion, the Vice President stated in interview:

> You don't need a meeting! Perhaps once or twice a year . . . all that talk and yapping about, don't get jobs done! I did everything and never used to go to the meetings. (Interview Vice President, 6/13/03)

Administrative mechanisms, such as "job descriptions", were irrelevant in Club B as the chair and even vice-chair were wholly inactive in committee meetings, with the secretary actually chairing meetings, and there were ill-defined and/or ill-understood rules of operation. Club B, being in a continuous state of conflict, showed a significant imbalance in its use of control mechanisms with very little agreement or acceptance of administrative mechanisms. The conflict was primarily between founding members (approximately half the committee) and "new" committee members who had not had experience or knowledge of the club's operations since its inception. For newer members, they wanted to make their own contribution to developing the club and not be constrained by a Constitution that was created decades ago. This resulted in conflict among the group, with the following interview excerpt being some recognition of this:

> The large majority of people on the committee now have lost that aim. They look at shows and nothing else . . . because they haven't been involved from the start. (Interview, 4/23/03)

This also begins to highlight the controlling nature of the identification founding members had with the club, or with what the club used to be. One of the interviewees revealed her immense emotional attachment to the club and cited this as the reason she had never stopped helping the club develop, even during times when she was not officially on the committee as this excerpt from the interview shows:

TB: So do you feel a sense of belonging to this club?

Gill: Mmmm (nodding in agreement)

TB: Loyalty?

Gill: Definitely.

TB: Can you explain why?

Gill: Why? [pause] . . . I suppose in a sense it's almost like a child. And you don't abandon children.

TB: Why do you feel this club is like a child?

Gill: Because I was a founder member, basically. I was there at its birth and it's a sense of pride because you've formed something: all those years ago . . . pride in belonging to something that is so well recognized and well thought of. Because when you've given birth to a baby, you don't dispose of it just because you can't happen to be part of it. So I didn't want to see the club fold so if anybody asked me for help I was prepared to do it. (Interview, 3/19/03)

Club C seemed to have a good balance between formal (administrative) mechanisms, such as their internal rule book (the "Bible"), agendas/ minutes and National Governing Body rules, and informal (social and self) control mechanisms, such as the use of various forms of capital, avoidance, emotion, and identification. As a result, there was little overt conflict within this group, and the committee organized a significant number of events for its membership each year and appeared to operate smoothly. However, a few months after the fieldwork for this research finished, there was a significant change in leadership in Club C, with the Chairwoman resigning after fours years of service. An email from her indicated that the change may lead to conflict within the committee when she stated:

Well, we had the AGM and I resigned, as I said I would. The new committee has its first meeting soon and yes, feathers will fly! There will be lots to sort out—lots of shouting I think! (Email, 11/14/04)

While there was a balance between formal and informal controls in Club C, this did not mean there was no conflict or animosity within the group, but that control was perhaps much more subtle than in the previous two cases (with the conflict latent and more difficult to observe). Although participant observation recorded no significant or direct objection to her leadership of the committee/club, one of the interviewees clearly stated (2/4/05):

I don't agree with the way she runs the club but it is not my place to say anymore. There are others too who think she is too rigid, too

> strict and don't like the way she's done things—but you know, she's
> doing it her way and that's that . . .

For example, she sometimes coupled emotion with her use of the agenda/
minutes as a tactic to get meetings started. For example, during one
meeting, she started by saying: "could we get started, I have some rather
sad news to tell before we get down to club business" (field notes WHRC,
8/15/03). This served to draw the attention of all committee members,
and she proceeded with her news and committee business seamlessly.
Likewise, control mechanisms could overlap such as emotion and identification when exercised as a self-control. Emotion has been acknowledged
as pivotal in the achievement of organization control (e.g., Fineman, 1993).
While emotional work has traditionally been viewed as conducted for
organizational purposes and by the direction of management (Hochschild,
1979, 1983), Callahan (2000) realized that it is also possible for individuals to control their emotions for personal reasons or in response to commitment to the organization rather than simply at the command of
management. Similarly, emotion has been linked to identity in organizations by Albert, Ashforth, and Dutton (2000) who suggested that identity
is crucial in determining how and what an individual thinks and feels
although they have also indicated that the relationship is ill understood.
Drawing on the work of Simon (1945), Thompkins and Cheney (1985,
cited in Barker, 1993) noted the effect of identification in organizations
to limit the range of alternatives considered in decision making, highlighting "organizational identity" as a mechanism of control that serves to
limit the perspective of organization actors.

This notion that identification with an organization controls/limits
actors' perception and therefore range of actions from which they may
choose is evident within each of the case studies in this research. However,
in contribution to the literature on the role of identification in organization control, this study highlights the diversity of this mechanism. While
Alvesson and Willmott (2002) focused on how identity is formed, reveal-
ing the importance of discourse to identity regulation and control, they
also concentrate on management's intentional attempt to influence this
process in describing organization control. Within the committees in this
study, identity was mainly evident as a self-control mechanism and served
to influence individuals both tactically and strategically. It can also be
argued that personal identity and identification with the club could serve
as systemic mechanisms of control as the individual, or contribution of
the individual, gradually became part of the history of the club. In Club
C, personal identities consistent with identification with the organization,
and consistent over time, served to provide a strong systemic mechanism
of control that suggested the character of the club, committee, and its
serving members.

Identification with an organization can also have negative consequences, leading to conflict and difficulties in controlling and coordinating organization activities. In Club B, founding and long-standing members strongly identified with "their" club. However, the remaining committee members did not identify with the same image of the club that the long standing members held. This caused considerable friction between the two groups, and many conflicts could be traced to this significant difference in identification. For example, one interviewee suggested that the long standing members constantly referred to the founding principles of the club and stated in an interview:

> They are always banging on "have you read your Constitution!?"— well, no I haven't! [laughing]—so what! They really hold the club back, they don't want to try anything new or different or do anything other than the way it used to be. (Interview, 6/30/03)

Overall, Club C demonstrated very little conflict focused on goals or the direction of the organization. Likewise, there was very little observed personal conflict. Committee members seemed to accept the operational procedures of the committee and its role in the larger structure of equestrian sport within the region and country. They were respectful of the leadership of the Chairwoman of the committee. Similar to Club A, she created administrative mechanisms to provide guidance and control within the group. However, whereas the Chair of Club A created the agenda mechanism to enforce her authority to direct the club, she created mechanisms which took the emphasis of control away from her. For example, in creating the "Bible," it was possible for her to refer to this document when making decisions that enabled her to avoid responsibility for difficult decisions.

Conclusions

Broadly, we have attempted to introduce the reader to the concept of organization control, a subject of recently renewed interest in the mainstream management literature (see Delbridge and Ezzamel, 2005; Wilmott, 2005), but that has not been the focus of sport management scholars. From early, mainly positivistic, conceptions of control to the more critical and postmodern theories, researchers have still offered a limited focus on "management control." This chapter has sought to offer a more holistic view of control and suggest that any study of control should reflect the active role played by all organization members in organization operations.

In using Hopwood's (1974) framework as a basis, a wider lens through which to see what control mechanisms operate within small voluntary sport organizations, preliminary results of this study suggest that administrative, social, and self-control mechanisms operate simultaneously. While there were administrative controls (e.g., agenda), it was social and self-controls that appeared to influence members significantly. Administrative control mechanisms were enforced or at times completely ignored to suit an individual or the group. The enforcement of these mechanisms was possible through the knowledge of values and norms developed over time through socialization in the committee and/or through long standing members' knowledge of and identification with the values and norms upon which the club was founded. For example, committee members in Club B resented the "iron fist" leadership of their chairwoman but nonetheless accepted that she was able to make rules/decisions and essentially was the most powerful individual in the group. A significant form of control at the time of participant observation was the history and tradition, accepted and encouraged by the majority of long-standing committee members, which served as significant resistance to change and acted as a control discouraging innovation and new developments.

Although this research presents previously uncharted territory—control in sport organizations—it is a snapshot and demonstrates only a small period in the organization's history observed through participant observation. Arrow, Poole, Henry, Wheelan, and Moreland (2004) provide a useful review of literature that has demonstrated the temporal perspective and importance of longitudinal studies in small group research. Cardinal, Sitkin, and Long (2004) provided an interesting account of the first ten years of the creation and evolution of control mechanisms in a commercial company. In addition, an important factor in understanding control in the organizations in this study was the historical development of the clubs, committees, and individual roles within the committees. Given the importance of time and historical development, it would be useful to examine small voluntary sports clubs from their inception through ten or even fifteen years of their development to compare with the present study that had to rely on historical data to provide evidence of past developments. This would go some way to validating some of the assumptions and inferences made in this study based on historical data and how it has affected the present control mechanisms found. Also useful would be comparisons to organizations of different sizes/structures/contexts, such as professional sport organizations and National Governing Bodies to develop a more advanced understanding of how modern sport organizations are controlled. Finally, change in control mechanisms during periods of significant change may give insights, from inception through development of new control mechanisms as they are introduced.

References

Agarwal, S. (1999). Impact of job formalization and administrative controls on attitudes of industrial salespersons. *Industrial Marketing Management*, 28(4):359–368.

Albert, S., Ashforth, B.E., and Dutton, J.E. (2000). Organizational identity and identification: Charting new waters and building new bridges. *Academy of Management Review*, 25(1):13–17.

Altheide, D.L. (1996). *Qualitative Media Analysis*. London: Sage.

Alvesson, M., and Willmott, H. (2002). Identity regulation as organization control: Producing the appropriate individual. *Journal of Management Studies*, 39(5):619–644.

Anthony, R.N. (1965). *Planning and Control Systems: A Framework for Analysis*. Boston: Harvard Business School.

Anthony, R.N., and Dearden, J. (1989). *Management Control System*. Homewood, IL: Irwin.

Anthony, R.N., and Young, D.W. (1988). *Management Control in Nonprofit Organizations*. New York: McGraw-Hill.

Arrow, H., Poole, M.S., Henry, K.B., Wheelan, S., and Moreland, R. (2004). Time, change, and development: The temporal perspective on groups. *Small Group Research*, 35(1):73–105.

Ashby, W.R. (1956). *An Introduction to Cybernetics*. London: Chapman and Hall.

Ashforth, B.E., and Saks, A.M. (2000). Personal control in organisations: A longitudinal investigation with newcomers. *Human Relations*, 53(3):311–339.

Barker, J. (1993). Tightening the iron cage: Concertive control in self-managing teams. *Administrative Science Quarterly*, 38(3):408–437.

Burns, T., and Stalker, G.M. (1961). *The Management of Innovation*. London: Tavistock.

Byers, T., and Slack, T. (2001). Strategic decision-making in small firms in the leisure industry. *Journal of Leisure Research*, 33:121–136.

Callahan, J. (2000). Emotion management and organizational functions: A case study of patterns in a not-for-profit organization. *Human Resource Development Quarterly*, 11(3):245–267.

Cardinal, L.B., Sitkin, S.B., and Long, C.P. (2004). Balancing and rebalancing in the creation and evolution of organizational control. *Organization Science*, 15(4):411–431.

Chua, W.F., Lowe, T., and Puxty, T. (1989). *Critical Perspectives in Management Control*. London: Macmillan.

Cohen, C. (1995). Striving for seamlessness: Procedural manuals as a tool for organizational control. *Personnel Review*, 24(4):50–57.

Das, T.K. (1989). Organizational control: An evolutionary perspective. *Journal of Management Studies*, 26(5):459–475.

Delbridge, R., and Ezzamel, M. (2005). The strength of difference: Contemporary conceptions of control. *Organization*, 12(5):603–618.

Ferner, A. (2000). The underpinnings of "bureaucratic" control systems: HRM in European multi-nationals. *Journal of Management Studies*, 37(4):521–539.

Fineman, S. (1993). *Emotion in Organizations*. London: Sage.

Fineman, S., and Sturdy, A. (1999). The emotions of control: A qualitative exploration of environmental regulation. *Human Relations*, 52(5):631–663.

Fortado, B. (1994). Informal supervisory social control strategies. *Journal of Management Studies*, 31(2):251–274.

Garfinkel, E. (1967), *Studies in Ethnomethodology*. Englewood Cliffs, NJ: Prentice-Hall.

Gertosio, C., Mebarki, N., and Dussauchoy, A. (2000). Modeling and simulation of the control framework on a flexible manufacturing system. *International Journal of Production Economics*, 64(1–3):285–293.

Giddens, A. (1984). *Constitution of Society*. London: Polity Press.

Green, S.G., and Welsh, M.A. (1988). Cybernetics and dependence: Reframing the control concept. *Academy of Management Review*, 13(2):287.

Gupta, A.K., and Govindarajan, V. (1991). Knowledge flows and the structure of control within multi-national corporations. *Academy of Management Review*, 16(4):768–792.

Hochschild, A.R. (1979). The sociology of feelings and emotions: Selected possibilities. In: M. Millman and R. Kanter (Eds.), *Another Voice*. Garden City, NY: Anchor.

Hochschild, A.R. (1983). *The Managed Heart: Commercialization of Human Feeling*. San Diego: University of California Press.

Holy, L. (1984). Theory, methodology and the research process. In: R.F. Ellen (Ed.), *Ethnographic Research: A Guide to General Conduct*. pp 13–24. London: Academic Press.

Hopwood, A. (1974). *Accounting and Human Behaviour*. London: Prentice-Hall.

Jermier, J.M. (1998). Introduction: Critical perspectives on organizational control. *Administrative Science Quarterly*, 43:235–256.

Johnson, P., and Gill, J. (1993). *Management Control and Organizational Behaviour*. London: Paul Chapman Publishing.

Jorgensen, D.L. (1989). *Participant Observation: A Methodology for Human Studies*. Applied Social Science Research Series, 15. London: Sage Publications.

Kelman, H. (1961). The processes of opinion change. *Public Opinion*, 25:57–78.

Kendall, J. (2003). *The Voluntary Sector*. London: Routledge.

Kirsch, L.J. (2004). Deploying common systems globally: The dynamics of control. *Information Systems Research*, 15(4):374–395.

Lawrence, P.R., and Lorsh, J.W. (1967). *Organization and Environment: Managing Differentiation and Integration*. Boston: Harvard University Press.

Leisure Industries Research Centre (2003). Leisure Forecasts 2003–2007. Sheffield, LIRC.

Manz, C.C., and Simms, H.P. (1989). *Super Leadership: Leading Others to Lead Themselves*. Berkeley, CA: Prentice-Hall.

Meyer, J.W., and Rowan, B. (1977). Institutionalized organizations: Formal structure as myth and ceremony. *American Journal of Sociology*, 83:340–363.

NCVO (National Council for Voluntary Organisations) (2000). The A to Z of the voluntary sector. *Research Quarterly*, 9.

Nichols, G. (2001). The UK voluntary sector. In: C. Wolsey and J. Abrams (Eds.), *Understanding the Sport and Leisure Industry*. Essex: Longman, Pearson Education Limited.

Oliga, J.C. (1996). *Power, Ideology and Control*. London: Plenum Press.

Ouchi, W.G. (1980). Markets, bureaucracies, and clans. *Administrative Science Quarterly*, 25:129–141.

Ouchi, W.G., and Johnson, J.B. (1978). Types of organizational control and their relationship to emotional well being. *Administrative Science Quarterly*, 23(2):293–317.

Pennings, J., and Woiceshyn, J. (1987). A typology of organizational control and its metaphors. *Research in the Sociology of Organizations*, 5:73–104.

Perrow, C. (1995). Why bureaucracy? In: *Foundations of organizational communication: A Reader*. White Plains, NY: Longman.

Poulantzas, N. (1973). *Political Power and Social Classes*. London: New Left Review.

Pugh, D.S., Hickson, D.J., Hinings, C.R., Macdonald, K.M., Turner, C., and Lupton, T. (1963). A conceptual scheme for organizational analysis. *Administrative Science Quarterly*, 8(3):289–315.

Reed, M.I. (2001). Organization, trust and control: A realist analysis. *Organization Studies*, 22(2):201–228.

Robson, K., and Cooper, D.J. (1989). Power and management control. In: W.F. Chua, T. Lowe, and T. Puxty (Eds.), *Critical Perspectives in Management Control*. London: Macmillan.

Salaman, J.G., and Thompson, K. (eds.) (1982). *Control and Ideology in Organizations*. Milton Keynes: The Open University Press.

Simon, H. (1945). *Administrative Behavior: A Study of Decision-making Processes in Administrative Organization*. New York: Macmillan.

Simon, H.A. (1957). *Administrative Behavior: A Study of Decision-making Processes in Administrative Organization* (2nd ed.). New York: Macmillan.

Simon, H.A. (1976). *Administrative Behavior: A Study of Decision-making Processes in Administrative Organization* (3rd ed.). New York: Free Press.

Slack, T. (1997). *Understanding Sport Organizations: The Application of Organization Theory.* Champaign, IL: Human Kinetics.

Spreitzer, G.M., and Mishra, A.K. (1999). Giving up without losing control: trust and its substitutes' effects on managers' involving employees in decision-making. *Group and Organization Management*, 24(2):155–187.

Tankersley, W.B. (2000). The impact of external control arrangements on organizational performance. *Administration and Society*, 32(3):282–304.

Tompkins, P.K., and Cheney, G. (1985). Communication and unobtrusive control in contemporary organizations. In: R.D. McPhee and P.K. Tompkins (Eds.), *Organizational Communication: Traditional Themes and New Directions.* pp 179–210. Beverly Hills: Sage. 179–210.

Weick, K.E. (1979). *The Social Psychology of Organizing.* New York: McGraw-Hill.

Willmott, H. (2005). Theorizing contemporary control: some post-structuralist responses to some critical realist questions. *Organization*, 12(5):747–780.

15

Sport Clubs—Computer Usage—Emotions

Markus R. Friederici and Klaus Heinemann

The three keywords in the title of this contribution point to the problem that we wish to address, as well as to the program by which we wish to deal with the problem. Many studies have already elaborated on structural peculiarities of voluntary organizations, including sport clubs; the consequences of computer usage or digital data processing have been analyzed in many and controversial ways in the relevant literature; and on the sociology of emotions—including emotions in organizations—there has been a considerable number of publications especially in recent years. Therefore, there is nothing new that we can contribute on these themes. Rather, we wish to attempt to analyze the connections between these three thematic elements, or to be more precise, to show the influences the introduction of computer technology or techniques of information processing can have on the various emotions typically found in sports clubs, and how such changes in the emotions in turn affect the interactions and functioning and the network of social relationships in sports clubs. Although there are a number of studies on the consequences of computer usage in other types of organizations, here the question arises in how far results that are valid in commercial enterprises can be transferred to nonprofit organizations in general, and sports clubs in particular, given the peculiar structural differences that exist.

These three thematic elements—sports clubs, computer technology, and emotions—therefore represent the building blocks that we seek to connect to one another in order to gain new understandings of the way in which emotions in sports clubs have perhaps changed with the usage of computer technology, and how they might further change. By this, we hope to derive new understandings of a sociology of voluntary organizations, a sociology of technology, as well as a sociology of emotions.

To begin with, however, there are certain limiting parameters that need to be defined:

1. We will provide a brief introduction to each of these three thematic elements. In doing so, we are not seeking to provide a complete and comprehensive representation of the current state of the art in each area; rather we will seek to highlight only those aspects that appear to be especially useful in examining the problem that we have described.

2. With this problem, we are approaching new territory. Although there are clearly established understandings of the consequences of computer usage in organizations, these do not take into account voluntary organizations, and they often exclude an examination of emotions. Our reflections, therefore, are in part largely hypothetical, and only partially substantiated with our own empirical findings. Several publications point to changes in the emotional relationships between actors as a result of (increased) digital communication (Bühl, 2000, 2001; Charwat, 1994; Sadek and de Mori). The assumption might, therefore, be made that such influences can also be identified in sports clubs, though in modified form to account for the particular structures of this type of organization.

3. From empirical research (cf. Heinemann, 1999; Heinemann and Puig, 2001), we know that sports clubs take on varying forms from one country to the next—this applies to their function, the meaning of voluntary work, the type of integration of the members, the participation in democratic processes, and the relevant organizational culture. For example, in a comparative study of the situation of sports clubs in Germany and Spain, it became apparent that in Spanish clubs, a feeling of solidarity was less pronounced than in German clubs, i.e. the service provider mentality is stronger in the Spanish context (cf. Heinemann and Puig, 1997). Furthermore, in each country, as is well known, different emotions are valued differently and in turn communicated in varying ways. The German language has ca. 350 terms with which to express emotions, English ca. 250, Spanish ca. 450, and Chinese ca. 650—this is also a good indicator of the cultural effect of feelings, since it is questionable whether we can develop feelings for which we have no words. Such country-specific and cultural divides cannot be considered in this contribution. Our reflections, therefore, restrict themselves to the context in Germany, not least because we can thereby resort to various

empirical studies (including our own) and many personal experiences that relate to the three thematic elements that seem to us to be absolutely necessary in thinking about the (after all only) hypothetical statements about the consequences of computer usage on various emotions.

4. Even if it appears as if at various times our reflections give the impression that we are predisposed to the (culturally-)critical consequences of computer technology, this is not the case. We are not interested in value judgments in the sense of good or bad, but in the comparison of advantages and disadvantages. This is particularly the case since these are developments that cannot be controlled, far less changed. Rather we seek to draw attention to unforeseen and unintended effects of developments in digital information processing; because they are unforeseen and unintended, the consequences are not discussed.

Thematic Elements

First Thematic Element: Voluntary Organizations

Typical characteristics of voluntary organizations often include the following:

1. They are nonprofit organizations, and any profits that do arise are therefore used for the purposes of the organization. For this reason, the expression "Not-for-Profit" Organization is appropriate, since surpluses are (or can be) generated; but this also means that:

2. the aims of the organization become the motive for both membership and involvement;

3. they have to have a democratic decision-making structure; and

4. their most important resource is voluntary work, usually on the part of the members.

From these characteristics, there are certain important things to note regarding voluntary organizations in relation to our topic: they represent a curious mixture of structural elements of formal organizations (such as state administrations or industrial corporations), as well as structural elements of a social grouping.

- While sport clubs have as their aim the enabling of sport for its members, the relationships within the clubs are not clearly related to specific functions. Behavior in a club derives to a far lesser extent from the aims and rational rules of the organization than is the case in commercial enterprises or public administrations. Cooperation in a club is not only centered on a specific aim, but has far more expressive characteristics. The higher the identification with the aims, values, and traditions of the club, the more pleasant the atmosphere in the club's work, the greater the motivation of the honorary office-bearers, and the readiness to resort to informal agreement for action—and there is less need for things to be explicitly determined. Regulations are initially created through the interplay between participants; this stabilizes the image that the actors create of themselves and others, as well as those actions that have shown themselves to be successful.

- In the context of sociological organizational research, the question as to whether sports clubs are to be categorized as service organizations or mutually supportive societies has been addressed from an early stage (Heinemann, 1998, p. 85f.). This discussion highlights the fact that it is difficult to categorize sports clubs on the basis of their structural particularities. Sport clubs are marked by a distinctive feeling of subjective belonging of their members, who take responsibility for one another, do not measure their involvement on a rational cost/usage basis, or, on the basis of incentive and contribution, calculate and check whether involvement pays for itself, at least not in the long term. Personal trust and consensus determine the decisions and action of the actors in these circumstances.

- Social structures do emerge, but these do not have the same degree of formalization as is typical for formal organizations. Since a club can generally be organized less on the basis of a division of labor than, for example, a commercial company, there is only a relatively minimal level of coordination required.

- Although there are some formal authority structures, influence and effectiveness remain dependent on the personality and powers of persuasion of the office-bearers. The mix of the somewhat contradictory particularities of social groups and formal organizations can manifest itself in different ways in different types of clubs. Clubs can approximate toward the characteristics of social groups or the features of a formal organization. In how far one or the other of these is the case depends, among other things, on the size of the club, its age, the number of sporting activities on offer, and the interests of the membership. However, it is worth remembering that (1) in Germany about 35% of clubs have less than 100 members (and many of those less than 50 members), and even this size increases the likelihood that group-like circumstances develop, and (2) larger clubs often structure themselves into departments, subgroups etc., in which such group-specific characteristics can equally well develop (Heinemann and Schubert, 1994).

- Sanctions are usually only of an informal nature—for example, in the form of a reprimand, an ironic comment, a joke, a demonstrative silence, a sudden change of topic, or inattentiveness. The more diffuse the relationships, the more the sanctions are, so to speak, targeted in a moralistic way at the person concerned.

One can also formulate it as follows: sports clubs are, in contrast to other organizational types, "communities of interest" (Heinemann, 1998, p. 90), in which members are bound by the common interest in movement, communication, and sociability, and in which membership, cooperation, and the fulfillment of tasks is largely determined by the kind of face-to-face relationships between the members that exist and the emotions involved. Similarly, studies on, among other things, the emotional mood in sports clubs (Heinemann and Schubert, 1994) show that the vast majority of members interpret "their" club as a mutually supportive society. Quite simply, a sport club is not just a social object—in other words an institutionally distinct place of social order—but also a place of community, in which people come together who not only pursue a common interest, but who also develop feelings of belonging and solidarity. The club can, therefore, also be described as an organizationally demarcated, group-oriented coalition (Heinemann, 2004). In German this is expressed with the word "Verein" (club) derived from the term "Vereinigung," meaning community. Translation of the term into other languages is difficult, in that the often somewhat diffuse and emotionally-laden connotations are lost.

Second Thematic Element: Computer Usage

In the meantime, there are many academic publications that deal with the economic, political, cultural, and social applications and effects of computers (Bühl, 1999; Castells, 2001, 2004; Rammert, 1990). If one attempts to distill the relevant particularities of computer usage for our theme from these publications, one ends up with an impression of the effects of digital information processing in sports clubs; this is, therefore, described in some detail below:

1. *Changes in knowledge and thinking.* The Internet produces an intensification and expansion of knowledge. But this expansion is not only of a quantitative nature; rather it is worth noting the "technicalization" of this knowledge, i.e., it is knowledge that is acquired

primarily for efficient usage. It is no longer important to know how things work, but how to use them appropriately. The purpose of computer usage is, therefore, often simplification, standardization, differentiation, acceleration, and improvement of work routines, or reducing time and money costs. The odd thing is that technology does not become stranger to the user even if the way in which it works becomes stranger: the acceptance of a technology that one does not understand, but the functionality of which one has to trust unequivocally increases. Technology is accepted more, the less it is understood.

The division of labor, for a long time a way of increasing efficiency, is not removed through computer technology, but rather increased. There follows an increasing segmentation into ever new specialists, because these technologies are functionally open and, therefore, suited to ever more applications. However, this division of labor no longer follows fixed patterns with their own consistency, but rather the division of labor is spontaneous, in a way that is closely related to the technological changes and the mutations of applicability. Mintzberg (1979) described this type of organization beautifully using the term "adhocracy."

2. *Computer usage and decorporealization:* Evolution has determined that humans perceive the world with all five senses equally, incorporate these in interactions, and use and communicate about them. And because this is the case, these five senses—as is especially apparent in visual and bodily contact—are subject to many social and cultural rules (for example, as means of communication, as cultural symbols, as objects of societal control) in the types of individual behavior (singularly, as well as in combined form), such as in bodily contact and gaze. One only needs to visualize all that can be expressed and communicated with a look, with various smiles, and with various forms of bodily contact to realize the extent of the achievement of appropriately communicating externally in suitable codified forms emotions that always only affect us internally, as well as the extent of the achievement of other people who read these emotional codes correctly. For example, one has to learn to differentiate between "artificial" and "real" smiles, to work out whether it is a (perhaps, ironic) grin or a (perhaps, encouraging) smile, (perhaps, shameful) making fun of someone or a (perhaps, provocative) come-hither-smile—and we all know the consequences and problems that can arise from an incorrect decoding and interpretation of such facial expressions. It, therefore, becomes clear how hopeless it must seem when the multiplicity of such forms of emotional expression are to be communicated on the Internet, or when moods with sound

simulations (e.g., "harrumph," "cough," and so on) and action words (e.g., "laugh," "choke," "surprise," and so on) relativize, caricature, reinforce, or diminish a written statement (cf. Döring, 1999, p. 45). That the body is of importance in face-to-face communication, and distinct from gestures and facial expressions, can be seen by the fact that people generally find it easier to lie on the Internet (for example, by not describing themselves completely accurately) when compared to a face-to-face encounter. We are left with images with no bodies.

We can only understand the world through our senses. We can strengthen our senses with microscopes, stereoscopes, robots, or hearing aids, but we can always say: that which is beyond our senses remains hidden. Our senses define the parameters of our consciousness.

On a computer, perception and communication are reduced to, at most, two senses: the perception of what appears as text and image on the computer's screen. However, this is not simply a reduction of our sensory perception. In English, for example, one can interpret terms such as "senseless," "out of one's senses," and many more in equivocal ways. This also works in German, for example, "Sinnlos" and "von Sinnen sein." On the one hand, there is the loss of perception through our senses, and on the other hand, there is the overlapping and ordering of this perception with a "sense," in other words an assessment that determines something as "containing sense" or "senseless," i.e., that vests it with "reasonable" interpretations, but also with emotions. Heller (1981), at least, makes us aware that cognition can never be separated from emotions.

In this three-way relationship of information—interpretation—emotion, there is not only a selection of sensory perception of reality, but also its construction in "significant–insignificant," "important–unimportant," "up–down," "belonging–excluded," "ugly–beautiful," "permitted–prohibited," and so forth. Our senses produce sense or meaning not simply through obvious or subliminal actions, but rather structure reality into component parts; value-driven interpretations and emotions then use these to create a meaningful pattern. The senses give the brain fragmentary information that, like the small pieces of a puzzle, are put together to create a complete picture of reality. In a similar way, people who lost their sight as very small children, but who through medical advances are given their sight in adulthood, can still not "see." This is because their brain has not learned early enough to give meaning to the optical signals it is receiving. But with the primacy of digital information, the cognition of "senseless" becomes more precise: a fluid, diversified, unstable image of reality that is open to interpretation. Digital processing of information succumbs to the primacy of cognition. The extent to which this happens can be shown by the receptivity of computer games that glorify violence—reality, in these circumstances, remains digital. These games communicate neither the emotions nor the meanings that would force themselves on us if we were to witness similar scenes in real life.

The consequences that arise from this become clear when we make ourselves aware of the meaning of face-to-face relationships: they share the same coordinates of space and time. The interaction of computer users however, is in variant, nonshared spaces; in many cases, it is asynchronous, so that a physical and contemporaneous presence of the participants is unnecessary. The other is not here, but somewhere. Information can be transmitted, but the existence of the person behind that information diminishes in significance—even toward nothingness. Instead of consciousness and the feeling of face-to-face interaction, there is the abstract advantage of a multipersonal interaction, but one that is restricted exclusively to cognition.

Third Thematic Element: Emotions

The characterization of the particularities of voluntary associations, including sports clubs, makes it clear that the quotidian reality of a sport club can only, with difficulty, be imagined without emotions. Feelings of togetherness and belonging, friendship and enmity, sympathy and antipathy, identification with the club, commitment to a team or to athletes, feelings of mutual trust, but also mistrust and ill-will, are obvious. In addition, there are joy and fulfillment, but also frustration in the course of voluntary cooperation, as well as feelings, such as solidarity or exploitation, annoyance at excessively long committee meetings and the apparently "stupid" arguments of others, the disappointment after a defeat in a vote, and the frustration with internal politics.

However, we do not wish to claim that similar feelings cannot be found in other types of organizations. However, we maintain that such feelings are key for achieving the aims of a sports club, since they derive from constitutive characteristics of voluntary associations and do not represent ignorable concomitant characteristics. That is why emotion-work and the management of emotions play such a key role in clubs, although not in the form described by, for example, Hochschild (1979, 1983): a forcibly commercialized emotion-work with the identifiable consequences of alienation and so on. Rather, we mean the many forms of informal emotion-work between club members: to be there for others, listen, encourage, console, feel empathy, sympathy, and so on can all be examples of this. The term emotion-work is used to denote the application of those strategies that in the relevant area—in this case sport and associated organizations—secure positive and avoid negative emotions (or prevent their having an effect). Emotion-work describes those efforts and techniques with which an individual deals with their emotions "reasonably," in order to externalize the "positive" ones, suppress the inappropriate ones, and develop those that have as their purpose the influencing of other people's emotions for one's own purposes. It is often difficult for people to speak about their emotions, not least because people in western European countries, more so than in Asian contexts, have learned, in the course of their cultural socialization, to control their emotions, i.e., to do emotion-work. It is, therefore, distinctly possible that neither trainers nor athletes have any interest in showing their emotions publicly, so that the emotional expression that is observed does not necessarily represent the real feelings that are being experienced. After all, openly displayed disappointment of a trainer can bring additional motivation for the athletes in the struggle for the ball, or a euphoric expression of support by the trainer on a difficult ascent in the Tour de France can lead to the cyclist mobilizing the very last reserves of strength to enable the achievement of a decisive lead. Possibilities and limits of a codification are, among other things, bound to the vocabulary that a language offers: we have to force our constantly changing, context-dependent inner feelings of varying stability into the stiff corset of such terms as a language allows for the expression of emotion. Expressions of emotion are furthermore dependent on language ability, physical control, the perception of reality, and so on of each individual.

This is not to say that in clubs, the mechanisms of emotional management that Hochschild (1979, 1983) describes, such as selection when choosing new members of a club, or the executive committee, or the cooperation in a commission, are not effective: clearly, in how far these members can be emotionally integrated, or as it is described in colloquial terms, there is the "right chemistry" between individuals, plays a role. In many clubs, existing members need to vouch for a new member. This is undoubtedly another reason why it can be shown that many clubs are in and of themselves homogenous, closed societies: people would rather stay "among themselves," precisely because they understand each other "better" emotionally. Maintaining this internal homogeneity is the reason many clubs rely on new members joining as a result of word-of-mouth recommendations (cf. Heinemann and Schubert, 1994).

It is, however, difficult to research emotions sociologically, because there are so many, and yet it is hard to provide equally valid statements about each one. It is also impossible to order systematically the multiplicity of our emotions: the listing of possible emotions in clubs alone makes this clear. How often efforts have been expended (in vain) on such a classification is shown by, for example, Vester (1991) in a summarizing portrayal of the many attempts to define and standardize emotions. Compare also the differentiated and theoretically-based system by Heller (1981). Despite this, a classification of emotions is worth suggesting that underpins the context of the emotions in sport and sports clubs, and the circumstances in which they arise (cf. Heinemann, 2001a).

- *Activity-related emotions.* Emotions are included in this category that emerges from the actions themselves. Feeling and action go hand in hand. Many emotions arise in the course of action and are experienced as part of the action. Joy and disappointment, success and failure, fulfillment and bliss, pride and despair, "membership feelings," "sport feelings," and "spectator feelings" can all serve as examples (cf. Friederici, 1998). These are feelings about the action—whether in sport or in voluntary service—that are not complementary to a cognitive judgment about the action, but are essential experiences that accompany the action itself.

- *Emotions of commitment.* These describe emotions of belonging, involvement, and identification: emotional connections to one's own club are a clear example of organizational commitment. Terms such as faithfulness to the club, loyalty, identification, solidarity, and so on represent such emotional commitments, but emotional commitments to sport apparatus and rooms are also examples for such commitment emotions. The geographical location of a sport club, the rooms that are available, the architectural features or the image (for example, being up-to-date technically) all influence the creation and intensity of commitment emotions. Bale (1989, 1993) alerts us to the fact that members of clubs can also develop such commitment emotions at sporting venues (in which they achieved many victories and had to suffer many failures), at "their" clubhouse (built with their own strength and the crystallization point for club-life), and at the spatial environment of the sporting complex (where one is at home and that can act as a prop for one's own identity-construction). The emotional connection to a club is often also a positive emotional connection to the stadium or the clubhouse. The connection is mirrored by negative emotional moods at away games, in other words "spatial-affection" on the one hand, and "spatial-phobia" on the other. Fans feel "at home" with their team in their home stadium: they can identify with it, they can feel comfortable and secure there. One's "own" stadium creates feelings of security, belonging, and well-being; the stadium of one's opponent, however, communicates feelings of strangeness, unease, and exclusion.

- *Emotions in social relationships.* Many emotions are based on typical relationships and interaction of sports clubs. Friendship and enmity, jealousy and envy, disappointment and annoyance with others are emotions that develop in the relationships between members of a team and its opponents, in relationships to trainers, between club members and so on. Special forms of emotionally-laden relationships are to be found between genders (Rastetter, 1994) or different ethnicities. The problems associated with interpreting emotions are complicated, in particular by culturally-specific peculiarities and ethnocentric value-systems. For example, are tears a sign of sadness or joy? Depending on people, tribe or culture, the indicator "lachrymal secretion" can have many different emotional causes analyzed by social scientists from an ethnocentric perspective. Freud (1972, 1978) and Vester (1991) focus in their work on the influence of culturally-specific behavioral standards on emotional state, which in turn influence or suppress/repress action dependent on culturally-determined norms. A particular form of these relationship-emotions is the emotional relations in groups: cliques, circles of friends, members of commissions, an executive committee or a team. The "we-feeling"—often a definitive marker of a social group—is just one example that shows that groups develop an affective general mood; team spirit, a community mentality, mutual understanding, and internal cohesion are further examples. These groups develop a common affective feeling that achieves that which is important for the members of the group through consistent selection and interpretation.

- *Emotional mood in clubs.* Organizations also have feelings (Albrow, 1992, p. 313), i.e., emotions develop not only within a person; rather they are also characteristics of organizations and, therefore, simultaneously a central aspect of their achievement. Clubs have an emotional mood or an "emotional image." This is evidenced by quotidian experiences, for example, if this club is described as cold and impersonal, while that one is dominated by feelings of solidarity and belonging, or that in one mistrust and fear and in another get-up-and-go and optimism prevail.

Sports clubs are also primarily about achieving goals in the best possible way. On the basis of the structural particularities of this type of organization, we can assume that emotions can contribute to a special extent to a sport club fulfilling its tasks in a better way, thereby reaching its aims more effectively. Equally, emotions can help members to pursue their interests and desires more easily. These are two distinct (functional) classes of emotions. The identification of these as "instrumental emotions" is appropriate in this context. Those emotions that in this context are positive and those that are negative in this double sense, can only be decided on a case-by-case basis and using empirical studies. In any case, one must bear in mind this outstanding functional meaning of emotions in clubs when asking what broader consequences arise from computer usage, if computers subdue or suppress these various (instrumental) emotions—that given the reflections on digital information processing and incorporealization seems most probable.

Following the enunciation of these three thematic elements we can be more precise about our original question, i.e., what consequences do the aforementioned typical characteristics of computer usage or digital information processing have on the various emotions in the structural peculiarities of sports clubs? To what extent such changes happen is surely connected in the first instance to the form and intensity of the use of these technologies. That, then, is our next topic.

Computer Technology in Sports Clubs

Computers are currently an essential component in the completion of many tasks that arise in sports clubs. This is apparent externally in the Internet presence of a club's website in which its history, offers, activities, venues, regional context, directions, and specific features that the executive committee wants to promote are elaborated. Furthermore, programs that allow digitalized membership lists and the administration of members' details, calculations of members' financial contributions, financial transactions, the entire financial administration (including budgets and accounts), the preparation of meetings, the distribution of agendas and minutes, stock records, the production of leaflets and posters, sending out of club news, the preparation and conduct of competitions, the coordination and control of human resources, the creation of lists of sporting achievements, and records are all a part of this work. Using the Internet, members can quickly access these and other information. Perhaps even more importantly, tasks and achievements can now be contemplated that would at one time have been out of the question, of which an Internet presence, continually updated and expanded, is but one example.

The main advantages of computer usage are, therefore, notably "time" and "money." The costs associated with implementation of computer technologies are generally recovered quickly when one bears in mind the costs that are saved, such as postage, informational materials, telephone costs, and so on. When thinking about "time," similar savings become apparent: at first there is a need for a lot of time in order to use the programs that the computer has, but once they have been set up, the usage of the computer saves a notable amount of time, for example, through electronic postings, processing of text and tables, acquisition of information, and so on. The significance of computers in the administration of sports clubs is, in the meantime, so great that many tasks could no longer be completed without one. Evaluating interviews with volunteers has shown that many clubs would no longer survive without a computer; many of the interviewees argued that the competition with private sports and leisure organizations forced clubs to make drastic savings, offer new services, and engage in new forms of marketing, all of which would not be possible without a computer (Friederici, 2006). The sports clubs and their volunteers have, therefore, taken steps that they can no longer realistically reverse. The decision to integrate computers into the working practices of sports clubs has, thus, created an inertia that on the one hand eases the pursuance of a particular direction, while on the other hand hinders fundamental changes of direction. The many (obvious) positive effects of computers, especially in the area of saving resources, produces inertia that not only eases a particular path, but also makes a change of direction in a sequence of events almost impossible.

Emotions in Computer Usage

In analyzing the connections between computer usage and emotions, one can differentiate between two perspectives: first, the emotions that relate to the technical machine itself—the computer with its potential—the (programmable) power and, especially, also the many malfunctions. For example, technology can irritate because it does not function the way one wants it to (accompanied by repetitive work "demanded" by the machine or programs), or create pleasure when one has finally managed to "wrest" a particular achievement from it. We know, for example, from technology studies, that the relationship to technology is by no means just sober and objective, restricted to the cool analysis of use, function, and costs. Instead, it is entwined with emotional connections and dependencies. Manifold experiences—success and failure, achievements and efforts—are projected onto computers and condensed to an emotional attachment to a physical thing (Heinemann, 2001b). Second, there are emotions that arise from the usage of computers that lead to the acceleration, standardization, and expansion of areas of work in the network of social relationships. In the following section, it is only this second category of connections between computer usage and emotions that we wish to deal with.

Emotions as a Consequence of Transition

From empirical studies we know that in many clubs members of the executive committee are often of retiring age or beyond (cf. the extensive representative studies by Emrich, Pitsch, and Papathanassiou, 2001; Heinemann and Schubert, 1994). Because digital information processing is a comparatively young technology, many of these people will not have grown up with this technology and will, therefore, not necessarily have the knowledge required to appropriately estimate the potential of a computer and then operate it appropriately. Existing experiential and knowledge gaps can, therefore, contribute to a feeling of dissatisfaction and resignation. New computer programs that can increase efficiency, can, because of the demands they place on the user, also lead to a fear of failure that, among other things, can lead to falling back into old (but known) patterns of behavior. I (Friederici) recall an interview with the director of an athletics- and sports-club, who, despite newly-installed image-manipulation software and appropriate training, after a few failed attempts, returned to cutting out pictures and cartoons that accompanied notices and leaflets with a pair of scissors, and sticking them onto the original that was then photocopied. The operation of the copier (in terms of color intensity, size, and format) was, the director said, as complicated as the computer's program, but he said it sufficed him to only engage with all this technical stuff once.

In addition, the change from traditional to digital administration can create situations of excessive demands, since, for example, to analyze membership profiles, all the relevant details have to be entered into the appropriate program, which initially costs a great deal of time—time that is then not available for other activities. Furthermore, interaction with a computer can give rise to many varied reactions. The positive feeling of having communicated important information to all the relevant people simultaneously contrasts with the negative feeling when the computer program shows an error message in regard to one of the recipients or the entire process stops for no apparent reason. For example, the conversion to a digital database for the members requires the disposal of the card-index system that has been nurtured with handwritten notes over many years. The emotional connection to the card-index box can be so strong that, despite recognizing the necessity of the change, negative emotions can result. In addition, positive effects for emotional relationships can arise in the course of virtual communication. Because patterns of behavior acquired in the course of socialization in the usage of computers can also be applied in organization contexts, computer experts can achieve a status that, in the eyes of other members, makes them indispensable, and thereby produces positive feelings, such as being special and useful.

Changes in Knowledge Structures

Expansion and Objectification of Knowledge. The use of a computer brings an enormous expansion of knowledge and its immediate availability, for example, regarding membership profiles (age, gender, residence, sporting activities, sporting achievements, level of usage of different offers) or developments over time; beyond this, one can also quickly acquire important information for the club through the Internet that previously could only be acquired with great effort, or not at all.

For example, the computer becomes the memory of the history and contemporary situation of the club. Individual memory, but memory filled with experiences and emotions ("do you remember when . . . ," "I often think of . . . ," "I'll never forget that," "I can barely believe that we succeeded in that . . . ," "Was it really like that?"), is replaced by the lodging of factual information cleansed of emotions and memories.

We want to illustrate the consequences that can arise in these circumstances using two examples. The first example deals with changes in emotional states of mind, that—empirically proven (cf. the studies on organizational cultures by Heinemann, 2004; Heinemann and Schubert, 1994)—the representation of a club on an Internet web page can have. The images that each individual member of the club has derived from the puzzle of manifold experiences, memories, and stories that, perceived through the five senses, through interpretation and togetherness and relationship emotions are put together to produce an image of "my" club. We consciously note "five" senses because the construction of perception and reality includes, for example, the smell of the seat, the stuffy atmosphere in sports halls, the memory of weather conditions, rain, low temperatures, many forms of physical reaction and bodily contact, pain, and pleasure.

This image of the club consists of told and experienced stories—about the "founding fathers," the surmounting of critical situations and conflicts, the way that one communicates and makes decisions, the language style that has been adopted, the relationship networks, the successes and failures of "our" team or the individual, including the many connections to the sporting venues, and so on. This all remains subjective and individually different—there is not "the" club, but just these various images that, perhaps, in common experiences, conversations, and stories told and retold are cemented and adapted.

The representation of the club on a website objectifies this subjective image and, at the same time, cleanses it of individual interpretations, emotional assessments, and personal experiences. It becomes just a piece of condensed digital information—extremely selective, but "publicly appealing." Commitment and relationship emotions are suppressed: in this more objective image, there is no longer room for them. The distance between the subject and the (digitalized) object "sports club" has grown.

The second example relates to the particular meaning of the casual togetherness and the purposeless communication of groups as a special form of socializing—often derided as club mania, but of special meaning for the relationship emotions and the emotions in groups. The typical feature of such socializing is that it relates to specific individuals and assumes parity between partners. This can be described as the "democracy of socializing" (Richter, 1985). Sporting experiences—including those from long ago—and many other experiences in a club are recalled, reconstructed, and represented in all their highs and lows. Within limits, one includes one's own involvement, reports on joys, pride, insecurity, fears, and disappointments. One puts oneself in the place of others—such as the chairperson, the trainer, the (sporting) opposition—and "knows" what could all have been done better. One speaks of things that are not necessarily allowed to be official or public. In doing so, such subcultures in turn acquire a specific emotional position: one "opens oneself up" and at the same time has to trust that one's contribution will remain confidential. Whereby it is often the case that those achievements of bygone years that were perfectly natural become, through repeated telling and imaginative exaggeration, such tremendous achievements that they can only sensibly be told to one's equals, in order not to create the suspicion of megalomania. Examining facts objectively stored by the computer has the capability to destroy such illusions.

The question is, therefore, what influences digital information processing has on sports clubs as a place of community feelings; in other words: to what extent does the emotional climate change because of the factualization of communication? These effects must not be exaggerated because the aforementioned forms of socializing remain—at least potentially—despite technicalization. But changes, even if only on the margins, do take place that one should note. For example, if we revisit the example of the Internet presence of a club: it is not just information that is presented, but interaction with the club that is permitted—for both members and nonmembers—including members registering for contests, finding out about competition results, informing oneself about decisions and current developments; nonmembers can even, via the Internet, register as members. Interaction is "incorporealized" and simultaneously becomes an interpretationless and emotionless communication of information.

In light of the description of the first thematic element and the high value of face-to-face relationships and the associated emotions in sport clubs, such incorporealization of communication as illustrated in these two examples must have significant changes in the functional operation of the club, as well as in the emotional state of the members.

Increase in Efficiency. The usage of computers, as already explained, is meant to (1) lead to an increase in efficiency and therefore, (2) lead to new forms of labor division. In analyzing these effects, either the structural limits of computer usage in voluntary organizations or their consequent problems become apparent.

From the aforementioned mix of two different and ultimately incompatible structural principles, there develops a number of dilemmas: division of labor and formalization, for example, must not be taken too far, since otherwise the tasks that need to be fulfilled lose their motivational strength. The division of labor cannot be seen only under the perspective of efficiency and functionality, but must also be seen from the point of view of emotional integration. Because of this, the division of labor in clubs is usually smaller than would make sense from an efficiency perspective. Meetings cannot only be seen from an efficiency perspective, but also serve social integration and communication—these activities are, therefore, connected to activity-related emotions and commitment feelings. Similar reflections apply in terms of a formalization of developing tasks. Formalization limits the space for decisions and actions of the individual and can therefore have a demotivating effect. A problem is created that can be termed a time-paradox: on the one hand, the amount of time volunteers spend on work can be reduced and more efficiently organized through organizational regulation or individual commitments, but also through delegation to paid staff, use of technical measures, division of labor, and a clear circumscription of tasks. But with the reduction in time commitments, both the integration with the group and the possibilities for self-fulfillment diminish, both of which are significant motivating factors in voluntary work. This results in an organizational dilemma: it is possible to limit the amount of work of volunteers as described above, but the integration into the group is reduced, as is the power of socialization, which in turn restricts the space for the workers to act and interpret their tasks (Horch, 1987).

Simultaneously we need to consider that a special form of activity-related feelings is "work feelings," which can especially be identified in the work of voluntary workers. Joy and disappointment, success and failure, fulfillment and feelings of happiness, pride, and dejection are typical. These are feelings that accompany voluntary work—not as a cognitive judgment about the work itself, but as an essential experience in the work. Since not only membership but also being a volunteer is a voluntary activity, work feelings are surely an important motivational factor when taking on such tasks, and one should not carelessly destroy them.

But if—with increasingly functional division of labor and standardization—the motivational power of the task at hand is diminished, since the individual is only fulfilling an ever smaller selection of tasks of the many that exist, thereby losing a meaningful connection to the whole, then we can estimate the effects of digital information processing on the activity-related emotions: this is because it is precisely this enlargement of the functional division of labor, formalization, and standardization resulting from the various forms of computer usage that, after all, is the main purpose for using a computer. As we have shown, computers are designed for specific new forms of division of labor, standardization, and the acceleration and relief of working processes. The question arises, therefore, in how far the activity-related emotions of office-bearers are influenced through precisely these circumstances—perhaps positively since digital information processing relieves people from routine work that fails to motivate participation, while more systematic information about the club that is useful for the work becomes possible, but also negatively, because the individual's expression of freedom, action, and interpretation are restricted and possibilities for self-expression are reduced.

New Division of Labor and Specialization.   It has already been explained that cooperation and fulfillment of tasks are to a large extent determined by individuals, and that leadership is based on personal charisma, authority, and the control—in the first instance—of personal relationships. This form of "coincidental" development of standards and work routines is prevented with the use of a computer. A computer requires new abilities and thereby creates a new type of specialist and new forms of division of labor, a division of labor that is spontaneous and variable, depending on the speed of technological change and the expansion of possible usage, for example, as a result of new programs. This can have many consequences, of which we will describe two:

1. As already pointed out, it will often not be the chairperson or a member of the executive committee that can operate this new technology, but another member of the club who—perhaps from professional involvement—knows how to use it. But it is also possible that external consultants are brought in, which is often necessary to create an attractive website. The displacement of competencies must also lead to a displacement of respect (status) and influence (power). Presumably, this is not without consequences for the emotional situation in a club, at least, if following the thesis of Kemper (1978), who makes deductions about emotions in organizations from judgments about the extent to which status and power in an organization are seen as appropriate or inappropriate. Kemper's "Social Interactional Theory of Emotions" takes as its particular focus the interaction that is primarily determined by the two variables of power and status. Power in this context, as with Weber (1956), means the opportunities for an actor to implement their will even in the face of resistance from others; an actor who exercises power determines, delegates, forces, and urges. Status, on the other hand, has already been earned and is usually accompanied by high esteem, recognition, and respect.

   In the course of an interaction, therefore, status and power dimensions are displaced, something that, depending on an individual's estimation of the situation as appropriate or inappropriate, is interpreted and substantiated with corresponding emotions. For example, during a meeting with a trainer, an athlete is praised for something that is not a result of their work, but that of a computer program. The athlete "achieves" a gain in status as a result of the trainer's praise, but the athlete feels it to be inappropriate. The athlete is embarrassed. If the athlete was responsible for the increased status (perhaps through a lie told in advance) then perhaps s/he would not only be embarrassed, but also experience shame. In this way, with help from interactional analysis that examines the dimensions of status and power, many varying emotions can be classified.

2. The computer-related technicalization of club tasks can accelerate a process that can be described as professionalization, or the substitution of voluntary work with full-time paid staff. The employment of full-time paid staff can change the decision-making structure of a club. Volunteers try to preserve their influence within the organization, which is facilitated by, amongst other things, the decision-making powers, the possibilities of formalization, control of duties and methods of work of the employees, and the concentration of decisions within the voluntary executive committee. In each individual case, the level of trust and the expectations that volunteers and employees bring to the situation is important (Lincoln and Zeitz, 1980). This, too, can be connected to comparable change in the work and commitment emotions that we have mentioned above in relation to Kemper.

Widening of Access to Knowledge.   Knowledge, as Max Weber (1956) said, is power. Therefore, the control of access to various forms of knowledge and the breadth of the accessible knowledge is an important tool of the exercise of power and the influencing of decisions, for example, in democratic votes. In these circumstances, as has already been explained, informal agreements—and, therefore, also the informal sharing of knowledge—play an important role. This form of control and access to knowledge, and informal agreements based on this, can be made more difficult through two factors: on the one hand, that (at least in theory, insofar as all the recorded information is made available to all the members) the use of a computer broadens the knowledge base, but on the other hand, different groupings in a club can use the computer to quickly and reliably coordinate their positions and behavior (for example, in votes). This can contribute to a depersonalization of debates and decisions if the decision makers have the possibility and intention of making only selective information available. After all, the use of a computer can influence democratic principles in that the ownership and the associated possibility of exchanging information have a selective character: there are those who can exchange information using the computer and those who are excluded from this exchange. Two groups of actors are, therefore, formed, differentiated from one another by an information deficit. This stigma leads to a strengthening of the (already existing) factor of limited rationality (on the basis of missing insight and knowledge about the state of affairs) through the use of the computer—at the very least for the group excluded from the virtual communication. The emotional consequences for the group are—on the grounds of a lack of empirical data—speculative, but it can be assumed that the informational disparity leads to decisions or voting behavior that cannot be understood by other actors—that in turn can lead to negative emotions that do not influence the democratic principle of decision making, but do impact on the emotional climate in the group, the "we-feeling," the affective mood that is carried by all, the team spirit, the sense of community, mutual understanding, or internal cohesion.

Decorporealization

Images without Bodies.   We would also like to introduce this section with an example, in which the term decorporealization is taken literally. In times gone by, in many cases until the beginning of the 1980s and often even beyond this, the membership fees were usually collected on a monthly basis by the treasurer, often by making house-to-house visits and asking for payment of the appropriate amount. Membership of the club was "corporealized" or embodied in this person, and one could, if short of money, request a postponement—after all, everyone knew one another. Cancellation of membership happened in communicating to the treasurer that one no longer wanted to (or could) pay the membership fee. However, later, the amounts were taken from the bank account of the member (or, in the case of children, of the parents). The club and membership were no longer "embodied" or symbolized through a person, but reduced to a banking procedure. Missing payments, tracked through the computer, were automatically requested in writing (right through to a formal collection procedure). If one wanted to cancel membership, one now had to do this in writing within the time frame specified by the club's regulations. The number of passive members, therefore, rose dramatically. Heinemann and Horch (1991) were able to show that this apparently insignificant change had significant consequences for the integration of the members into the club—this was a small but important step toward viewing it as a service-provider.

Depersonalization of Expectations.   Positions in a club are not very differentiated and their tasks and responsibilities are hardly standardized. In place of standardization and specialization, one finds a relatively high level of personalization of expected behavior. Since a club can generally be organized less in terms of division of labor than, for example, a business, there is only a relatively minimal need for coordination. Where coordination is required, it cannot happen through orders or planning, because there is little inclination to follow orders in clubs, and the necessary structure for formalization is missing that planning and programming would require. Rather, we can identify self-determination in informal meetings, in the context of general meetings or specially formed committees, and we can find that a typical form of coordination is leadership based on personal charisma and the persuasive ability of individuals. But if membership, cooperation, coordination, leadership, and the development of structural patterns in clubs are significantly developed through the idiosyncrasies of the people involved and through informal face-to-face relationships, then the dominance of the cognitive and every form of incorporealization must change this characteristic of clubs and, therefore, also their emotional reality. Emotions of commitment are reduced or can no longer develop to the same degree, relationship emotions are factualized, and the emotional climate in an organization is displaced by a service provider mentality.

Loss of the Foundation of Trust.   Finally, we wish to draw attention to the special meaning of trust in the context of sport and sporting organizations. Trust plays a central role, particularly in sport clubs. If one trusts others, then one can depend on not being exploited by those who jump on every bandwagon, that rules and agreements are kept to, or that the relationship is not taken advantage of one-sidedly. Collective action and the production of club-goods are only possible on the basis of trust. Trust in clubs is therefore constituted in a different form than in many other social contexts (cf. Kramer, Brewer, and Hanna, 1996, p. 358). When trust is created between members in clubs or between members of a team it means that (1) athletes/members are regarded as more cooperative and more trustworthy than nonmembers; (2) one is more likely to assume that they will behave according to the norms, values, and rules; and (3) the fear of exploitation is assumed to be lower. In this way, a "depersonalized trust" is created, a trust that is no longer based on an assessment of a person, but on a social classification in a collective, such as membership in a club.

Now, trust is not necessarily a feeling. However, we know from empirical studies that trust can also be based on emotions, especially when it grows out of an identification with a cause, emanating from people and an organization. On the other hand, trust is linked to emotions in three ways: (1) feelings arise when trusting someone else, (2) feelings are usually created when someone else puts trust in one, and (3) apart from anything else, nobody is emotionally untouched when trust is broken or abused. So trust is connected to activity-emotions as well as to relationship-emotions.

Trust develops when the individual—integrated in social relationships or a group—has experienced rights and made use of these, or when it is based on relationships, including those that exist out of sport activities. Trust is, therefore, related to, among other things, the size of the group pursuing sport with one another, the frequency of contact, the extent of the relationships (in other words, in how far the other person is also a friend, work colleague, or club member), what emotional connections exist between parties, and the extent to which the behavior or wounding is observable.

But if because of digital information processing this frequency of contact and the emotional ties between people are reduced—as we have shown with many examples—then the question arises as to how such a "depersonalized" trust can be achieved. This can then lead to weak points developing in clubs, as can be observed in the many reports about drug abuse, corruption, mismanagement, internal politics, fraud, and so on. Trust needs to be transferred in an appropriate and functionally-capable form in relation to the technology being used and be included in the organization's implementation of control mechanisms.

A Case Study: The Changed Role of the Coach

To close, we wish to illustrate our reflections by using a concrete case, namely one that deals with the changes that a coach experiences in the course of the use of new computer-generated recording, measuring, and data processing technologies. The coach, of course, is the person who, on the basis of his professional knowledge, ability, and experience, is responsible for the improvement of the sporting abilities of the athletes entrusted to his care, for the preparation for competitions, and for giving care and advice in the course of the competitions.

The coach faces totally clear expectations in relation to the results of the work done (from the club, audience, and, generally also from, athletes). The primary task is to optimize the performance of the athletes or team s/he are entrusted with, and thereby ensure victory in sporting competitions. Successes—objectively measurable and visible to everyone, and, therefore, obvious—but in particular failures, are clearly ascribed to the competency or incompetence of the coach (Coakley, 1978, p. 216f.; Edwards, 1973, p. 133f.). However, at the same time, there are usually manifold emotions that develop between coaches and athletes—friendship, sympathy, and, not rarely, also dislike and hatred—which cannot be irrelevant to the coach. Again, at the same time—and this is, therefore, not a "coincidental" phenomenon of emotional connections between people, but structurally necessitated—normative orientations are presumed, such as result from ethos and legitimation of the sport, from basic societal values, but also from the expectations of other relevant groupings, such as the parents, the school, or the friends of the athlete(s). The coach is also expected to take responsibility for the consequences of the training methods employed on the development of the athletes and the sport they have been entrusted with, a responsibility that can be in competition with the "real" training tasks.

But there are questions about the extent to which the trainer can deal with all the aspects of a task in the light of developments described in the following example: slalom skiers from Germany spend the summer in the Andes with their coach (it is, after all, winter there), in order to prepare themselves for the next (northern) winter season. With special cameras, a trained expert records the movements of the racing skier on the way down the mountain. This recording is then sent (via the Internet) to a distant sports center in a university in Germany, where further experts using the appropriate programs analyze it. In this way, mistakes in the tiniest detail—often not even visible to the naked eye and certainly not interpretable—such as certain movements (e.g., the position of the arms, the way in which turns are completed), are identified and suggestions for corrections communicated to the coach/athlete via the Internet. These suggestions are realized; the corrected movements are again recorded, transferred, and analyzed for their effectiveness, until an "ideal movement" as defined by the computer program has been achieved.

Here we can see a concrete example that reflects what has been described generally about the usage of computers: a new division of labor is created that corresponds to the progress of recording and analytical technology as well as in the further development of programs and their appropriate use. Neither the coach nor the athlete now know how it all works because they hardly know the details of the programs and, for example, the biomechanical theories that underpin them; they can now only trust that the information they are sent is optimized toward improving performance. The human connection to information is lost, and the information is exclusively cognitive. Whereas, in earlier times, a contemporaneous presence of the relevant people was important, now there is a noncontemporaneous nonpresence. This results in the fragmentation of competencies and a displacement of decision-making responsibility from the coach to a computer program, or those who have the expert knowledge to operate these programs, which in turn leads to a shifting of hierarchies. In this way, the competency of the trainer is, on the one hand, (technically) expanded, since at any given moment (in cooperation with the athlete), it becomes possible to decide which training recommendations are to be implemented in which form, while on the other hand the reliance on third parties increases, since for an efficient use of the computer, numerous technical experts (programmers, media specialists, data analyzers) need to incorporate their knowledge and skill.

It can be assumed that this form of using technology: (1) fails to meet either the trainer's or the athlete's needs for social interaction; (2) creates dependencies since there is a compulsion to acquire and process knowledge in order to be—and remain—competitive; and (3) creates expectations (optimization of performance, calculable success).

All three factors can bring negative emotions in their wake: the diminishing of face-to-face relationships is accompanied by a partial incorporealization of the social relationship between the coach and the athlete, since in processing digital information emotions can only be transmitted in a limited form. The dependency on the computer arises from the sense that, without the transfer of complex information, an improvement in performance hardly seems possible, and it is precisely this (noticeable) necessity of usage that is influenced, as well as the emotional status of the individual (thinking of the feeling that arises when the computer is out of action for a prolonged period, or the Internet is not accessible) and the emotional relationship between those that depend on the information. For example, a computer program can make precise suggestions for change in movement, but information that might perhaps explain the factual details or that arises in relation to quotidian events, such as altered training conditions or the estimation about potential opponents can be misinterpreted without facial expressions, body language or emphases, and can, therefore, result in initiating unintended emotions. In particular, stylistic language in texts, such as double negatives or sarcasm, can cause additional misunderstandings. Misunderstandings can also arise in text-based communications if a "sender" encodes emotions that the "recipient," because of a reduced sensitivity, is not aware of or cannot decode. As well as missing or variant experiences, reasons for the resulting virtual communication error (and the related consequences) can also be cultural-social differences or missing intellectual processing and interpretational abilities. Virtual communication is also lacking a key element, namely the reward, connected with a pat on the back, the encouragement that lets an athlete know that the coach is supporting them, the winking of an eye, or the facial expression that helps to dissolve emotional tension, such as disappointment, frustration or anger.

What does this mean for the trainer and the relationship between the coach and the athlete? A typical effect for trainers is the general uncertainty of success of their training methods, for which they need to take responsibility with all the (uncertain) consequences. This insecurity must now, at least partially, be transferred to a trust in the effectiveness of the computer's recommendations. However, the division of labor may change: the coach remains responsible for the success or failure—and that is the question here, as in other comparable situations when decision-making ability and responsibility are no longer in one and the same hand. We can also question what happens when a party processes and communicates information in a quasi-objective form between a coach and an athlete yet is cognitively oriented and not present. From various studies we know how trainers react in situations that they experience as typical (cf. Bette, 1984; Cachay and Gahai, 1989; Edwards, 1973, p. 172; Heinemann, 2006; Hendry, 1972, p. 528; Ogilvie and Tutko, 1970; Patsantáras, 1994). The question is, how will these reactions change under the impression of digital information processing? One can assume, among other things, that activities become more directed to what was earlier described as emotion-work, in order to compensate for deficits in this area that are of necessity brought about by the processing of information that is restricted to the cognitive level.

Concluding Remarks

With the problems that have been addressed in this chapter, a wide field of interesting and important studies has been revealed, in particular regarding the unintended effects of the use of computer technology on the emotional state, in other words, on circumstances that have been seriously neglected, at least in social science research (on sport). In addition, if computer usage or digital information processing really has the effects on emotions described in this chapter, and if emotions cannot be separated from face-to-face relationships for the integration of the members, for functional and working methods in clubs, then the question arises how structures are stabilized, authority founded, division of labor organized, formalization and control possible, sanctions implemented, and so on, if the emotions that are almost essential components (as described in the first thematic block) are pushed into the background.

At the very beginning, we noted that our reflections are moving on thin ice, and that the danger of falling through the ice could only be diminished through a few of our own empirical findings, the transfer of results from comparable studies, and through many personal views and experiences. While empirical research dealing with these questions would be very desirable, this is only likely to happen with great difficulty, since (1) the process of introducing computers into sports clubs as described here is already very far advanced and the (often only small) changes that have come about as a result are difficult to identify retrospectively; (2) such effects overlap with other influences that also lead to changes, for example, in club structures, and such effects are difficult to isolate from one another; (3) many of the influences on emotions arising from computer usage are often the result of many small changes in the various tasks of the club based in the employment of digital information technology, that only really have an effect when seen in total, so that individuals are hardly aware of them, especially since these are always long-term creeping processes, in which one often forgets that it used to be different; and finally (4) one cannot overlook that—especially in the "male-culture club"—there are rarely reflections on emotions, and they are discussed even less.

Perhaps these are also the reasons why the themes discussed here have not (yet?) been researched more systematically.

References

Albrow, M. (1992). Sine ira et studio—or do organizations have feelings? *Organization Studies* 13: 313–329.

Bale, J. (1989). *Sports Geography*. New York: E. and F.N. Spon.

Bale, J. (1993). *Sport, Space and the City*. London: Routledge.

Bette, K.-H. (1984). *Die Trainerrolle im Hochleistungssport. System-und rollentheoretische Überlegungen zur Sozialfigur des Trainers*. Sankt Augustin.

Bühl, A. (1999). *Cyberpunk: Dystopien am Ende des Millenniums Reihe: Studien zur Science Fiction, Band 3*. Münster: LIT-Verlag.

Bühl, A. (2000). *Die virtuelle Gesellschaft des 21. Jahrhunderts. Sozialer Wandel im digitalen Zeitalter*. Opladen: Westdeutscher-Verlag.

Bühl, A. (2001). *Computerstile. Vom individuellen Umgang mit dem PC im Alltag*. Opladen: Westdeutscher-Verlag.

Cachay, K., and Gahai, E. (1989). Brauchen Trainer Pädagogik? *Leistungssport* 19/5.

Castells, M. (2001). Das Informationszeitalter. *Band 1: Der Aufstieg der Netzwerkgesellschaft*. Leverkusen: Leske und Budrich Verlag.

Castells, M. (2004). *Das Informationszeitalter (3 Bände). Volume 1: Der Aufstieg der Netzwerkgesellschaft*. Leverkusen: Leske und Budrich.

Charwat, H.J. (1994). *Lexikon der Mensch-Maschine-Kommunikation*. München, Wien: Oldenbourg.

Coakley, J.J. (1978). *Sport in Society, Issues and Controversies*. St. Louis: Mosby.

Döring, N. (1999). *Sozialpsychologie des Internet*. Die Bedeutung des Internet für Kommunikationsprozesse, Identitäten, soziale Beziehungen und Gruppen. Göttingen: Hogrefe.

Edwards, H. (1973). *Sociology of Sport*. Homewood, IL: Irwin.

Emrich, E., Pitsch, W., and Papathanassiou, V. (2001). Die Sportvereine. Ein Versuch auf empirischer Grundlage. *Schriftenreihe des Bundesinstituts für Sportwissenschaft*, Volume 106. Schorndorf: Hofmann.

Freud, S. (1972). Jenseits des Lustprinzips. Massenpsychologie und Ich-Analyse: das Ich und das Es. *Gesammelte Werke*, Volume 13 (7th ed.). Frankfurt aM: Fischer Taschenbuch Verlag.

Freud, S. (1978). *Das Ich und das Es und andere metapsychologische Schriften*. Frankfurt aM: Fischer Taschenbuch Verlag.

Friederici, M.R. (1998). *Sportbegeisterung und Zuschauergewalt*. LIT-Verlag, Hamburg.

Friederici, M.R. (2006). *Virtuelle Emotionen? Über die Folgen der Computernutzung in NPOs* (unpublished manuscript).

Heinemann, K. (1998). *Einführung in die Soziologie des Sports*. Schorndorf: Hofmann-Verlag.

Heinemann, K. (Ed.) (1999). *Sport Clubs in Various European Countries.* Schorndorf/Stuttgart: Hofmann-Verlag/Schattauer.

Heinemann, K. (2001a). Emotionen in Sportvereinen—Entwurf einer funktionalistischen Theorie. In: *Sportwissenschaft* 31/4.

Heinemann, K. (2001b). *Die Technologisierung des Sports—eine sozioökonomische Analyse.* Schorndorf: Hofmann-Verlag.

Heinemann, K. (2004). *Sportorganisationen—verstehen und gestalten.* Schorndorf: Hofmann-Verlag.

Heinemann, K. (2006). *Einführung in die Soziologie des Sports* (5th ed.). Schorndorf: Hofmann-Verlag.

Heinemann, K., and Horch, H.-D. (1991). *Elemente einer Finanzsoziologie freiwilliger Vereinigungen.* Stuttgart: Verlag Siebek-Mohr.

Heinemann, K., and Puig, N. (1997). Aspectos sociológicos de las organizaciones deportivas. *Apunts—Educación y Deportes*, 49(3).

Heinemann, K., and Puig, N. (2001). Sportvereine in Deutschland und Spanien. In: K. Heinemann and M. Schubert (Hrsg.), *Sport und Gesellschaften.* Schorndorf: Hofmann-Verlag.

Heinemann, K., and Schubert, M. (1994). *Der Sportverein—Ergebnisse einer repräsentativen Untersuchung.* Schorndorf: Hofmann-Verlag.

Heller, A. (1981). *Theorie der Gefühle.* Hamburg: VSA.

Hendry, L.B. (1972). The coaching stereotype. In: H.T.A. Whiting (Ed.), *Readings in Sport Psychology.* London: Kempton.

Hochschild, A.R. (1979). Emotion work, feeling rules, and social structure. *American Journal of Sociology* 85: 551–575.

Hochschild, A.R. (1983). *The Managed Heart: Commercialization of Human Feeling,* Berkeley: University of California Press.

Horch, H.D. (1987). Personalwirtschaftliche Aspekte ehrenamtlicher Mitarbeit. In: K. Heinemann (Ed.) *Betriebswirtschaftliche Grundlagen des Sportvereins.* Schorndorf: Hofmann-Verlag.

Kemper, T.D. (1978). *A Social Interaction Theory of Emotions.* New York: Wiley.

Kramer, R.M., Brewer M.B., and Hanna, B.A. (1996). Collective trust and collective action: The decision to trust as a social decision. In: R.M. Kramer and T.R. Tyler (Eds.). *Trust in Organizations. Frontiers of Theory and Research.* London and Thousand Oaks, CA: Sage, pp. 357–389.

Lincoln, J.R., and Zeitz, G. (1980). Organisational properties from aggregate data. *American Journal of Sociology* 45.

Mintzberg, H. (1979). *The Structuring of Organizations.* Englewood Cliffs, NJ: Prentice-Hall.

Ogilvie, B.C., and Tutko, T.A. (1970). Self perceptions as compared with measured personality of selected male physical educators. In: G.S. Kenyon (Ed.): *Contemporary Psychology of Sport.* Chicago: The Athletic Institute, pp. 73–78.

Patsantáras, N. (1994). *Der Trainer als Sportberuf—Entwicklung und Ausdifferenzierung einer Profession mit einem Rückblick auf das altgriechische olympische Ideal.* Schorndorf: Hofmann-Verlag.

Rammert, W. (Hrsg.) (1990). *Computerwelten—Alltagswelten. Wie verändert der Computer die soziale Wirklichkeit.* Opladen: Westdeutscher Verlag.

Rastetter, D. (1994). *Sexualität und Herrschaft in Organisationen. Eine geschlechtervergleichende Analyse.* Opladen: Westdeutscher Verlag.

Richter, R. (1985). *Soziokulturelle Dimensionen freiwilliger Vereinigungen. USA, Bundesrepublik Deutschland und Österreich im soziologischen Vergleich.* München: Minerva.

Sadek, M.D., and de Mori, R. (1998). Dialogue systems. In: R. de Mori (Ed.). *Spoken Dialogues with Computers.* London: Academic Press, pp. 523–561.

Vester, H.-G. (1991). *Emotion, Gesellschaft und Kultur: Grundzüge einer soziologischen Theorie der Emotionen.* Opladen: Westdeutscher Verlag.

Weber, M. (1956). *Wirtschaft und Gesellschaft.* Tübingen: J.C.B. Mohr (Paul Siebeck).

Index

AAS, *see* Attendee-awareness sponsorship

Academic fundraising
athletic program fundraising effects
data sources, 19–20
donor recruitment by successful athletic program, 30
findings, 20–22
linkage of giving decisions, 26–28
success effects on giving, 28–30

Administrative control, organizations, 274, 278–279

AIRS, *see* Attendee improved relationship sponsorship

AIS, *see* Attendee-image sponsorship

Armenia, *see* Eastern European countries

Attendee-awareness sponsorship (AAS), 257, 259

Attendee-image sponsorship (AIS), 259

Attendee improved relationship sponsorship (AIRS), 261

Attendee-use sponsorship (AUS), 260

Audit Committee, International Olympic Committee, 215

AUS, *see* Attendee-use sponsorship

Australia, environment protection for recreational sport, 88–89

Azerbaijan, *see* Eastern European countries

Baseball, *see* Major League Baseball; National Association of Professional Baseball Leagues

Belarus, *see* Eastern European countries

Berlioux, Monique, International Olympic Committee, 209

Bird Larry, free agency, 191, 202
Bourdieu's theory
  doxic, 45
  habitus, 46–48, 50
  linkage with neo-institutionalism,
    44–46, 49, 55–56
  overview, 43
  sociodicy, 45
Bosman, Jean-Marc, European
    Court of Justice case, 128

CAS, see Court of Arbitration for
    Sport
C5ICB, see C5 Index of
    Competitive Balance
C5 Index of Competitive Balance
    (C5ICB), 158–159
Champions League, see European
    football leagues
Channel member-targeted
    sponsorship, 260–262
Clemson University, winning and
    donor support, 17–18
Coase Theorem
  competitive balance, 154
  complex league
    complication types, 161–162
    promotion and relegation
        systems, 164–165
    tournaments, 162–163
    win dispersion, 162
  environment protection, 85–86
  prospects for study, 169–170
  simple league
    characteristics, 155
    competitive balance ratio,
        161
    perfect competitive balance
        versus perfect competitive
        dominance, 156–157
    performance persistence,
        155–156, 160–161
    prize concentration, 155–156
    summary statistics

C5 Index of Competitive
    Balance, 158–159
D-index, 161
Gini coefficient, 160
Goossens's index, 158
Herfindahl Index of
    Competitive Balance,
    158–160
Lorenz Seasonal Balance
    Curve, 158, 160
M-index, 161
Quirk and Fort ratio,
    157–158
Spearman rank correlation
    coefficient, 160
standard deviation, 157
  win dispersion, 155–156,
    158–159
talent distribution, 154
Coercive isomorphism, organized
    sport participation, 45,
    51–52
College and Beyond dataset,
    17
Community/government-targeted
    sponsorship, 263, 265
Competitive balance
  Coase Theorem, 154
  definition, 149
  economic power distribution,
    153
  financial determinism, 153
  importance, 149–150
  Rottenberg invariance
      proposition, 154
  uncertainty of outcome, 151
  winning probability, 152
Computer technology
  decorporealization
    depersonalization of
        expectations, 306–307
    images without bodies, 306
    overview, 292–294
    trust loss, 307–308

knowledge
  access, 291–292, 305–306
  coach case study, 308–311
  division of labor and
    specification, 304–305
  efficiency increase, 302–304
  expression and objectification,
    300–302
  prospects for study, 311
  sport club–computer usage–
    emotion interactions
  computer impact, 291–294,
    298–299
  emotion characteristics,
    294–298
  limiting parameters in study,
    288–291
  overview, 287–288
  voluntary organization
    characteristics, 270,
    289–291
Concern for self-maintenance,
  organizations, 53
Consumer-targeted sponsorship,
  257–258
Control
  administrative control, 274,
    278–279
  conceptualizations, 269
  power
    conceptualization, 270–271
    control relationship, 271–273
  rationality, 269–270
  self-control, 274–275, 278–279
  social control, 274, 278–279
  voluntary organizations
    characteristics, 270
    dynamics of control, 276–278
    formal versus informal control
      mechanisms, 278–280
    identification in control,
      280–281
    prospects for study, 281–282
    study design, 275–276

Cournot-Nash equilibrium,
  European football
  leagues, 132
Court of Arbitration for Sport
  (CAS), International
  Olympic Committee
  interactions, 222
Czech Republic, see Eastern
  European countries

Decentralization indicator, sports
  economy institutional
  reform, 113
Decorporealization, computer
  technology
  depersonalization of
    expectations, 306–307
  images without bodies, 306
  overview, 292–294
  trust loss, 307–308
D-index, competitive balance
  measure, 161
Director General, International
  Olympic Committee, 210,
  212
Donors, see also Economics and
  finance
  behavior modeling, 31–32
  trends in giving, 23–25
Doxic, Bourdieu's theory, 45

Eastern European countries
  (EECs)
  commercialization of sport,
    101
  financing of sport, 102
  institutional economic reform
    formal versus informal rules,
      103
    governance assessment,
      106–109
    quality measures, 104–107
    requirements, 103–104
  sport participation rate, 102

Eastern European countries
(EECs) *(continued)*
sports economy institutional
reform
building of institutions,
110–111
central Eastern European
countries, 114, 116
economic governance quality
correlation, 120–122
institutional economic reform
comparison, 116–119
prospects for study, 122–123
transition indicators
aggregated indicator, 114
decentralization indicator,
113
findings, 115
legislation index, 111–112
liberalization indicator,
113–114
privatization indicator,
112–113
EBRD, *see* European Bank for
Reconstruction and
Development
Economics and finance
athletic program fundraising
effects on academic
fundraising
data sources, 19–20
donor recruitment by
successful athletic
program, 30
findings, 20–22
linkage of giving decisions,
26–28
success effects on giving,
28–30
donor behavior modeling, 31–32
donor trends, 23–25
Eastern European country
institutions, *see* Eastern
European countries

football league, *see* European
football leagues
fundraising models
independent model, 33
integrated model, 33–34
private model, 33
overview, 5–6, 8–9
prospects for study, 10, 34–35
research interests in sports,
6–8
EECs, *see* Eastern European
countries
EMMS, *see* Employee/
management motivation
sponsorship
Emotion
activity-related emotion, 296
commitment emotions, 296
formal versus informal control
mechanisms in voluntary
organizations, 278–280
individual identification in
organization control,
280–281
mood in clubs, 297
social relationships, 296–297
sport club–computer usage–
emotion interactions
computer impact, 291–294,
298–299, 300–308
emotion characteristics,
294–298
limiting parameters in study,
288–291
overview, 287–288
voluntary organization
characteristics, 270,
289–291
transition consequences, 299–300
Employee/management motivation
sponsorship (EMMS), 263
Employee/management
relationship sponsorship
(EMRS), 263

Employee/management-targeted
    sponsorship, 261, 263
EMRS, *see* Employee/management
    relationship sponsorship
EMS, *see* Environmental
    Management System
Environment, *see* Outdoor
    recreational sports
Environmental Management
    System (EMS), forests,
    83
Estonia, *see* Eastern European
    countries
Ethics Commission, International
    Olympic Committee, 218
European Bank for Reconstruction
    and Development
    (EBRD), Eastern
    European country
    institutional reform
    analysis, 103–108, 110,
    116
European football leagues
  competitive balance, 166–169
  economic theory
    benchmark case with no
        sponsorship, closed labor,
        and product market
    Cournot-Nash equilibrium,
        132
    demand function, 133
    dominance of large market
        team, 133
    equilibrium wage, 133, 135
    overview, 130–131
    profit maximization,
        134–135, 145
    talent demand, 132,
        134–135, 145
    total cost function, 131
    wages in profit maximizing
        league versus win
        maximizing league, 135,
        146

broadcasting and sponsorship
    modeling
    dominance of large market
        team, 136
    profit maximization,
        136–137, 146
    talent demand, 136
Champions League with open
    labor market and
    broadcast rights
    dominance of large market
        team, 140, 147
    overview, 128, 137–138
    profit maximization,
        138–139
    talent demand, 139
    wage equilibrium, 139–140,
        147
comparison for leagues,
    142–144
empirical validation, 140–142
maximal sum of win
    percentages, 141, 148
revenue function, 129
win probability and
    maximization, 129–130,
    135
historical perspective, 128
Events, *see* Pan American Games
    and International
    Olympic Committee
Executive Board, International
    Olympic Committee, 210,
    212–214

Finance, *see* Economics and
    finance
Finance Commission, International
    Olympic Committee,
    214–215
Football, *see* European football
    leagues; National Football
    League
Free agency, 191, 194

Fundraising, *see also* Economics
    and finance
  athletic program fundraising
    effects on academic
    fundraising
    data sources, 19–20
    donor recruitment by
      successful athletic
      program, 30
    findings, 20–22
    linkage of giving decisions,
      26–28
    success effects on giving,
      28–30
  models
    independent model, 33
    integrated model, 33–34
    private model, 33

Gini coefficient, competitive
    balance measure, 160
Glasnost, Soviet reform, 100
Gokomsport, Soviet system,
    100–101
Goossens's index, competitive
    balance measurement, 158

Habitus, Bourdieu's theory, 46–48,
    50
Herfindahl Index of Competitive
    Balance (HICB), 158–160
HICB, *see* Herfindahl Index of
    Competitive Balance
Hockey, *see* National Hockey
    League
Human capital theory, general
    versus specific skills,
    192
Hungary, *see* Eastern European
    countries

Identification, individuals in
    organization control,
    280–281

Individualization, organization
    theory, 47
International Olympic Committee
    (IOC)
  Charter, 212, 218, 221, 223
  environmental concerns, 83
  functions, 207
  governance
    Administration, 208–209
    Audit Committee, 215
    commissions, 214–215
    definition, 207–208
    Director General, 210, 212
    directors, 210–211
    elected athletes, 217–218
    Executive Board, 210,
      212–214
    finances, 210–211
    foundations, 211–212
    improvements, 224–225
    levels, 208–209
    management of management,
      212–216
    meetings, 213
    metagovernance, 222–224
    organization chart, 211
    President compensation, 209
    regulatory mechanisms
      agency theory, 219
      Court of Arbitration for
        Sport, 222
      Ethics Commission, 218
      harmonization of regulation,
        219–222
      International Sports
        Federation, 216–217
      membership, 217–218
      World Anti-Doping Agency,
        220
    staff, 209–210
    Swiss law, 221–223
  scandal, 207, 216, 224
International Sports Federation,
    International Olympic

Committee interactions,
216–217
IOC, *see* International Olympic
Committee

Kazakhstan, *see* Eastern European
countries
Kyrgyz Republic, *see* Eastern
European countries

Latvia, *see* Eastern European
countries
Leagues, *see* Competitive balance;
European football
leagues
Legislation index, sports economy
institutional reform,
111–112
Liberalization indicator, sports
economy institutional
reform, 113–114
Lithuania, *see* Eastern European
countries
Lorenz Seasonal Balance Curve,
competitive balance
measure, 158, 160

Major League Baseball (MLB)
competitive balance, 165–168
minor league affiliates, *see*
National Association of
Professional Baseball
Leagues
descriptive statistic, 179
team owners and business
interests, 184–185
winning percentage and
Lieberman technique
regression, 180–182
Mimetic isomorphism, organized
sport participation, 45,
52
M-index, performance persistence,
161

Minor league baseball, *see*
National Association of
Professional Baseball
Leagues
Mississippi State University,
winning and donor
support, 17
MLB, *see* Major League Baseball
Moldova, *see* Eastern European
countries
Mood, *see* Emotion
Multiplex ties, network
perspective, 69
Mythic, neo-institutionalism,
45

Nagano Declaration, environmental
concerns, 83–84
NAPBL, *see* National Association
of Professional Baseball
Leagues
NAS, *see* Nonattendee-awareness
sponsorship
NASSM, *see* North American
Society for Sport
Management
National Association of
Professional Baseball
Leagues (NAPBL)
demand variation hypotheses,
177–178
transaction cost hypotheses,
176
vertical integration in Major
League Baseball
choice equation, 178–179
controls in analysis, 185
overview, 173–176
ownership structure effects,
186–187
prospects for study, 187–188
regression analysis, 180–182
weighted least squares
analysis, 182–184

National Basketball Association
    (NBA)
  competitive balance, 165–168
  free agency, 191, 194
  organization specific training
      and player salary
    data description and sources,
        193–197
    empirical model and variables,
        197–198
    overview, 192–193
    player efficiency rating,
        195–196
    prospects for study, 201–202
    regression analysis, 198–201
    summary statistics, 198–199
National Collegiate Athletic
    Association (NCAA)
  athletic operating expenses
      versus alumni giving, 17
  basketball tournament success
      and financial support,
      18
National Football League (NFL),
    competitive balance,
    165–168
National Hockey League (NHL),
    competitive balance,
    166–168
National Survey on Recreation
    and the Environment
    (NSRE), 82
NBA, see National Basketball
    Association
NCAA, see National Collegiate
    Athletic Association
NCIS, see Nonattendee community
    involvement sponsorship
NDCS, see Nonattendee-
    distribution commitment
    sponsorship
Neo-institutionalism
  linkage with Bourdieu's theory,
      44–46, 49, 55–56

  mythic, 45
  overview, 43
Network
  definition, 62–64
  interorganizational network, 61
  matrix conversion, 75–76
  nodes and lines, 63–64
  properties, 72
  structure, 61
Network perspective
  advantages, 62, 67
  definition, 62
  departments, 69–70
  individualistic, reductionist
      approach, 64–66
  networks within networks,
      69–71
  organizations, 76–77
  overview, 67–71, 73–76
  practical applications, 77–79
  prospects for study, 79
  structural, holistic approach,
      64–66
  ties
    intensity and directionality,
        68, 74–75
    multiplex ties, 69
    presence, 74
    structural changes, 71, 73–74
NFL, see National Football League
NHL, see National Hockey League
NIRS, see Nonattendee improved
    relationship sponsorship
NIS, see Nonattendee-image
    sponsorship
Nonattendee-awareness
    sponsorship (NAS), 257,
    259
Nonattendee community
    involvement sponsorship
    (NCIS), 263–264
Nonattendee-distribution
    commitment sponsorship
    (NDCS), 261

Nonattendee-image sponsorship (NIS), 259–260
Nonattendee improved relationship sponsorship (NIRS), 261
Nonattendee-use sponsorship (NUS), 260
Normative isomorphism, organized sport participation, 45, 52
North American Society for Sport Management (NASSM), origins, 1–2
Norwegian sport, *see also* Sports City Program
  clubs, 38
  funding, 38–39
  Norwegian Olympic Committee and Confederation of Sports, 38
NSRE, *see* National Survey on Recreation and the Environment
NUS, *see* Nonattendee-use sponsorship

Organization theory
  control, *see* Control
  networking, *see* Network
  organizational field, 44, 51–53
  overview, 2, 4–5
  participation in organized sport, *see* Sports City Program
  prospects for study, 9–10
  research interests in sports, 2–4
  volunteer staff–professional staff relationship, *see* Volunteer staff
Outdoor recreational sports
  definition, 81
  environment preservation
    Coase Theorem, 85–86
    collective action, 87–88
    overview of concerns, 81–84
    prospects, 93–94

public policy, 88–90
sport subculture targeting, 91–93
tragedy of the commons, 84–85
voluntary cooperation, 90–91
participation trends in United State, 81–82

Pan American Games, *see* Volunteer staff
PER, *see* Player efficiency rating
Perestroika, Soviet reform, 100
Performance persistence, competitive balance, 155–156, 160–161
Player efficiency rating (PER), 195–196
Poland, *see* Eastern European countries
Power
  conceptualization, 270–271
  control relationship, 271–273
Privatization indicator, sports economy institutional reform, 112–113
Prize concentration, competitive balance, 155–156
Profit maximization, European football league economic theory
  benchmark case with no sponsorship, closed labor, and product market, 134–135, 145
  broadcasting and sponsorship modeling, 136–137, 146
  Champions League with open labor market and broadcast rights, 138–139
Professional Staff, *see* Volunteer staff

QF ratio, *see* Quirk and Fort
    ratio
Quirk and Fort (QF) ratio
    complex league, 162
    North American major leagues
        and European club
        football, 165
    simple leagues, 157–158

Race, player compensation effects,
    192
Reflexivity, organization theory,
    47
Rogge, Jacques, International
    Olympic Committee,
    209–210, 212, 215
Romania, *see* Eastern European
    countries
Rottenberg invariance proposition
    competitive balance, 154
    definition, 7
Russian Federation, *see* Eastern
    European countries

Salary, *see* Wages
Samaranch, Juan Antonio,
    International Olympic
    Committee, 209, 216
SCP, *see* Sports City Program
Self-control, organizations,
    274–275, 278–279
SGMA, *see* Sporting Goods
    Manufacturers
    Association
Slovak Republic, *see* Eastern
    European countries
Slovenia, *see* Eastern European
    countries
Social control, organizations, 274,
    278–279
Social network theory, 62
Sociodicy, Bourdieu's theory,
    45

Soviet Union, *see also* Eastern
    European Countries
    glasnost, 100
    Gokomsport, 100–101
    perestroika, 100
    sports economy collapse,
        100–103
Spearman rank correlation
    coefficient (SRCC),
    performance persistence
    measure, 160, 165–166
Sponsorship
    characteristics, 250
    classification schemes, 249
    definition, 248, 250
    European football league
        modeling, *see* European
        football leagues
    research resources, 247
    resources, 251–253
    typology of activity
        attendee-awareness
            sponsorship, 257, 259
        attendee-image sponsorship,
            259
        attendee improved
            relationship sponsorship,
            261
        attendee-use sponsorship, 260
        channel member-targeted
            sponsorship, 260–262
        community/government-
            targeted sponsorship, 263,
            265
        conceptual framework,
            253–254
        consumer-targeted
            sponsorship, 257–258
        definition, 249–250
        empirical use, 264
        employee/management
            motivation sponsorship,
            263

employee/management
    relationship sponsorship,
    263
employee/management-
    targeted sponsorship, 261,
    263
nonattendee-awareness
    sponsorship, 257, 259
nonattendee community
    involvement sponsorship,
    263–264
nonattendee-distribution
    commitment sponsorship,
    261
nonattendee-image
    sponsorship, 259–260
nonattendee improved
    relationship sponsorship,
    261
nonattendee-use sponsorship,
    260
objectives, 250–251, 255–257
targets, 250–251, 254–255
theoretical use, 264, 266
Sport club, *see* Voluntary
    organizations
Sporting Goods Manufacturers
    Association (SGMA),
    82
Sports City Program (SCP)
aims, 39
funding, 38–39
growth, 39
organization, 39–40
participation
    Bourdieu's theory
        doxic, 45
        habitus, 46–48, 50
        linkage with neo-
            institutionalism, 44–46,
            49, 55–56
        overview, 43
        sociodicy, 45

coercive isomorphism, 45,
    51–52
mimetic isomorphism, 45, 52
neo-institutionalism
    linkage with Bourdieu's
        theory, 44–46, 49, 55–56
    mythic, 45
    overview, 43
normative isomorphism, 45,
    52
organizational field, 44,
    51–53
supply and demand, 53–55
survey data, 40–43
SRCC, *see* Spearman rank
    correlation coefficient
Staff, *see* Volunteer staff
Standard deviation, competitive
    balance, 157
Subculture, targeting in
    environment protection
    for recreational sport,
    91–93
Supply and demand, organized
    sport participation,
    53–55

Tajikistan, *see* Eastern European
    countries
Talent demand
    competitive balance, 154
    European football league
        economic theory
        benchmark case with no
            sponsorship, closed labor,
            and product market, 132,
            134–135, 145
        broadcasting and sponsorship
            modeling, 136
        Champions League with open
            labor market and
            broadcast rights, 139
Ties, *see* Network perspective

Transition economies, *see* Eastern
European Countries
Trust, loss in decorporealization,
307–308
Turkmenistan, *see* Eastern
European countries

Ukraine, *see* Eastern European
countries
UN, *see* United Nations
United Kingdom, environment
protection for recreational
sport, 89
United Nations (UN),
International Olympic
Committee interactions,
223
University of Oregon
athletic program fundraising
effects on academic
fundraising, 18–19, 21–22,
26
donor recruitment by successful
athletic program, 30–31
Uzbekistan, *see* Eastern European
countries

Voluntary organizations
characteristics, 270, 289–291
control
characteristics, 270
dynamics of control, 276–278
formal versus informal control
mechanisms, 278–280
identification in control,
280–281
prospects for study, 281–282
study design, 275–276
sport club–computer usage–
emotion interactions
computer impact, 291–294,
298–299, 300–308
emotion characteristics, 294–
298

limiting parameters in study,
288–291
overview, 287–288
Volunteer staff
motivations and incentives,
229–230
professional staff relationship
data collection and analysis,
231–232
organizational design effects
clarity, 233–234
communication, 237–239
control struggles, 234–236
coordination, 233, 239–240
leadership, 236
planning, 236–236
organizational theory, 230
Pan American Games case
study, 230–231
personal resource effects,
240–241
prospects for structural factor
studies, 241–242

Wages
European football league
economic theory
benchmark case with no
sponsorship, closed labor,
and product market
equilibrium wage, 133, 135
profit maximizing league
versus win maximizing
league, 135, 146
Champions League, 139–140,
147
National Basketball Association
organization specific
training and player salary
data description and sources,
193–197
empirical model and variables,
197–198
overview, 192–193

player efficiency rating,
196–196
prospects for study, 201–202
regression analysis, 198–201
summary statistics, 198–199
WAS, *see* World Anti-Doping
Agency

Win dispersion, competitive
balance, 155–156,
158–159, 162
World Anti-Doping Agency
(WAS), International
Olympic Committee
interactions, 220